Henry
LAMB

Henry LAMB

The Artist and his Friends

KEITH CLEMENTS

REDCLIFFE
Bristol

First published in 1985
by Redcliffe Press Ltd.,
49 Park St., Bristol

© Keith Clements

ISBN 0905 459 55 5

Typeset by Photobooks (Bristol) Ltd.,
Printed by Biddles Ltd., Guildford

Contents

List of Illustrations

Colour:

Black and White:

Edie McNeill 1909 (Tate Gallery, London)
Dorothy Lamb 1912 (Whereabouts Unknown)
The Sentry 1906 (Spink & Son Ltd)

between pages 114–115   In France and Ireland:
The Anrep Family 1920 (Museum of Fine Arts, Boston, USA)
The Lake 1911 (Private Collection)
Phantasy 1912 (Tate Gallery, London)
Breton Cowherd c.1910 (Private Collection)
Death of a Peasant 1911 (Tate Gallery, London)
Edie McNeill 1911 (Southampton Art Gallery)
Irish Girls 1912 (Tate Gallery, London)
Marie-Joseph Favennec 1911 (Whitworth Art Gallery, Manchester)

between pages 146–147   Bloomsbury and Stanley Spencer:
Leonard Woolf 1912 (Private Collection)
'When will he realize what he makes us SUFFER?' 1912
   (British Library)
Lytton Strachey and Clive Bell c.1910/11
   (Stone Gallery, Newcastle-upon-Tyne)
Ottoline c.1910 (Private Collection)
Lytton Strachey c.1912
Lytton Strachey c.1912/13 (Private Collection)
Katherine Cox 1911/12 (Private Collection)
Carrington c.1926/27 (Private Collection)
Stanley Spencer 1920 (Whereabouts Unknown)
Dear Hay Lane 1922 (Whereabouts Unknown)
Football Edition 1926 (Private Collection)
The Tea Party 1926 (Private Collection)

between pages 178–179   Second Marriage and Later Work:
Evelyn Waugh 1930 (Private Collection)
Lamb and Lady Pansy on honeymoon 1928
The Artist's Family 1940–3 (Tate Gallery, London)
Tea Things 1932 (Birmingham City Art Gallery)
River Ebble, Wiltshire 1937 (Fitzwilliam Museum, Cambridge)
Rt. Hon. Neville Chamberlain 1939
   (National Portrait Gallery, London)
Fatigues, Canadian Forces 1942 (City Museum, Stoke-on-Trent)
The Artist's Wife 1933 (Tate Gallery, London)
Afternoon Walk 1949 (Private Collection)
Self Portrait 1950 (Private Collection)
Self Portrait 1951 (National Portait Gallery, London)

Dust Jacket Design: Keith Clements

Acknowledgements

My warmest appreciation and thanks to Robin Plummer, Dean of the Faculty of Art and Design at Brighton Polytechnic: the existence of the research for "Henry Lamb" I owe to his initial inspiration; my thanks too, to Norbert Lynton, Professor of the History of Art at the University of Sussex; each has given invaluable advice, detailed criticism and great encouragement throughout; to Julian Freeman, Exhibitions Officer at Brighton Polytechnic, my thanks for much information and many stimulating discussions on topics of mutual concern; to Robert Haynes, Head of the Department of Art History, who in the early stages helped focus the material; and to colleagues in the Department, contact with whom has been helpful in countless, indefinable ways. For some financial assistance I am indebted to the Polytechnic and to East Sussex County Council.

The whole book has been enriched by unfailingly enthusiastic support from the artist's widow, Lady Pansy Lamb who has graciously granted permission to reproduce copyright material, letters and paintings; and from her daughter, Henrietta Phipps, and family. Whilst it is difficult and inevitably invidious to single out individuals from the many relations, friends, collectors and institutions contacted all of whom have responded so willingly, special mention must be made of Lord and Lady Moyne and family, Dr and Mrs Christopher Turton, Richard Morphet, and Peyton Skipwith and the Fine Art Society.

Others to whom I am indebted, including those galleries who granted permission to reproduce works in their collection, are: Aberdeen City Art Gallery; W. G. Plomer, Agnew's; Anastasia Anrep; Dr Igor Anrep; the late Edward Ardizzone; the Army Records Centre; Mark Arnold-Foster; A. Eldon Edington, The Arts Club; Dame Peggy Ashcroft; Beryl (Su) Atkins; Barbara Bagenal; The Cooper Art Gallery, Barnsley; Dr Wendy

Baron; Rose Battye; the late Sir Cecil Beaton; George Behrend; the Ulster Museum and Art Gallery, Belfast; Professor Keith Bell; Professor Quentin Bell; the late Sir John Betjeman; Birmingham City Art Gallery; Dr Ann Bishop; David Bonavia; Gabriel Bonavia; Hilda, Mrs Ferrucio Bonavia; K. L. Bonavia; Dr Michael Bonavia; Mary Adshead, Mrs James Bone; Helen Hall, Boston Museum of Fine Arts; Russell Cotes Museum and Art Gallery, Bournemouth; Nicholas Raine, Western Orchestral Society, Bournemouth; Liz West and Learning Resources, Brighton Polytechnic; Bristol City Art Gallery; the Headmaster, Clifton College, Bristol; Don Carleton and Elizabeth Harlow, University of Bristol; the British Architectural Library of the RIBA; the British Council; M.A.F. Borrie, Department of Manuscripts, the British Library; the Newspaper Library, British Library; Humphrey Brooke; Nicholas Brown; Dr Peter Bullough; Richard and Angela Burrows; Fitzwilliam Museum, Cambridge; the Principal and Bursar, Homerton College, Cambridge; Marion Stewart, King's College Library, Cambridge; the Bursar, Newnham College, Cambridge; Guy Lee and M.G. Underwood, St John's College, Cambridge; Dr R. Robson, Trinity College, Cambridge; David Fraser-Jenkins and Anne Grierson, National Museum of Wales, Cardiff; the late Richard Carline and Nancy Carline; Noel Carrington; Gwen Castle; Lord David Cecil; the Central Office of Information; the Chelsea Art Club; the Chelsea School of Art; Susan Chitty; Sir Thomas Chitty; Francis Farmar, Christie's; the late Lord Clark; George Clive; Lady Mary Clive; Barbara Constanduros; Frank Constantine; the Contemporary Art Society; Jilly Cooper; Priscilla Copeman, Courtauld Institute; R. A. Clarke, Coventry City Libraries; Daniel Cowin; Angus Davidson; Cecily Langdale, Davis & Long Company; the Department of the Environment; Nicolette Devas; Diana and Tristan De Vere Cole; P. J. Day, Librarian and Keeper, the Devonshire Collections; Patricia Diamand; the DMS Watson Library, University of London; Anthony d'Offay; Cesar Domela; Shamus Donald; R. W. Draper; Eithne Waldron, Curator, the Hugh Lane Municipal Gallery of Modern Art, Dublin; John Hutchinson, the National Gallery of Ireland, Dublin; St Columba's College, Dublin; Trinity College Library, University of Dublin; Lady Olwen Carey Evans; Lady Enid Faber; Diana Farr; Dr Dennis Farr; Emile Favennec; Sir James and Lady Bice Fawcett; Olivia Fetherston-Dilke; James Fitton; Penelope Fitzgerald; W. W. Foot; the late David Garnett; Oliver Garnett; Jonathan Gathorne-Hardy; William Gaunt; Thomas Gibson Fine Art; Sir Ian and Lady Caroline Gilmour; Mrs V. Gilmour; Dr Mark Girouard; Kathleen, Mrs L. A. Godfree; the Headmistress, Godolphin's School, Salisbury; the Headmaster, Gordonstoun, Elgin; Professor Sir Lawrence Gowing; Elizabeth Graham; the late Duncan Grant; Frank Kelsall, Surveyor of Historic Buildings, GLC; the Guardian; Assistant Registrar, Guy's Hospital; Allan Gwynne-Jones; Trinita Japp,

Acknowledgements

Mrs Hall; Barbara Strachey, Mrs Halpern; Lord and Lady Hambleden; Norah Hartley; Edward Harvane; Major Hargreaves, the National Trust, Hatchlands; J. F. Hayley; Professor Thomas and Mrs Ann Hewer; Sylvia Hickson; Lady Anne Hill; Hogarth Press; John Holmstrom; Michael Holroyd; John Boyden, Curator, Hove Museum of Art; Louis and Jacqueline Hubert; John Bernascori, University of Hull; Sybil Schuster, Mrs Hutton; Lady Elspeth Huxley; the Department of Art, Imperial War Museum; the late Professor Derek Jackson; Guy Jamieson; Juliet Jamieson; Professor Wladyslawa Jaworska; the late Admiral Sir Caspar John; Poppet John, Mme. Pol; Romilly John; Vivienne John, Mrs White; Gilbert Kennedy; Professor Charles and Mrs Ann Kennedy; Mary, Mrs George Kennedy; Richard Kennedy; James Kirkman; Howard Kopet; Armand and Betty Lacroix; Felicia Lamb, Mrs Palmer; Professor Hubert Lamb; Lady Rose Lamb; Valentine Lamb; Vanessa, Lady Ayer; Department of Fine Art, University of Leeds; Lloyd George Memorial Museum; the London Library; Lord and Lady Longford; Sir Anthony Lousada; Hon. David and Lady Cecilia McKenna; Brigit Macnamara, Mrs Marnier; Chetham's Library, Manchester; Jane Farrington, Sandra Martin, Julian Treuherz, the Manchester City Art Gallery; Ian Bailey, the Manchester Grammar School; D. F. Cook, the Medical Library, University of Manchester; the Whitworth Art Gallery, Manchester; Catherine Martineau; Jonathan Meuli; Kay Melzi; Professor Donald Mitchell; Lady Diana Mosley; Ferdinand and Julia Mount; Julienne Favennec, Mme Narvor; National Art Gallery, Wellington, NZ; Kai Kin Yung, Registrar, National Portrait Gallery; Stone Gallery, Newcastle-upon-Tyne; David Woolfers, New Grafton Gallery; Norah Schuster, Mrs Nicholls; Rosemary Olivier; Alan Overton; Ashmolean Museum, Oxford; E. J. S. Parsons, Bodleian Library, Oxford; R. A. C. Parker, The Queen's College, Oxford; Senior Bursar, St Hugh's College, Oxford; Oxford University Press; Senior Tutor, Wadham College, Oxford; H. G. Pitt, Worcester College, Oxford; Kevin Pakenham; Hon. Thomas Pakenham; Trekkie Parsons; Frances Marshall, Mrs Partridge; Brian Allen, the Paul Mellon Centre for Studies in British Art; Sir Peter Pears; Phaidon Press; Yves Philippe; C. Picken; Sir Harry Platt; Hon. Reuben Pleydell-Bouverie; Professor John and Mrs Mary Postgate; Anthony Powell; Lady Violet Powell; Isobel, Lady Radnor; Julia Rushbury, Mrs Ramos; Professor Philip Rieff; Professor Giles Robertson; Rochdale Museum and Art Gallery; Paul and Clarissa Roche; Guy Roddon; Gavin Ross, Edinburgh College of Art; Sir John Rothenstein; Sidney Hutchinson, Constance Parker and Norman Rosenthal, the Royal Academy of Arts; Maud, Mrs Gilbert Russell; Richard Cusden, Salisbury College of Art; Sheffield City Art Galleries; Richard Shone; Murray Watson, the Slade School of Art; Eva Olesen, Sotheby's; Southampton City Art Gallery; Frances Spalding; the late Gilbert Spencer; the late John

Stanley-Clarke; Stoke-on-Trent Museum and Art Gallery; Michael Stone, University of Sheffield; Amy and Vincent Summers; Elizabeth Inglis, University of Sussex Library; Sarah Fox-Pitt, the Tate Gallery Archives; the Tate Gallery; Mary Taubman; Ellen S. Dunlap, Humanities Research Center, University of Texas; Thames & Hudson; N. M. Tremlett; Romilly Turton; Ruth Conway, Mrs Verney; Carol Hogben, Victoria & Albert Museum; Julian Morrell, Mrs Vinogradoff; Justin Vulliamy; Kitty West; Charles Whaley; George White; G. B. H. Wightman; Tony Cooper, Richard Wade and Valerie Warren, Wimbledon Lawn Tennis Museum; and Professor Irving Younger.

Acknowledgement is also given to the following institutions and individuals who have allowed me to use unpublished sources. Letters by Henry Lamb, and others, to Lytton Strachey are in the Strachey Papers at the British Library. Henry Lamb's letters to Lady Ottoline Morrell and Dora Carrington are at the Humanities Centre, University of Texas. And his letters to Richard Carline are on microfilm in the Tate Gallery Archives, London, as are letters by Augustus John to Henry Lamb.

Walter Lamb's letters to Clive Bell when originally consulted were with the Charleston Papers at King's College Library, Cambridge, as were letters by Vanessa Bell and drafts by Duncan Grant. The Charleston Papers are now in the Tate Archives. The diaries of Leonard Woolf are at the Library of the University of Sussex.

Stanley and Gilbert Spencer's letters to Henry Lamb are in the possession of Lady Pansy Lamb and are also on microfilm in the Tate Archives.

Correspondence between Henry Lamb and the Ministry of Information and the War Artists' Advisory Committee is in the Department of Art at the Imperial War Museum, London.

Letters to Lawrence Haward by Henry Lamb, and others, are at the Manchester City Art Gallery.

Henry Lamb's letters to Guy Roddon are in the possession of the recipient. Some private sources wish to remain anonymous.

For photography, my thanks especially to George Deacon, Paul Hicks and Zul. For transcribing the text to typescript, my gratitude to Veronica Symons, for indexing to Maureen Webley; from The Redcliffe Press to Michael Abbott for his patience, perception and sensitivity in editing the text and to John Sansom for general guidance and support.

The whole is dedicated to my family: to daughter Vaila and son Gavin who, while growing up, have had to live with my preoccupation and whose tolerance of which has helped me feel a little less guilty; and to my wife Jackie who, amongst innumerable tasks, acted as interpreter for the Breton dialect, and whose profound interest, encouragement and criticism has been a constant inspiration.
Newhaven, Sussex
1984

Introduction

In 1960, when Lamb died he was known, had been well known, but few of his paintings were remembered and his work, like that of most of his contemporaries, was unfashionable. Worse, he had painted many portraits, and portraiture then was passé and unpopular.

Since the nineteen-sixties, British Art of the early twentieth century has been steadily rediscovered and increasing scholarly attention devoted to that remarkable generation of artists. Also since Lamb's death, almost twenty five years ago, painting has seen a resurgence of interest in figuration and a concomitant revival of portraiture, especially in England.

One effect of this has been that many pictures, hitherto relegated to museum cellars or hung unobtrusively in private collections, or even left in portfolios, have now had the dust swept off to reappear in galleries and salerooms. Detailed research has been launched into the work of students of the Slade School of Art – first the men, then the women; the flamboyant figures of Fitzrovia, the reticence and *intimité* of Camden Town, the brief blasts of the Vorticists, and the multifarious influences of Post-Impressionism. This welter of scholarship has made it look as though no artist of consequence nor any drawing, painting, or merest *pochade* from such an intensely fertile period in British art and letters could possibly have escaped notice or been uncatalogued.

As well, the spate of related biographies, memoirs and letters grows, seeming to invest some of the principals with a near-fictional fascination suggesting, because of such exceptionally well-authenticated minutiae, that there could be no other character awaiting rediscovery nor any relationship remaining unexplored, undocumented, unanalysed. Bloomsbury, in particular, from seeming an aloof but influential elite, now appears, from the formidable body of literature by and about them, to be less a group and more the centre of an ever widening circle of friends – and enemies.

There was however one surprising omission in the story of this generation of artists. In histories of the art of his period, Henry Lamb would be mentioned, acknowledged, but receive limited critical attention. In biographies he was a handsome, moody, mercurial figure flitting from friend to friend, recalled more for the diversity and fame of his remarkable associations than for his intrinsic qualities or his own achievements. Apart from exhibition reviews and an occasional article, nothing has been published on him since a slim monograph of 1924.

In portraiture, there are two kinds of artist: portrait painters and painters who paint portraits. Of the former, in Lamb's lifetime, William Orpen would have been one of the wealthiest and most succcessful; amongst the latter, the father figure of Sickert looms large. There are, too, those who span something of both worlds, like William Nicholson, or Augustus John, or Henry Lamb: for he was more than just a portrait painter, and the range of his work and interests was far wider and more varied than generally supposed. He was a prolific artist, and there is a Lamb in most public collections in Britain and some in America, but the majority are in private possession. His work shows radical changes of style though oddly, perhaps because of the consistently idiosyncratic use of colour, a Lamb, from any period, is almost unmistakable.

As a man, he was unusually sensitive, highly intelligent, widely read, cultured and deeply musical. He was courteous, gentle, affectionate and caring, selfless and enabling to others, often inspiring in them the greatest affection and respect. But he could be difficult, obtuse, unreasonable in his determination to be independent, and in personal relations, sometimes edgy and impatient. Yet relationships were important to him and he had some lengthy, exciting and enriching friendships. Places too, even though he came to dislike some of them and was never a distinguished landscape painter, were also significant in his development as an artist and as a person.

Hence, the shape of the story that follows.

I never met Henry Lamb, although I now feel as if I had. His famous portrait of the infamous Lytton Strachey is an indelible memory from a first, boyhood visit to the Tate Gallery. However, later, in 1951, or possibly 1952, I did catch sight of him at the Private View of the Royal Academy Summer Exhibition, in what I now know to have been an alien environment. He was amongst, as he might have said, 'a covey' of Academicians – James Fitton, Ruskin Spear, Alfred Munnings and the then President, Gerald Kelly, were in the group. Slight, spare, lean and alert, he looked exactly like the self portrait drawings of about the same time. Crowds he abhorred, especially on formal occasions: 'I don't enjoy any kind of collective festivities', he once wrote, a feeling that remained with this sociably intimate and very private person.

I

Manchester

1885 – 1905

ONE

THE LAMBS

———

'I'm in no hurry to go to Manchester, a return to my greatest and most seismatic vomit', wrote Henry Lamb some thirty years after he had left. 'The place is more mean, sordid and shrunken looking than is possible to remember or imagine and practically all its associations have for me a very ugly side', he complained, again airing his prejudices on a previous return visit. The unhappinesses of his formative years remained a persistently painful memory, making the city both an object for his disaffection and a symbol of his frustration. Ever after he was haunted by the nagging recollection of first, the Grammar School, then Medical School: each he felt to have been largely a hindrance: the former, unavoidable; the latter, through parental pressure, a wrong turning from which he was to escape. But, above all, Manchester was identified with family life. 'O, why did I never have the chance of associating with some indulgent sage during all those years I was frantically trying to set up some hostile standard to those I have been reared under and no longer respected?' he asked after leaving home.

One of seven brought up in a large house at Fallowfield, a tree-lined residential suburb three miles or so to the south of the city near the university and popular then with well-to-do professional people, Henry – the third son and fourth child – was actually born in Adelaide in 1883. For ten years his father held a Chair in Mathematics at the University of South Australia until, in 1885, the

Lamb family returned to England and settled in Manchester. In any biographical summary, Henry Lamb's birthplace becomes a conspicuous irrelevance, for not once does he ever recall Australia.

Certainly Manchester, 'the scene of my tempestuous early struggles', as he dramatically described it, was significant in his evolution as an artist even if, ultimately, it is only accountable as a negative force against which he reacted so vehemently. From some of the blackened Victorian edifices that remain – perhaps shored up alongside and overshadowed by imposing redevelopments or isolated in a wasteland of potential redevelopment – it is not too difficult to visualise what an alien and depressing environment the industrial and commercial capital of the North of England might have seemed to a romantically inclined, artistically talented young man growing up at the turn of the century. Though the city has nourished many artists and designers, to Henry, despite the possible advantages of an academic background and despite, too, the consolations of the Hallé orchestra, exhibitions at the City Art Gallery, and a lively local patronage in the arts, Manchester then may still have seemed a provincial backwater.

Henry's father, Horace Lamb, had his origins firmly in the north. The son of a Stockport cotton mill foreman, he was a pupil at Stockport Grammar School and a student of mathematics at Owen's College, Manchester, until, in 1869, he left to complete his studies at Trinity College, Cambridge. Three years later he was back in Manchester, again at Owen's College, as a Fellow and Lecturer, during which time he met an Irish girl, Elizabeth Mary Foot, employed as companion to two middle aged Mancunian spinsters. In 1875 Mary married 'her little lamb' – a family joke thereafter – and the newlyweds departed for Australia.

A decade after, on being appointed to a Chair in Mathematics at Owen's College, Horace Lamb resumed his long association with that institution. As an influential professor he showed a gift for administration and was one of the tutors instrumental in the translation of the College into the Victoria University of Manchester, as it was first known in 1903, by which time son Henry was a student at the Medical School. Professor Lamb in a distinguished academic career – he was knighted in 1931 – wrote several notable scientific articles and papers of which the best known, *Hydrodynamics*, published in 1895, was probably his most important contribution to the study of

4

mathematical physics. It still ranks as a landmark in the history of the subject. A former colleague described him as 'a man of great personal dignity, somewhat awe-inspiring to youth, but on closer acquaintance kindly, humane, humorous, highly cultured, (he read French, German and Italian) conservative in temper, with wide interests and many contacts.'[1] Such a father, said to be 'a rather grim intellectual' with a large family and an impressive home, can only appear the stereotype of a Victorian patriarch. Henry himself never subscribed to the official, public opinion of his father and privately maintained a cautious, sceptical attitude, developing an almost patronising tolerance of him in his old age.

Of his mother Henry was unkindly, but perhaps accurately, critical, once describing her as meeting him 'with a prepared expression of spontaneity' and on another occasion as being 'very puffed up by [his] temporary success'. Mrs Lamb seems to have been singularly lacking in confidence and quite unsure of her social role, believing that her husband's position demanded certain appearances that she was continually at pains to keep up. She came from a large, well-known Irish family with a wealthy background. Her great, great grandfather, Lundy Foot, in the latter half of the eighteenth century, had made a fortune from producing and retailing snuff and tobacco in Dublin where her father, Simon Foot, was a solicitor and Justice of the Peace. She was one of eight daughters and seven sons, a family that 'encountered more adversity and tribulation than is found in many marriages' with a series of personal tragedies against a background of 'a troubled Ireland throughout their lives'.[2] The sad and straitened circumstances of her branch of the Foot family in the 1850s are a likely reason for Elizabeth Mary's departure from Dublin to seek employment in Manchester. It may too, partly account for her being so sensitive to social status and obsessive about the cultivation of airs and graces, attitudes that increasingly alienated her son Henry. A neighbour recalled her as 'kindly but an awful snob – both Professor and Mrs Lamb liked everything to be terribly proper.' A cameo of family life at Fallowfield – and a pertinent comment on the intellectual climate of the then college – was left by a Cambridge contemporary of Henry's elder brother Walter, Alfred Ainsworth, appointed in 1902 to Owen's and a young colleague of the already eminent Horace Lamb: 'Manchester is damnable', he wrote,

'Its unsafe to have opinions here which do not agree either with those of the Guardian or of some Professor or other, unless of course you are a Professor . . . Lamb's father is very nice, much more like the university Don than any other member of the staff here . . . I went to supper there on Sunday. After a smoke we went into the drawing room. Lamb [Walter] has three sisters, I went to sit next to one, but before I could begin to talk to her Prof. Lamb & a younger son [Henry] & another guest & I somehow began to talk. It seemed like the usual thing: & those three poor girls sat there for two hours without moving or speaking, except to laugh when they thought they ought from a cue that came from somewhere, perhaps Mrs. Lamb.'[3]

Mrs Lamb remains a somewhat shadowy, negative figure yet her twittering was to be a quite positive irritant within the family, particularly to Henry who became so sickened by his mother's hypocrisy and pretentiousness and so frustrated by the formality and conventions of home that for many years he was provoked into unconsciously seeking refuge by 'adopting' families with values more fundamental than his own. Having escaped in 1905, he was ever reluctant to return to the awesome restrictions of Fallowfield. Following one, rare visit, he confided how he had been 'possessed' by 'an awful whirl of feelings . . . most of them oppressive & painful'. Invariably it was a debilitating experience: as well as going back physically, that intimidating, claustrophobic atmosphere did terrible harm to his psyche making him uncomfortably aware of his personal regression.

Henry's relations with his parents were in no way helped by his decision to abandon medicine, a profession into which he had been dragooned by a father who, having struggled to overcome the disadvantages inherent in his own modest background and having succeeded as an academic, was highly unlikely to give his blessing to a speculative career for his youngest son. Oddly enough, the fault, indirectly, was father's: at Easter in 1904, when Henry was in his second year as a medical student, Professor Lamb took him on a tour of Italy that inspired and stiffened his resolution to become a painter. It was some time before the Lambs were quite reconciled to their son's pursuit of art. Years later, when they appeared to be accepting the idea, Henry remained defensive and cynical: 'My family, on seeing some newspaper praise of my pictures, discovered a new affection for me and threatened to invade my peace: so I had to spurn them discreetly once more.'

Partial reconciliation between father and son came about in a curiously ironic way when, in 1913, the University of Manchester commissioned Henry to paint his father's portrait in recognition of his having held the Chair in Mathematics for twenty-eight years. 'I have been stirred by news from Manchester', he reported, 'I am to paint my father for that bloody university after all . . . the pay will be good – at least £100, and I must determine to dispatch the thing rapidly before I succumb to the surroundings. There will be some amusement but of a rather ghostly kind – and infinite horror'! Sittings were in 'a large light room' at the university: 'in spite of many an evil presage' he made an auspicious start and the work began 'to go in a favourable direction. My design appears splendiferous', he announced, 'scarlet & pink robes: yellow-downshire wall behind with a death-trap of a Manchesterian view through a window at the back: in the middle of all that mon petit bonhomme d'un père sits in a tetrahedral pose. The expression should be an excruciating mélange of eminence and diminuitive pomp: but it will be difficult.' And difficult it became. At first, father sat well enough – 'when amused' – and was 'enthusiastic about the occasion'; but later 'the professor . . . developed a formidable garrulousness' and, complained Henry, 'I simply can't paint and talk simultaneously'. Eventually, the portrait 'came to a doubtful conclusion owing', as the artist put it, 'to very unfortunate conditions of time and surroundings.'

The Artist's Father – or 'Professor Horace Lamb, FRS, DSc', as the painting was called originally – was presented to the university at a large gathering in the Whitworth Hall in November 1913. Even allowing for the predictable platitudes that are usually trotted out on such official occasions, some of what was said at that ceremony points up a little of the polarity of attitude existing between father and son. As one of Professor Lamb's oldest colleagues observed, 'It seems to me to be especially appropriate that the portrait of the man whose judgement – if it erred at all – did not err on the side of revolutionism should be painted by one, and that his own son, whose style of painting if it errs at all – does not err on the side of conservatism.'[4] The Vice-Chancellor of Leeds University – better known as Professor Michael Sadler, an active patron of contemporary British art and later to be a sitter to Henry for another official commission – considered it 'a great thing to have obtained for the University "a portrait by one of the greatest of the young painters"'.[5] In conception the painting now seems quite traditional and not unlike many others of the *genre* but at the time because of the lightness of key and the studied stylisation, it may well have appeared very modern. The handling reveals a candour avoiding any of the slick tricks of the formal, professional portrait trade, especially in its Edwardian twilight; and the knowing, unsentimental vision that informs the fine likeness sets it above the conventions of its period, ranking it among the best of Henry's pre-1914 portraits. In compositional unity however, it is less successful: the parts remain disparate, never satisfyingly relating to each other nor making a cohesive whole. The view through the window in the background – from Henry's jaundiced description known to have actually been there – is irritatingly obtrusive and, with its artifice like a painted theatrical curtain, fails to convince; and those vermilion robes which he said he was 'doomed to include' are never properly integrated. Harmony may well have prevailed at an earlier stage but perhaps from impatience, doubt, or loss of nerve, the artist has allowed the anecdotal business to become a distraction. It is a weakness that may be attributable in part to his being somewhat daunted and not a little perplexed by the nature of the commission and increasingly irritated by the sitter and the setting.

Professor Lamb, as both student and tutor, was connected with Manchester University for more than forty years until in 1920, at the age of 71, he was appointed to an Honorary Fellowship at Trinity, his old Cambridge college. Here too, there is another portrait by Henry of his father, done in 1927. It is one of his finest drawings, combining spontaneity, simplicity and delicacy of treatment: the eyes are still alert and questioning, the mouth suggests parsimony, but the artist – then in his mid-forties – seems to be underplaying his perception of the sitter as if betraying some slight softening of attitude, although no such change was ever consciously revealed. The Professor, for his part, eventually became quite approving of Henry Lamb, the painter, even admiring his skill and success and, in his declining years, promoting him to the top of the family pecking order.

But Henry never properly relaxed his suspicious reserve of either mother or father. Though his boyhood had sometimes seemed mitigated by memories of holidays in the Lake District and in North Wales when his father, 'normally austere and shut up in his study all day, would unbend, and they would all go for long walks together', family gatherings were generally an anathema to him and he would make his return visits to the fold as brief and infrequent as possible. Apart from Manchester itself holding out what he called 'a store of pestiferous attractions', life at home was no more promising, '"frosty" manner being one of the peculiarities of the establishment – just a curious little botanical rime quite normal and spontaneous at certain moments . . . and puzzlingly like a true frost.'

With such continuing antipathy, it is not surprising that Henry attended neither of his parents' funerals. In 1932, replying to condolences after the death of Professor Lamb, he wrote, 'My father's end seems to have been as well contrived (according to his ambitions) as the rest of his existence. But as far as I was concerned he was defunct several years ago.'

Henry's relations with his various brothers and sisters were scarcely easier. When in 1913, his eldest brother Ernest – who early on he had dismissed as 'rather dull and ordinary' – was appointed Professor of Engineering at London University and, in the same year, his other brother Walter became Secretary of the Royal Academy of Arts, Henry was moved to comment cynically: 'I foresee some bright and brotherly reunions as soon as . . . I settle there too'. Ernest came to pay his respects some weeks later but was treated as an intruder and 'dispatched . . . exactly 3 minutes after arrival'. Walter, on the other hand, took a somewhat paternal, admiring interest in his more adventurous younger brother, particularly in their early years away from home. Less assertive, less independent, Walter Lamb always kept in touch better with the family although, from his own account, he could hardly have relished visits to Manchester any more than Henry. 'This city is entirely peopled by gnomes', he once wrote from home, 'They stream along the streets, knotted together by their twisted limbs into one viscous continuity'. At Cambridge, Walter had been editor of 'The Cambridge Review' and his first major publication in 1914 was a study of the prose-form in Thucydides; in 1924 he edited *The Discourses of Sir Joshua Reynolds* and a decade later wrote a seminal history of the Royal Academy. He also translated Plato and occasionally wrote poetry; but he was wanting in imagination and creatively impotent: his literary works were either analytical interpretations or straightforward historical accounts, never springing from the roots of genuinely original thought. In theory, because of Walter's near lifelong association with the visual arts, Henry should have had most in common with him; but in practice, their dispositions were poles apart and despite the crossing of their professional paths they were to meet only occasionally.

Of Henry's sisters, Helen, the eldest, married a schoolmaster but was widowed young, afterwards becoming a Don at Newnham: appropriately, he had always thought her 'a bit schoolma'm-ish'. Peggy was the most popular relative with him until she took the veil and was virtually estranged through living most of her life in a Belgian convent. Lettice, overshadowed by an academically dazzling flock of Lambs, was downgraded as 'tiresomely silly' and placed unfairly at the bottom of the class. It was his youngest sister Dorothy who, more than any of the family, remained mostly an exception to his indifference and hostility. She had kept father amused for a few of the sittings whilst his portrait was being painted; and when Henry returned for the unveiling and presentation he recorded how the maturing Dorothy 'was *lovely*, a charming creature, much nicer than I have ever known her to be, and so wonderfully recovered from a morbid self-conscious period' and, having 'learnt to dress simply & amusingly . . . & now quite direct & unaffected & of course quite intelligent', she inspired in him an arousal of more than ordinary fraternal affection: observing her with a surprisingly sexual eye, he confessed, 'She ravished me by sitting up on the back of the drawing room sofa with her feet on the seat & playing her Greek peasants fiddle'. At that time, in the autumn of 1913, when Henry had seemed to be emerging from the depression of a year before yet still despairing of establishing a happy, permanent relationship with the opposite sex, he quite irrationally contemplated an unconventional liaison with his favourite sister: 'Dorothy describing her journeys and adventures in Greece with such a romantic summary . . . made my heart beat mad with new projects', he wrote, wondering whether 'we two could get on together; she seems intelligent & active & not obstinate – idle for the moment and contemplating matrimony for a sustenance or a fixture at least. I feel much inclined to try her companionship and *she* wants to introduce me to Greece'. The easier prospect of sister, mother, wife, lover and friend, all apparently available in one single person, was an alluring fantasy, a momentary temptation while he was still recovering emotionally. In noting with pleasure how attractively Dorothy was growing up, he found her engaging combination of elfin prettiness and alert, wide-eyed wonderment so appealing to his aesthetic sensibilities that he was moved to paint her portrait. Despite, or perhaps because of, the feelings she engendered in him, the result is weak and unremarkable.

The profound fascination soon passed; but brother and sister remained fairly close: during the First War, while Henry was away on active service, Dorothy stayed sometime in his studio in Hampstead; and afterwards, in 1920 when she married, she had a house nearby in Arkwright Road. It was here, in her absence and while his own studio was occupied, that Henry stayed, ostensibly intending to work on a portrait commission. Since the proposition meant his stay might be a long one, the idea was quickly quashed, proving too much even for her sisterly love and she evicted him 'giving useless and very offensive reasons . . . After Dorothy's infernal beastliness', he declared, 'I hate being in this house & won't have meals here – my pride only giving way to the convenience of breakfast & in the evenings when not invited out I'm on the streets'. Henry, on reflection, blamed their disagreement on her first husband, Sir John Reve Brooke, a civil servant, whom he could hardly abide and thought unbearably pompous. Brooke died in 1937 and two years later she married Sir Walter Nicholson, another civil servant. In 1946, she was again widowed and left very well off, enabling her to be a generous benefactor to her second husband's old college, Balliol. She was godmother to Henry's younger daughter; and towards the end of his life he accompanied Dorothy on holiday to Italy. She was an inveterate, enthusiastic, knowledgeable traveller, a classical scholar, archaeologist and historian; as a writer, she combined these interests in *Pilgrims Were They All*, published in 1937, a study of 'Religious Adventure in the Fourth Century'. Henry continued to respect her and to share her interests: of all the family he was perhaps at his most intimate with Dorothy.

However aggressively disposed Henry felt towards his family, and whatever prejudices he held against Manchester, not all his experiences in that milieu were unpleasant and abortive. One particular memory he came to cherish was of his first significant encouragement in drawing from Joseph Knight, the newly appointed art master at the Manchester Grammar School, where Henry arrived as a pupil in the September of 1894.

Himself an old boy of the school, Knight was twenty-three when he began his teaching career there. Henry always respected him and never forgot his early encouragement, once calling him 'a most excellent &

discerning fellow'. In 1930, when he retired on severely limited means after being headmaster of the Bury School of Art for many years, Henry took an active and continuing interest in his welfare. Some measure of his affection and concern may be gauged from how Henry, though never really prosperous and at that time supporting a young wife and family on the uncertain and variable income from painting, was fully prepared to be of financial and very practical help to his old art master. Knight was a competent if unexciting artist, remaining somewhat provincial in practice and being for several years Vice-President of the Manchester Academy of Fine Arts. When the City Art Gallery bought three of his etchings he recalled unassumingly having known the collection since boyhood and 'to be represented in it then was something of a dream . . . now' it was 'a pleasure and an honour'; and after retirement, when he again turned to oil painting, the Royal Manchester Institution presented a still-life of his to the Gallery. Despite his limitations and his modest, self-effacing personality, he was undoubtedly a caring and inspiring teacher. For young Henry the new art master's arrival must have been like a door opening, providing a welcome antidote to the academic rigours of school, the formal demands of preparing for university entrance and, above all, the frustrations of home. The art room would have been a much needed outlet for at least one of the abilities of this many-talented pupil who, in addition to having some precocity in drawing, was highly intelligent, scholastically able, and showed a special aptitude for music.

This last he seems not to have studied in any formal sense though he is said to have attended piano lessons privately and everyone testifies to his exceptional skill: 'I have often thought that he might have had a career as a musician had he done nothing with his painting or his medical work', commented Henry's old friend Lawrence Haward, Curator of the Manchester City Art Gallery from 1914 until 1945; and Kenneth Clark, who first met Henry in the thirties, wrote how he 'greatly enjoyed his company, not only because of his intelligence but because he was deeply musical'.[6] As a young man, Henry was as much a part of the musical as of the artistic circles in Manchester; he claimed that the main reason for his not pursuing a career as a professional pianist was because his hands were slightly webbed, preventing him from stretching a full octave.

At the Grammar School Henry won no prizes and always felt outshone by his academically brilliant family; but he was invariably 'above average' overall in his class, succeeding in being top in Drawing in his first year and top equal in the Classical Fifth; 'he went up the Classical side and then had three years in the Mathematical Sixth'. In specialising in Mathematics and Science, he could only have continued studying art by attending the 'Optional Classes, without additional fees' taken on Saturday mornings by Joseph Knight. Henry was a good gymnast and enjoyed cycling; but he took the tram daily from Fallowfield to the school which then was in the city centre, in Long Millgate, in a building put up in 1870, adjacent to what is now Chetham's Music School on the site of the original foundation. The forbidding facade remains virtually unaltered, still conveying the tradition of inculcated learning associated with the Victorian school. In the 1930s the Grammar School moved to its present site, by coincidence not far from the Lamb family home in Wilbraham Road. Regrettably, no artwork by Joseph Knight's promising pupil has been discovered but, when Henry left in 1901, unwillingly to study medicine, he would have taken with him some proficiency in drawing and an already smouldering ambition in art.

The earliest record of a Henry Lamb drawing is 1903, two years after he had entered the Medical Faculty of Owen's College: dated and signed in fake oriental script, 'H.T.L.' (his middle name was Taylor), it was the first of three cartoons 'By our Special Japanese Artist' reproduced in 'The Manchester Medical Students' Gazette' of 1904 and '05. Stylistically, and temperamentally these little excursions into pseudo-orientalism are quite out of character for, apart from sketches inserted in letters, Henry rarely indulged in caricature publicly, although in this instance there is some vague affinity with an odd pen and ink drawing of *Lytton Strachey and Clive Bell criticising works of art*, done about 1910, which is similarly satirical and lightheartedly witty. In the Manchester cartoons the target for comment is the Dean of the Medical Faculty:[7] in *First Impressions of Physiology* he appears as a gargantuan, menacing figure leaning on his pointer, in a lecture hall, before a ludicrously Lilliputian audience – the Japanese theme is carried through to the extent that the Dean resembles some sinister samurai resting on his sword. In *Second Impressions of Physiology* of a year later, the Dean has become a relatively insignificant, distant figure declaiming at the far end of an

13

even larger lecture hall to an inattentive audience – a smiling young man seated at the left in the forefront of the drawing, ignoring the lecturer and turning to his fellow student to whisper behind a cupped hand, is Henry himself. The third, done in his last year at Manchester, portrays his *bête noire* looming large again but flying high above the roofs of the Medical School in an imaginative exercise called *A Vacation Nightmare.* Each of the cartoons is typical of student humour revealing an impatience with the formal lecture and an irreverence towards authority, in this case, in the shape of the Dean, whose sharp diminution and ultimate banishment to fantasy reflect something of Henry's discontent with medicine and perhaps his determination to escape although he participated in university life variously and conspicuously.

In October 1904 the 'Gazette' reported a recital to the Musical Society at which Henry contributed piano solos, opening the programme with a group of Beethoven's Bagatelles:

> 'Mr. Lamb played these well, showing a thorough grasp of their conception, though failing in clearness of execution of the more rapid passages. As his later solos he played an exquisite Intermezzo and a fiery Capriccio – both by Brahms. In the first of these he created the exact atmosphere requisite and rendered its subtle charm with great delicacy, and in the Capriccio . . . he showed considerable technical skill.'[8]

He was, too, an active member of the Debating Society and, in February 1905, attended a Women's Rights meeting at which Miss Pankhurst was asked to move the motion, 'That this house is in favour of equal opportunities for men and women in professional, political, and industrial life'; but Henry supported an amendment that effectively moderated the proposal to 'sympathies with women in their attempt to obtain equal opportunities', thus aligning himself with a more cautionary, less radical attitude.[9] In the light of his early experience of the emerging feminist movement, it is noteworthy that a portrait commission of his after the First War – and a year or so after completing a portrait of his old Chemistry master, Francis Jones, on his retirement from the Grammar School – was to paint, also in Manchester, Margaret Ashton, a well known activist in the campaign for women's rights. The picture was presented to the university in 1923 and hung in the Debating Hall for many years; with that of Francis Jones, it is now in the permanent collection of the Manchester City Art Gallery.

Further to Henry's Debating Society activities, later in 1905, the 'Gazette' printed a lengthy paper supposedly given by him at a meeting on the twentieth of February. Whether it was actually presented remains conjecture but as an article it is certainly authentic, seeming to be the only piece he ever had published. Henry always maintained doubts about the expressive value of writing, once complaining how he hated what he called 'this confounded pen-art which comes in and damps all expression'; yet despite his reservations, the whole paper is both relevant and revelatory, giving remarkable insights into some of his persistent traits. Entitled *The Mesoblastic Layer* and sounding more like a learned scientific paper, it is in fact an ironic parody, described as 'an extract from Gulliver's Travel to the Island of Danglen', a barely concealed anagram of 'England'. Written in the first person the narrator, a visitor, 'having tarried for some time in this strange town of Mancity' – an obvious compression of 'Manchester' – 'was diverted by the many customs and peculiar institutions of its inhabitants' who have, what is unflatteringly and pointedly called, 'a natural torpor'. Like 'all the towns so far visited in the north of the island', he continues, 'if ever I stopped any man to ask of him some small matter . . . he would begin slowly to reflect on the answer, then he would set the clumsy machinery of his expression going; and so it was often a weary while before the actual articulation of the reply began . . . the vocabulary of these inhabitants is almost as limited as their intelligence'. He then ridicules the traditions and rituals of medical students who, in the 'Onion' (Student Union), greet the entry of each newcomer with 'a stamping of feet, thumping of fists, and a jingling of utensils'. He also suggests that the saying 'off his onion' may well derive from students who do not attend the Union of which Henry himself may not have been a fond frequenter since for most of his life he remained unwilling to belong to groups and organisations; as well he was ever impatient of group norms, always tending to sympathise with minorities and with the outsider.

The main part of the article is a detailed description of a student debate, the topic of which is never made explicit but seems basically about the merits of asceticism and the conflict between the puritan and the liberal. The final speaker, described as 'not tall but thin . . . his pale face mobile and expressive . . . a curious-looking young man . . . called Agnew. As this is the name of the wool-bearing quadrupeds of Danglen the appellation seemed scarcely inap-

15

propriate for on the top and sides of his head there was a fair-coloured fleecy growth'. None other than the hirsute Henry who, even before his brief bohemian phase, sported side-whiskers. Here, metaphorically, he holds up a mirror as if to draw a self-portrait in words seen through the eyes of the reader. Allowing for the flippant vein and satirical slant, the writing still shows how Henry was studying medicine under sufferance; and reading between the lines reveals a series of unguarded moments betraying attitudes that were to surface later. Youthful disdain permeates the piece; and the author, in the guise of 'Agnew' the heroic outsider, goes on to show a surprising narcissism, almost conceit: 'To some he was known as a musician, to others as a painter . . . a few declared that he was of an extremely amiable disposition, a clever and ingenious fellow of many parts'. But, 'the great majority of students . . . looked askance at him, and he enjoyed little popularity there'. Among the members of the assembly 'Agnew was held in very bad odour, and had a great reputation for immorality'. Finally, they vote, 'in the name of decency', as to whether they can 'tolerate the concupiscence and immorality of Agnew any longer' and declare that he 'should be thrust forth from their midst'. Thereupon, he is unanimously ejected 'apparently more pleased than ever . . . and entirely sensible of the extreme honour they were paying him; nothing could be more gratifying . . . than to be ejected from this assembly as something unclean'.

Apart from illustrating the obvious conflict between medicine and the arts, and taking account of the natural ebullience and rebellious spirit of youth, some of Henry's enduring characteristics may be construed from this singular exposition. His play upon the family name is in itself an ironic reminder of his habitual resistance to being herded and his reluctance to subsume his individuality – a not uncommon trait among artists, of course – but again, it is reflected in his cynical references to the sports of what he calls, 'Crossal' and 'Ticker' – respectively, Lacrosse and Cricket. He always disliked team games, feeling temperamentally ill disposed towards their corporate competitiveness, although he took regular exercise, often strenuously, throughout his life. His mistrust of the church – any church – his revulsion from any form of organised religion, his hatred of self-righteousness, all are underlined in his reference to 'those who hide their cowardice behind the smug trappings of religion and piety': certainly he was agnostic, some said atheistic. He also maintained an unwavering aversion to dealers in art, any entrepreneur who might conceivably profit – literally – from his artistic productions. Neither was he one bit more kindly disposed towards critics, 'tastemakers' as he called them, anyone who might attempt to influence his aesthetic judgement: 'I have come to the conclusion', Agnew decides, 'that in this island of Danglen there exists, just as in our own England, a certain species of obnoxious persons who, having received what they are pleased to term a Liberal Education, imagine themselves to be thereby provided with intelligence, and therefore regard themselves as authorities or persons of "taste" in all branches of culture'. Finally, the humour pervading the article is typical of the wit that infiltrates his letters, sometimes sardonic, occasionally manifest in an imaginative, diabolical practical joke.

'Agnew's' fictional expulsion from the 'Onion' was an uncanny anticipation of Henry's own voluntary departure from medicine and Manchester barely a year later, in the summer of 1905. Although he left university before completing the course and without a degree, at no stage was he an inadequate student – quite the contrary, in fact, for his academic record was consistently creditable. In 1903, he was a medallist in 'Practical Histology'; the year after, he gained his Intermediate 'Anatomy and Physiology' with 70.9 per cent; and later in 1904, was awarded a University Scholarship in 'Medicine'. Adding these successes to his numerous extra-curricular activities – the existence of which suggests that his medical studies may have been done with some ease – it can be seen what a distinctive and energetic student he was and how his eventual choice of career could not have been made lightly.

NOTES

1 *Dictionary of National Biography* 1971.
2 Foot *What's My Line?* p.70.
3 Alfred Ainsworth – Lytton Strachey: 29 Nov 1902. Ainsworth was a Cambridge Apostle and close friend of the philosopher G. E. Moore, guru of the Bloomsbury group. Ainsworth was a brilliant scholar and lectured in Latin at Manchester 1902–3, taught Greek at Edinburgh 1903–7, and in 1908, became an Inspector of Schools with the Board of Education. E. M. Forster sketched a portrait of him as Ansell in *The Longest Journey*. (Levy *Moore* pp.209–11).

4 'The Manchester Guardian' 21 Nov 1913: Dr Arthur Schuster. In the 1930s, Schuster commissioned Henry to paint a portrait of his wife. He himself, later knighted, was painted by Orpen for the Royal Society. Also at the ceremony was Professor Rutherford, the nuclear physicist, who 'added a few words as to Professor Lamb's success as a teacher and worker in the field of science, and of his personal kindness.'

5 'The Manchester Guardian' 21 Nov 1913.

6 Lord Clark – author : 22 Oct 1977.

7 Sir William Sinclair MA MD MRCP

8 'The Manchester Medical Students' Gazette' Dec 1904.

9 'The Manchester University Magazine' Feb 1905.

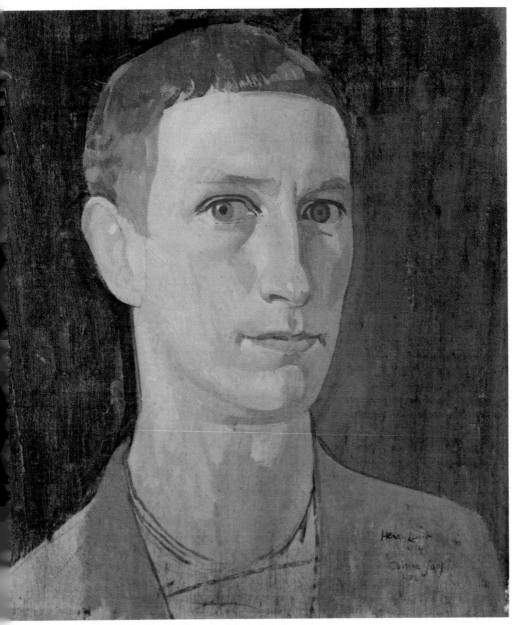

lf Portrait *1914* *Oil on panel* *36.8 × 31.8* *National Portrait Gallery, London*

Fisherfolk, Gola Island *1913   Oil on canvas   82.1 × 102.6   Private collection*

TWO

FRANCIS DODD

———

During his last months at Medical School Henry became increasingly active as an artist, advertising his aspirations in a number of ways. Prior to publication of the lengthy literary explosion, *The Mesoblastic Layer*, the editor of 'The Medical Students' Gazette', in the February number of 1905, had 'noticed with pleasure three examples of Mr. Lamb's work now hanging in the Spring Exhibition at the City Art Gallery. This we believe, is a unique achievement for a Manchester University student, and we offer him our heartiest congratulations on this distinction.' Attention was also drawn to the 'specially executed' portrait drawing reproduced in the same edition, the first of three published portraits of members of the university staff done that year. The other two reached a wider audience, being also printed in 'The Manchester University Magazine', in the June supplement of which, the editor commented on the artist 'rapidly making a name for himself, especially by his pencil sketches . . . Although he is leaving Manchester, we hope in our next volume, to be able to produce more of his excellent work.' Some editorial collusion might just be construed from the almost excessive attention given to 'Mr. Lamb' by the 'Gazette'; but, aside from his distaste of any kind of publicity often to the extent of actually avoiding it, and also any form of connivance being totally out of character, in this instance he was not even on the editorial committee, some of whom he had satirised quite savagely in *The Mesoblastic Layer*.

The three 'university' portrait drawings are the earliest examples discovered of Henry's more serious artistic intentions. Certainly they show what a competent, if unspectacular, draughtsman he was even before leaving Manchester, shortly after his twenty-second birthday. He was then at an age when most artists would be indicating their potential if not actually putting some achievements behind them: for this reason alone, he could hardly be thought precocious, in any normal sense; but on the other hand, considering his relatively late start in art, and bearing in mind that he had spent most of the previous three years ostensibly studying medicine, the drawings are remarkably confident and well realised. Without other, earlier evidence to illustrate the stages in his development, one 'misses the beginning of the picture', as it were, but no student, even with the insight and intelligence indicated by Henry's academic record, could have produced such worthy results without a great deal of practice, persistence and encouragement. In each portrait, the relationship between head and body is well made, though only one includes the hands. They are described as 'pencil sketches'; but it is difficult to be sure of the exact medium used: From the reproductions, the texture suggested is broader than pencil alone, and one of the originals that survives is certainly in conté – or similar crayon – heightened with white, interestingly a method Henry was to use quite frequently in drawing portraits. Though a traditional and fairly sophisticated way of rendering form – from Holbein onwards – it is rarely handled with conviction or subtlety by the novice, suggesting more experience of drawing than indicated by Henry's academic record.

Some credit for the relative maturity of these early drawings must be attached to Francis Dodd, who had arrived in Manchester around 1895, while Henry was still at school. Nine years older than Henry, Dodd – no one ever seems to have called him Francis – had studied painting at the Glasgow School of Art until, in 1893, he won the Haldane Travelling Scholarship enabling him to visit Italy. On his way there, as a gauche and bluff student, he called on Whistler in Paris and met with a friendly but amused reception: 'the sight of the young red-haired lad struggling to get a roll of his masterpieces out of his hip pocket greatly entertained Whistler, who became interested in his work', advising him to study Tintoretto in Venice.[1] Perhaps he did so. However it was more likely Whistler himself who left his mark on the young Dodd, possibly stimulating his interest in etching: but whereas the 'master' attacked his work *con brio* seeming to pirouette round his subject matter with calculated grace and style searching for its essence, Dodd became an increasingly complex plodder. Whistler practised the art that conceals art and sought to achieve the sublime serenity of his ends with ever greater economy of means, truly confirming what Arthur Koestler has called 'the infolding process' – the tendency for the mature artist to work towards an ultimate simplicity by way of implication rather than over explicit statement.[2] By contrast, Dodd deliberated and worried his work, betraying more and more his honest sweat and lack of imagination, mainly in portrait drawings, innumerable examples of which either line the walls of Oxbridge colleges or are stored in the cellars of the Imperial War Museum, faithfully accurate but desperately dull records of distinguished academics and servicemen. The National Portrait Gallery in London, with its criteria for acquisition as much historical as aesthetic, also has several in the permanent collection.

Nevertheless, in those early years in Manchester, and at first in London, Dodd had a warmth and vitality in his work that sadly he was never to recapture: at the same time, he was for Henry a distraction from medicine and an inspiration to his art. They probably met through Joseph Knight. Dodd, fresh from his continental experiences soon became well-known and influential in Mancunian art circles although, as an artist, he was by no means an immediate success. His circumstances were well described by Alfred Ainsworth, Professor Lamb's young colleague:

'Lamb's younger brother [Henry] . . . took me to see Dodd last week. He's living alone in a large house, doing his own cooking & washing. We sat in the kitchen in front of the stove & talked scrappily & disconnectedly, for we didn't hit the right vein . . . quite readily. He's a little depressed, for he's got but little money, & has several people dependent on him. But he seems to be able to get out of his worries & become interested . . . quite easily . . . I liked some of his pictures: but he seems to have little of what I call emotional powers'.[3]

Dodd was doomed, by the restrictions of his puritan upbringing – he was the son of a Wesleyan minister – and by his largely prosaic nature, to become a dogged topographer. Certainly his staid, sober beginnings provided him with a sound grounding in the virtues of the work ethic and his reliability and dedication to drawing were indisputable; but clearly those same virtues were to become a straitjacket and inhibiting to the more imaginative demands of being an artist. Thus he could never erase, nor disguise, nor completely rise above the confines of his background. If Dodd's mature style of drawing were definable, it would approximate to a kind of Edwardian conservatism of which, perhaps not unexpectedly, there is more than a hint in Henry's 'Medical' portraits: they have an untypical tightness and containment never again to be seen in his work and strongly reminiscent of Dodd himself, though there is no evidence that he ever taught Henry.

However, the embryo artist would have learned by example from the older man, for Henry's artistic activities were fairly considerable well before he made the break with medicine. Early in 1904, brother Walter recalled taking a friend up to the bedroom they shared and Henry showing 'all his oil and pastel follies, with much lecturing to an apparent willing novice in the mysteries'. Doubtless Henry would have been encouraged in his diversion by Dodd and at the time there must have been some mutual admiration between them. One side of this friendship is recorded in a fine, surprisingly vigorous, portrait of Henry by Dodd. Dated 1905, the recalcitrant medical student is seen to have abandoned medicine, at least in spirit; the longer locks (mentioned by 'Agnew'), the flowing tie and velvet jacket, all suggest his capitulation to art and predestine *la vie de bohème*; on his knees rests a large book, seeming as much a practical as a theatrical prop; the eyes, bright and attractive, gaze ahead, anticipating a more exciting, self determining future: already, Henry looks as if in the Quartier Latin and about to break into a Puccini aria. Something too, of the youthful narcissism evident in *The Mesoblastic Layer* is suggested in this lively, rather romantic, remarkably revealing portrait.

Sometime between 1903 and '05 in Manchester, Henry must also have met, and been encouraged by, Muirhead Bone, Dodd's brother-in-law, a not dissimilar artist who had been a student with Dodd at the Glasgow School of Art. Bone was from the Highlands and Dodd, though having such strong and long connections with Manchester and in personality seeming the stereotype of a brash northerner capable of telling broadly funny stories, was actually born in Holyhead and spent most of his early life in Scotland. As well as having Scottish backgrounds and being related by marriage, there is a strange stylistic affinity between the work of Bone and Dodd, despite the differences in subject matter: each was competent in both landscape and portraiture; but Bone became best known for his often vast, highly complex townscapes, and Dodd as a meticulous, reliable portraitist.

Much of their work now appears dour and depressing, as if conceived in a presbyterian gloom: that Bone, too, came from a strictly puritan background and was brought up as a 'wee free' is not altogether surprising for, as artists, they seem to represent the obverse of the joyous, sensual, passionate, spontaneous avenue explored by other contemporary Scots, painters such as Fergusson, Peploe, and Redpath, who looked more to Matisse and inhaled a breath of the Mediterranean, as if to celebrate a revival of the 'auld alliance'. Both Dodd and Bone drew and painted extensively in France – and Italy and Spain – but even in the Latin landscape the warmth and sunshine seem overcast with the shadow of John Knox. The brothers-in-law were also prolific and successful etchers and engravers, many of their drawings being highly elaborate preparations for printmaking and, when translated into etching or drypoint – or often a combination of the two, their work regained a visual 'edge', subsequently acquiring a period interest; but for the most part, despite their skill and precision as craftsmen, even when not simulating the deliberations of the needle, they made unusually heavy weather of the process of drawing.

Francis Dodd and Muirhead Bone belong very much to the later eighteenth, early nineteenth century tradition of topographical draughtsmanship in Britain; but however much a 'nonconformist' upbringing may have contributed to their becoming conformist artists, each had a highly developed sense of helping others and consistently and effectively showed a kindly disposition towards fellow artists. Neither seems to have been too formidably nor aggressively ambitious and in carving their own safe, unadventurous, conservative careers they became influential members of numerous art clubs and societies. Both were busy with enough commissions, first as stalwarts of the New English Art Club, then as official artists in the First and Second World Wars, and as pillars of the establishment through election to the Royal Academy – Bone was knighted in 1937. As regular committeemen and exhibition organisers they were continually enabling to their contemporaries: in 1919, Bone instituted a fund to commission and purchase pictures for the Imperial War Museum – in which scheme Henry was to be included; and Dodd was ever encouraging Henry to join some group or other, or send something to a mixed exhibition, usually with little success. 'Dodd writes wanting to nominate me for the Society of Portrait Painters & also for the XII', reported Henry in 1911, 'I wrote back temporising'. And a month later he mentioned receiving, 'Another letter from Dodd wanting me to become a member of the NEAC which I refused. C. J. Holmes [then Director of the National Portrait Gallery] had offered to second me. Since I am anxious for that institution to come to a quiet end, there's no use my supporting it, even on the ground of the little it has supported me.' Henry was always cynical of art institutions and detested the whole para-phernalia of exhibiting his pictures. Any notion of institutionalised art was so abhorrent to him that for a large part of his life he maintained his independence and avoided joining anything: in spite of becoming well-known and being eligible, he was fifty-seven before elected to the Royal Academy. Informally, and in small groups, he was sociable enough; but formal occasions he refrained from when at all possible and was always resistant to being organised. Dodd, on the contrary, with a breezier bonhomie, enjoyed organisations and, being less confident, clearly needed the support of an identifiable and properly constituted brotherhood of artists. He was, too, more wholeheartedly – and perhaps realistically – involved in the art business than Henry was ever disposed to be. In the early days, he would sometimes generously take charge of Henry's haphazard affairs: 'With all the fervour of benevolence for which his sect are noted', wrote Henry in 1913, 'Dodd came . . . & took away a large bundle of sketches (drawings & oil paysages) to sell to his Lancashire & Glasgow dealers'.

When Dodd first arrived in London – a year ahead of Henry – his gaucheness, heartiness, and general lack of sophistication, were something of a disadvantage socially; but with his art, he soon established himself by a one man show and election to the New English, and for Henry, was to prove a helpful bridge between Manchester and the metropolis: 'The kind Dodd asks me to stay with him when I come to London', he wrote. Yet at times, some strain must have been put upon Henry's loyalties since few of Henry's first acquaintances in London seem to have had much regard or respect for his older friend who was soon to become another butt for Bloomsbury and a joke to Augustus John. After the opening of the New English summer exhibition in 1907, Augustus reported to Henry that, 'the dauntless Dodd turned up . . . and . . . complained bitterly about one of his gimcrack views of decaying London districts, being hung between two rival "yallers" and got it changed. He pointed out to me a picture of Rothensteins & said with much solemnity "Why that's all out of perspective" I answered "So's yours" and he fetched up one of his weak titters.'[4]

The impact of Augustus' bravura bohemianism, painterly panache, and relatively avant-garde attitudes to art, must all have emphasised to Henry how dull an artist dear Dodd really was; and as a person his idiosyncrasies and inadequacies were frequently ridiculed by Virginia Stephen (one of the 'Bloomsberries' whom Henry was to see something of before she became Mrs Woolf in 1912), who made a great play of the derogatoriness implicit in that single syllable of a surname: 'Dodd a little New English Club artist, half drunk, and ecstatic, wishes to paint my portrait', she announced in the summer of 1907, 'and I am to sit in the afternoon from 2 to 4.30. Alone?', she added.[5] That he ever painted 'half drunk' is probably quite untrue; 'little' could only refer to his limitations as an artist; and 'ecstatic' is a cruel dig at his naive enthusiasm and plodding sincerity, obvious targets for some of Virginia's less charitable 'flights of mind', for Dodd was conspicuously lacking in any of the incisive intelligence and perceptive wit that endeared Henry – initially and albeit briefly – to the Bloomsbury group. 'Friend – brother – citizen', she called him sarcastically;[6] and referring superiorly to Dodd's deficiency in the social graces, related how she had, 'Such a night last night – Dodd feeling compelled, as a Blacksmith's grandson, to tell Lady Ottoline that he was – constipated!'[7] Virginia continued to make mock of him but agreed, not without unkind comment, to sit for her portrait. As the sittings wore on between October 1907 and July 1908, she complained to her sister Vanessa, 'I have Dodd tomorrow . . . O, Misery'.[8] Nor was she impressed with the result although one drawing now in the National Portrait Gallery is remarkably lively and potent and untypical: 'Dodd writes that he is much pleased with his print of me, and will send me a copy', reported Virginia in August 1908, 'it looked rather too stout, so he added flounces to the dress. The only good part was the line of the skirt – so my vanity once more will be shocked.'[9]

Dodd's unacceptability to Bloomsbury was amazingly maintained. Dora Carrington, liaison of Lytton Strachey and an intimate of Henry in the twenties, called 'Mr. and Mrs. Dodd . . . ghosts from

Henry's past. A terrible couple!'[10] And in the early thirties, Henry, in London on his way to lunch with David Garnett, then a 'younger' Bloomsbury writer, meeting Dodd by chance invited him to join them; to Henry's chagrin and absolute disgust, Garnett ignored Dodd throughout the meal: as a consequence, Henry dropped Garnett forever. Often he had a touching loyalty to old friends, seeming never to have betrayed ingratitude for the help and kindness he received from Dodd, despite their diverging careers and their fundamentally differing attitudes to both art and living. Whatever the weaknesses in Dodd's work, and whatever his personal shortcomings, for Henry – marooned in medicine in 1905 – the contact with this academic, disciplined draughtsman must have been some compensation for his lack of formal training and further flamed his resolve to be an artist.

NOTES

1 *Francis Dodd RA*, obituary, 'The Manchester Guardian' 19 Mar 1949.
2 Arthur Koestler *The Act of Creation* Pan Books 1970, pp.339–40.
3 Alfred Ainsworth – Lytton Strachey : 26 May 1903.
4 Augustus John – Henry Lamb : 25 Jun 1907.
5 Virginia Woolf – Violet Dickinson : 3 Jun 1907; *Letters* Vol.1, p.297.
6 Virginia Woolf – Lady Robert Cecil : early Mar 1908; *Letters* Vol.1, pp.323–4.
7 Virginia Woolf – Lytton Strachey : 25 Jun 1909; *Letters* Vol.1, p.399; and *Woolf*–Strachey Letters p.34.
8 Virginia Woolf – Vanessa Bell : Oct(?) 1907; *Letters* Vol.1, p.316.
9 Virginia Woolf – Violet Dickinson : 1 Oct 1907; *Letters* Vol.1, p.313.
10 Carrington – Lytton Strachey : 27 August 1929; *Carrington: Letters and Diaries* p.418.

II

Chelsea and Montparnasse

1905 – 1911

THREE

EUPHEMIA

At the end of his last term of Medical School in the summer of 1905, Henry went to the University Ball with a local lass of uncertain origins who was to become a *femme fatale* of the English art world and of near international notoriety. The alluringly attractive Nina Forrest was then, according to Henry, a virgin and a protegée of prostitutes in the Greenhays quarter, a district of Manchester comprising 'a few streets in which the women . . . would sit in their dressing gowns on the doorsteps calling across to one another'. It was cleared up later by a conscientious police official with the result that prostitution increased and spread all over the city. She and Henry used to visit an old nurse whom some supposed to be her mother but he was 'convinced she could not have been owing to the conformation of her face about the temples'. Though from Lancashire, she was said to have been born on a boat to Bombay; but she had no trace of a regional dialect and spoke with what Henry called 'a superior accent'. Her father, Arthur Forrest, was recorded to be 'of independent means'. From all accounts, she was 'inordinately fond of romancing and never would be believed' hence the inconclusiveness of her shadowy background. Known by several names, the most enduring was that given her by Henry: since she reminded him so much of Mantegna's Saint, he christened her 'Euphemia'.

Euphemia's appearance at the summer Ball was evidently

sensational. Her own wardrobe was negligible and a friend from Manchester recalled her borrowing a dress from Mrs Lamb to attend a concert with Henry; but the dress she 'adapted' to wear to the dance was so scant and of such daring decolleté that it caused consternation among the conservative crowd of provincials. From that fateful evening, Henry was plunged into a deeply divisive affair. It was a relationship that lingered, more often unhappily, for over twenty years, at first alternating acrimony with passion, later smouldering in a corner of Henry's life, occasionally to flicker inopportunely.

The young couple – he thought her sixteen or so, she claimed nineteen – absconded as soon as term ended, arriving in London somewhere in July, 1905, to lead a precarious existence at a variety of addresses. Henry's ambition to become an artist and his urge to escape from home had been helped by the gift of a stipend for a year from the wealthy father of Gustav Alexander, a friend from schooldays. Mr Alexander was generous and kindly but unostentatious and, being a refugee, had a reticence that many learn and some never quite lose. Crucial to Henry's future was that he 'was of a very charitable disposition' and, 'No deserving case, whether a charity, education institution, or private distress ever went from him without substantial aid'.[1] The Alexanders were among the first of several families Henry was to 'adopt' for he had been a regular visitor to their home at Didsbury, near Manchester. Mrs Alexander was especially fond of young Henry, treating him like another son and once taking him, with Gustav, on holiday to Brighton where, away from his brothers and sisters, he slept for the first time in a room of his own.

Henry's other spasmodic, modest income during these initial months in London was from 'The Manchester Guardian' which, between August 1905 and the end of 1906, published some of his drawings. In illustrating a few anniversaries and current events he became their 'man in London'; but precisely how remains uncertain although several possibilities arise: C. P. Scott, proprietor of the 'Guardian', lived near the Lambs at Fallowfield, was a governor of the Manchester Grammar School, and a sitter to Francis Dodd; James Bone, brother of Muirhead, was London editor of the 'Guardian' and an admirer of Henry's work; and Ferrucio Bonavia, musician and music critic contributing occasional articles to the 'Guardian', was friendly with both Henry and Walter Lamb. With these connections alone, it would have been surprising for his talents not to have been used in some tangible way.

The 'Guardian' drawings are unique to Henry for two distinct reasons: thereafter, he became a persistent painter, seeming never again to prepare drawings for publication; and architecture was rarely to be the sole or dominant feature in his work – the human condition and human situations were to become his métier. The first drawing published, on the front page of the 'Guardian' on Saturday, 12th August 1905, is by far the best and really the most interesting. The subject, Westminster Hall, was in the news as the setting for a luncheon to be given 'by members of both Houses of Parliament to the French admirals and officers' and must have been done, either on the spot or certainly from sketches and observation there, while 'work was going on . . . in preparation for the immense banquet; no number of people could look too large for the quiet, dim place', ran the caption, 'Decorations have been put up on the walls, but it is still a dim place and grey.' Despite the forbidding prospect, the young artist responded to his commission with great gusto and the drawing smacks of a celebratory relish betraying none of the struggles of a raw recruit: the line and structure are assured with a vitality and directness worthy of an experienced illustrator. The then crude demands of line block reproduction on newsprint have still not coarsened what must have been a sensitive and spontaneous original and though Henry soon came to dislike London, it seems as if the metropolis was, for a moment, an inspiration.

His second commission was to make a drawn interpretation of Turner's *Death of Nelson* for a 'Guardian' supplement published on 21st October as 'an anniversary study' of 'The Battle of Trafalgar' hardly the most exciting task since Henry appears never to have been a copyist, always preferring to work from life or from sketches done on the spot: the result is competent and professional looking, but of only marginal and documentary interest. Next month he made a portrait study of the King of Greece, a guest at Windsor Castle, surely done from a photograph since it was published to coincide with the subject's arrival in Britain. A week later, Wren's House in Botolph Lane was to be sold and was featured with an apparently original, straightforward though not unpleasing drawing. But Henry's initial enthusiasm must have waned a little as he had to rely for sources increasingly on photos and engravings: neither the 150th anniversary of the birth of Mozart, nor the bicentenaries of the birth of Benjamin Franklin and the death of John Evelyn, would have allowed him any scope to exercise his special talent as a perceptive portraitist. Although some of the later drawings published in 1906 may well have been done on the spot – including one of Sayes Court, Evelyn's house at Deptford – his career as an illustrator was brief. Apart from his likely disenchantment with the work, doubtless he felt it was diverting him from his intention of becoming a painter.

Another noteworthy drawing from this first winter in London, though unpublished, relates to the 'Guardian' series. Dated 1906, it has been called 'The Sentry', for lack of a specific title; now identified as Cumberland House, a building put up in the 1760s on the south side of Pall Mall and later altered to accommodate the old War Office before it moved to Whitehall, the drawing may well have been commissioned to accompany an article that was never printed, for the site must have been under discussion by the government of the day since the building was soon to be demolished – the eastern half in 1908 and the western in 1911–12 – to make way for the present headquarters of the Royal Automobile Club. Heavily hatched with pen and black ink over a pencil basis, it looks as though Henry has tried to make the drawing look less topographical and more pictorial, perhaps with the intention of exhibiting it, especially as, unlike the published drawings all of which are merely inscribed 'H.L.', that of Cumberland House is signed in full. Henry was never quite at ease nor at his fluent best with pen and ink, after this early period in Manchester and London, considering the countless drawings he made throughout his career, ink is used in relatively few and mostly before 1920.

In spite of Mr Alexander's generosity, and although the 'Guardian' work would have produced a few, occasional coppers – Scott was reputedly 'the meanest man on earth and paid his journalists a pittance'[2] – poverty was a recurring problem for Henry and Euphemia throughout that winter of 1905 and '06. 'What that couple lived on I do not know', wrote Bernard Leach, the potter, whose family had known the Lambs in Manchester and who was then an art student at the Slade.[3] By historical implication and popular assumption, Henry is always associated with the Slade School of Art; but, despite his soon getting to know many of the students and his drawing continuing to reflect the Slade tradition, there is no record of his ever having studied there, although it was not uncommon

32

occasionally for outsiders to attend classes without signing the register. It has been suggested that Euphemia too, may have studied at the Slade; but again, there is no record of her attendance. More likely, in order to supplement their slender means, she used her abundance of natural attributes resourcefully as a model.

An unaffected English beauty, Euphemia had a perfect sense of theatre enabling her to fall into any pose instinctively, with absolute ease and conviction: though 'a great romancer, prone to exaggeration', visually, she retained an elegant simplicity that lent itself admirably to pictorial portrayal. Some women thought her 'rather gross with a booming voice', even 'fat and ungainly'; most men found her irresistible, calling her husky speech 'seductive' and her figure 'devastating'; in truth, she was of medium height, slim, with long legs, and charmingly proportioned. In renaming her, Henry, Pygmalion-like, had set her in something of a classical mould. She was to be a model to many other artists but at first, in London, he often drew her. One of the studies from this difficult period is both a lovely drawing and a lovely portrait, sensitively conveying the deeper feelings suggested by the sitter in repose. Pensive, sensual, Euphemia looks down and away to her left, a vulnerable angel contemplating human fallibility. Done with style and grace and without a trace of that dour conservatism noted in the Manchester 'medical' portraits, this particular drawing is a masterwork ranking not only with the best of the Slade tradition, but also, in echoing perhaps Raphael or Rubens, looks back to a much older, longer tradition, and could hold its own in the company of any great draughtsman.

Whilst Henry's drawing made great strides as soon as he came to London, paradoxically, his emotional life regressed dramatically. On the one hand, he had successfully freed himself in order to realise his ambition; on the other, he was frustrated by a tempestuous entanglement that was a disaster almost from the beginning. Euphemia should have been an ideal partner for an English artist; she and Henry seemed, on the face of it, complementary; but in reality, temperamentally, they were totally incompatible. 'She used to fight with him terribly, using dinner plates and knives in their battles', a friend recalled, 'her temperament being such that fights were necessary to her. She had a knack of saying exactly the things she knew would most rile him.'[4] Apart from the sheer worry of survival, such ructions and continual tension would have heavily over-

33

shadowed the elation of escape: for Henry, in no time, the frustrations of home were replaced by the stresses and strains of an impossible relationship.

Worse, in the spring of 1906, Euphemia discovered she was pregnant. Neither she nor Henry had ever seemed to show regard for convention until, on the tenth of May, they were married at 'The Register Office in the District of Chelsea'. The witnesses to the inevitably unconventional wedding were brother Walter, then near the end of his final year at Cambridge, and Augustus John, a formidable friend, teacher and refuge, whom Henry had met during that winter of discontent. Bride and bridegroom had proffered the same address – 13 Trafalgar Studios, Manresa Road, now the site of the Chelsea School of Art – and then almost immediately vanished from London. At some time they stayed in a cottage on the Wiltshire Downs and it seems likely that it was there and then that they made their escape – for a honeymoon, of sorts, although they were penniless. Henry had no fond memories of the area: some years later when Lytton Strachey was prospecting for a country retreat, he warned him, 'Marlborough & Avebury are both quite near my old establishment with Euphemia. Do beware of the downs: I used to find them so depressing to live among', admitting, 'but perhaps I didn't give them a fair chance'. The cottage where the newly-weds lived was at Shepherd's Shore, near Calne, between Beckhampton and Devizes: remote, isolated, what should have been an idyllic setting in blissful circumstances proved disastrous, and the atmosphere was fraught throughout.

Meanwhile, Walter, worried at Henry's disappearance after the wedding, wrote from Cambridge to his friend Clive Bell in London, in June 1906, 'I should be glad if you could renew your acquaintance with my brother Harry, who has set up for himself as an artist at 125 Cheyne Walk, Chelsea', adding with concern, 'I dare say he feels a little lonely . . . I know he is on the look-out for any job which will put something into his pockets'. Clive, he thought, had shown the right measure of sympathy towards his wayward brother and only the month before had complimented him on his attitude, giving him a Bayswater address where he thought the young Lambs might be hiding: 'As to my brother's affairs, I confess it is pleasant to find one person at least who takes what I hoped would be the general view. Other friends have no doubt meant kindly, but have not been kind enough to stop there.' Euphemia and Henry were finally found early in July, back in Chelsea, by Clive's wife-to-be, Vanessa Stephen, sister of Virginia.

Vanessa may have had a vested interest in finding Henry again. They had first met in the autumn previous, soon after Henry had come to London and at about the time she conceived 'The Friday Club', a meeting place for painters, where they could discuss their work, listen to lectures, and hold exhibitions. She herself was then a fledgling artist, beginning to make her way independently after three years at the Royal Academy Schools and a brief attendance at the Slade. Four years older than Henry, Vanessa must have been intrigued by this attractive, articulate, talented newcomer, even to the extent of making a tentative arrangement to share a studio with him: whether Henry intended to extricate himself from his ill-fated liaison with Euphemia is merely a guess; but, just before Christmas 1905, the two painters met for about an hour at a teashop in the King's Road to discuss the plan, 'Lamb in his corduroys, smoking a pipe', as a naive and fascinated Vanessa described, 'and I thought with joy how shocked all my friends and relations would be if they could only come in and see us! But our conversation was most innocent and all about Miss Forrest.'[5] Euphemia too, had attended the Friday Club, surreptitiously at first, for there is mention of her at one meeting concealed behind a curtain. 'Unluckily she was discovered, much to the indignation of the more strait-laced members.'[6]

Vanessa had refused Clive Bell's first proposal of marriage in July 1905 but accepted in November, a year later, and they married the following February. It is difficult now to imagine Henry ever talking intimately with Vanessa or to envisage any romantic, even intellectual, attachment between them in view of his subsequent disenchantment with most of the 'Bloomsberries'. Any plans they discussed in that teashop in Chelsea came to nothing. Henry attended the Friday Club for some years but seems not to have had any particular contact with Vanessa. She evidently made several attempts to gain entry to the address in Cheyne Walk; but when eventually she met with success she also met with no encouragement from the tenants, as Walter explained to Clive, she 'found my brother there with his wife in the studio. It seems they were lurking there all the time. I hope he was polite to her. Do you think he is all right in his intellects? Or is it that we are just too right in ours?'[7]

It was Virginia, Vanessa's sister, who developed such a surprising fascination for Euphemia. With a feigned irritation and ennui, she would complain of being 'landed with Miss Forrest' who 'sits vaguely in the drawing room for hours, and forgets whether she had tea or dinner last, whether children have meat or wine. My head spins with her stories; until I say sternly "Miss Forrest take my advice and learn Greek" it is like a nightmare.'[8] She likened both Euphemia and Henry to 'a stunted kind of nightmare' claiming to be unable to 'even take a psy . . . gal interest in them'.[9] And after the wedding she announced, 'Lamb and Nina have finally drifted into marriage. At the Friday Club last week, we sat and listened to this kind of thing . . . "Well, Nina. Are you married?" Nina: "Oh no, I'm not married. That is I am married. I think I was married yesterday, and I was so hungry the whole time, and I had a new blouse, and a cake." '[10] Imaginatively, wittily, cunningly, Virginia caricatures Euphemia's apparent scattiness and by selectively sketching an outline of her conversation, suggests an unfeeling, uncaring creature, vague, diffident, prone to whims and incapable of decision. In all this, there is some truth: Euphemia, especially when young, was apt to be too susceptible to intuition, excessively reliant on the irrational, and over impulsive; but it was the outcome of these traits that so regularly aroused Virginia's instinct for gossip. It is unlikely that Euphemia's intellect alone would have held her interest: rather it was Euphemia's amorous adventures that so intrigued Virginia, who, unconsciously, may have seen in her a fascinating reflection of another self, the possibility of an alter ego, a more extrovert, passionate reverse to the containment of her own private life. She may even have viewed with some envy this woman of the world who Maynard Keynes said had had more sexual life than the rest of Bloomsbury put together.[11] Sexually, Euphemia seemed so at ease and her frequent changes of partner were to be in such contrast to the constancy of Virginia's lifelong marriage and to the physical boundaries that she proscribed for herself, boundaries that seem only to have been transgressed through imaginative projection and through fiction. Doubtless Virginia encouraged Euphemia in her willingness to embroider stories of her affairs; but for many years she continued to refer to 'Nina' with astonishing curiosity and to weave her own fantasies around the already fantastic exploits of the amazing Euphemia: how 'interesting . . . impure women are to the pure', she wrote in 1920, 'I see her as someone in mid ocean, struggling, diving, while I pace my bank', adding superiorly, 'One may console oneself though by the brainlessness of the exercise. One dip is all that's needed.'[12]

Soon after Henry married Euphemia she had a miscarriage. From then on they more or less went their separate ways, at times exchanging glances in a loose labyrinth of extraordinary inter-relationships, later to recover from their wounds in opposite corners. Euphemia pursued a wayward, tortuous path which – at least until the First World War – crossed and re-crossed that of the Café Royalists in London and the habitués of the Café Lilas in Paris. It was probably in Montparnasse – where the Lambs stayed with the Johns in 1907 – that Augustus John became most inspired by her 'mercurial presence . . . with her pale oval face and heavy honey-coloured hair' and made countless studies of her. 'She was comedian and model to him: he admired her body, was amused by her exploits' and became infatuated.[13] There too, and at the same time, she fell into the arms of Duncan Grant, then an art student in Montparnasse. In a café there, in the spring three years later, another British painter, James Dickson Innes, is said to have fallen in love with her: 'Together they made their way, largely on foot, to Collioure . . . Euphemia dancing in the cafés to help pay for them.'[14] She was not really a dancer but, motivated by the desperate need of money and aided by beauty and a natural ability to move well, she survived. Innes is always identified with landscape painting but around 1910, possibly stimulated by his new-found passion, he attempted some large-scale figure compositions à la Augustus John's own enormous 'decoration' *Lyric Fantasy*. Earlier, in 1908, in London, she had modelled for the sculptor Jacob Epstein, for whom Euphemia's 'very English looks' must have had great appeal: he was to make several busts of her, in the first of which she looks upwards, showing part of the arms and breast and, as Richard Buckle suggests, it 'could only be a modern portrait of a modern woman', perhaps echoing something of Augustus John's vigorous view of her as a feminine feminist, soon to be liberated. In another of the busts, Epstein seems close to the classical ideal that first attracted Henry, 'not only because of the way it is cut off traditionally below the shoulders, but also from the delicacy of its modelling, its reticence and the life it breathes [it] might almost be a work of the Florentine "Quattrocento".'[15] Epstein also made an atypical sculpture commissioned by Lady Ottoline Morrell in 1909 using Euphemia – less as a portrait subject and more as a model – for a garden figure in which she becomes an essay in carving, this time

37

reminiscent of Egyptian or possible Early Greek sculpture. Buckle called it 'unique among Epstein's surviving carvings, the rest of which are conceived in far more monumental terms . . . The formalised archaic treatment of rippling drapery in contrast to the little modern sleeves of Euphemia's clinging dress is strange too.'[16] A cast of the 'Quattrocento' head and shoulders is in the Tate Gallery where there is, as well, a rather strange painting of Euphemia by Ambrose McEvoy, a Slade contemporary of Augustus John and a sitter to him in 1903, and husband of another sitter to Epstein in 1909: 'originally the right hand portion of a picture called *The Ferry*', Euphemia appears in a quite different guise – fey, wistful, uncharacteristically full of innocent wonderment, bereft of the firm bone structure and simple strength stressed by other artists, seeming more like an ungroomed Pre-Raphaelite beauty. Euphemia was a model to many artists in the London and Parisian art world: she may well be the seated girl in a pastel drawing by Christopher Nevinson of the Café Royal, in a history of which she is mentioned, rather extravagantly, as one of a 'floating population of models' and linked to another 'who was desperately in love with a different man every week.'[17]

Not all of Euphemia's loves were artists; but they were usually creative, invariably intelligent, and certainly wealthy and successful. She would dominate any gathering, inspiring jealousy in women – making some singularly unhappy – and in men, enduring devotion and incredible loyalty. 'I remember that the last time I ever saw Augustus John at a disastrous dinner party given by John Russell', wrote Penelope Fitzgerald, 'the mention of Euphemia was almost the only thing that seemed to "get through" to the grand old man – I believe he was truly fond of her.'[18] Nicolette Devas, daughter of Francis Macnamara, a poet and later liaison of Euphemia's, has left a rich, revealing, dubiously fantastic, scarcely credible but deeply affectionate portrait of her sometime 'adopted aunt':

> 'Though I knew she had been Francis's mistress, it did not bother me. I was entranced by her exotic beauty and envied her bold confidence. In her "marvellous ginny voice" deep and hoarse, I would now call it sexy, she instructed us in mancraft. She lived for men. The life appeared rewarding: she chucked Schiaparelli cast-off clothes across the room for us to grab, and in other ways was generous too. Pound notes and hundred pound notes were kept in the top of her stockings: when she patted her thigh with a crackling noise, we could expect a tip.'[19]

Henry too, mentioned how Euphemia 'was always well supplied with money' and that he would 'find her fingering notes', though this would obviously have been a memory from after they separated for in fact he thought her very mean, probably a jaundiced view since so many others have testified to her near cornucopian generosity and extravagance. Apparently she had an abundance of warmth and openness but was at times a victim of her own impulsiveness; yet she was a great survivor with a tremendous obtuseness and tenacity: hence some of the exceptional and prolonged wrangling when Henry was desperate to divorce her in the twenties. She herself remarried in 1935 but divorced again eight years later.

Euphemia must also have been connected – sometime around 1907, in Paris – with the arch-occultist, Aleister Crowley in whose *Confessions*, first published in 1929, she is described under the pseudonym 'Dorothy' as one who,

'would have been a *grande passion* had it not been that my instinct warned me that she was incapable of true love. She was incomparably beautiful. Augustus John has painted her again and again, and no more loveliness has ever adorned any canvas. She was capable of stimulating the greatest extravagance of passion . . .

She was, in addition, one of the best companions that a man can possibly have. Without pretence of being a blue-stocking, she could hold her own in any conversation about art, literature or music. She was the very soul of gaiety, and an incomparable comedienne. One of my most delightful memories is the matching of our wits. It was rapture to compete with her in what we called "leg-pulling", which may be defined as inducing someone to make a fool of himself. We carried this out with all due regard for honour and good feeling; we never did anyone any harm, and we often did people a great deal of good . . .

(She had a husband round the corner, but one ignores such flim-flam in Montparnasse.)'[20]

Flim-flam, more or less rhyming with Lamb, seems a curiously Freudian slip, for the 'husband round the corner' could then only have been Henry. That Euphemia was capable of great kindness and friendship was also mentioned by Betty May, 'Tiger Woman' as she was called, one of the models frequenting the Café Royal before the First War. 'I used to sit at a table by myself', she recalled, 'with a cheap drink, coffee or lager, in front of me to justify my presence, my head resting on both hands, watching the parties of artists and models at the top end of the room . . . I tried to imagine what it must be like to be made love to by one of those great men, and I envied the models who were priveleged to sit with them'.[21] After getting to know Euphemia, Betty May too, came under the spell of Crowley, the self-styled 'Beast 666', and recorded how 'very kind she was to me during this awful period . . . I can never be grateful enough to her for it.'[22]

That Euphemia had a sense of fun was noted by Nevinson, another British painter studying in Paris in 1907, who remembered how, in the

'rue Delambre, Augustus John taught Euphemia Lamb to ride a bicycle. I am ashamed to say I giggled at the sight of Lamb (or was it Innes?) exquisitely dressed, with yellow French novel under his arm, watching while Euphemia, a lovely ash blonde, in black velvet, a yellow-scarlet muffler, and a great display of black silk stocking, curvetted and staggered down the road, with John, in corduroy trousers, jersey, golden ear-rings, and carrot beard and hair, dashing after her.'[23]

The ubiquitous Euphemia, as Virginia said, 'was very attractive to a good many people' and became such 'a well known character'[24] that her story is inextricably woven into the fabric of early twentieth century art and society. One of her last and longer lasting attachments was to Morton Sands, of partly American descent and brother of the wealthy Ethel, patron, painter, and pupil of Sickert who, in 1915, painted her portrait – a masterpiece of sympathetic honesty and skill for, previously, her lack of good looks had prompted Henry to declare, in one of his more cruel asides, that he would have to be a martyr to despair and take the improbable step of marrying 'Ethel Sands & have no worry about my material future', as he put it so brutally. Euphemia's friendship with Morton may well have been platonic but nevertheless was the likely reason for a protracted schism between brother and sister that was never openly discussed yet was mysteriously healed after Euphemia's death early in 1957.[25] On hearing the news Henry was moved to write to her family,

'a line of sympathy and an assurance of old but still living affection . . . I wish I could adequately offer you a word of condolence. But Euphemia was unique & I always feel grateful for the privelege of having been so closely associated with so much of beauty & genius & glorious energy of character. I think I have never met anyone who knew her & who didn't feel these same things about her – with admiration & gratitude. In this way I like to think something of her wonderful tonic influence is disseminated imperishably among us all.'[26]

NOTES

1 *Bernard Calman Alexander*, obituary, 'The Manchester Guardian' Oct 1910. His son, Gustav Alexander was a pupil at the Manchester Grammar School 1894–9, and was an Honours Classics Scholar at Corpus Christi, Oxford. He was a benefactor to the University of Manchester; and in Nov 1928, presented Henry Lamb's portrait group *The Japp Family* to the Manchester City Art Gallery.

2 Hilda Bonavia – author : 18 Jun 1980 (interview).

3 Leach *Beyond East and West* p.31.

4 Lord Moyne – author : 5 Jul 1977 (interview).

5 Vanessa Bell – Margaret Snowden : 21 Dec 1905; Shone *Bloomsbury Portraits* p.27.

6 Shone p.27; also Shone *The Friday Club* 'The Burlington Magazine' 1975.

7 Walter Lamb – Clive Bell : 13 Jul 1906.

8 Virginia Woolf – Violet Dickinson : undated/end Mar 1906; *Letters* Vol.1, p.218.

9 Virginia Woolf – Violet Dickinson : undated; *Letters* Vol.1, p.219 (published as Apr 1906 – Henry and Euphemia were married on 10 May 1906).

10 ib.

11 V. Woolf *Diary* Vol.2, p.54.

12 ib.

13 Holroyd *Augustus John* p.321.

14 Holroyd p.451.

15 Buckle *Epstein* p.54.

16 Buckle p.52.

17 Deghy and Waterhouse *Café Royal* p.157.

18 Miss Penelope Fitzgerald – author : 16 Dec 1978.

19 Devas *Two Flamboyant Fathers* p.79.

20 Crowley *Confessions* pp.575–6; Holroyd *Augustus John* p.324.

21 May *Tiger Woman* p.45.

22 May pp.146–7.

23 Nevinson *Paint and Prejudice* p.47.

24 Virginia Woolf – Violet Dickinson: 27 Apr 1914; *Letters* Vol.2, p.705.

25 Baron *Miss Ethel Sands and Her Circle* pp.268–70.

26 Henry Lamb – Dr Christopher Turton : 7 Feb 1957.

FOUR

AUGUSTUS JOHN

'I explored about 6 taverns . . . and not finding you and no more taverns had to lunch in melancholy solitude', wrote Augustus John to his newly-found friend – and fan – Henry Lamb, in the flush of their mutual admiration. They must first have met in London most likely towards the end of 1905.

Then nearly thirty, a rising success as an artist with the skill in drawing of an old master, a roving eye alert both to the avant-garde in art and to any attractive woman, a notorious bohemian with a flamboyant, trend-setting appearance and a dominating, persuasive personality, Augustus seemed a heaven-sent star destined to light the way for a beginner. 'I saw a tall man with a reddish beard, in a velvet coat and brown trousers, striding along', wrote Nina Hamnett, then herself a starry-eyed student; 'he was a splendid-looking fellow and I followed him down the King's Road'.[1] With such credentials and such potential it is hardly surprising that in him Henry should find a model, albeit temporarily, for his art and to some extent for his life: Augustus' example focused the former, giving it direction and purpose and a professional 'edge'; and broadened the latter, by introducing him to a lifestyle of which hitherto he could only have dreamed.

Away from the provincialism of Manchester, the conservatism of Medical School, and the claustrophobia of home, Henry soon discovered that, apart from the terrible ructions with Euphemia, the

42

excitement at his independence was easily dulled by the sheer struggle of becoming an artist. Like any serious student he was often daunted by the awesome difficulties of concentrated, disciplined drawing and was regularly plagued by lengthy periods of agonising self-doubt: 'the sight of my recent products fills me with dejection', he complained; 'my pictures. . . deject me beyond sufference', were variations on a theme of woe that he was to cry in these early years. Art had no simple, straightforward *raison d'être* and, unlike the clear-cut objectives and essentially practical and social justification of medicine, was relatively amorphous. He quickly found how deceptive it all was, even years afterwards being reminded how easily in painting he had been 'led away into the old snare' by departing from his arranged scheme and, losing confidence in what he had already accomplished, 'began', as he put it, 'cowardly copying the mean literalities of the effect'. Later he was to call his first efforts, 'early works of blundering seeking & education', asking, 'how many blunders to be repeated before I can express the beauties of everyday's imagination!'

Until his arrival in London, Henry had shown pronounced talent in drawing and, having regard for his limited experience and training, quite remarkable competence: from the contact with and example of Joseph Knight and Francis Dodd he had learnt a modicum of technique and developed considerable skill; but effectively, it was the meeting with Augustus John that gave him, especially in his drawing, the technical fluency and confident professionalism which he was never to lose.

In the autumn of 1903, Augustus, in partnership with his ex-Slade student contemporary William Orpen, had founded the Chelsea Art School in the Rossetti Studios in Flood Street. Sessions began, not with the traditional academic year, but with the calendar year. No records of enrolment nor registers of attendance have been discovered but, from the fearful warning to 'intending students' that 'no application can be considered later than the 31st December', and from the progress evident in the few of Henry's drawings remaining from this period, it seems probable that he began studying there in January 1906, perhaps explaining why, by the end of the year, Henry had given up drawing for the 'Guardian'. The aims of the Chelsea Art School as portentiously outlined in the prospectus, though not inconsistent with the uplifting intentions of any art school at the turn of the century, were closer to the fifteenth century

43

and Cennino Cennini's 'loftiness of spirit' than to the earthier bohemianism of Augustus; and that he – and his partner Orpen – should subscribe to the convention of segregating the sexes in life classes is, in retrospect, laughable. Augustus is said to have rather enjoyed his teaching – at least, at first, for doubtless his approach was as fitful as his more usual attitude to life – and Henry was fortunate to attend at a time when his tutor still had an active interest in the school: he 'stressed the value of observation . . . discouraged the use of red chalk because it tended to make a bad drawing look pretty. Every line should carry meaning, nothing be left vague. Students were taught to cultivate precision . . . to draw with the point and to perfect what he called "the delicate line".'[2] Not that this makes him sound innovatory. Any teacher of drawing over the past few hundred years might have been in absolute agreement; but Augustus' method seems to have included as much of the dynamics of demonstration and example as of verbal instruction. Wyndham Lewis has described one of Augustus' dramatic, return visits to a life class at the Slade when he made a drawing watched by the students:

> 'a tall bearded figure, with an enormous black Paris hat, large gold ear-rings . . . a carriage of the utmost arrogance, strode in and . . . sat down on a donkey . . . tore a page of banknote paper out of a sketch book, pinned it upon a drawing board, and with a ferocious glare at the model . . . began to draw with an indelible pencil.'[3]

Allowing for Lewis' tendency to exaggeration and his own sense of theatre, it is some indication of the kind of teaching that Henry would have had at the Chelsea Art School. He never mentions Orpen whose 'chief contribution . . . was a series of lectures on anatomy' and his part in Henry's education appears to have been negligible.[4] In view of his training in medicine, Henry may not have attended any anatomy classes for he would have arrived with more than an art student's superficial knowledge of the subject. Consequently, it is surprising how he became steadily less confident in drawing from the nude. Bernard Leach recalled Henry's first appearance at the school:

> 'Augustus came in late straight from some party looking well groomed and remarkably handsome, picked up a drawing board, and instead of using it sat behind this new student and watched him for half an hour. They talked and Augustus invited Henry to his home.'[5]

Henry, eight years younger, was equally taken with Augustus. Though older than the average student, artistically he was still at an impressionable age and, to relieve the brimming adulation of his idol, Henry wrote admiringly to Augustus who, flattered but modesty cautious and slightly embarrassed at the reverence bestowed upon him, replied, 'Your letter thrills me somewhat. I'm not a Master – yet . . . I hardly believed you really had faith in my possibilities – in my will – I'm so glad'. Augustus had a studio above the school and at one stage, when Henry was desperate for a roof over his head, he was invited to stay there: 'You shall certainly have a corner found in these studios – no difficulty about it', he wrote.

At first, Augustus was a genuine inspiration. The progressive effect on his drawing – and on his appearance – is dramatically illustrated in three Lamb pencil self-portraits of 1906. One in particular – from the longer hair and beard and the more confident handling, probably the last – is a perfect complement to that of Euphemia discussed above; yet it is more vigorous, more extrovert, perhaps more self-conscious and indulgent and, because of Henry's transformed appearance, it is difficult to separate discussion of the treatment from that of the character portrayed for the dynamics of the drawing derive very much from the changed image of the artist who has not only acquired a full-blooded Rubenesque technique but has begun to look a little like Rubens himself. In the superb drawing of Euphemia, there was a hint of Rubens at his most subtle and serene but here, in the self-portraits, Henry displays a panache hitherto unseen and obviously inspired by his new master. Though many of Augustus' figure compositions owe a good deal to Poussin and Puvis de Chavannes, until around 1908, it was Rubens and to some extent Rembrandt – 'the squalor of the Dutch, rather than the noble rhetoric of the cinquecento', as Wyndham Lewis called it – who were as likely to serve him as stylistic models. As with 'Euphemia', the dry, more tentative, restrictive line of Henry's Manchester portraits of a year and two years before, has been warmed, expanded and enriched to a robustness bordering on the baroque. Unlike the masterly interpretation of Euphemia, however, the hair is a shade overworked with some slightly irritating arbitrariness; and the sides of the face and neck are described by a cluster of lines that seem not so much searching for form as echoing some of Augustus' own mannerisms. The drawing also lacks the absolute precision and directness of Augustus at his spontaneous best, an approach he certainly advocated in his teaching. Thus, despite the progress evident in these early self-portraits, and despite their rarity and historical interest, ultimately they fall a little short of the impeccable balance, simplicity, and satisfying completeness of 'Euphemia'.

Nevertheless, whatever the weaknesses in some matters of detail, the self-portraits have a remarkable biographical – autobiographical – interest and significance, clearly demonstrating Augustus' initially powerful impact on Henry, both as a draughtsman and as a person. They also show how much Henry was in love with the idea of being an artist for, if the technique in the drawing tends towards the baroque, then the sitter looks positively rococo. He is enjoying his new guise immensely and the narcissistic streak hinted at in 'The Mesoblastic Layer' and also perhaps by Dodd in his portrait of Henry is here exposed more fully. Vanity was not for long nor very seriously a trait associated with him: only for a few youthful years – what at the onset of middle-age he called his *'beaux jours'* – was he at all concerned with his appearance. In London, moving in more sophisticated circles, he was probably encouraged to cultivate his image and although neither Augustus, nor later, Lytton Strachey or Lady Ottoline Morrell, were exactly fashion conscious, they were very definitely idiosyncratic in their sartorial tastes and always conspicuous by their dress and accessories. All of this, whatever the aesthetic merit of the result, must have soon heightened Henry's awareness of style.

At first, Henry could not afford to indulge in modishness; but he could let his hair grow and sport a beard. He is said to have had his ears pierced and to have worn gold ear-rings, a logical step for a follower of Augustus. Later, when Henry could afford to have clothes made to measure, he would compare notes with Lady Ottoline on the foibles and fancies of his wardrobe. 'My new hat is come & seems a failure', he complained, 'The brim is not at all what I ordered & the felt the wrong colour, but it should improve with wear.' And significantly, before a return trip to Manchester, he seemed content to travel in his 'untidy velvets', declaring, 'I must forgo the glory of my green suit.' To Lytton Strachey too, he sent what he called a 'very malfondu sketch' intended to represent his 'newest costume with thick velvet coat (marron & braided) & shiny top boots a la Cosaque.'

In addition to being younger than Augustus, Henry was some few inches shorter, and though strikingly handsome – many thought beautiful – his relatively diminutive stature limited the success of emulating his swashbuckling master who, not unlike Picasso, at heart remained something of a child. With a rumbustious sense of theatre, he loved playing a part and adored dressing up: 'Even John has abandoned his coat tails & wears yellow boots & rolled up trousers', remarked Henry in 1911; and before, mentioned having seen 'John . . . looking rather prosperous with a cigar in his mouth & sitting up very stiff in his brand new little turnout.' The various roles assumed by Augustus – and in which he cast others – would begin as fiction, steadily take on some meaning and, because of his complete immersion in the part and of his absolute conviction, become factual and believable. Not that his act was ever superficial: his best-known, longest playing role, that of the gypsy, was supported by genuine passion and scholarship and he became thoroughly acceptable to the Romany world. Sickert too, another associate of Henry's, began his career as a professional actor and in everyday life had more than a little sense of theatre: but whereas Augustus would adopt a conspicuous guise, Sickert's penchant was rather for disguise and his performances were infinitely more subtle and discreet. Nina Hamnett recalled travelling from Newhaven and being met by Sickert in Dieppe:

'I did not recognize him at first as he wore a sailor's peaked cap, oilskins, and a red spotted handkerchief round his neck. He was always difficult to recognize if one had not seen him for some time. He might appear with an enormous beard like a Crimean veteran or he would dress himself in very loud checks and a bowler hat and look like something off a race-course.'[6]

Sickert obviously enjoyed being incognito and his changes of character – as were his changes of studio, another predilection shared with Augustus – were closer to the surreptitious tactics of espionage than to the bravura of Augustus.

None of these dramatics was truly Henry. Above all he was consistently true to himself and in retrospect this phase of no more than a year or so, was so out of character as to be like an aberration: the *persona* he adopted now appears alien and unconvincing, especially in comparison with the breadth and depth that Augustus could bring to any part he chose to play. Moreover, Augustus had a Celtic flair for poetic exaggeration and a weakness for self advertisement that very soon was altogether too much for Henry, whose natural reticence and English instinct for understatement were affronted by what he felt to be insensitivity and lack of reserve. Even many years later, in the early thirties, Julia Strachey remembered how his 'panache' came in for 'severity' from Henry when Augustus,

> 'talked about his scheme for voyaging round the world. When he got up to go, in his flowing overcoat and scarf flung over his shoulders, he threw out his arm with a generous gesture and bid everyone a hearty goodbye.
> "Are you starting out already?" asked Henry, startled.
> "No, not yet, in the Autumn," barks Augustus, whose theatrical leave-taking reminded Henry of some grizzled Viking chief bidding farewell to his good comrades on the beach.'[7]

As soon as he recovered from the impact of Augustus, Henry cast off the flamboyant trappings and resumed his more modest image. He found he could easily dispose of the superficial appurtenances, but he could never quite eradicate from his drawing the effects that had once seemed so beneficial and yet were to remain as indelible as the pencil Augustus had used to demonstrate at the Slade in the early 1900s. To him, the awesome influence was like some dread disease from which for many painful years he sought to purge himself: even in the twenties, he would still complain of a sketch getting 'infected with something of Augustus' brazenness': in Henry's sober, more mature view, an incurable contamination. Neither had he a higher opinion of the man: when Henry's infatuation turned to resentment, he warned Lady Ottoline, 'I wish you . . . joy of your visit to almighty John . . . I thought him unbearable the last evening I was there', going on to deplore Augustus' excess of 'power & cold wit . . . & his lack of humanity'.

Henry's wit was devastating though far from cold; he had a great sense of humour and was capable of tremendous bawdiness – much of which he shared with Lytton Strachey – but the John household was rarely the setting for much fun for Henry. Romilly, Augustus' son, recalled him drawing up his will before leaving to enlist in 1914. 'Everybody particularly wished to know to whom he had left his conduit', an appropriate euphemism for penis, 'a joke', Romilly admitted, 'I did not understand and which I do not think Lamb much appreciated', despite the earthy compliment to his libido.[8] But in visiting the Johns, Henry also had to compete with the moodiness of the 'maitre' himself: 'I think Augustus' threatened breakdown is all fiddle-de-dee – just some of his melodramatic methods', commented Henry, 'I suppose he is quite plainly & slowly breaking up if not down'. Eventually, Henry's visits were contrived to avoid the master of the house, whose sudden return to the family fold would generally hasten Henry's departure, 'now', as he put it, 'that tarantula Augustus has reappeared in his customary nimbus of boredom, silence, & helpless gloom.'

But, however incredible it might seem with hindsight, Henry must briefly have been carried away by the daring and independence of the mighty Augustus and entered the vast and varied John circle so willingly and wholeheartedly that at one point, when he was at an unusually low ebb and at his least rational, he envisaged a commune of sorts consisting of the Johns, the Morrells (to whom he was introduced by Augustus in 1909), the Maitlands (whom he was to meet in Paris in 1907 or '08), and Henry himself: 'Could we not form a discreet sort of colony . . . in couples?' he asked, suggesting magnanimously, 'For the sake of symmetry I could double myself no doubt at suitable intervals.' In some ways, his proposal already had its prototype for the John family was then the nucleus of a complex series of interrelations within which Augustus was a dominating but sometimes distant patriarch, conveniently absenting himself when his restlessness demanded: he was always to have an entourage; but usually they were settled at a safe distance allowing him to satisfy his continual craving for mobility and freedom.

During 1907, Henry, possibly with Euphemia, either accompanied or followed the Johns to Paris, where, although his reason for crossing the channel was simply to further his studies in art, he became deeply enmeshed in an intricate pattern of fluctuating relationships. It was not his first visit to the city for he would have seen something of it three years before with his father en route to and from Italy; but certainly, his initiation into the Parisian art world began sometime during 1907. Prior to the First World War, nearly every British artist of note studied for a while at one or other of the many *académies* or *ateliers* and submitted to the critical judgement of Paris, that international 'laboratory of the twentieth century', that 'cultural Klondike', as it was dubbed by Harold Rosenberg.[9] Among those with whom Henry was to have some greater or lesser, friendly or abrasive, contact were, Wyndham Lewis, who called this period in Paris, 'its late sunset', finding that he could not write of it with

49

suitable restraint; to him, Paris 'was the greatest humanist creation of the French . . . expansive and civilised, temperate in climate, beautiful and free . . . It is dangerous to go to heaven when you are too young. You do not understand it and', he admitted afterwards, 'I did not learn to work in Paris.'[10] Having left the Slade in 1901, Lewis travelled widely in Europe and was to spend one summer in Brittany with Henry. Another fellow student was the Irish architect, George Kennedy, then a painter who had also been at the Slade and was attending the Académie Julian where Henry may have studied as well: they had probably met previously in London and were to become lifelong friends. Another painter/architect, Maresco Pearce, 'the unequalled horror' of whose 'dreariness' was more than Henry could tolerate, was a rich student 'living with his terrible old mama in the Avenue du Bois'; and Maxwell Armfield, 'extremely handsome in a rather delicate & perhaps . . . effeminate way' who 'painted elaborate pictures in spotless tempera' and 'hinted at the same sort of sexual fantasies – jewelled & yet remote – in which Gustav Moreau excelled',[11] was there, as was Ian Strang, draughtsman and etcher, whose father William Strang is thought to have included a portrait of Henry as a waiter in the large group of actors, actresses and dancers at the Café Royal in 1913. Boris Anrep, a Russian, who arrived around 1908, studied at Julian's and became one of Henry's closest friends; and Augustus' sister Gwen, who had been living in Paris since 1898 and was later to become reclusive, Henry thought of as 'really quite a gay person who could be full of fun.'[12] In the April of 1907, Clive and Vanessa Bell spent part of their honeymoon there; but of the British colony in Paris, it was Duncan Grant whom Henry would have seen most of, since they were fellow students at 'L'Ecole de la Palette'.

'La Palette' was a small *académie*, at first situated 'somewhere not far from the quays on the south side of the river towards "Invalides"', wrote Duncan Grant in a memoir,

> 'A little place then & not above 20 students . . . It was not supposed to be run for profit, the fees were to go entirely for rent & models & heat.'[13]

The school had been started by the anglophile French artist, Jacques-Emile Blanche, friend of the francophile English artist, Sickert. Blanche was a competent, conventional painter, probably best known in England for his sympathetic portrait of Aubrey Beardsley, done in Blanche's house near Dieppe and now in the National

Lytton Strachey *1914   Oil on canvas   244.5 × 178.5   Tate Gallery, London*

The Kennedy Family *1921*　*Oil on canvas*　*112.8 × 82.1*　*Private collection*

Portrait Gallery. 'Blanche took his position very seriously', recalled Duncan,

'He came at least twice a week . . . & for him it was obviously a pleasure. He was not a great painter though possibly now an underrated one . . . He could be disgustingly bitter & unfair to Matisse, Derain, Picasso, Utrillo . . . On most days I spent the afternoon at the Louvre . . . Blanche would sometimes take his students there . . . and talk about the pictures & give his criticisms of any copy a student might be doing . . . Blanche's remarks were to the point . . . Generally I found him a stimulating & exciting professor.'[14]

Duncan began there in September 1907 but, during the following year, 'La Palette' became so successful that in the summer vacation it moved to larger premises in the Rue du Val de Grace, off the Boulevard St. Michel, in the heart of Montparnasse. On his return in the autumn he found that,

'an international reputation had descended on it . . . Rows of Swedish ladies & gentlemen . . . were painting in what they conceived to be the style of Matisse . . . The studio was enormous & very pleasant, in what must have been once an old stable.'[15]

The building has since gone but it was there that Henry began his studies in Paris.

Blanche acknowledged later that many came to the school because they 'were mainly attracted by the glamour of Montparnasse';[16] but it was also, from the nineties until 1914, a district where many British artists and writers congregated. Doubtless Henry, as he had been at the Chelsea Art School, was one of the more serious and talented students at 'La Palette'. None of the work he did during this first spell in Paris seems to have survived but a series of life drawings discovered in his Hampstead studio after he had vacated it in the late twenties and done probably on a subsequent visit are of interest, if only because appearing less typical. They are larger, more vigorous and a great deal broader – possibly even cruder – than his portrait drawings of the same period. Using mainly chalk, probably conté, rather than his more customary pencil, Henry has treated the model very much as a vehicle for study. Usually, his line is searching and sensitive; but each of these drawings, whilst realising the form boldly and being admirably descriptive, is almost aggressive, certainly impatient, as if he resented the time spent on them. 'I draw steadily at these tiresome posed figures in the academies & of course refresh my knowledge in this way', he wrote from Paris, complaining, 'But it's not very inspiriting'. Nor was he ever apparently at ease in a life class despite his exceptional knowledge of anatomy and his natural skill in rendering the human figure: extraordinarily, he developed a ridiculous, unwarranted feeling of inferiority in drawing from the nude, so much so that he came to begrudge the effort involved. 'I have been working a little better today', he reported on another trip to Paris, 'but I don't think these academy drawings are much use to me . . . my existence here has been tediously insignificant'. Yet when he first came to working out and painting figure compositions he had to admit to the value of the academic tradition of studying the nude: 'What drawing I did recently in Paris was only enough to confirm the need for incessant life study', he confessed afterwards, 'how fettered I feel without it just now.'

Of the teaching at 'La Palette' Henry made no mention but he must have created a good impression since he seems to have been welcome there to work whenever he was in Paris, once saying how, 'The "Palette" people were very polite & generous' inviting him 'to make use of the studio & models as much as I liked.' Publicly, Henry acknowledged a debt to his tutor but, privately, retained reservations and was suspicious of him as a person: after one visit he mentioned that, 'Blanche was there & addressed me with infinite urbanity'. Blanche himself recorded how 'Lamb and Duncan Grant are kind enough to assure me that they did not waste their time there.'[17]

In this first year in Paris, Henry stayed in a tall tenement, 7 Rue Cels, in a narrow street off the Avenue du Maine, adjacent to the Cimitière du Montparnasse, and a few minutes from 'La Palette'. 'Drama seemed constantly in the air', recalled Duncan Grant, who was somewhat out of sympathy with the frequent changes of partner among the British colony. The phantasmagoria of 'La Ronde' was not properly to his taste and, by nature of a gentler disposition, he would have preferred to be less a part of the network of terrible entanglements between his student contemporaries, fellow artists, and their models, wives and mistresses. 'That Lamb family sickens me', he complained, 'and that man John. I'm convinced he's a bad lot.'[18] Not that Duncan ever hinted at taking a moral stance to the affairs of the John family and friends, for he was himself to become a pillar of Bloomsbury who evolved their own, perhaps more subtle, but no less complex, pattern of relations. However, as Michael Holroyd has pointed out, Augustus was always separated from the Bloomsbury painters and 'ill-at-ease in their tidy educated presence'.[19] Thus Duncan, with his more delicate constitution, weary and distracted, felt threatened and clearly was unequal to the boisterous pace set by 'the formidable John'. His cousin, Lytton Strachey, in trying to console him, reminded Duncan that, 'The dangers of freedom are appalling!'[20] Euphemia too, was conspicuous among the *amours divers* and, like Balzac's succubus, bore down upon the unwilling and hapless Duncan who reported to Lytton: 'Henry has left Nina perhaps for ever', adding defensively and with some bitterness, 'and the white haired whore still goes on eating "*crèmes nouveautés*"'.[21] But Duncan, after moving 'high over the heads of the world into a delightful green studio' with a comfortable armchair, declared himself 'indifferent to them all and sometimes completely happy'.[22]

Henry stayed for at least another year. So did Euphemia, apparently, though under different circumstances, as Walter, on a visit to Paris in April 1908, informed Clive Bell,

'I found my brother, who appears to be doing some very fine drawings, but to be making no money & to be under the necessity of changing his abode about twice a week: whereas his wife, while changing the circle of her friends about every ten days, persuades them to maintain her always in the same set of rooms. She seems to be on fairly amicable terms with him, but is meditating divorce'.[23]

The ever susceptible, overly flirtatious Augustus had continued to be intrigued by the beautiful Euphemia although he was married to his first wife Ida. Henry had grown fond of Ida John but, tragically, was not to know her for very long. In March 1907, he went to music hall with her the night before she entered hospital to give birth to a son. Following a straightforward delivery, complications set in and she was moved to a Maison de Santé in the Boulevard Arago. Within a week Ida had died and was cremated at the Cimitière Pere Lachaise. Augustus was too drunk to attend the ceremony but Ambrose McEvoy, though also heavily under the influence, arrived in Paris the same morning and, with Henry, was a witness at the crematorium. The ashes were then placed in a box and taken back to Augustus and a memorial service was held later in Henry's room.[24] The sad, macabre story ended nearly five years after when Henry described how he had, 'met A. E. J. on Waterloo platform in a scrimmage of people . . . looking bleary & debauched & said he was travelling 1st. because he had an urn with him . . . at Poole we found each other & went to a pub for a carriage. J & I drank of course while waiting: then we came back to the station & got our luggage on board. J. flabbergasted me when they bumped a dull looking wooden box beside the coachman by suddenly announcing that it contained Ida's ashes.'[25]

The death of Ida brought Henry closer to Augustus' mistress, Dorelia, who, for at least a year, had been living with the John family in a *ménage-à-trois – ou peut-être plus*! In that spring of 1907, in Paris, Henry fell deeply, desperately in love with her and began a protracted affair of *grande passion* that was to fluctuate almost until his second marriage: for twenty years he clung to the romantic notion that somehow, eventually, he would wrest Dorelia from, as he put it, 'the August clutches'.

At first the affair is said to have been encouraged by Augustus who conceded that Dorelia thrived under Henry's 'sunny influence'. The arrangement seemed mutually convenient: Augustus continued to be fascinated by Euphemia whom he renamed 'Lobelia', a name Henry called her for a while as if unconsciously accepting his wife's capitulation to the spell of his master. Thus briefly, the Lambs and the Johns pursued an agreeable *échange*, at times slightly resembling a quadrille but without its formality and predictability; though the respective partners, never having subscribed more than nominally to marital convention, still preserved their instinctive rights to independence and, whenever they felt inclined, took up the options to diverge from any absolute symmetry in the pattern of their relations.

But spontaneously, naturally and easily as it had all begun, this *entente cordiale* soon disintegrated, developing into a profound cause of aggravation between Henry and Augustus with Dorelia *au milieu* and Euphemia moving on to fresh fields. Certainly the two men became unfairly critical of each other's work; yet any disagreements on matters of art were mild in comparison with the fundamental differences that erupted over their respective attitudes to and treatments of Dorelia. It was Henry's continuing involvement with her that became the real reason for the rift between Augustus and himself. After visiting her once when she seemed seriously ill, Henry reported that, 'John's alarm was naturally exaggerated by past experience' and they 'made an amnesty for these peculiar conditions'; and when she was in need of recuperation, Henry wrote, admitting, 'Certainly she deserves a rest & holiday' but that perhaps, 'travelling with Augustus is rather a doubtful way of getting it.' Without Dorelia's magnetism and her undeniable tact and patience, it is unlikely the two painters would have seen much of each other. As it was, Henry visited more often when Augustus was elsewhere, and fond as he was of the many children when young – 'a favourite with us boys because of his propensity for mild practical joking', recalled Caspar John[26] – as they grew up, rather than 'the zany Rom . . . & those most obstreporous girls', it was Dorelia he came to see. The family always called her 'Dodo', as did all who knew her intimately; and Dodo she was to both Augustus and Henry who, mixed with their more mature affection, shared an image of her as the supreme mother-figure, an ideal haven of sympathy and blissful security. Beyond that, however, any similarity between their views of her ended.

To Augustus, she was forever a remarkably tolerant, stable mother to his extensive family and a welcome refuge from the ravages of excess. But as an artist, he uncharacteristically distanced himself and formalised her features in an often restrained and disciplined way. Having successfully translated the once-secretary Dorothy McNeill into the enigmatic Dorelia and invested her with Romany origins, he drew her considerably taller than she was in fact; and invariably, he painted her rather respectfully as a symbol of woman, elegant, ethnic, with the nobility and simplicity of a peasant. She was his model more consistently and for longer than any other yet, in his countless renderings of her, she rarely appears nude recognisably as Dorelia and her sexuality is always stylised and diffused. By contrast, in his many studies of Euphemia she is usually nude, or nearly so, and he fairly relishes maximising her sexuality revealing, with dazzlingly virtuoso draughtsmanship, an unashamed, earthy eroticism. Normally for Augustus, every beautiful woman must be attainable; but in his art, Dorelia remains the embodiment of the eternal mystery of all women, inscrutable, inviolable, La Gioconda incarnate. In his vision of her, he created an uneasy equation, an incompatibility, between his art and his life: it was an inevitable condition of Augustus that fact and fiction should intermingle; but for those close to Dodo who were only too aware of the actual disparity for many years in the relationship between the artist and his model, it could be an unconvincing and ironic portrayal, since her seeming serenity often masked great unhappiness and despair.

It was particularly this aspect of Augustus' fiction that so antagonised Henry. After finding the Contemporary Art Society's spring exhibition of 1913 such a 'depressing affair', he reported, '*Tout le monde en sort mal* . . . except only Gwen John . . . *Le grand maître* himself is horribly represented by that damned picture of Dorelia smiling.' Perhaps largely because of his emotional involvement with Dodo and his resentment at the apparent injustices in the love stakes, Henry came to hold an unjustifiably low opinion of his rival's painting. While visiting Newnham in 1910, Henry's sister Dorothy showed him Augustus' recent portrait of the classical scholar, anthropologist and lecturer, Jane Harrison, which he 'disliked' on sight, '& much more when Jane herself appeared'; and in 1912, he claimed to be bored stiff with '*le maître . . . et son oeuvre nouvelle!*' There was however, the occasional truce: in the same year, after one of their more relaxed encounters, Henry remarked on how Augustus had been 'perfectly delightful' showing him 'the few things he had in his studio, which I criticized . . . & exchanged loving glances at table just as though there had never been a cloud between us', promising, 'I shall go & see his large cartoon in Chelsea as he asked me.' Momentarily, Henry was moved to proffer an olive branch and to re-establish some kind of rapport, 'just as in the best of the old days'. Sometimes, from a mixture of nostalgia and pity, his resistance would weaken and he would see Augustus in a pathetic light: 'There is no doubt he pines for comrades & is sick of his chance pub acquaintances', wrote Henry in one of these moments, asking, 'but will he ever consider the unidealistic demands of friendship? I feel as though I could be a better friend to him now than I ever was, but much doubt whether he has not become inaccessible enough to make this feeling presumptious.' Nevertheless, any chance of a reconciliation soon passed and hostilities were resumed with perhaps greater animosity. Historically, their relationship implies subservience of the younger to the older: in old age, when they settled to a grumbling tolerance of each other, the reverse was probably true.

Henry is credited with saying, 'I should have been Augustus John.'[27] It can only be supposed, since the flush of excitement from their first meeting faded so quickly and ever after Henry was at such pains to disengage himself from any influence on his work, that he was referring wistfully to the possession of Dorelia. Certainly he thought that he alone could properly appreciate and adequately cherish her, whose precious qualities – '*du rayonnante de beauté, vigueur, gaîté,* as he described them – were merely taken for granted by the unworthy Augustus whom he once called, in a fit of pique and an excess of unkindness, 'that disintegrating troll'. Dorelia's 'charms accumulating like the banked fortunes of some capitalist' were utterly wasted on the errant Augustus: 'That old wreck is a millstone round her neck from which', wrote Henry, 'she recovers in quite a few days' absence.' She was a tonic, the rejuvenating effects of which he was inspired to describe – after staying '4 nights' when 'J. was not there' – as 'some tremendous affirmation of that Spring that glimpsed on me with curious early rays . . . & not all the lapis lazulae of Giotto or emerald of Fra Angelico could ever colour it'; and 'in the course of some endless conversations', he 'thought her as supreme as ever', declaring, '*que celle-la m'assomme de ses boutes*'. Though he contrived to be a near neighbour to Dorelia, she was never reliably nor easily available either as companion or model and, unhappily for Henry, the qualities in her that he so admired were to remain mostly prospective. A letter from her would make him 'more *éperdument amoureux* than ever'; and with a telegram, 'telling me to meet her at the station at 8', he would be over the moon: 'Imagine the volcano in my soul!' he wrote, 'All that beautifully established Rumpelstiltzkin's self-possession gone at a blow!' There were consolations, of course, when later that evening he 'conducted her home to a very copious bed'; and again he confessed, 'Dorelia did come . . . we walked through divine woods & lunched in an exquisite pub & I got . . . quite drunk. Then I had another evening with her all alone . . . It was more than the expected comble'. Though a later 'visit was a triumph while it lasted' he felt afterwards what he wryly diagnosed as 'complete catalepsis sulphurealis'; and too often the brief ecstasy would be negated by a prolonged anguish that left him frustrated and depressed: 'my . . . greatest gloom . . . was not lifted by the immediate discovery that Dodo was only here for a day more', he complained; 'I have had some glimpses of her. But in spite of some occasional gleams I cannot escape from the terrible feeling of a great cloud descending – dark & immoveable.'

Dorelia shared with Henry a consuming interest in music and they accompanied each other in piano duets. She read a great deal but rarely volunteered discussion of her reading matter: she was not especially articulate nor given to loquacity. Much of her time was devoted to domesticity, to the many children, and to coping with 'Augustus & a mass of people'. Possessively, Henry thought her home too often 'heavily beslimed & beset for a long time with various male & female slugs . . . It is strange', he noticed, 'how D. willingly inflicts herself with such trials.' For relief she would turn to tending the walled garden full of flowers, another interest she and Henry shared; and when it all became too much, even for her remarkable forbearance, she would uproot herself and disappear for days, sometimes staying with Henry. Their relationship was probably most passionate before the First War and perhaps more poignant after, when Henry returned. He was always solicitous of her: in 1912, following the death of her young son Pyramus, he noticed how she,

> 'looked well & strong enough at first glance but . . . soon saw she was much changed. She has lost a lot of hair & the rest is gone terribly white: there is also a new look, something weak, & bewildered & profoundly cynical. I do wish there was someone near her now to cheer her: in the crowd at meals & after she was too bravely merry in a way I thought awfully hectic.'

Something of this transition – apart from the obvious passing of time and the ageing process – may be noted in the very incomplete cycle of Henry's drawings of Dorelia. They may also reveal a little of his changing attitude to Augustus and his efforts at emancipation from the dreaded influence. An early, full-length drawing, probably of 1907, could at first be a John. Inscribed 'Dodo', she sits, looking down, turning her head towards the artist and leaning forward with her left hand raised as if in a placatory gesture. Though seated, she seems to be moving as Augustus often drew her – in a state of becoming rather than being and essentially romantic. The vigorous line is strongly reminiscent of Augustus' own vitality and spontaneity. Dorelia wears her customary long dress of which Henry, with powerfully rhythmic lines, makes great play. The figure too, is elongated à la John and it is just possible that the two artists may have shared the model and drawn the same pose, so similar are the style of drawing and the interpretation of the sitter. The few other drawings by Henry of Dorelia from this earlier period are more intimate close-ups – head, head and shoulders with the occasional suggestion of a hand – indicating the more personal, private view he was to have of her; and all the subsequent drawings show this same intimacy and increasing warmth. That they all seem unfinished may be due simply to expediency and for very practical reasons: moments together were generally snatched, becoming more spasmodic and uncertain as the years passed and hardly ever being ideal for sustained sessions of drawing. Augustus was never really able to be critical of the affair but he would make the occasional 'sarcastic' remark to Dorelia with regard to Henry seeming 'indispensable'. Even though Henry's visits were always within full view of the John household, whether 'his highness' was there or not, meetings elsewhere became increasingly clandestine. Not surprisingly, Henry appears to have made few paintings of Dorelia for it is highly unlikely that circumstances were often suitable for portraits in oils.

Augustus had a virtual monopoly of Dorelia as a model. His sister Gwen painted her 'with extraordinary tenderness' and 'an almost impersonal pity' when they stayed together at Toulouse in the autumn of 1903. Although it was several years before these gentle, sensitive portraits were completed and several more before they were exhibited, they were in conception whilst Dorelia was 'trustfully unaware of the scarring realities of life' and before Augustus had so forcefully imprinted his personality on her.[28] Thereafter, any other artist had to compete with the image '*le maître*' had created. In fact, his projection of her is still one of the most famous images in British painting, an inescapable truth that was a recurring source of irritation to Henry, who resented the popular success with which she had become virtually inseparable from her creator. That the object of his continuing affection should be permanently identified with his rival in both love and art was unfair, unsettling, and profoundly damaging to his ego.

Some comparison between their respective views of Dorelia is inevitable but sadly unsatisfactory and ultimately unequal. For Augustus, her image was the work of a lifetime: at first she was a subject for essays in the art of portraiture, gradually becoming more of a vehicle for formal exercises and stylistic improvisation. Typically, he simplified her form and features, frequently posing her quite dramatically against the skyline. He chose to do so deliberately, consciously, but he also had the freedom and opportunity that were denied Henry whose drawings of her are relatively slight and among

59

some of the least important of his whole oeuvre in so far as his development as an artist is concerned. To dissociate Dorelia from the image created by Augustus and to approach Henry's view with an unprejudiced eye is virtually impossible; and so perhaps his more delicate interpretations are most interesting for their biographical import, since they seem to touchingly trace the barest outline of a relationship and suggest the pathos of a dwindling love affair, despite Henry's attempts at discretion by referring to Dodo as 'a certain lady whose name must be veiled even from our biographers.' As the pencil almost caresses her features, his view becomes steadily cosier: devotion shines through and seems evident in every mark. It was possibly this caressing, symbolically bringing the artist closer to his model, that produced drawings more strongly tonal than usual, a technical trait rarely associated with Henry for as a draughtsman – and like Augustus – he characteristically used line to describe and interpret form. His drawings of her done in the 1920s are still fairly tonal but much lighter and gentler in conception and somewhat reminiscent of the brothers Spencer, particularly Gilbert Spencer's subtle, searching portrait drawings. In the immediate postwar years, Henry was seeing a lot of the Spencers – and their work – and it seems he was able at last to cure some of the 'infection' from Augustus. In these later studies, Dorelia reads, rests, dozes, or gazes as if contemplating the uncertainty of the middle years; a tinge of sadness creeps into her expression and hint of tiredness hangs over their execution, reflecting something of the despair at the impossibility of there ever being a future together. Once, she was seriously tempted to take the plunge and leave Augustus – for a while, if not forever: 'It was no use' wrote Henry,

'the rain & the hopelessness of the houses seemed to penetrate her & she wanted to turn back at Salisbury. Although I carried out the plot to programme, waiting till the last minute at Upavon before springing it on her she flatly refused – not till next day giving the reason – "we should never have been able to get away".'

That was in the summer of 1926. By the autumn, Henry had not entirely given up, saying, 'there is a fair chance of it all coming off some day when that strange woman is less perplexed & all our nerves less raging.' But it never did.

NOTES

1 Hamnett *Laughing Torso* pp.26–7.
2 Holroyd *Augustus John* p.200.
3 Lewis *Rude Assignment* p.119.
4 Holroyd p.200.
5 Leach *Beyond East and West* pp.31–2.
6 Hamnett p.165.
7 Julia Strachey *Diary* : summer 1934.
8 Romilly John – author : 28 Jul 1979 (interview); R. John *The Seventh Child* p.53.
9 Harold Rosenberg *Tradition of the New* McGraw-Hill 1965, pp.209–10.
10 Lewis p.112.
11 Grant *Paris Memoir*.
12 Mrs Mary Taubman – author : 7 Apr 1979 (interview).
13 Grant.
14 ib.
15 ib.
16 Blanche *Portraits of a Lifetime* p.264.
17 ib.
18 Holroyd p.322.
19 ib.
20 ib.
21 Duncan Grant – James Strachey : 25 Apr 1907.
22 ib.
23 Walter Lamb – Clive Bell : 23 Apr 1908.
24 Holroyd p.305.
25 Henry Lamb – Ottoline Morrell : 6 Apr 1912.
26 Caspar John – author : 24 Sep 1979.
27 Leach p.31.
28 J. Rothenstein *Modern English Painters* Vol.1, p.167.

FIVE

BORIS ANREP

———

'I have had to believe in his glory & support the strain of his drawbacks practically single-handed all these years', wrote Henry to Lytton Strachey in 1912, on discovering that his two friends had met at last: 'I never expected you would take to him so quickly; hurrah! . . . it is not comfortable to be enthusiastic alone . . . *Now* I can laugh about him without the distressing feeling of disloyalty.'

Boris von Anrep was an exact contemporary of Henry's and, like him, decided to become an artist relatively late in life. Born in Russia, he was first a student of law in St. Petersburg before arriving in Paris in 1908 to enrol at the Académie Julian. Here the two mature students struck up a friendship: 'I had a warm feeling towards him', wrote Boris in 1960, on hearing of Henry's death, calling him, 'my old friend of my youth and one of the first English friends I had.' Henry too, naturally warmed to – and retained his affection for – this irrepressibly ebullient, refreshingly spontaneous, fantastically open and engaging emigré who at various times he described as, 'bulging with inconsequent gaiety', brimming with 'invincible bonhomie and generosity', and overwhelming him 'with an avalanche of geniality'. Boris had more than a little of Augustus' sense of theatre, with the classical instincts of a clown and a genius for comedy to which Henry, when young, happily responded. Lady Ottoline Morrell recalled his being 'clever, fat, good-hearted, sensual . . . full of youthful vitality and Russian gaiety'; and Frances Partridge remembered him, even in his sixties, 'wearing an elegant suit of lichen-green Irish tweed, the trousers tapered round his massive legs, and black Italian shoes with perfectly square toes, made of the softest leather. Next morning, however, he appeared for breakfast in a cowboy shirt in gorgeous red and green checks, and to remind us of its beauty he several times during the day lifted his pullover from over his stomach to reveal it, while an ineffable smile spread over his broad Slavonic features.'[1]

But, unlike Augustus who indulged in lengthy moods of gloomy introspection, Boris was more consistently jovial and the kind of silences to which the master was prone were hardly conceivable in his company. 'Perhaps he will prove just the required magnet to draw me out of myself', thought Henry, recounting how,

'Anrep arrived . . . & relieved me from a melancholy state of mind. How easy it is to forget the power of personal charm & the unreasonable qualities generally. When I went to meet this fellow, all his attributes passed my mental muster duly & without excitement till the elusive member of the rank appeared. What an astonishment & what pleasure! There was the same animal just so high & just so broad, with same hat & the same trousers, the same high voice & just the same rare intelligence & powers: all this I could expect & recognize without delay & without emotion. But immediately this other thing – the spirit & charm, which one knows & doesn't know, which answers no summons but seems to wait until one is napping before appearing, flushed, making dull things beautiful & horrors acceptable!'

Sometimes though, Henry found Boris rather a handful, complaining that in his whirlwind presence, 'everything is upside down including my head' for, intellectually and physically, he was exceptionally energetic and courageous, seeming never to be daunted by feelings of inadequacy or inexperience. His acute intelligence, volatile mind, and fertile imagination, embracing an extraordinary range of interests and abilities, were a stimulus to Henry, hugely extending his own cultural orbit. Certainly, Boris was a European man, perhaps an international one. His enthusiasms encompassed influences from east and west as well as a Mediterranean enrichment of his Slavonic background: 'He is indeed a wonderful fellow & I learn to appreciate him more wisely', conceded Henry, in 1911,

'There is in him so much to learn – from his fresh points of view, & particularly from his amazingly genial character, his kind & never weak treatment of others – that I feel it mean to entertain the feelings of irritation which his tendency to overbearing sometimes provokes. What he doesn't understand in me seems not worth vindication against his predominance in other qualities. Oh, si vous aimez mieux, what he can learn from me could be got otherwise by subsequent incarnations, while I feel that this is my unique chance of *fixing for ever* certain elementary essentials, if not of acquiring new ones!'

Whilst deriving great pleasure from Boris' agile mind and diversity of interests and talents; and whilst admiring his quick grasp of any problem – artistic, philosophic, practical – Henry always enjoyed his exuberant, idiosyncratic use of English. As a schoolboy, he had been sent to Great Missenden in Buckinghamshire to learn English but, although he became conversant in several languages, it was some years before English came to him naturally and fluently. Even so, he never lost what Frances Partridge called, his 'Borisisms' and, as she wrote, 'His conversation is always a delight with a brilliant choice of words, surprisingly modulated in tone.'[2] Henry was ever keen to share with other friends his appreciation of Boris; but it was not until towards the end of 1910 that he was to meet Henry's old sparring partner Augustus, an event so entertaining to Henry that almost at once he wrote to Lytton Strachey,

'I give you verbatim Anrep's account of his first meeting John in Paris 2 days ago: (at dinner)
"If you could creep in my heart & memory which you honoured by some particulars of your relation to John's – you would fell sike & poisined by the byle which turns round in me when I saw first John. That was a night-mare, with all the appreciation of his powerful & mighty dreadedness, & some ghotic beaty, I could not keep down my heat to some beastly & cruel & vulgar lock (look) of brightness which I percived in his face & demanour . . ."
This seems to me a perfect description of all that part of him which some inexplicable vanity prevented me from acquainting you with.'

Boris, like Henry, was penetratingly perceptive of people and always alert to their mannerisms and affectations. 'Some day', he wrote to Lytton, 'you must meet Anrep if only to face the crisis of learning from him how N[ijinsky] shake's one's hand.'

As a regular theatre and concert-goer, Henry was caught up in the wave of enthusiasm for the Russian Ballet that began in Paris in 1909 and '10, and soon spread to London culminating in 1911 with the arrival of Diaghilev and the Imperial Russian Ballet Company at

Covent Garden. Though not without his reservations concerning some of the performances, Henry became quite a fan, marvelling especially at Nijinsky: 'I am still doting on that lovely serpent', he confessed to Lytton, 'He did nothing very perventi that evening (Les Sylphides, Cléopatra, Spectre de la Rose, Prince Igor) – his dances seemed all quite simple & straightforward: but when he walked on & off with that skirt-bearing gait I couldn't help squirming. I thought the Chopin things the best, it was such a pleasure to know the tunes & be used to the costumes. The more gaudy decors bored me with their badness after a second's surprise.' Mentioning how he had heard that Nijinsky was, 'Actually . . . very short & rather insignificant', which he believed 'to be impossible for a person of those proportions', he admitted to having been 'twice at the Russian ballet' in one week; after dismissing Stravinsky – 'The elaborate new thing (l'Oiseau de feu) is rubbish' – he went on to express his continuing admiration for the dancing, adding, 'Nijinsky thrills me more than ever in the old things.'

Early in 1910, with the encouragement of Boris, Henry began reading Dostoievsky whose novels by then had been translated into French: '"Pauvres Gens", he wrote, 'seems perfectly charming – his first published thing', but 'L'Esprit Souterrain' he found 'a disturbing tale', describing it as 'a diabolic work . . . Certainly it dispenses with the necessity of reading any Nietzsche' and calling it 'more than a prototype to Also Sprach Zarathustra, even the first part recalls it at once – style as well as ideas. Isn't the *writing* dazzling?' During the summer of 1911 Henry received a copy of Gogol's 'Ames Mortes' in thanks for which he said he was 'trying to read in his spare moments', thinking it at first 'grand' with 'such gigantic power of caricature & irony, magnificent, magnificent . . .', though when finished calling it 'very unequal' and admitting how,

> 'nearly all my pleasure in it vanished when I discovered with Anrep, by comparison with a Russian copy, that a good 3rd of the French is the invention of the translator, who, being paid by line or page has bolstered up his two volumes with useless recapitulations at the beginning of each "Chant", long senseless footnotes, & endless "tables des matieres" with repetition of the recapitulations – all this as well as numerous "amplifications" in the actual text of the original.'

But his interest in Russian literature never really waned: he 'finished the all but eternal War & Peace', mentioning incidentally that

'Tolstoi's son who has recently made the Anreps' acquaintance greets me with an ape-like grin at the sketch-class' in Paris, 'but I repel him with an august frown'. Henry found 'those . . . historical dramas – terribly moving' and, in the 1920s, reported how he was 'reading Gorki's two autobiographical books with the greatest fascination.' In 1912, he became so enthusiastic about the Russian 'invasion' that he began calling Lady Ottoline, 'Ottolinotchka'; and in London, with Leonard Woolf, Adrian Stephen (Virginia's brother), and Saxon Sydney Turner (another Cambridge Apostle), he began learning Russian. After a few weeks he reached what he called 'the critical stage' explaining, 'the brilliant first canter is over & one's early good intentions almost lost sight of: we can talk about the gardener's hat & feather mattresses but are still far from Tolstoi: the grammatical complications are simply stupefying – to me & Adrian: Turner just smiles indulgently at the first second & then knows them for ever the next.'

Boris Anrep, as well as influencing Henry, played no small part in the extraordinary interest in all the Russian arts that swept Europe in the years immediately before the First World War although some connections – certainly between France and Russia – had been made towards the end of the nineteenth century. Many Russian artists had studied in Paris and, by the time Boris arrived, there were already several hundred French Impressionist and Post-Impressionist works in Russian collections, so that he was by no means unprepared for some of the more recent developments in French art. Whilst a law student in St. Petersburg, he had mixed in literary circles and begun to make some reputation as writer; and at first in Paris, while struggling to become a painter, he 'was absorbed in composing & illustrating lengthy cosmico-epico-ethico-didactic poems' that Henry described as 'very wild & apocryphal' and which he helped translate into English despite what he called 'the fatigues & uncongeniality of the work'. Thus Boris was well-placed to act as something of a cultural go-between the two countries and when the Russian journal 'Apollon' was first published in 1909 – with editions in French and Russian – Boris became the Parisian art correspondent, trying, as he put it, to spread the gospels of the avant-garde 'among thinking artists in Russia'. He also contributed some of his poems, announcing to Henry, 'rather pomposo', that he had had '"literary success" in Petersburg. "Men of note expect me to be a prophet & I have but to foretell my own grandeur"'. In 1914, he reviewed Clive

Bell's *Art* for 'Apollon'. In thanking the author for sending him a copy which he 'read with avidity' Boris wrote from Paris:

'Of course the main idea of it: about the significance of the form being the thing in art cannot be denied and I only too strongly appreciate that you put down this principle in a harsh and polemical language I hope it will produice [sic] its effect in England where I think people need much more enlightening than anywhere else.

There are of course some points in which I don't quite agree with you. And of which I will have the pleasure to speak to you very soon as in [a] few days. I leave for London where I will stay a cuple [sic] of months'.

Above all, Boris became best known as a mosaicist. Before 1914, a few commissions – notably from Augustus John and Ethel Sands – and the first of several schemes for Westminster Cathedral had begun to establish him as a unique artist in that medium. Henry played a part in encouraging patronage although, in any contractual negotiations, he was always alert to see that the artist was not exploited. But it was not until after the First World War that Boris' talent for this exacting medium blossomed fully, making him one of the best known and most sought after exponents in Europe. 'I live in France, and work for England', he used to say, and, ironically, the removal of his main workshop to Paris in 1926 coincided with the start of a whole series of major projects in London that included the Bank of England, the Blake Room at the Tate Gallery, the Greek Cathedral, and the entrance to the National Gallery, as well as numerous smaller private commissions.

In the early years in Paris, while steadily improving his drawing and design, Boris gradually acquainted himself with the techniques of mosaic, an apprenticeship helped by visits to Ravenna and Rome. Before studying at the Académie Julian he had visited Ravenna with an older Russian artist, Stelletsky, one of several chosen by Boris to represent his country when in 1912 Roger Fry invited him to organise the Russian section of the Second Post-Impressionist exhibition in London. Despite his seeming to be in touch with contemporary art, Boris' initial selection proved a disappointment to Fry and too passé for his modernist taste. Fry's intention had been to show the most recent developments in European art but, instead of Goncharova and Larionov – whose work arrived after the opening of the exhibition – or Malevich and Tatlin, Boris at first chose artists who more properly belonged to late nineteenth century symbolism, reflecting the influence of Moreau, Puvis de Chavannes, and the Russian,

Vrubel. After seeing the exhibition at the Grafton Galleries, where Henry was himself modestly represented in the British section with a small version of the full-length *Portrait of Lytton Strachey*, he wrote to his sitter, 'I knew even the Anrep drawing you thought too much of an illustration: I wanted to know what you thought of them in that milieu', and asked, 'Did you peradventure admire any other Russians – isn't Stelletzki amusing?'

This contact through Boris with the work of the Russian painters – and doubtless, as well as seeing their work, Henry would have met some of them in London or Paris – may partly explain why in 1911 and 1912 he was tempted to digress temporarily to the mood of the *fin-de-siècle* with a few insouciant, somewhat effete compositions of female nudes grouped by the sea or lakeside. These delicate confections seem quite out of character and, chronologically, a curious departure: had they been done some three or four years earlier under the influence of Augustus, who had looked so closely at Puvis, they would have fitted more naturally into the sequence of Henry's progress as a painter. But no artist's development is ever quite as logical or sequential as it is often written, Henry's closer acquaintance with Russian symbolist painting simply diverted his attention briefly from a near exclusive concentration on portraiture and genre subjects to an atypically decorative style. It was a phase too, that came at a time when he was experimenting with tempera which, he said, 'I have just learnt from Fry.' For Henry ever to acknowledge indebtedness to Roger Fry was an event in itself in view of their more usually acrimonious relationship. 'It's a lovely medium but *very* slow', he reported; but only a few days later having had what he called, 'the experience of this doubtful début in the new medium', he described how he had made himself 'quite ill over the damned little picture sitting over it for 6 & 7 hours a day . . . indeed I am not made for minute work I think. And as yet I don't see how to use tempera at all sketchily or freely. The design must be very determined & life studies will be necessary.'

This was in February 1911. In January, Henry had spent a week in Paris with Boris, attending life classes, probably at 'La Palette', when he confessed that, 'drawing from the nude . . . has more than excised my last drop of life out of me'. It was some of these drawings that he used as a basis for his trials with tempera although his excursions into decorative symbolism really owe more to Puvis than to the study of nature. One in particular, *The Lake* – for which a watercolour study done in the spring in Britanny is in the Whitworth Gallery, Manchester – is so close in style and composition to Puvis de Chavannes' *Young Girls at the Seaside* of 1879, now in the Louvre, that it would be remarkable for Henry not to have made some detailed study of it. There are too, distinct echoes of Augustus' own decorative schemes, as well as a possible affinity with Maurice Denis, especially his *Bathers* of 1899, and in this context it is noteworthy that,

'Denis had a great following in Russia, which he visited several times during this period [1905–1910], for his work more than that of any other French painter was sympathetic to the Petersburg Symbolist school of literature among whom he found ardent supporters; works and articles by him were frequently reproduced in their magazines.'[3]

Henry would have had his attention drawn to Puvis by Augustus when he first went to Paris in 1907 although little or no influence on his work seems evident before 1911. 'I long to work harder at my technique', he wrote then, 'anything to equip myself better for the pursuit of the glorious mental improvisations which choke each other with such desolating profusion during moments of health & bien être.' One of these 'improvisations' he struggled with on and off for at least the first half of 1911 was in fact *The Lake*, on which he 'worked so long & hard that', he complained, 'my eyes & head are stupid from it' and 'the excitement prevented me from sleeping.' The picture was begun while Henry was staying at the 'Dog Inn' at Henley-on-Thames and working nearby in a makeshift studio at Peppard Cottage, Lady Ottoline Morrell's country retreat. It was intended for her brother, Lord Henry Cavendish-Bentinck, 'a noble lord of my acquaintance', as Henry called him, who 'has commissioned me to do a nude for him; my head teems with ideas', he wrote, 'but I pine for the real flesh – someone to look at & grasp; without these & with my present smatterings of anatomies & classical recollections, I shall only be able to go on turning out sort of Bouchers.' Henry rather relished the idea of producing something mildly titillating to suit 'milord Henry'; but the painting had a difficult birth and, while still in progress, he transported the canvas to Britanny from where he announced he was 'working fairly hard, but so hampered for want of models. My figures do look so hideous & lifeless – so crude', he wrote: 'Now . . . I plan a great winter's work in Paris drawing nudes all day & night – not chance poses so much as studies for figures already imagined.' Two days before he thought he had 'finished a picture for Lord H.' but then felt so 'dissatisfied with parts of it' that more than half he 'scrubbed away' and it was not until a week later he reported, 'Lord H's picture is done & gives me some pleasure – among more blushes. I think it the most *complete* of my productions'.

Because of the subject matter and its associations, *The Lake* might have had a hint of sensuality; but the result is quite unerotic. So too, in the gentle, inconsequential atmosphere of the painting is there no suggestion of the dis-ease with which Henry troubled over the unfamiliar territory of the content and its treatment, nor of his inexperience with the technique of tempera. The traumas of its lengthy gestation are lost in the relaxed undulations of the design and shrouded in a symbolist nimbus.

During the summer of 1911, Boris went to stay with Henry in Britanny. 'Anrep gave me great encouragement in my work, seeing great advance both in my drawings & colour sketches', he wrote to Lady Ottoline, adding, 'but chiefly he liked my picture for Lord H. . . . I like it too, now, & wish it were for you instead of him'. As if taking up the suggestion, Ottoline bought *The Lake* before her brother ever saw it. On the back, its title is chalked in Russian indicating that she complied with Henry's urgent request of the beginning of 1913 when he mentioned that he and Boris were 'sending a few things to an exhibition in Moscow' the following week: 'Will you kindly lend me . . . the 2 nudes & baby in front of a lake'? he asked, 'The things will be away about 8 weeks.' That he should have chosen to be represented by this particular picture seems quite significant since he must have deemed it one of his more suitable efforts to be shown in the company of what he envisaged as contemporary Russian painting: moreover, it provides further confirmation of his interesting, though short, links with Russian art via Boris.

After *The Lake* had found its way into the Morrell's collection, Henry was no nearer completing his commission until, a month later he announced being 'at a moonlight picture of nudes which amuses me greatly & might suit Lord Henry's taste.' This second attempt known simply as *Two Nudes* also remained with Lady Ottoline, as did a watercolour study of the same subject. Henry had thought 'the drawing of it classical', a surprising epithet in view of the lack of both structure and definition in the design: the form is fudged and the

70

figures considerably less anatomical and less convincing than those in *The Lake* which, in any case, appears to have been based more concretely on a particular Puvis; but, like the tinkling of a Palm Court orchestra, *Two Nudes* has a certain period charm that somewhat compensates for its amorphousness.

However, despite the overt femininity of the two women, they are slightly androgynous, a judgement influenced in part by Henry's own confession at the time when his 'anxiety to inquire into certain planes of male anatomy' led him 'to indulge in some long nude séances before the glass'. This, he wrote, 'came of trying to make nude compositions without models . . . I was able to reflect profoundly on my natural composition: it wasn't quite cheering. Of all degenerate male forms I have never seen my equal: not a trace of muscles round the chest: the hips too wide; arms & legs quite round & covered with female skin. Not that I can deny the aesthetic charms of certain passages, it is the type which desolates me. A great damning question seems to mock every undertaking – "how could a creature of those proportions effect anything?"', he asked.

These personal and private investigations may have affected Henry's renderings of the female nude but more surely were used as a basis for what seems to have been one of his few essays involving male nudes: *Phantasy* was first shown at the New English Art Club Summer Exhibition in 1912. 'The Times' called it 'very clever' noting perceptively that,

> 'These two nude figures with a horse come from M. Picasso, who can invest such themes with a curious significance not expressed in words. But Mr. Lamb seems to have taken the theme without himself knowing quite clearly what it meant, and the picture is an expression of his taste in art rather than his feeling towards nature.'[4]

Henry had been disappointed with the Picasso show in London in 1912 but in the previous year mentioned spending what he called 'a dutiful afternoon at the dealers' shops' in Paris, and seeing 'an exhibition of early Picassos at Vollards' which he thought 'charming enough – especially a nude boy carrying a baby & also a nude girl pouring water into a saucer'. The rest he considered very slight, and complained that 'none were framed or shewn with a trace of respect for the painter.' There is no documentary evidence proving that he ever met Picasso but it is likely that at some time between 1907 and 1911, with perhaps Augustus John, Wyndham Lewis, Duncan Grant

71

or Clive Bell, Henry would have visited his studio. As well, he would have seen more of Picasso's work at Gertrude Stein's in the Rue de Fleurus, as did Augustus, Lewis, Epstein, Fry and Lady Ottoline. Although Henry was always averse to Matisse, he remained a persistent admirer of Picasso – at least of the pre-Cubist work – and it is significant that in the February of 1912 he received some postcard reproductions from Paris that 'exceeded everything' he could imagine. 'The Picassos & Greco simply rivet one: it is impossible ever to forget such lovely visions', he wrote enthusiastically, adding, as if to convince himself of the paramount importance of drawing, 'and surely they show that *in the end* colour must be an *accessory* expression.' Presumably the reproductions were in monochrome but the images must have been powerful enough to inspire Henry to improvise on one of the themes that Picasso had explored in his 'Blue' and 'Rose' periods – horses and riders.

Phantasy was begun at a time when Henry was riding a good deal, which may have encouraged him to tackle such untypical subject matter. These male nudes, in comparison with his renderings of the female nude, seem somewhat epicene, though clearly deriving from life studies of conspicuously masculine models done earlier in Paris; but the reservations that Henry had expressed about his own anatomy have subtly infiltrated the two main figures and almost certainly the head in three-quarter view is an adapted self-portrait merged with memories of Nijinsky in *L'Apres-Midi d'une Faune.* Could the other figure have been influenced by observations of Boris? A third, far distant figure of indeterminate sex rides a prancing horse like Uccello's 'St. George'; and all is set in a lunar landscape predominantly, and appropriately, blue. The painting succeeds in its strong drawing and design, strengthened further by delineation, again reminiscent of Picasso: but whereas Picasso integrates the line expressively, Henry uses it as a binding afterthought, a demarcation between areas of form and colour; and, unlike Picasso, whose figures move freely without concern for an audience, the poses in *Phantasy* have a curious coyness, as if a prude might be peeping or a censor lurking.

Despite the pertinent criticism in 'The Times', *Phantasy* was well received: Charles Aitken, of the Whitechapel, later Director of the Tate, wanted to buy it but 'had little money'; Lady Ottoline was interested and, though continuing to prefer her 'old blue one', as Henry dubbed the *Two Nudes*, wrote a cheque for it on behalf of her brother – for whom she really considered it unsuitable. However, the 'tangled question of the Horse picture' was 'happily solved' when Robert Ross bought it for the Contemporary Art Society: 'I will return your £30 as soon as I am paid', wrote Henry to Lady Ottoline, apologetically, 'I'm sorry your brother is feeling dissatisfied. I will of course do him another picture.' Whether Lord Henry was ever satisfied remains a mystery but, through the CAS, *Phantasy* found its way into the permanent collection of the Tate.

For Henry, creatively, *Phantasy* turned out to be a cul-de-sac. Yet, he thought it the best of his divertissements saying that, even before its completion, compared with *The Lake* and *Two Nudes*, it was 'already better'. In isolation, this apparently illogical digression has a logic of its own, and shows a development from Puvis, via the Russian symbolists, to the early symbolism of Picasso. On the other hand, in relation to his work in portrait and genre painting, it underlines how temperamentally ill-suited he was to transposing and stylising natural form into anything other than an identifiable setting; and only then was he wholly convincing when there was some deeply felt, expressive purpose, as for example, the results from his experiences in the First World War. Usually he was too interested in individual psychology and the nuances of inter-relationships between people ever to be at home in the more generalised, suffused, ethereal realms of symbolist painting. 'No. Symbolism doesn't occur in my works, unless sometimes as an afterthought or discovery, such as academics manage to find in favourite masterpieces', he was to write in old age, adding, 'but I don't mean to exclude poetry, or appropriate adjuncts especially in a portrait'. Certainly, his portraiture was affected, indirectly: that of his father of the following year might not have been as stylised but for this experimental detour; and there is a discernible influence on his genre painting done soon after in Ireland where, in the winters of 1912 and '13, he was to produce a formidable body of work that included one masterpiece which combined perfectly his observation of nature and his understanding of people.

Sometime during 1910, Boris Anrep rented a studio in Paris that was to become – apart from the years of occupation – his main mosaic workshop until his death in 1969. Situated on the Left Bank, Boulevard Arago, with a hospital at one end, a prison at the other, and a convent in the middle, is a long, wide, tree-lined avenue spanning a quiet part of Montparnasse. No. 65, known as 'La Cité Fleurie', is still a compact complex of *ateliers d'artiste* each opening onto a courtyard. Though now flanked by tall blocks of flats the site has been spared redevelopment and remains a unique example of *vieux Paris*. Studio 6, in which Boris worked, had a small apartment where he also lived from time to time and where Henry often stayed, although neither as easily nor ideally as he would have wished. 'Anrep's room is occupied', he complained, 'so I shall have to poke up in some semi-reputable & wholly unclean hotel'; fearing the worst, he admitted, 'I do so dread those bug-ridden Paris hotels.' But even when staying chez Anrep, Henry was apt not to find the conditions to his liking – either for living or working: '65 Bd Arago doesn't abound in the comforts of privacy so I have sallied forth to write', he reported ungraciously; but even at the café where he chose to sit, he found himself 'fallen into a nest of loud-voiced Swedes'; and in the day, Boris was so busy that Henry went to life classes.

The studios at 65 Boulevard Arago are still used by artists, several of whom recall Boris with respect and affection. The Dutch Constructivist, Cesar Domela – an associate of Mondrian, Arp, Moholy-Nagy, Pevsner and Herbin – settled there in 1933. While deploring the 'apartheid' to which groups of artists became prone in Paris, Domela well remembered how Boris acted as a lively catalyst, tactfully bridging gaps between opposed ideologies.

Tact is not a trait immediately associated with anyone of Boris' disposition; but his warmth and good nature always seem to have come uppermost in his relationships – at least with men. After a difficult time in Brittany with Boris, Henry described how he had been 'particularly comforting with his worldly tact during a small crisis'. But when he came to establish any enduring relationships with women, tact seemed quite to desert Boris. Here, his cultural attitudes and personal convictions remained obstinately Victorian, even un-European, and somewhat out of step with his more advanced views on art which, despite appearing to stop short of Cubism and Fauvism, nonetheless just lifted him into the twentieth century. In later life, he was to become cynical of Picasso, whom he called, 'a clever crook, who cashed in by "épatant la bourgeoisie" – a couturier, a Dior, always thinking up new models.'[5] However, in dealings with the opposite sex, Boris was either totally unaware of the emergent movement for emancipation or simply chose to ignore it: to his absolute amazement, no woman was ever willing to subscribe for too long to his overbearing masterfulness nor to put up with his unconventional penchant for two 'wives' – or 'associations', as he preferred to call them. Monogamy was never properly to his taste and eventually he became quite disenchanted with the whole idea of the married state: from the wisdom of maturity, he decided, 'There's no sense in marriage; I prefer *collages* – associations that everyone knows about.'[6]

During 1908, Henry himself had become 'associated' with Helen Maitland, a young music student in Paris: born in California, of Scottish parentage, she had been brought up, first in America, then spent much of her youth travelling in Europe chaperoned by her widowed mother. Henry must have successfully by-passed 'Ma Maitland' as he politely called her, and extricated her daughter, like 'La Fille Mal Gardee', to make some charming drawings and at least two interesting paintings, none of which seem to have met with the sitter's approval. In them she is revealed as a pretty, rather dreamy, perhaps fey girl dressed à la mode de Dorelia. Inevitably, in Paris then, Helen had become caught up in the John family and it is not too far fetched to see her as briefly a substitute in Henry's life for the frustratingly unavailable Dodo. Nurturing was in Helen's nature and, though only in her early twenties, she had an air of someone more mature than her years: to describe her as maternal is possibly too definitive but Gerald Brenan has observed how, 'she seemed to have been born with a greater gift for leisure than other people', and whilst an 'admirable *causeuse*' was also a good listener.[7]

There was something aristocratically Russian, perhaps faintly Chekhovian, in the image of Mrs Maitland and her daughter drifting around Europe, before Helen ever encountered Boris and made any connections with Russia. She may well have first met him in Edinburgh where she stayed for some time and where, too, Boris studied at the College of Art in the winter of 1908–09. Also in Edinburgh then, staying in Doune Terrace was Henry, painting a portrait of his beautiful hostess, Mrs Jamieson, the young wife of a local solicitor and distant cousin to Helen Maitland. It is tempting to assume some causal connection between this and Henry's commission to paint the full-length portrait and it may well explain the more practical reason for his wintering in Scotland. Sittings began early in the November of 1908 with numerous studies in pencil and watercolour from which eventually the painting had to be completed because of the changing appearance of his 'Scotch lady', as Henry referred to her: Elizabeth Jamieson was pregnant at the time and whilst posing tried to disguise her condition with the folds of an 'Empire Line' dress; but in the finished picture she appears 'wasp-waisted' and typically Edwardian. Evidently the portrait became rather a race against time for she gave birth to a daughter in the following summer. Henry also made drawings of the first child, another Elizabeth, who was just two when he began painting her mother. The portrait of Mrs Jamieson is one of the artist's earliest surviving oils and surely his largest – over six feet in height: ambitious in scale it is, nonetheless, modest in conception and unremarkable as to pose and treatment. Bearing in mind that he was still struggling, such a size would have been a challenge and stretched his ability: clearly he had difficulty with part, particularly the drawing of the left arm that rests uneasily on the hip and looks to have been repainted several times over, never quite satisfactorily. The pose is not dissimilar to the one he used for Ede McNeill in Brittany nearly three years later when somehow he managed, with more experience, to make the contrivance convincing. Mrs Jamieson is simply and obviously posing and, competent as the result is, its chief interest now lies in the date and in the imaginative potential of the biographical background, still a subject of amused speculation amongst the younger generations of Jamiesons who remember how well and warmly Henry Lamb was always spoken of by his sitter, even in old age – she lived to be ninety-four. Inevitably, the young artist would have had an admiring eye for the lovely Elizabeth Jamieson; but whether there was more to the relationship remains tantalising conjecture.

Music was Helen Maitland's first interest – indeed her main talent – and in Florence she had studied singing and the violin. Boris was really no musician but was never beaten by his own incompetence: to make himself more attractive to Helen he is said to have set about learning the piano. Henry, of course, was a proficient pianist, but his place in Helen's life was soon superseded by the amazing Anrep, despite his then living with a Russian girl, Junia, another 'association', who nevertheless was known as Mme von Anrep. Thus, for a while, Boulevard Arago housed an uneasy ménage with which Boris seemed happy enough but which soon ill-suited the women: Henry noted 'poor Junia . . . in a curious state – rather nervous & irritable';

yet he showed little sympathy for Helen, describing her as 'not increased in sensibility or diminished in conceit.' With the occupation of France in 1914, the situation was resolved. When Helen came to London, Junia returned to Russia, and Boris, having been a reserve Cavalry Officer in St. Petersburg, joined the Russian Army. He showed exceptional bravery 'riding with a party of cossacks' in battle and counted himself 'very lucky to remain safe though in the midst of fires and other opportunities of a prompt end', as he described it: 'I was an officer of communication between two neibouring [sic] corps and had to dash all by myself on a splendid horse . . . The dead in the fields does not seem very grim [sic]. Everything is done in such a simple way that one does not feel any exaution [sic] from the actual fight.' Boris was decorated for his part in the Russian campaign but, years later, was to dismiss it as, 'just Ball*et*, just Ball*et*, men running forward and then falling down, just Ball*et*.'[8]

During the war, Helen gave birth to Boris' daughter, Anastasia; but it was not until a son, Igor, was born that he put aside his prejudices and married Helen. For some years they lived mostly at No. 4 Pond Street in Hampstead where he set up another mosaic studio and 'invariably went to and fro from London to Paris in grand style by Train Bleu, as he did between Paris and Venice' ordering materials for his workshops.[9] Just as he seemed on the brink of success as an artist and just when his domestic life looked settled and straightforward, so the marriage became complicated by the continuing presence of a distant relative of Boris', Maroussa Volkova, an eighteen year old girl who, after the war, he had brought back with him from Russia. Gerald Brenan described her as,

> 'very lovely . . . in the Circassian style with dark eyes and hair and a creamy complexion, but she was both indolent and unintelligent, though as she grew older she developed into a genuine and original person with a taste for finance. He made her his mistress and seemed to think it quite proper for him, as a Russian aristocrat and artist, to keep a concubine on the premises and that Helen, who had a Victorian distaste for sex, could have no reason for objecting. She accepted the situation without protest and was always kind to Maroussa, but still it rankled.'[10]

Helen tolerated the triangle until the end of 1925, by which time it began to 'rankle' too much: uprooting herself from Pond Street she deserted Boris forever to live with Roger Fry, remaining with him until his death in 1934. She had become attracted to the much older and very famous Fry in the previous year, a fact that appears less surprising in the light of her intellectual pretentions which had grown since the early years in Paris. Before meeting Henry, Augustus, and Boris, her knowledge of the visual arts had been negligible but, encouraged by the contact with this circle, she developed what eventually became to many friends irritatingly mandarin views on art and artists. Henry hardly welcomed the new liaison and, for him, this last twist in the Anrep tale was the irony of ironies: that his one-time girl friend should have married his one-time best friend to end up with his all-time enemy was only feasible in fiction. Shortly after he reported entertaining 'Helen & Roger & Ma Maitland . . . in various groups' and 'thought Roger amusing & picturesque but really', wrote Henry, 'he has the bigotry of a common proselyte, the observation of a bat & about as much sense of direction & range of flight.'

Meanwhile, Boris, who until then had always seemed oblivious to the effects of what Henry called his 'amatory wanderings' and had been content to ignore any tensions within his own ménage, took Helen's departure badly, and, at first, was quite distraught. Little wonder he became so disillusioned with marriage. However, he soon recovered: he still had Maroussa – his 'consort' as he called her – who was to become, both technically and commercially, an invaluable assistant to his expanding mosaic business. Helen's departure, temporarily an emotional setback, heralded a boom in his fortunes as a mosaicist along with his establishment of a personal style in that very demanding medium. Previously, Henry had felt that it was as a colourist 'where his chief originality' lay; but, after the debacle, on seeing at Anrep's studio '3 or 4 small plaques intended for table tops which seemed (even in artificial light) really lovely', Henry thought he had 'never liked anything of his so whole-heartedly: there was no appearance of that misty, cussed, Russian meandering eccentricity which half spoils all the old ones', he wrote. Being married to Helen might well have been too much of a containment even for Boris' independent spirit since the gap she left was soon filled with a tremendous burst of creative enterprise resulting in a remarkable series of highly original mosaics in which he imaginatively combined the exacting demands of traditional craftsmanship with his inventive flair, spontaneous wit and good-natured irreverence and, in the process, truly finding himself as an artist.

One of the projects by which Boris is perhaps best known is the mosaic floor in the National Gallery in London, a series upon which he worked for some thirty years. His uniqueness of personality shines through and transforms what might have been a merely decorative, mundane solution to a design problem. The vestibule landing, completed in 1933, is especially interesting since it portrays eleven of Boris and Henry's famous contemporaries and friends playing the part of Classical Muses, Gods and Goddesses, though Henry himself is not included: by the thirties, he and Boris, were still friendly, but no longer the familiars they once had been. The likenesses to Diana Mosley, Christabel Aberconway, Mary Hutchinson, Clive Bell, Osbert Sitwell, Virginia Woolf, Greta Garbo, and Lydia Lopokova, amongst others, are remarkably recognisable once the onlooker is aware of the theme. The result is not only an amusing and intriguing interpretation of well-known personalities of the period but also succeeds as a brilliant design well-suited to its purpose. In 1952 Boris added other areas to the scheme incorporating more portraits of famous figures including Augustus John, Bertrand Russell, T. S. Eliot, Winston Churchill, Edith Sitwell, as well as the up-and-coming ballerina Margot Fonteyn, the young film star Loretta Young, and the young astronomer Fred Hoyle. The portraits are a compliment to the sitters in the sense that to have been included was a little nearer to being immortalised; at the same time, like tableaux in a theatrical parody, they are affectionately debunking.

Boris came to admire many things English, particularly English literature: 'after Anrep's tirade against Plato', wrote Henry from Brittany when Boris had left, 'he picked up the Shelley Symposium & was so captivated that he took it off in the train with him.' He was ever an admirer of Blake and must have been a natural choice to design the floor of the original Blake Room at the Tate Gallery. In his selection of texts integrated with Blake motifs, Boris reveals more than a little of his tastes and inclinations: 'He who desires but acts not breeds pestilence', and 'If the fool would persist in his folly he would become wise', could almost be Boris talking; and 'Expect poison from standing water', could be a testimony to his creative energy. Despite the official nature of this and many other commissions Boris continued to be thoroughly himself – at least in his secular art. In 1923, Roger Fry, before any hint of his liaison with Helen, had noted in an article on *Modern Mosaic and Mr. Boris Anrep* that, 'for all the apparent inflexibility of the medium it is possible to be as witty and mischievous in the grand style of monumental design as in any other. I say as witty', he continued, 'I might have said more witty – for there is a peculiar piquancy in Mr. Anrep's sly allusions to the more trivial details of life.'[11] Fry, then, was referring mainly to some of the private commissions from which Boris was beginning to make a reputation. In these already he had injected new life into an ancient craft by formalising motifs from modern life, such as motor-cycles and telephones, and creating a timeless comment on the more opulent, sometimes frivolous, aspects of society in the twenties. But in the religious commissions, though always aesthetically exquisite and beautifully crafted, and despite his avowed atheism, the hand of God seemed to inhibit the more playful hand of Anrep, and the imagery and interpretation owe more to tradition than to innovation.

Henry, in 1920, painted a fine portrait group of *The Anrep Family*, set in their house in Pond Street. Helen, seated, leaning forward looking at the artist as if about to speak, is really the pivot of the composition which spreads across a 'landscape' shaped canvas. Young Igor, like the Dancing Master in a Degas painting of a ballet rehearsal, clasps a walking stick that stands almost as high as he does; and Anastasia, also standing, holds her mother's hand while looking at her father who slumps resignedly on the sofa alongside his wife to the left of the picture. In the background, by a large window overlooking the garden, the slender Maroussa works at a mosaic spread over a massive table. A pair of steps standing open behind the family near the centre of the room help link the various elements in the design which was made up from several pencil studies of the separate figures. Henry did at least two studies in watercolour and one in oil of the whole arrangement but in the final version omitted a dog from the extreme right, perhaps deciding that it blocked the flow round the picture.

Arguably the least successful part is the portrait of Boris. Judging from reminiscences and photographs it is very like: his physical characteristics, his good-nature, his sensuality are all there, impeccably drawn, immaculately painted; but a static, silent image may be inadequate to conveying the varieties of intellectual and physical energy that were essentially Boris and the result seems but a pale shadow of the man as experienced. Beside his clasped hands, the tools of his trade lie on a cushion; yet despite several visual references to his life and work, he fails to come alive in any painterly sense. Of course, the medium of painting itself, with neither sound nor kinetic movement, begins unequal to the problem of rendering the multifarious facets of such a vital and complex character; and perhaps, in any case, Henry was not the painter to do this – Augustus, on form, might well have come closer to realising the dynamics of Boris, though he seems never to have tried. No, Henry was better at painting less restless, more contemplative people, like Lytton Strachey for example, whose exceptional mental agility was complemented by his legendary physical inertia. Boris may have intended to be a co-operative sitter but is more likely to have proved a frustrating, far from ideal model. Although he shared with Henry an enthusiasm for the more individualistic sports of tennis, fencing, riding and swimming and always played intensely, even while actively involved he appears not to have forsaken dialectical exploration: 'we go for long swims discussing the developments of philosophy with the short remnants of our breath', reported Henry from Brittany. Communication was never a problem for Boris in whichever country he landed: he was such a volatile, expressive talker; and if words ever failed, gesticulation and sheer exuberance would overcome any linguistic limitations. Thus it may not be too surprising that Henry should have perceived all this in his friend Boris; yet so much of it eluded him in the painting of *The Anrep Family*.

NOTES

1 Partridge *A Pacifist's War* pp.200–1
2 ib.
3 Gray *The Russian Experiment* p.62.
4 *The New English Art Club* 'The Times' 25 May 1912.
5 Partridge pp.200–1.
6 ib.
7 Brenan *Personal Record* p.81.
8 Partridge p.52.
9 Justin Vulliamy (catalogue introduction) *Boris Anrep* 1973.
10 Brenan pp.80–1.
11 Fry *Modern Mosaic and Mr. Boris Anrep* 'The Burlington Magazine' Jun 1923.

Henry Lamb as a boy. c.1898, in Manchester
City of Manchester Art Galleries

Second Impressions of Physiology 1904
Self portrait and fellow student at a lecture by
the Dean of the Medical Faculty, University
of Manchester

Professor Horace Lamb *1913*   *Oil on Canvas*   *122 × 105.4*
The artist's father
University of Manchester

Francis Dodd Henry Lamb *1905*   *Oil on canvas*
City of Manchester Art Galleries

Euphemia *1906   Pencil on paper   29.5 × 23*
Lamb's first wife
Private collection

Self portrait *1905   Pencil on paper   35.8 × 25.4*
Ashmolean Museum, Oxford

Dorelia *(Dodo) c.1907/8   Pencil on paper*
Augustus John's second wife
Fitzwilliam Museum, Cambridge

Edie McNeill (A Girl's Head) *1909*   *Black chalk on paper*   *35.5×29*
Dorelia John's younger sister
Tate Gallery, London

Dorothy Lamb *1912   Oil on canvas*
Lamb's sister
Whereabouts unknown

The Sentry (Cumberland House,
Pall Mall) *1906   Pencil, pen, grey ink
and wash   25.1 × 34.9*
An unpublished drawing for the
Manchester Guardian
Spink & Son Ltd

III

Doëlan and Donegal

1909 – 1913

SIX

LA FAMILLE FAVENNEC

———

'I have little time to feel lonely now with these beautiful amiable people about me, my studio for privacy or the depths of the country & sea', wrote Henry in the summer of 1911 after settling in for another spell with the Favennec family at Doëlan, a tiny port on the southern coast of Brittany.

For impecunious artists a continuing attraction of the area was the cheapness of living. Brittany, like Cornwall, geographically and economically, was out on a limb having been bypassed by major industry and commerce so that for many years it remained one of the most backward and consequently poorest regions of France. As well as being cheaper than Paris or London, its primitiveness was also an appealing antidote to the stale sophistications of the city and painters and writers could identify easily with the basic simplicity of the peasant's lot unsullied by the encroachment of civilisation. Doëlan, at the mouth of a small river near Pont-Aven, between Concarneau on the west and Lorient to the east, is in a district that had been popular with painters since at least the 1860s: Whistler – as a land or seascapist more usually associated with limpid views of the Thames or of Venice – had been one of the first to realise the pictorial potential of the rugged Brittany coast. A generation later, many British painters – several soon to be connected with the Newlyn school, again in a situation similar to Cornwall – having studied in Paris, 'set off for Brittany in 1881 . . . to paint in the open air and to paint ordinary people in harmony with their surroundings.'[1] Henry La Thangue, Blandford Fletcher and Stanhope Forbes stayed in and around Quimperlé, a few miles inland from Doëlan. The year after, Edwin Harris and Elizabeth Armstrong, later to become Mrs Stanhope Forbes, were painting at Pont-Aven. In 1883, the year before his death, Bastien-Lepage, 'the apostle of French naturalism', popular in England and a prime influence on both the Newlyn and Glasgow Schools, was at Concarneau; so too were the Scots, James Guthrie and John Lavery, and it is significant that 'the most vital period of the Glasgow School' began around 1885; and another disciple of Bastien, George Clausen, was also in the district painting the peasants in their setting in a similar, naturalistic style. In fact, 'in those days there was hardly a village in Brittany which was not occupied by one or two painters' and 'at Pont-Aven they simply swarmed – English, French, Americans and representatives of almost all nationalities.' Yet, recalled Edwin Harris, 'This little village, shut in on all sides by the wooded hills, was then, and probably still is, a most unhealthy spot in which to make a lengthy habitation.'[2] Another visitor during the summer of 1886 was the English illustrator A. S. Hartrick: 'Why Pont-Aven became a great resort of painters I cannot say', he wrote, noting how, 'The landscape round about the village is not very attractive or varied' but it was in Pont-Aven that Hartrick, as 'a somewhat green youth, an art student and a foreigner', met the great Gauguin, 'a man of the world . . . nearly forty years of age',[3] who was to become the most famous artist to stay and paint in the region.

Gauguin's formidable influence – and that of his followers – linking aesthetic theory with both the character of the landscape and the sentiments of the way of life permeated the district for over twenty years, even until Henry was there. 'One is struck by the fact that practically all the painters who became in any degree involved with the Breton group went through a phase, long or short, of submission to the personality of Gauguin, or to the collective atmosphere, or both at once', wrote Wladyslawa Jaworska in his detailed study of the place and the period.[4] Admittedly he was referring to when Gauguin was actually there; but there is no doubt that Gauguin's attraction was magnetic and enduring: the sheer power of his presence and the force of his intellectual arguments were sufficiently strong to linger long after he and his disciples had left. Like some colossus, he cast his enveloping shadow across the area and, as with Arles and Van Gogh and the environs of Aix with Cezanne, it became virtually impossible to interpret the peasants and the countryside and coast unaffected by the imagery and stylistic innovations of Gauguin and *l'école de Pont-Aven*.

Henry was no exception. His artistic antennae responded to the vibrations of the new environment at once, although he must have arrived with some preconceptions. By 1907, four years after his death, Gauguin's pictures were being shown regularly in Paris; Henry must also have seen more in London in 1908 and '09; and towards the end of 1910, thirty-seven were on view at the first of the Post Impressionist exhibitions. Yet soon after this considerable exposure of, for then in London, such an avant-gardist Henry was saying, 'Thanks to my disillusionment about Gauguin at the P.I. exhibition . . . I need no longer hold out my left hand to these French moderns except as far as sketching from nature goes.' Thus the influence was quite shortlived but remarkably intense.

Perhaps it was the increasing attention given to the work of Gauguin during Henry's apprenticeship that provoked his going to Brittany, though he would have found himself at the tail-end of a tradition. Rather less idealistically too, his ever present shortage of funds might have encouraged his migration to the coast. 1909 is the earliest recollection of him at Doëlan. He had made other excursions from Paris: part of the summer of 1907 he spent with the Johns at Equihen, on the Normandy coast near Boulogne; and the summer following was again with the John family at Cherbourg, from whence, to relieve Dorelia of just one of her numerous charges, he took Caspar, then five, carrying him most of the time on his shoulders, on a walking tour of the Normandy peninsula. 'Glad to hear how you are getting on', wrote Augustus to Henry, 'yes – Caen is a stinking hole – I know it and its ugly inhabitants – In fact are not all these Normans rotten?' adding encouragingly, 'You'll be able to get a donkey at Bayeux . . . *Un embrassement pour mon brave Gaspard.*'

The earliest drawings and paintings of Henry's to have survived these summer sojourns *chez les Bretons* are dated 1910, although it seems reasonable to assume that some – and those most under the influence of Gauguin – might have been done the previous year and signed and dated when framed for exhibition, a practice not uncommon with Henry, as with many artists. The paintings are also among the earliest of his oils to have emerged despite his having wrestled with the medium many times over even before leaving

Manchester. At a glance, so reminiscent of Gauguin are these first Breton pictures that it seems as if the master himself had been beside Henry whilst he was working. A study, called simply *Boy's Head* when exhibited at the first Camden Town exhibition in 1911, is the most consistently Gauguin-esque though not necessarily the first chronologically. From reproduction – the original still untraced – this strong, stylised portrait of a young boy wearing a beret with slightly small eyes set wide apart in a broad, flattish face, wide mouth and full lips, looks so typically Breton – and, incidentally, a common Cornish physiognomy – that the features are generalised more than is usual in Henry's portraiture: his subject must have existed but is not a likeness known to any of the villagers of Doëlan – unlike most of the other Breton pictures which usually provoke a glimmer of recognition. Thus, a *Boy's Head* is less a portrait in any conventional sense and more a starting point for stylistic experiment and improvisation: furthermore, it could have been painted away from the model, possibly away from Brittany, and appears very much a study of a generic type seen through a filter of synthetism suggesting the style of Pont-Aven remembered rather than nature observed. Behind the head, the landscape is not exactly a background but is complementary, on an equal plane, the shapes of both figure and ground being simplified, flattened and interlocking, bounded here and there by a *cloisonné* line; and the sinuous trees wind their way round the head decoratively, yet as a structural and integral part of the whole design, in imitation of and as homage to Gauguin and his followers. The most strikingly original aspect of the painting is in the subtly effective use of reflected light, something that neither Gauguin himself, nor Bernard, Sérusier or Denis seems to have exploited. In Henry's 'portrait', the head is completely in shade, silhouetted against bright sunshine, the reflection from which illumines the face and features, not as Monet or Renoir used it to show the flickering, ephemeral nature of light, but as a formal strengthening of the composition.

Any number of examples from Pont-Aven might have served as models for Henry during this phase: one especially close in style and treatment to the *Boy's Head* is Maillol's portrait of his wife of 1894. Usually thought of as a sculptor, Maillol, after periods of working with Gauguin at Pont-Aven, had virtually to abandon painting because of failing eyesight. Prior to this however, during the 1890s, he produced several portraits – heads close-up set against natural or quasi-natural backgrounds – stylistically so similar to the *Boy's Head* that for Henry not to have seen some of them seems inconceivable. Two more of Henry's portrait heads of about 1910–11 – *The Girl of the Fields* and *The Lady with Lizards* – have possible echoes of Maillol: but in these the beautifully balanced, flat, abstracted shapes of the Breton boy have been supplanted by a more conventional rendering of form in a more conventional use of light; and in each, the sitter is clearly indoors, the head on a plane obviously in front of the background which, though less stylised, provides, in its decorative, tapestry-like pattern, a tenuous link with synthetism.

Nevertheless, any links were soon broken. Henry despised theories of art and never could subscribe to an aesthetic programme. Neither was he an intellectual painter: though highly intelligent, well-read and articulate, he remained mistrustful of art historians and critics and was probably happiest when his painterly instincts were stimulated by his acute perception and tempered with a modest sense of craftsmanship. Thus, as much by disposition as by age, he was really separated from the previous generation of artists who had painted at Pont-Aven and any principles borrowed or devices exploited were solely a means of gaining a foothold on the ladder towards a personal style.

Before seeming to abandon this style, Henry painted two tiny panels that charmingly combine his study of art with his observation of nature: *Breton Cowherd* and *Breton Peasant Boy*, despite the conspicuous presence of Gauguin, are on the way to a more personal response to the environment. Gauguin, in 1888, had painted a number of pictures of Breton youths bathing and wrestling among trees; and it is just possible that his *Naked Breton Boy* of 1889 might have been seen by Henry and inspired him. But whereas Gauguin often distorted his figures for compositional reasons, twisting them into near unanatomical arabesques if it suited his artistic purpose, Henry could never distort the figure to any great extent unless to indulge his occasional weakness for caricature and emphasise a trait of personality or human foible. Here, in these delightful Breton *pochades*, he follows the norms of academic proportion and adjusts to their modest scale by simplifying the figures and reducing the features to a minimum of suggestion. Apart from the subject matter and this degree of simplification, what most gives them their strikingly Pont-Aven look is the overall consistency of treatment which, as in the *Boy's Head*, makes little distinction between the figure and ground: the two are dovetailed, perfectly balanced, almost camouflaging each other in a counterpoint of light and shade, aided by the raised, near absent skyline, a device so beloved of the synthetists. The synthetists, however, used colour symbolically, emotively; here, Henry uses it more or less naturalistically: the boys' smocks really are a faded *blouson bleu*, the trees and hillside a variety of greens and browns; and even in the preponderant shade, the heat of the day is felt in the contrast between the parched yellow of the sunlit meadow and the bluish, purple shadow. Painted, probably *en plein air*, at Doëlan, in the orchard in front of 'Kersimon', the Favennec family home, the raised skyline in each picture might be, quite mundanely, as much due to the actual incline of the hillside and the contour of the landscape as to the influence of Pont-Aven. Of this setting, Henry wrote, 'The grass in the orchards & meadows is long now & the cows are kept picketted on narrow strips of over-grazed ground at the edges, feeding rather miserably from about 7 to 10 a.m. & then from 5 or 6 till dark. It is after tea when the boys are back from school & from the sea that one has most chance of sittings.' His models, two of the Favennec boys, pose as if for a snapshot, selfconsciously looking straight at him. Even the merest indication of features reveals his sympathy for youth and it was as well that Henry had an innate fondness for children for there were seven boys and five girls in the Favennec family at 'Kersimon'. He should never have lacked for models but seems always to have experienced difficulty in persuading anyone to pose: either they were too busy or too young. 'If I am to do any large Breton pictures', he soon realised, 'I shall have to learn how to coax the right people away from their work & sit for love or money.' As it happened, most of his Breton compositions were on a smallish scale and none of the work done in Brittany was really large.

Precisely how Henry discovered the Favennecs is uncertain. One connection is with the French painter Henry Moret who, in the late 1890s and early 1900s, had stayed at 'Kersimon' and painted in and around Doëlan. Born in 1856 in Cherbourg, Moret studied in Paris but thereafter lived in Brittany where he 'survives in memory as perhaps the best-known painter of all and a highly popular figure'.[5] Whilst to the world Gauguin is the most famous artist to have been associated with the region, Moret is the most well thought of locally. In 1888, he had worked at Pont-Aven with Gauguin and had become caught up in the synthetist movement which style his painting reflected until around 1900 when he 'was coverted to pure Impressionism'.[6] Moret's trial blobs of colour in the Impressionist vein are still very evident on the bare floor, walls and ceiling timbers of the attic room where he painted at 'Kersimon' and where Henry worked too, in what he called his *grenier*. With the patina of time, his paint mixings and palette scrapings merge harmoniously and historically with his predecessor's like a rich and subtle mosaic. A dormer window faces south overlooking the front yard and the orchard beyond; and to convert the room more adequately to a studio, the Favennecs inserted a skylight on the north although Henry complained that by midday it was 'at oven-heat & after 1 p.m. the sun beat in vertically'. As his easel gathers dust and the few pieces of furniture look virtually unmoved since he was last there in 1912, time seems almost to have stood still.

Henry could have met Moret in Paris, of course. Perhaps they never met and Henry heard of the Favennecs and the availability of a studio by chance through Moret's dealer, Durand-Ruel, whose gallery in Paris he would have frequented. The Irish painter Roderic O'Conor spent most of his working life in France, knew Segonzac, met Clive Bell in Paris, and was a close friend of the Pont-Aven painters Charles Filiger, who settled nearby at Le Pouldu, and Wladyslawa Slewinski, who, in 1910, bought a house at Doëlan. And before Henry went there, he had become friendly with Boris who, around 1909, had his portrait painted in Bacchanalian guise by Pierre Roy, son of Louis Roy, another Pont-Aven painter. There were too, the many London connections: in 1908 and '09, Henry used Augustus' old studio in Fitzroy Street where, nearly opposite at No. 19 through Sickert's famous Saturday afternoon gatherings of patrons and painters, he would have met Robert Bevan who, in 1890, had been at Pont-Aven probably with another English artist, Eric Forbes-Robertson, a friend of Filiger's. Another of the Fitzroy Street group, James Bolivar Manson – to be Director of the Tate Gallery in the thirties and to write two books on British painting – 'From 1905 onwards . . . often painted in Brittany and in 1907 . . . lighted upon Doëlan. The paintings he did of the village and its surroundings are among his most considered Impressionist works.'[7] One of 1907, *Summer Day, Doëlan, Brittany*, looks so close to a Moret of the same period that Manson could well have met him – or at least, seen some of his work.

Thus, innumerable possibilities arise as to how Henry found the

Favennecs but, for whatever reason, it is extremely unlikely to have been premeditated: he was rarely given to much planning or calculation in life and, since by 1909 was to all intents and purposes unattached, he had become used to following his whims. The strangest connection of all – and possibly the most fruitful with regard to the missing link – is the summer, either 1909 or 1910, he spent with Wyndham Lewis. Lewis, not yet the *enfant terrible* of the English *avant-garde*, nor the *bête noire* of Bloomsbury or scourge of the Sitwells, had a penchant for pamphleteering and, in a very un-British way, became prone to tub-thumping about matters of art, none of which could have been at all to Henry's taste. How they survived that sojourn together is a subject for speculation, since they seemed to have so little in common, thereafter communicating indirectly, via mutual friends, with rude forthrightness. On noting one of Lewis' pictures at a Contemporary Art Show in 1913, Henry called it 'a putrid thing' similar to those he had seen before; and he held no higher opinion of Lewis' art criticism after he had 'inspected . . . some bloody Germans at the "21 Gallery"' who had been 'cracked up by Lewis in a manifesto abjectissimo'. As he saw 'Poor old Lewis . . . proceeding ever upwards & onwards', Henry decided, 'it is no use trying to pretend that he is not quite damned'.

Lewis too, somewhat pompously, was moved to complain to Augustus at being maligned by Henry: 'Criticism being only valuable when it is disinterested, when one of the parties, between whom there is friction, pretends to impartiality, superiority, as with Lamb, the harm he may do is more to be redoubted than it would otherwise be', he wrote, 'I have no objection to people being saints. I naturally object to their being saints at my expense.'[8] But in Britanny, before he entered the arena of art politics with both feet, Lewis was wearing his author's, rather than his critic's or artist's hat, and recalled years later,

'My literary career began in France, in the sense that my first published writings originated in notes made in Brittany. Indeed, this period in retrospect, responsible for much, is a blank with regard to painting . . .

The coastal villages of Finisterre in which I spent long summers (one of them with the artist, Henry Lamb) introduced one to a more primitive society. These fishermen . . . brawled about money over their fierce apple-juice: when somebody was stabbed, which was a not infrequent occurrence, they would not call in a doctor, but come to the small inn where I stayed, for a piece of ice.'[9]

At a guess, 'the small inn' must have been the one known then as 'Peste' – why, no one seems to remember – by the slipway on the east side of the harbour across the water from 'Kersimon'. Boris stayed several times and is remembered locally; Lytton Strachey stayed once, briefly and disastrously, remaining in bed most of the time, his visit now forgotten. Neither is Lewis remembered although, in preparing material for his Breton stories published later as *The Wild Body*, he fairly immersed himself in the primitiveness of the society and was led to dramatise the life to a near unrecognisable extent. His fishermen, for example, bear little resemblance to those in the Favennec family and to the hardworking, relatively peaceable existence at 'Kersimon'.

There was, however, one dramatic event *chez* Favennec, a tragedy, that affected Henry profoundly and was the subject of one of his first major, though smallest, paintings. In the summer of 1910, he was witness to the sudden death of Mme Favennec. Cancer had constricted her throat and she quickly became unable to eat; deteriorating rapidly, when she died, she was emaciated. Death to the Bretons, like many other primitive societies, was manifest, understood and accepted as an inevitable phase in the cycle of experience: birth, birthdays, marriage, seasonal festivals, and death were emphases marking the steady evolution of changing generations yet blended with the rhythm of life and were part of the natural order. Despite all this, *la mère de famille*, having spent most of the fifteen years of her married life bearing and rearing children, was still in middle age and her widower, children and relatives were stunned; and mixed with their ritualistic, symbolic mourning was a deeper, personal grief and despair of people who felt cheated by the terrible loss and by the inexplicable injustice of God, Fate, or whatever ordinance they might summon to blame. As an atheist, Henry was a detached observer of the religious rites but felt more able to empathise with the family in their genuine shock and private sorrow for, already, the Favennecs had become a substitute for his own family. When, the year after, he wrote to the eldest daughter Marie, who by then had taken the main burden of domestic responsibility, he signed himself, '*croyez-moi toujours, votre espèce de frère tres affectioné*'.

As well as being humanly and sympathetically involved, Henry was moved to respond artistically, making many drawings of what he described later as 'grotesque scenes'. These studies became the basis of the painting that was to be his first critical success, 'Morte d'une Bretonne', or as it is always known now, *Death of a Peasant*. The canvas is surprisingly small, given the monumentality of the subject. The dead woman's head and that of her husband, near to life size, occupy most of the picture which is an impressively simple composition. Because of the cinematic-like close-up, the emotion is intensified: the death rattle and cries of bereavement are almost audible. In fact, like a film director, Henry focuses on the essentials in the story compelling the audience to participate in a way unusual in painting. Having abandoned any classical conventions of design, despite echoes of Mantegna, Henry seems to have deserted the Mediterranean; and in evoking the anguish of Grünewald, he perhaps comes closer to the Gothic and to the Northern Renaissance than at any other time in his career. Yet the treatment is quite contemporary and reflects something of the *angst* of Nordic expressionism and there is possibly some slight affinity – at least so far as feeling, mood and atmosphere are concerned – with Munch, particularly *The Sick Child*, of 1906–7, which by coincidence has often been hung not far from *Death of a Peasant* in the permanent collection of the Tate. Munch was frequently in Paris where Henry might just have seen some of his work; but, rather than a stylistic or historical link, any connection is more a chance one from the interpretation of a not dissimilar subject.

It is a subject with all the potential for cloying treatment but Henry effectively overcomes the pitfall of sentimentality. The tiny surface is packed with drama and the sense of tragedy is powerfully conveyed, nowhere spilling into melodrama. Painted with passion, expressiveness takes precedence over strict, academic accuracy and naturalistic illusion: though realised with precision, none of the features is especially well drawn and all contain an uncharacteristic element of naivity strangely matching the primitiveness of the setting. Tension is created and accentuated by the proximity of the heads: the man presses his forehead against the dead woman's, the noses making a wedge and visually forming a triangle of focus, the whole cradled and counterbalanced by the clenched, sharply drawn, angular hand of the man clutching a handkerchief, a conspicuous symbol of sorrow. Having renounced medicine, Henry took care to keep his art free from his previous training and experience, but perhaps in this instance, he could hardly avoid their coming together for, in the almost morbid attention given to the detail of the gruesomely rendered mouth, the choked throat and scrawny neck suggesting the pain of expiration, there is a sinister clinicalness.

Back in England the following winter Henry 'tinted . . . the dead woman with proper morbidity', as he described it; and in the spring of 1911, began a second version of *Death of a Peasant*, which he thought he would make 'convincingly finer'. Using tempera this time and later calling it 'a technical experiment – glazing over a monochrome grisaille',[10] he reported having 'more or less finished the "laying out" of Mrs F. it bored me greatly: & now I can't decide whether it's better than a Slade School Competition picture or worse than a museum piece by W. Rothenstein.' Despite such typical self-denigration, when he had 'finished the replica of dead Mrs F.', he began to feel he had been successful 'in spite of some roughness', and declared, 'it seems to me *incomparably* finer than the first version.' However, it was the first version that was bought sometime during 1911 by Michael Sadler from one of the Saturday afternoon gatherings at 19 Fitzroy Street, 'where Sickert . . . with his usual generosity', as Henry recalled, 'was good enough to vaunt it to prospective purchasers'. And it is this first version that was eventually purchased for the Tate and by which Henry is known, though, according to the artist, the tempera reworking was the first to be exhibited publicly.

The event in Britanny must have profoundly moved and inspired Henry for, in addition to the two versions of the near identical composition, he undertook, almost concurrently, another larger, quite different interpretation deriving from the same theme: called 'Mourners' when first exhibited – a title Henry himself preferred – it has been known latterly as *Lamentation*, unfortunately, since in neary every respect and by contrast with *Death of a Peasant*, *Lamentation* is lamentable. Here, the drama is merely melodramatic and any tragedy is reduced to theatricality. The participants – three of the Favennec family: the eldest daughter, Marie; the eldest son, Jean-Louis; and one of the younger boys, probably Prosper – like inadequate amateurs, go through the motions of playing their parts and, though strongly and well drawn from life, fail to convince. In the artist's attempt to convey emotion too explicitly they are contorted into caricatures of grief, leaving the audience unmoved and uninvolved, and the whole picture remains a curiously contrived montage of obstinately separate poses that never cohere.

Qualitatively, conceptually and technically, the 'dead Mrs F.' and the 'Mourners' are poles apart, yet were first shown together at the New English Art Club Summer Exhibition at the RBA Galleries in Suffolk Street in May 1911. Henry was in Doëlan when it opened but asked to be sent 'any criticisms . . . & of course all confidential gossip', saying to Lady Ottoline, 'I am aware of the exact merit of both pictures so don't fear to send anything disconcerting either way.' From his reaction, it is difficult to tell which affected him more, praise or blame. 'The Times' singled out *Death of a Peasant* for its treatment of a tragic theme 'with primitive simplicity' but felt it might be 'labelled Post Impressionist and condemned for its ugliness and crudity . . . It is, of course, an experiment, but one which was worth making, and is full of promise for the future.'[12] In the same article, *Lamentation* was referred to as, 'another experiment of the same kind, an attempt to represent grief as John Bellini represented it in his "Brera Entombments". Here, because the picture gives us no reason for the grief, it seems to be a little mechanical and forced. Primitive treatment of this kind needs a great and obvious theme to justify it. Here we have only phenomena without the theme.'[13] 'The Morning Post' was more unreservedly complimentary; but when Henry received the cutting from the paper which his mother had sent he complained bitterly to Lady Ottoline that it was 'a real pain to find armsful of praise for one'self at the end of all that desperate drivel', and then proceeded to berate Robert Ross who had written the piece: 'Good heavens! is *that* Ross?' he asked, 'Well if Fry & McColl suspect such judgement there is indeed something to be said for theirs (just as there must be something against a painting that pleases the writer of that contemptible article).' Ottoline reproached him for his outburst, thinking his attitude altogether too cavalier; but it was Henry's habitual response to critics and he remained unrepentant, replying that he had found 'The Western Gazette' 'certainly the most sensible' though even that was 'too limited by a decrepit hankering for the "pleasant in art" . . . The others I object to – not from silliness as you accuse me – but from hatred & contempt of their ignorant pretentiousness. (except the Times). There was no high fallutin indifference to fame about it.'

Neither was Henry any happier with dealers and exhibition organisers. At the NEAC show of the previous winter he had sold 'the small wooden panel', *Breton Cowherd*, for twelve guineas, and also a pastel drawing, but complained that 'the asses' had rejected one of his drawings and 'the fool at the desk' had been telling people that his other picture was not for sale. As he explained, 'in my present financial crisis I felt bound to close with the mean offer', adding cynically, 'I thought the red stars merely might help me a step towards a desirable eminence.' During the summer show, at the end of May, he heard that *Death of a Peasant* was sold – for £25. He also had various other modest sales and offers for his three Breton pictures at the first exhibition by the newly formed Camden Town Group – of which Henry was a nominal, reluctant, founder member – that opened in June at the Carfax Gallery in St James's: the offers included a second one of £17 10s. by another founder member, Spencer Gore, 'which I refused again', said Henry, 'more from curiosity as to the effect of inflexibility in such a case than avarice. I don't care whether he buys or nor; but I am anxious for him not to haggle with me in the future.'

Prompted by these mild successes, and the prospect of several commissions, Henry suddenly broke his stay in Doëlan and returned to England for a few days in the middle of the summer of 1911.

'I have been back here ten days – not alone this time', reported Henry from Doëlan after his return in July; 'a sudden enterprise made me carry off Dorelia's sister with me, I thought the main thing was to have a sitter always handy, & oh! how I have groaned since.' Dodo's younger sister Edie McNeill, as she seems to have been known, but Ede, as Henry always called her, had posed for him many times before her abduction to Brittany. One very lovely drawing of 1909 is especially characteristic of her and perfectly epitomises the period: dressed as if auditioning for Eliza Doolittle, or simply waiting in the wings of an Edwardian music-hall, from beneath the shadow of a large feather 'titfer', Ede pouts with indifference and stares vacantly past the artist. In an equally fine painting done at about the same time, Ede has lost the hat and her head is crowned with her hair piled high effectively focusing attention on the eyes which again are expressionless. Known as *Purple and Gold* – a title taken from the purple velvet dress edged with gold braid set against a pink and burgundy background – its colour was quite daring for Henry who, until then, had seemed more concerned with draughtsmanship and design; and its adventurousness also has the seeds of some of Henry's later, typical, and often astringent colour schemes. The painting and to some extent these earlier drawings of Ede still

97

reflect the impact of Augustus. Probably all were done in his old studio in Fitzroy Street, which Henry rented between 1909 and 1910, since, whilst there, he mentioned taking his 'picture of Ede across to Sickert's where it was much admired: it certainly looked better there than here'. The influence of Augustus is usually more evident in Henry's drawing than in his painting but *Purple and Gold* is quite strikingly reminiscent of any number of portraits '*le maître*' was painting in the early 1900s, particularly of his first wife Ida and, too, some of the first, more detailed studies of Dorelia. But Ede appears to have modelled rarely for Augustus and Henry was able to make her more identifiably his own – at least, in his art, since their relationship was evidently passionless. Only for art's sake could she have accompanied him to Doëlan: her phlegmatic disposition was a blessing as a model but a curse as a companion. Almost at once Henry regretted the impulse to which he had succumbed as a result of a sudden flush of relative wealth at the height of a long, hot summer.

On landing at Brest, Henry and Ede took a train to Quimperlé, the station nearest Doëlan, thence by pony and trap, finishing the last three miles from Clohars on foot. 'All the village seems intrigued at my arrival with a "*bonne amie*"', he reported, 'though the Favennecs received us charmingly . . . Poor Ede was very exhausted from lack of sleep & the heat of the trains.' After 'a lovely swim on arriving', Henry woke the next morning recovered from the journey, though depressingly aware of the drawbacks to his self-inflicted situation as it dawned on him what a fool he had been not to have foreseen at least some of the difficulties arising from the re-arrangements now necessary at 'Kersimon'. 'I'm very doubtful of the success of this venture with Ede', he admitted, since he was 'no longer in the familiar bosom of the lower classes; but leading' what he called, 'a nondescript & parlous existence'. Graphically he described their 'make-shift *ménage*' in the spare room, 'bordered by the lousy, bepissed beds of small boys', one of whom still had to sleep there at night. 'Two broken chests feebly attempt to be a table,' he complained, '& then we have to cook & eat & wash up . . . Oh my god!' Because Ede was so 'infernally slack & helpless', and 'also the slovenliest & least efficient creature' imaginable, Henry found himself 'breaking wood, making the fire, washing plates etc.' and planning what he called 'the commisariat', tasks which he thoroughly resented doing and to which he was quite unused: 'I have to . . . think out each day . . . as I have to think out each picture. To prepare materials for painting & for eating . . . all this is a great tax on my energies', he wrote in exasperation, asking, 'Can you see me squatting at the door disembowelling fishes within a ring of grinning boys & an outer ring of mangy cats & and a still outer one of mangier fowls'?

Apart from the physical horrors of the domestic arrangements, which Henry confessed he 'ought to have imagined more clearly before risking them', he had too, failed to anticipate how much Ede would be on his hands and what a dreary, 'scarcely inspiriting companion' she would prove. 'There is something in her which disgusts me profoundly – not counting a level of intellect & materialism of conversation most essentially banal', he decided, as he began developing positively malevolent feelings towards her; but, in resigning himself to disappointment in Ede as a helpmate, he was resolved to find consolation in her main *raison d'être* at Doëlan. 'I must just do one large portrait of her & not seek to be inspired by her as a type – I don't like her enough', he declared on settling to some kind of working routine. He began by making numerous drawings of her – head, half-length, full-length – in a variety of poses before deciding on the design of two paintings that he was to work on for most of the six weeks she was there. Having intended her stay to be a short one, as he worked, he became increasingly intrigued by his imported model: 'What then is the meaning of that curious subterranean look? is there depth of feeling somewhere perhaps?' he asked himself, noting that, 'When she is posing there is a certain grim romance in painting that serene mysterious brow which I know to contain flat thoughtlessness & no trace of imagination & the far-gazing eyes! I know that they are too short-sighted to see anything & that they are glad of it'. Ede's seeming immunity to feeling, or perhaps more surely, her inability to show feeling, proved her an ideal sitter for the tensions of painting portraits. After an auspicious start, a graph of their progress would look dauntingly mountainous and Henry recorded many a setback and change of direction before there was any 'hope of getting them & her off my hands' and, as he put it, 'send her back (unsoiled)'. His programme sounded ideal: 'a long sitting every morning . . . a scrappy lunch, then a lazy interval followed by a swim before tea; then a long sketching walk'; but, he complained again, 'the handicaps are many . . . I don't waste my feelings in regret for having brought her here but simply push on ferociously with the pictures in the hope of an early release.'

Just as Henry's concentration wavered and he was beginning to despair of both Ede and the portraits, in the middle of it all, in August, Boris arrived at Doëlan – his second visit that summer. Henry felt ambivalent about the intrusion: on the one hand, Boris was a most welcome diversion from, and for, his model; on the other, he was a distraction from work. 'If Anrep wasn't so confoundedly sociable & "obliging"', wrote Henry, after lunching together in the impossible discomfort of their makeshift room chez Favennec, 'I'd make him eat at his old pension across the water.' In fact, he stayed in a room just behind 'Kersimon' and they would dine at the pension in the evening. Fortunately, the larger of the two portraits 'delighted Anrep' who tried to persuade Henry 'to leave it as it was'. Despite this encouragement, in 'going in search of his original aims' with what he called his 'usual virtuous intentions', he started to lose much of the 'incidental charm'.

However, as soon as Boris left, he regained some of the sublimity which he suspected to have been accidental and made an almighty effort to finish both paintings. At one point he thought they were done and then found that most of a week's work went in 'scrubbings & replacements'. Always he was over-optimistic: after bracing himself for the final sittings he reported going on 'at a snail's pace' and being 'rather distracted from the endless women's chatter' in the next room from which he was only separated by a leaky, thin flooring. Yet he claimed to 'like making portraits more than other things' and even began to be more appreciative of the 'poor picturesque, kind-hearted Ede', his long-suffering, most 'resigned sitter'. Eventually, on September the ninth, after prolonged anguish over the final touches Ede departed. 'It's finished at last', he announced, although he was actually referring to his '*ménage*', the termination of which had at times assumed even greater importance than the completion of the portraits, since each was so maddeningly interdependent. With profound feelings of deliverance, having seen her off 'all but painlessly' from Brest at midnight, Henry returned to Doëlan, 'very tired from long travels, but so relieved & airy'. Some rumblings of guilt must have made him reflect on her willingness as a model for, 'After all I must be grateful', he wrote, 'the despised creature has repeatedly done me immense & rare services: it was only a pity that I could only accept them at the price of living with her at such close quarters.' And such are the quirks of human nature and the tricks of memory that only a day or so later, Henry, to his absolute amazement, received 'a note from poor Ede stranded for a day & night at Plymouth for lack of trains. She says she wishes she were back here – which surprises the opinions I had formed from her grumpy looks & ways. Indeed', he declared, 'I can say squarely – the same wish is not mine.'

The larger, near full-length portrait of Ede done at Doëlan and initially called simply 'Portrait of a Young Woman' fuses several influences from Henry's more experimental years and was perhaps one of his first paintings to establish the essentials of a style with which he was to remain chiefly identified until the later 1920s: half and full-length portraits in relevant settings, or groups of figures in a landscape, relatively stylised and tied not too concretely to natural appearances, painted thinly, smoothly, with precision, almost hard-edge and fairly flat but with gently modelled relief and close-toned, high-pitched colour. The subtle strength of this version of Ede probably owes most to Puvis, though the design, despite a raised skyline, is not unlike Augustus' portraits of figures standing against natural backgrounds: in fact, Henry's little oil study for the portrait, both in conception and in treatment, closely resembles a number of Augustus' own small, spontaneous studies of Dorelia and family and friends by the sea or lakeside in Normandy, Provence, North Wales or Ireland, though without his intuitive flashes of drama. In Henry's case, with Ede, any drama is implicit in the design rather than in the handling of the paint. The pose is monumental and quite classical. Like a sullen siren, she turns her back on the sea as if too bored even to bother luring fishermen to their fate on the rocks below. Her sultry stare is relieved only by a gleam of sunlight on the horizon above her left shoulder. Some overpainting of afterthoughts is revealed on close inspection but betrays little of the agony and uncertainty expressed so forthrightly during its evolution. Once Henry had decided on the design, he remained faithful to his original intention, as if he were giving very definite shape to his mind's eye, despite the difficulties of realising it. Of course, by then, he was familiar with the form and mien of his model: he had seen her often at the Johns' and drawn her many times before abducting her to Doëlan. Henry tried Ede in a variety of positions but it seems that one pencil drawing of the exact pose, a pencil and watercolour study of it in reverse, and a small oil study on a panel, formed the basis of the composition and were adequate to his embarking on the large canvas, which fine grain, despite minor revisions, is evident throughout most of the smoothly painted picture surface. Clearly,

101

from the study in reverse, he at first intended to surround the figure with more of a backdrop of rocks. On his solitary, exploratory walks along the coast and in the countryside, in between swims in the late afternoon and early evening, he had made careful drawings of trees and plants and rocks but relatively few have survived. During this summer of 1911, he mentions the sad loss of a full sketchbook which could have caused him to change his mind and simplify the background of Ede, reducing the rocks and plants to the barest, sparest symbols. The painting of the sea, particularly the right hand side, suggests that this may have been a fairly late change of mind. Otherwise, Henry was pretty faithful to the original pose.

From all accounts, including Henry's own descriptions of Ede, the pose embodies the essence of her. 'She always looked exactly like this', wrote Nicolette Devas, for whom Ede was periodically to be a substitute mother within the John household, describing her as,

> 'a much-needed Martha in the shifting population . . . The younger children took her for granted and fled to her in distress . . . she was docile and gentle in her ways . . . silent like her sister Dodo, gruff when she spoke, she was a thin, sad woman keeping to herself. With her black hair parted in the middle, and the John tradition of clothes, her black eyes and dark skin, she reminded me of an elegant Indian woman . . . she was ageless. With her reticence she revealed nothing, and her black eyes concentrated, it seemed, on the mystery of her soul.'[14]

There was a theory provoked by her reticence and circulated amongst the John family circle – obviously to fill the frustrating gap left by such sphinx-like inscrutability – that Ede was the original Virgin Goddess. The theory is only of moment because Henry, wittingly or unwittingly, always portrayed her as brooding and inviolable. Yet that statuesque stance in the larger portrait, when considered literally, borders on the contrived and ridiculous: who for long would perch so solemnly and precariously on the edge of a precipice? and isn't the pose almost banal? Nevertheless, the painting convinces rather as the conventions of opera convince; the formalisation and the poetry overcome the artifice. The whole picture is distinctly operatic, indeed very Wagnerian, and it is not impossible to imagine a *leitmotif* from *The Ring* reverberating round the cycloramic background as Ede contemplates the emptiness of existence. After she had left Doëlan, whilst Henry grudgingly acknowledged her help as a sitter, in calling her 'the unchangeable effigy of sloth & obstinacy', he clearly retained few fond feelings towards her as a person and the *Portrait of Ede McNeill* is a sad monument to the tragedy of her aimlessness.

When first exhibited, at the NEAC autumn exhibition in the year it was painted, 'The Times' thought it a 'very interesting portrait' but 'marred by a dull sky' and proceeded in a very schoolmasterly way to lecture him on the weakness of the background in relation to the strength of the figure:

> 'He has tried to achieve an equal finish throughout his picture and at the same time to make his background unobtrusive. But he has failed to find a convention for the sky, and it looks both empty and literal. But the failure is the result of an attempt to do too much & the figure, by itself, is finely conceived and thoroughly executed.'[15]

Henry too, thought he had failed. 'Alas it was once so beautiful!' he complained, before it went to the exhibition, feeling 'paralysed with dejection' because it was so '*échoué*'. Yet despite an unjustly critical review and his own bad opinion of the picture, Henry really had succeeded in unifying the figure with the background. The treatment of the sky, as that of the sitter, is stylised and simplified and the whole pleasingly consistent. No part remains opaque and the entire surface conveys a wonderful sense of space, distance and depth. What surprises especially is the colour which has an appropriately musical resonance, a beautiful balance of warm, light ochres, grey-white, and a delicate pale blue, possibly cerulean.

The other, smaller head-and-shoulders of Ede, with which he also thought he had failed, is no less an admirable likeness, but neither as analytic nor as interesting conceptually. Altogether a more conventional portrait. Though the two were worked concurrently, it is as if the experience of wrestling successfully with the one has resolved some of the problems with the other – but in a way, to its disadvantage: the deeper layers of meaning that so intrigue and triumph in the larger are here merely suggested and, being a more prosaic painting, it lacks the mysterious essence of Ede. 'The portraits have been more a gain in experience than actual successes', Henry decided after all, 'Both contain passages which make me blush to look at, & are better not remembered in bed: on the other hand I don't think I have done any heads . . . which have less uncomfortable souvenirs.' Exaggerating their defects, and mis-guidedly self-critical, he continued,

'Both are overworked & lack spontaneity & simplicity, the face of the larger one got so charged with paint I could scarcely work on it at the end: & in the last sitting an expression crept in which I had thought an unlikely danger: something like the vestige of an idea or ray of animation surely quite foreign to the creature.'

The larger *Portrait of Ede McNeill* was to be the last of Henry's major paintings with a Breton setting. Whilst he retained affection for the Favennec family, his inspiration and vision moved further from the environment; and though he continued painting at Doëlan into the autumn of 1911, his pictures owe little or nothing to the place itself. Of the landscape, he made numerous *pochades* in oil on small panels; and he would draw *les Bretons* as often as they could be persuaded to model; but in the summers in Brittany, he had worked through an intense, albeit brief, immersion in Gauguin, towards Puvis de Chavannes via an amalgam of influences including Augustus, of course, and in the process become more himself. Before starting the portraits of Ede, Henry, with for him unusual confidence, declared, 'I think I know where I am & about how far I may go: no clamours of "sensation" seekers or "admirers" shall deceive me.'

'I have been in better spirits; very happy indeed to be alone once more in my dear Favennecs' bosom', acknowledged Henry some days after dispatching Ede. Since she was such an able and obliging model, her stay at Doëlan had been an expedient, practical solution to an artistic problem; but socially, her presence had created other difficulties which Henry had completely failed to anticipate. The warm relationship that he enjoyed and to which he had grown accustomed *chez* Favennec was impossible with Ede there: she neither wanted to speak French nor participate in the day-to-day activities at 'Kersimon' and the surviving children remember her only appearing to empty *le seau de ménage*. With the household she had been highly unpopular and an intrusion. 'On my side', wrote Henry, 'I quickly resigned myself to her sordidness & all the nameless discomforts . . . but the Favennecs didn't . . . the importation of a female (*et une belle*) was held rather a slight to the nation, & the women of the family tried hard to make it unpleasant for us.' Because the Favennecs had no '*patente*' to give pension to lodgers he had been forced to eat alone with Ede, thus separated from the natural core of contact at mealtimes: they would have been, as

Henry put it, 'too conspicuous *à deux*' and incurred suspicion from the law. But now, *sans* Ede, he was free to join them at table and be absorbed into the family. For them, and for Henry, it was all easier and more rewarding when he was simply the adored centre of attraction: such a talented, intelligent, fluent-speaking, sensitive, handsome and engaging *étranger* was stimulating company and always welcome; but Ede, to the men and boys, had been a distraction for their hero; to the womenfolk and the girls – of all ages – she had been a rival.

Now, in the continuing hot autumn, the atmosphere at 'Kersimon' became lighter, more relaxed, and for a while Henry felt a return to normal *vis-à-vis la famille*. Before his bout of midsummer madness, he had loved the life in and around the little port and in between drawing and painting had happily involved himself with the family – at work and play. With Jean-Louis, the eldest son, 'my didactic friend' as Henry called him, he would often walk to the nearby mill where he worked, discussing European history and politics, art & morals; or spend a day at the threshing; and with the younger boys, when they were not farming or fishing, he would go swimming or 'waste time in top-playing'. Sometimes he would take the cart to Quimperlé and help with the shopping. 'The simple fare agrees with me wonderfully well & as yet I don't find myself pining either for roast beef or chocolate cakes', he wrote, and, with Ede away, reported, 'I keep on the best of terms with the Favennecs & am still convinced that they are the most civilized if the most *Spartan* family in the place.' Certainly, at 'Kersimon', there was a happy equation between gracious simplicity and genuine earthiness, the lack of which had so alienated him from his own home in Manchester.

Yet, fond as he was of the Favennecs, he remained uncharacteristically aloof from the locals generally. 'The other people I avoid', he admitted, 'especially in their depressing aggregate at markets & fetes'. After walking ten miles with Jean-Louis to a fete near Quimperlé, he was resolved never to go to another: 'it is beyond the fortitude of my spirits to watch the crowd being amused *to order* for so many hours', he declared. Although many of *les Bretons* posed for him – including Joseph Raoul, the village simpleton – he called them 'statues . . . not characters'. In developing quite unfairly strong feelings of disdain towards them, socially, he came to disregard them and seemed not to form any lasting attachments outside the family. The Favennecs, on the other hand, he thought always kind with

105

'virtues . . . rare enough in the neighbourhood' and clearly recognised their superiority over the other natives.

Latterly, too, he was not averse to the charms of the girls in the family who, in the years of his visits, had grown from mere gamines to nubile young women. The eldest, Marie, was safely married and settled at nineteen and, after her mother's death, had taken charge of the extensive, extended family. In the autumn, when Ede had gone, she gave birth – in the room next to Henry's – to a son, Yves-Philippe, named after her husband. 'With the sight of that strong woman resting & the fat urchin sleeping before me, the whole affair seems far enough removed from the investing horror & ignominy one is accustomed to in cities & their hospitals', wrote Henry, who was a helpful witness to the birth and made drawings of the baby. Marie had also modelled for him the previous summer: she was what he called 'the girl with the too long neck' in *Lamentation*; but, being pregnant in 1911 and with added responsibilities, so far as posing was concerned, was virtually *hors de combat*. Julienne, the youngest daughter, was then only thirteen but impressionable and old enough to develop quite a crush and remember Monsieur Lamb vividly. But it was Marie-Joseph, then just seventeen, who in particular took exception to Ede's presence and interpreted the intrusion as a personal affront, making no secret of her resentment by 'revealing her sentiments with a savage sincerity'. On arrival at the beginning of that summer, Henry had observed, rather superiorly, that 'she was perhaps a little dirty' but '*en dimanche* & after her weekly wash . . . looked sweet enough'. A pencil drawing done almost certainly on a Sunday and dated 1911, shows her *en coiffe de Doëlan* looking a little younger than her years, the beautiful Breton features nearly full-face, and the bright, broad-set eyes gazing with elfin gleam at the artist who, in these last weeks, was to remain neither detached from, nor unaroused by, his rapidly maturing model. In the interval between Ede's departure and his own, Henry must have succumbed to the seductive chemistry of heat and drought, and relaxation, availability and isolation, by filling the vacuum of indolence with a flirtation that raised both Marie-Joseph's and the family's hopes of a permanent union. 'I have the priveledge [sic] (sometimes ludicrous enough)', he wrote, 'of being on the stage of an intense family drama'; but he could not 'explain why M-Joseph was still a virgin!'

So the peace at 'Kersimon' was soon broken and his relations with the Favennecs changed. The possibility of such a liaison, with hindsight however ridiculous, produced an atmosphere of some anxiety within the family who were not exactly discouraging of the idea. But Henry's departure for Paris towards the end of October, effectively closed the door on any of their expectations. As if sensing that artistically and emotionally Doëlan was spent, he wrote at the time, hinting, 'it is very possible this is my last long visit here.' In fact it was to be his last visit. The lure of Donegal in 1912 and 1913, and the call to arms the year after, broke the spell forever. He was often to visit France again, but never Doëlan, though he corresponded and exchanged presents with his beloved Favennecs, keeping, what he called, '*mes souvenirs impérissables*'.

NOTES

1 *Artists of the Newlyn School* catalogue 1979 p.19.
2 ib. p.115.
3 Hartrick *A Painter's Pilgrimage* pp.29–30; quoted and paraphrased by Rewald *Post Impressionism* p.291.
4 Jaworska *Gauguin and the Pont-Aven School* p.181.
5 ib.
6 Jaworska p.186.
7 Baron *The Camden Town Group* p.170.
8 Lewis *Letters* pp.44–5.
9 Lewis *Rude Assignment* p.113 & p.116.
10 Henry Lamb – Tate Gallery : 22 Nov 1955; *Modern British Collection* Tate Gallery catalogue, p.367.
11 ib.
12 *The New English Art Club* 'The Times' 22 May 1911.
13 ib.
14 Devas *Two Flamboyant Fathers* pp.39–40.
15 *The New English Art Club* 'The Times' 22 May 1911.

SEVEN

GEORGE KENNEDY

———

'There is a certain divine strain in that profoundly unkempt creature, but it may take one lengthy probings to strike it', wrote Henry of his friend George Kennedy. Kennedy – the 'George' seems never to have been used amongst his friends – had studied painting at the Slade for two years until in 1906 he went to Paris and enrolled at the Académie Julian. He and Henry would certainly have met then, if not before in London, and their lives continued to overlap thereafter. It was partly due to this friendship that Henry was encouraged to make his first visit to Ireland in 1912.

Claiming that Kennedy was one of the very few 'who *does* know a thing or two', Henry invariably took his opinion seriously and looked forward to his arrival, mostly, for his criticism and advice for Henry's work. Yet, much as he appreciated Kennedy's comments, and enjoyed his company, he felt that two days was probably enough of him and had to admit difficulty in keeping what he called 'a plausibly attentive face' when his friend was slowly and lazily expressing his 'lumbering thoughts' and 'elusive ideas'. 'I should have been bored had he stayed longer', Henry confessed, although he was always prepared to overlook Kennedy's less bearable characteristics in order to elicit an opinion on his work in progress. Quite why, seems extraordinary. Engaging and endearing as Kennedy must often have been as a companion, as a critic, he was certainly imaginative but largely inaccurate. For a number of years he would

108

give his 'grandfatherly advice' appearing at Henry's studio 'in a vague nimbus' suggesting changes to pictures that Henry seems to have noted and probably made. When he first saw *Death of a Peasant* on the easel he disliked it, thinking it too literary and much preferred *Lamentation*, about which he made 'some valuable suggestions'. What could these have been and how much notice did Henry take? A preparatory study is vastly better and altogether more convincing, so perhaps Henry was led astray. Later, Kennedy was to prefer – perhaps with some justification this time – the first of Henry's two major war compositions, each of which is impressive and amongst the very best of his work: 'Irish Troops' is arguably the more exciting, imaginative and original; but in calling the treatment of the second, 'Troops on the Struma', 'pre-Raphaelite' he is so wide of the mark as to be guilty of a critical *faux-pas*. Having views so at variance with both contemporary opinion and subsequent judgements on Henry's work, and with such slender credentials as to his scholarship – other than a close acquaintance with the artist – it is still surprising that in 1924, Kennedy should have undertaken to write the first critical study of Henry Lamb. With customary modesty and self deprecation, Henry dismissed the little monograph as a 'book of reproductions which seems to me a very premature affair', and added wryly, 'at least I hope it will prove so.' After praising the companion study on Stanley Spencer in the series on 'Contemporary British Artists', he wrote, 'There are hardly any "dud" plates in his book, tho' mine contains half a dozen. The production is filthy. I mean the oppressive Englishness of the volumes & their perfect absence of taste', and added, 'Kennedy's introduction to me has some interesting moments.'

Kennedy was not really a writer although at Eton he had won the poetry prize. In his spare time, all his life, he painted: he was the son of a portrait painter, Charles Napier Kennedy; and he married the daughter of a Glasgow painter, Thomas Millie Dow, one of the first members of the New English Art Club. However, it was as an architect that Kennedy was to become well known and best remembered, a career he decided upon just prior to the First World War and which he resumed seriously soon after. One of his earliest projects was to redesign the Chenil Galleries, in the King's Road in Chelsea, above which he was to have his office for many years. He has sometimes been called 'the Bloomsbury architect' though, like Henry, his associations were much wider and his commissions more various. Yet, in his becoming a friend of Maynard Keynes, his Bloomsbury connections were certainly strengthened and he was to do a fair amount of work in Cambridge including, in 1925, an extension to King's College and, a decade later, the famous Arts Theatre, the planning of which is said to have 'presented unbelievably intricate problems' but which was eventually and successfully 'designed to harmonise with the traditional character of this very ancient part of the town.'[1] One of his last commissions was at Gordonstoun School in Scotland where, in 1939, he designed a boys' boarding house, described recently as 'an imposing wooden structure with sloping walls . . . still very much in use today'. While there, he was also involved in modifications to the interior of some of the older buildings and was to have undertaken other, more radical alterations and additions to the school but a sudden change of sponsorship and the outbreak of the Second World War intervened. During the war, when Gordonstoun was evacuated to Wales, Kennedy, ever resourceful, taught Classics and played the cello in the school orchestra.

According to his nephew Richard, Kennedy 'was a great believer in meeting people' but lacked 'the manner of a social lion'. He had too, 'a great admiration for business efficiency' and though without it himself, was not prevented from 'landing lucrative contracts'.[2] He was gregarious and loved talking and must have spoken a good deal about Henry and his circle, especially to his cousin, the writer Margaret Kennedy who, in 1924 – the same year as the appearance of the monograph on Henry – first published her bestselling novel, *The Constant Nymph*. She hardly knew either Henry or Augustus but vicariously wove her story round what she had heard of the early years of their bohemian ménage and included a character called Lewis Dodd, a moody young musician, based loosely on Henry though, understandably, he preferred not to acknowledge the connection. The book was an astonishing success going into many editions and being adapted for the stage.

Shortly after Kennedy decided to turn to architecture for a living, he stayed with Henry who, though pleased to see this 'most *aimable enfant*', was always wary of the effects of a long spell with him. While Henry agreed that Kennedy was capable of dragging him out of what he called 'a fit of the vapours', at the same time, when he was trying to work, Kennedy could be an alarming distraction. 'By far the gravest discount on my forces at present is the presence of

Kennedy', he wrote in sheer frustration, 'now I can hardly advance at all under the perpetual menace of his unanchored hulk bobbing aimlessly about me.' But it was this 'bobbing unanchored hulk' of which Henry made such play in his often witty, always affectionate portrayals of this 'original' – and the friendship survived. Kennedy had an engaging ungainliness that was further accentuated by his ill-fitting clothes which were chosen by his wife Mary and usually made 'by some frightful tailor who lives in the wilds of Donegal and makes working men's Sunday suits', wrote his nephew: 'No one would think from looking at him that Uncle George was an Old Etonian'.[3] Early in their friendship, when Kennedy was intending to be a painter and cultivating a more arty image, Henry noted him as a 'ridiculous creature . . . very much fancying himself as a sort of Pre-Raphaelite person à la Morris in a long black overcoat & a battered bowler' and made at least one delightful drawing of him in that guise; he also made other studies, mentioning early in 1911, having 'sketched him for an hour & then' going for a long walk; but few of these drawings appear to have survived and, what must be the definitive portrayal was to come later when, in 1921, Henry judged rightly that he could best do justice to Kennedy's awkwardness by painting him full-length, resulting in one of his most ambitious compositions and the second of his family groups.

In *The Kennedy Family* of 1921, the father, largest and most conspicuous, sits bolt upright, characteristically ill-at-ease. The rest of the family, then six in all, are gathered round, crammed into the picture with little or no room to spare. By compressing the group of figures into such a confined space, Henry effectively conveys the near claustrophobic atmosphere of the setting that he himself described as intended 'to represent any boarding house or temperance hotel – the sort of mouldy establishment' for which Kennedy had 'a fatal predilection', a curious and amusing inversion of his preferred taste as a professional architect. Despite the likely dinginess of the actual surroundings and the inevitably unkempt, shabby bagginess of Kennedy's suit, the colour of the whole picture is astonishingly light in key, almost sweet, gentle and lyrical, as though counterpoint to its gloomier associations.

Before the First War, Henry had also made studies of Mary Kennedy: in 1913, soon after she married, he reported, casually, doing 'two heads of Madame . . . with as much non-stylistic enthusiasm as you can prophesy'. On first meeting Mary, he thought

111

her 'undoubtedly a sublime creature'; but after she had sat to him he had to confess being nonplussed: 'I cannot undertake to describe Mrs. K', he wrote, 'partly because . . . I was quite unable to unravel her principal mysteries. Certainly she is a delightful *copain* – silent & with a great deal of sensibility. But I suspect she has a rather diminutive coefficient of everything & some arid tracts of Scotchness' though a 'smile that buggers all suspicion'. Months later, he was to recall a dream 'in which Madame G.L.K. appeared a most magnificent personage' thinking 'it must be true'. Yet in the family portrait, there is no aura of fantasy around Mary nor any trace of that disarming smile. Indeed, in the finished picture, she looks distinctly uncomfortable and nearly as ill-at-ease as her husband. Why does she kneel, semi-recline, or crouch beside him so awkwardly and anxiously? Moreover, realistically and maybe mundanely, her pose is almost impossible anatomically and, though largely obscured by the two boys standing beside her, she mars the visual relationship between the parents and remains the least satisfying part of the whole composition. Judging from the preliminary studies, in both pencil and watercolour and in oil, it would seem a design problem that has never quite been resolved; yet, in Seurat's *Le Chahut*, for example, no one is unduly worried at the absence of legs on the male dancers! Doubtless Henry was concerned to maintain a rhythmic flow in the disposition of the heads, Mary's making a significant link in the design although her body is in such relative disproportion – she appears even smaller in the studies – and it all contributes to the wit and quirkiness of this highly original painting.

The compact, albeit crowded, design has a unity but it is always to the bulk of the patriarchal Kennedy that the eye returns for, as well as occupying more of the picture space, dramatically he dominates the group. He looks like a heavier, less agile Jacques Tati, and some of the humour comes from the clownish clumsiness with which he displaces his ill coordinated legs and feet to accommodate safely on his lap the youngest in the family. Of the other children, Henry must have made studies, but few are extant. A small pencil drawing of a baby's head is almost certainly of the third son, Alexander Millie (Sandy), who died young: in the group, he obscures mother's lower half while resting his right arm and hand on father's left knee; but the drawing, being in profile, could not have been directly in preparation for the painting. A more important and precise preparatory study is an oil of the eldest son John who, in the family group, stands to his father's right leaning against him. Clearly, in its own right, it is one of the best, simplest and most sensitive heads that Henry ever did and was reproduced by Allan Gwynne-Jones in his book on *Portrait Painters*, where he described it as 'very beautiful' and complimented the artist on his restrained use of colour, his 'extreme sensitiveness of . . . perception and his strong and delicate draughtsmanship.'⁴ This portrait of John Kennedy – originally called simply *A Child's Head* – is indeed one of Henry's most satisfying combinations of spontaneous brushwork and profound observation; attractively handled, impeccably crafted, it is a subtle fusion of precise drawing, direct painting and characterisation. Gwynne-Jones, later, likened it, not inappropriately, to Hals, even Rubens. From all accounts, it is an excellent likeness and Henry has not only captured the elusive charm of the volatile, cherubic sitter, but also the generic quality of boyishness.

Something of this freshness has been lost – or perhaps intentionally sacrificed – in the finished picture, for *The Kennedy Family* is a fairly stylised, highly polished painting, its treatment – and to some extent its design – owing a little to the influence of Stanley Spencer although, as discussed later, a connection that may have been more mutual and interdependent than generally supposed. The surface rendering of the 'Kennedys', like that of the smaller 'Anrep Family' of the previous year, is absolutely immaculate and the colour glows intrinsically, independently of any accidental, textural effects, the properties of which seem rarely to have interested Henry. Yet the handling is positive and consistent and there is little evidence of alteration. A year after completion, it was shown in Henry's first one man exhibition at the Alpine Club Gallery in London and was bought by the Behrends, patrons who were to be regularly supportive of Henry and his work. Kennedy himself reproduced it in his monograph on Henry; and it has also been shown in Pittsburgh, Melbourne and Johannesburg. Nevertheless, despite its quality, its charm and idiosyncrasies, it has not been among the handful of Henry's more familiar works and deserves to be better known. *The Kennedy Family* is a still unique and amusingly affectionate tribute to a lifelong friendship.

In view of his Irish ancestry and his friendships with, first, Augustus, then Kennedy, it is still surprising that Henry should not have gone to Ireland before 1912. Earlier that year he had had some connection by being tentatively and reluctantly involved in a mural project commissioned by Sir Hugh Lane and destined for the Dublin City Art Gallery. With his habitually cavalier attitude toward patrons and his mixture of indifference and arrogance to the business of art, Henry took great pleasure in leading the interested parties up the proverbial garden path. Charles Aitken, then Director of the Whitechapel Gallery, was the London liaison of the scheme for which Henry, had he been less obtuse and more motivated, would have received £100: 'I have to meet Walter Bayes & Cayley Robinson who are to co-operate with me in some way', he wrote; 'I mistrust the whole affair: Lane is such a slippery creature.' Significantly, *they* were to co-operate with *him*, but he said he would 'like to do a subject from Irish Mythology' and started reading 'Irish stories in search of a subject'.

That was in March, 1912. By May, with about four days to go before Lane's competition, Henry reported that he had 'absolutely nothing done: of course a miracle of productiveness may happen though not if my stomach or liver can help it'. He also mentioned, 'Aitken showing signs of a pitiable distraction' and hoping that Henry had not forsaken the mural competition. Then, in June, he wrote, how he had been 'working every day at this Irish design gradually becoming more engrossed in it. I was too late for the actual competition', he admitted, '& too late for some sort of extra adjudication that Aitken arranged but I'm in correspondence with Lane who seems anxious to get at it. Even if he underpays me I feel anxious to try my hand at it on the large scale. I go to his house tomorrow to meet Lady Gregory. The work has been heavily handicapped – by relapse of health, & then by domestic revolutions.' Lane, however, was destined never to receive his design. Henry, having transported it to work on in Ireland, reported that he had 'been making a desperate effort to finish a sort of mural painting on a large sheet of brown paper' and that it was 'very nearly done. The interest has been almost entirely technical & really I do feel much wiser for the experience though the result is most boring. The subject is too slight & vulgar to support the long struggle which I didn't foresee . . . so I had better dispose of it to Clifton for £1,000 the day I return.' Clifton, of the Carfax Gallery, may never have seen it either although, the following week, Henry announced that

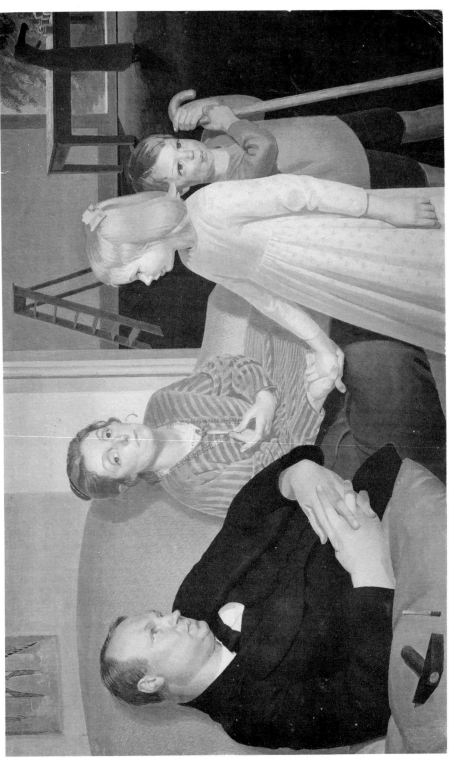

The Anrep Family 1920   Oil on panel   34 × 51   Museum of Fine Arts, Boston

The Lake *1911*   *Tempera on canvas*   *61.5 × 46.2*
Private collection

Phantasy *1912   Oil on canvas   86.5 × 61*
Tate Gallery, London

Breton Cowherd *c.1910* *Oil on panel* *35.5 × 25.4*
Private collection

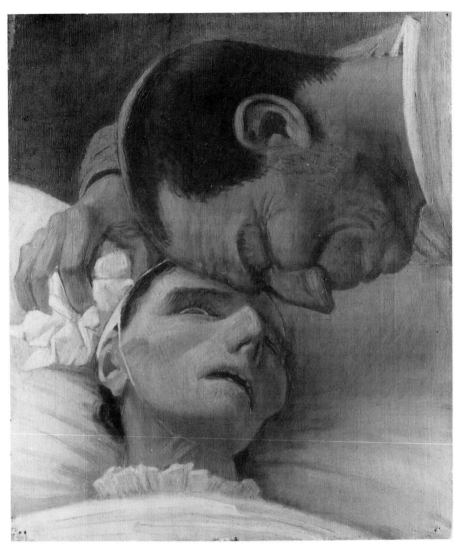

Death of a Peasant *1911   Oil on canvas   37 × 32*
Tate Gallery, London

Irish Girls *1912   Oil on canvas   75 × 69.5*
Tate Gallery, London

Opposite: Edie McNeill *1911   Oil on canvas   127.5 × 76.2*
Southampton Art Gallery

Marie-Joseph Favennec (Study of a Girl's Head) *1911*
Pencil on paper   28 × 25.4
Whitworth Art Gallery, Manchester

he had finished his 'most bloody decoration' which he thought 'only fit to bait slimy old Clifton with . . . unless', he added, 'I could get some cigarette firm to purchase it'.

Another artist involved in the Dublin scheme was Augustus who, on and off for several years, struggled to complete an enormous composition which was never really finished: when, in 1915, he heard the news that the ill-fated Lane had been drowned aboard the 'Lusitania', he abruptly stopped working on it altogether. However, Augustus was more naturally disposed to mural painting although he failed to finish almost everything; but Henry, even allowing for his usual self-deprecation and his often wildly inaccurate judgements on his own work, was never a 'decorative' artist: consistently, his *forte* was easel painting and after the Lane affair he seems never to have been tempted again – apart from a minor digression, collaborating with Kennedy in a fresco experiment on the walls of 'Cashelnagor', Kennedy's house at Gortahork, near the coast of Donegal.

When Henry first went to Ireland, in September 1912, he stayed a few weeks in Middletown, in the north west of Donegal not far from 'Cashelnagor', and put up at McBride's Hotel which he complained was too social. The weather hardly improved the whole time he was there though he managed to get some sketching done. He made the acquaintance of most of the local girls and children who could generally be persuaded to sit but were not to be relied on since the girls, especially, came in the hope of bagging drawings of themselves: as they would not accept payment he had to use his camera – so he said – but, when painting, he seems never to have had recourse to photographs. Among his fellow guests at McBride's was the former parish priest, there for a holiday, *'un très bon enfant,* but over 6 feet high, immensely stout, & O mon dieu! a devil of a snorer'* who quite disabled Henry from sleeplessness. Another of the guests, there with his wife and unpopular with Henry, was Jack Yeats, the brother of W.B. 'I find myself positively resenting his interruptions', wrote Henry, making an unflattering caricature of Yeats. Yet he continued to thrive, though overcome by a dullness that encouraged him to make friends and have flirtations in the villages and, as he put it, 'to drift, as usual, towards the lower classes'. Despite warming to the general amiability of the people, after the more taciturn Bretons, he was overwhelmed with their volubility: 'heavens!' he declared, 'how these Irish gabble! they fly

115

over the ground like a grass-fire in wind; scorching, but never consuming the rocks.'

In the November of 1912, Henry moved on to stay with Kennedy at 'Cashelnagor' taking with him some oil sketches of heads that he had done at the hotel. These were much admired by his host, who encouraged Henry to send two of them to the third exhibition of the Camden-Town Group that opened in December at the Carfax Gallery, run by the much maligned Clifton. Each exhibit he called simply, but unhelpfully, 'Study of a Head' though one, almost certainly, was of Charlie Gallagher, a well-known, roaring, pugilistic Irishman who had been persuaded to sit for his portrait: it, or a similar study, was in Kennedy's collection for many years. Again, on the evidence of this one, it is difficult to enthuse about and impossible to be in agreement with Kennedy. Indeed, in comparison with any number of Henry's portraits from any period, it seems a merely competent, unexciting study for what could have been a dynamic painting.

Strangely too, in treatment and tonally, this study of Charlie Gallagher bears a surprising resemblance to many of the landscape studies Henry made in Donegal – and, later, elsewhere on the mainland of Ireland. He himself dismissed them as 'a small bunch of *pochades* . . . each of which cost a chill' and mentioned the unparalleled difficulties of coping with such subjects in that climate: 'the weather is hopelessly bad', he wrote, but the darkness was 'the most upsetting thing: it makes it almost impossible to invent good colours'. Certainly, these *'paysages* sketches', as he called them, are modest and not unpleasing; but they reveal little of the richness of the countryside and, much as he responded physically and emotionally to the Irish landscape and admired the spatial, bracing qualities of the open air, none matches his feelings nor conveys a sense of place.

Henry stayed at 'Cashelnagor' until the end of the year and again in the spring and summer of 1913; but his most rewarding experience in Ireland, and one of his richest artistic sources, was to be his discovery of Gola, a tiny island off the coast of Donegal. As he reconnoitred the island weekly with the groceries boat and gazed at it longingly from the mainland, Gola had become a Promised Land: 'I find myself in a paradise', he declared on his first trip in the autumn of 1912; 'There are mountains, a lake, rocks, cliffs, caves & white strands: the people are more lovely & even more angelically dispositioned than on the mainland &', he added, 'certainly more sensible.' To provide for him, he said he had persuaded 'a lovely giantess' who must have been the mother of the McGinley family with whom he stayed and who seemed to replace the Favennecs in his life at this time. Even when Henry was there, Gola had a dwindling population with a mere handful of inhabitants. 'I have a bed-room & immense sitting room in the principal house – a new 2-storied erection', he reported soon after his arrival which, because of storms and rough seas, had been 'infinitely delayed'. With the weather little better during his first few days there and everyone working in the fields, he was not able to draw and paint immediately but at least had a chance to get his bearings and observe his new setting. 'The harvest & potato work will be finished at the end of the week & then they all promise to sit for me', he wrote, 'So I should pass a month agreeably enough even if the weather is bad: at present it is brilliant, only too breezy. The wind never drops, it is always practically a gale no matter from what quarter. This makes outdoor sketching out of the question & so I have made very few *"pochades"*.'

The Golese kept their promise, enabling Henry to fill sketchbook after sketchbook with drawings of the islanders. If anything, they seem more vigorous and more urgent than most done in Brittany although – because of the Celtic connections, a similar physiognomy, and circumstances not unlike Doëlan – some of this work has been mistaken for Breton. In the enthusiasm at discovering, on the edge of Donegal, his Shangri-la, he waxed eloquent, comparing the two places and peoples: 'surely I never saw such beauties before – easily eclipsing the Bretons: & then the colours!' he exclaimed. He had made little of the Breton landscape and, the year before at Doëlan, during the last weeks, had retreated from the people as subject matter for painting. But in Gola, though his essays in pure landscape were as undistinguished as those of the mainland, somehow, in responding to both island and islanders and relating the two, integrating them in a sensitive, unforced, convincing way, his art took a great step forward. Islanders, being literally so exposed to the elements, have an extreme awareness of weather and become conditioned to its vagaries. Even the portrait heads Henry did in Gola seemed to show this awareness. A study called *Irish Girls*, now in the Tate, includes a minimum of background and may have been part of a larger composition, but the figures, wrapped against an Atlantic gale, press to the left of the canvas, looking downwards, upwards, a third turning, looking back, all, in trying to cope with an insistent, restless wind, give a fine feeling of race and place. Another example, in pen and wash, of a woman and child sheltering against a wall, though not an especially good drawing, expresses, almost expressionistically, the islanders' vulnerability to storms.

The following year, 1913, Henry arrived in Gola earlier, towards the end of August, announcing, 'After a preliminary scowl my Elysian island has admitted me once more to all its private charms & I feel certain that "all will be well with me" independently of what I may be fortunate enough to produce here.' His intuition was right. Fate smiled on him and the sun shone for the first week or so enabling him to see Gola, literally, in a new light: he had returned with 'a new courage' though felt ambivalent about the 'miraculous weather', complaining, 'The place is not really quite so beautiful when sparkling with fine weather as in its normal & sinister attire & yet one needs the vague & powerful stimulus of the light.' In his absence, the kindly McGinleys had tried to improve his working conditions by putting a window in the loft: but he was less than appreciative, thinking it 'ridiculously small' and grumbling of 'a vile reek from the byre beneath' which caused him, in the middle of September, to flee from the island panic stricken that his studio was giving him typhoid. The doctor on the mainland sent him back 'full of physic & some reassurances' and, as part of the cure, he began potato digging two half-days a week 'with favourable effects'. Meanwhile, the McGinleys enlarged the skylight, handsomely illuminating his loft and allowing him, because of the warm winds, to sit all day with the window open.

Fond as he became of the McGinley family, Henry said he sometimes found 'the society of the other natives intolerable'. However, he is supposed to have formed a romantic attachment with one of the local girls, Kathleen; and also to have had an affection for Sheila McGinley, daughter of his hosts. Under his supervision, Sheila came to London shortly after the outbreak of war in 1914, to be a patient in Guy's Hospital, where Henry had resumed his medical studies and where he arranged her observation and treatment for suspected tuberculosis, a disease, then, not uncommon in islands with a preponderantly damp climate. Apart from the ever bleaker economic prospects, the incidence and spread of TB largely accounts for the dwindling population of islands off the coasts of Ireland – and Scotland – and the drift to the mainland leading, in the case of Gola, to its eventual abandonment.

Having enjoyed the isolation of the island and, evidently, the company of the McGinley's, Henry began to find, on this second visit, that he had become too accessible to others in the neighbourhood. 'Writing is the greatest problem', he reported, 'for in addition to my usual struggles, I have to survive the interruptions of visitors any time after my lamp is lit. These incursions are most dreary affairs. I had looked forward to them in the beginning as opportunities for sittings: but I have an unsatisfactory lamp and have come to hate sketching at night. I hate the inroads on my privacy still more. The ennui of the conversations is indescribable & eventually induces a state of coma in me . . . Of course there are charming & amusing people on the island & I can generally find them when I want. It is the embarrassing visits to me and inspections of my sketches which I dread.' As usual, he tried to persuade his London friends to come over, but only Kennedy, from 'Cashelnagor' nearby, did so. Soon, though, with the potato crop just coming to an end, sitters were at last available and he was again able to draw them in daylight.

It was then, in the middle of October 1913, that Henry began working out his Golese *pièce de résistance*, the magnificent, monumental, *Fisherfolk*. A rich, harmonious, moving and poetic marriage of figures and landscape, *Fisherfolk*, as the perfect summation of his experiences in Gola, is undoubtedly his best Irish picture, and – if it is possible and useful to single out a seminal work – perhaps his best painting of all. Though the studies were done in Gola, the canvas had 'to survive the . . . interruption of transplantation . . . miraculously well' and most of it was painted back in London. By one of those perverse twists of irony, in view of Henry's failure to produce anything for Lane's Dublin scheme, *Fisherfolk* is as well suited to mural decoration as anything he ever did: stylised, unified, gently rhythmic, sensitively handled with delicate, subtle colour. Puvis again comes to mind, possibly Maurice Denis; but any influences have been thoroughly assimilated, worked through, and it is essentially Henry Lamb. Privately, and appropriately, he called it his 'Gola Sonata' and it is perhaps the most overtly musical of any of his pictures, so musical, in fact, that the sweep of the composition seems almost symphonic in its grandeur. The figures are grouped perhaps a little artificially and self-consciously, but are so at one with the land and seascape and so exquisitely related to the background, that the whole becomes a unity and totally convincing. The potato harvest seems over, there is respite from the fishing: men, women and children relax together for a moment before the winter closes in, before the long nights and terrible storms. A 'scowl' in the weather threatens but holds off and there is a lull in the wind, an uncanny stillness, a characteristic of islands like Gola, in which such exceptional silence, sounds may carry for miles and even voices be heard across a bay. This atmosphere of ruminative calm, this pause for reflection on the toils of a routine existence, seems beautifully evoked in *Fisherfolk* which, as a sort of homage to Gola, is a fitting summary of Henry's feelings about what he called his 'half loved – half dreaded little exile'.

NOTES

1 'The Architect and Building News' 14 Feb 1936, pp. 216–9.
2 R. Kennedy *A Boy at the Hogarth Press* p.2.
3 R. Kennedy p.76–77.
4 Gwynne-Jones *Portrait Painters* p.36 and pl.139.

IV

Bloomsbury and Hampstead

1910–1914

EIGHT

THE BLOOMSBERRIES

———

As early as 1905, when Henry first came to London, his brother Walter had introduced him to several of the circle who were to become the nucleus of the so-called Bloomsbury group. He might also have met some of them even earlier and would certainly have known of them in 1902, when Walter, Henry's senior by a year, left the Manchester Grammar School to read Classics at Trinity College, Cambridge, where, as an undergraduate, his contemporaries included Lytton Strachey, Clive Bell, Leonard Woolf, and Adrian Stephen, brother of Vanessa and Virginia Stephen who were to become, respectively, Mrs Bell and Mrs Woolf. Intellectually, or at least academically, Walter Lamb could hold his own with this Cambridge circle; but his lack of creative ability left him wanting and, although he was prone to self-reassuring fantasies, he rarely indulged in or had the capacity for imaginative flights of fancy, one of a number of reasons for his soon parting company with the 'Bloomsberries', for whom, for continuing intimacy and respect imagination became a priority.

Another reason, that also contributed to his becoming a figure of fun with the group, was his mistake in proposing to Virginia Stephen in the summer of 1911, a year before she married Leonard Woolf. Unlike Henry, Walter had no way with women and was always ill-at-ease in their company, remaining misunderstood for much of the time: 'I gave an approving smile to some young ladies', he wrote to Clive Bell in their undergraduate days, 'but could not be sure, on thinking the matter over that I left them quite clear as to what it was that pleased me.' And in congratulating Bell on his engagement to Vanessa Stephen in 1906, he admitted having said 'some hard things . . . of her sex. But at worst', he continued, excusing himself, 'that was about women in general, and I always took care to say I had never known any of them at all well. The truth is, I am very awkward with them'. So awkward was he that his protracted and diffident courtship of Vanessa's sister Virginia was conducted more through Bell than openly with the object of his affection and admiration herself. 'About Virginia: I suppose she must have told you that she thought I thought she disliked me', he confided to Bell, having just seen enough of her 'to wish to know her well; I fancy she has qualities of mind for which I am always looking & mean chiefly her kind of imaginative, constructive humour. Yet I hardly ever see her, and when I do, things are so destined that we do not talk together . . . if I concerned myself with her *feelings* at all – as I doubt . . . it would be to chafe at the fact that she neither liked nor disliked me', and he resolved to 'try not to be so timid'. But, eight months later, Walter reported that he had had his 'first good talk with Virginia' as a result of which, he found himself in complete agreement with Bell about everything he had said concerning her mind, though he expressed surprise at 'how friendly she made herself appear' and wondered at her patience, regretting the infliction of his 'dulness on her vivacity'.

At some distance, Walter continued to worship Virginia's icy beauty and creative intellect: he envied her ability to write 'well and entertainingly' and, after reading an article by her, asked, 'I wonder how long she takes over a piece like that, or how the style compares, God help me, with my fifty pages a week.' Eventually, after some five years of tentative overtures, he confessed, 'I am in love with Virginia, and have told her so. She does not love me. She seems touched, and treats me with perfect nobility and grace. I go on hoping.' Vain hope, however. Walter's interest in what seems now a most unlikely, impossible match was doubtless genuine enough but was further inflamed by the diabolical Bell himself who obviously enjoyed his role as a 'go-between' giving assurances of Virginia's continuing interest and pointing up her virtues to her faint-hearted suitor. As well, he would have derived some impish pleasure from translating the confessions of Walter to his wife Vanessa and to his sister-in-law herself, who used them as ammunition for invective.

Walter, in failing to lead Virginia anywhere near the altar incurred some of her most acid gibes: 'How anyone has the face to be so magnificently egotistical one can't conceive', she wrote to Lytton Strachey, 'he lives in the centre of domes upon domes of bubbles.'[1] And years later, on a visit to Manchester, she described to Vanessa, the University people she met as 'somehow like Wattie [Walter], provincial, smug, destitute of any character, hopelessly suburban, yet trying to live up to the metropolitan intellect.'[2]

So not for long, did Virginia treat Walter 'with perfect nobility and grace'. Unable to resist debunking foibles and affectations, she found admirable material in him, keeping up a remarkable flow of invective over the years: 'Vanessa & Virginia were abominably rude to me', he complained to Bell; and only days later, wrote, 'I should hate to think I had a quarrel with any of the Stephens: but I thought the behaviour of the ladies so strange that I saw something must have happened of which I was unaware.'

Walter's relations with men were perhaps marginally easier. At the turn of the century, Cambridge was, as a contemporary put it, 'suffused with the golden glow of homosexuality in its most creative aspect';[3] and as an undergraduate, Walter had been one of the young men to whom Lytton Strachey had expounded what Michael Holroyd has called 'some of the special virtues and advantages of that love which passes all Christian understanding'.[4] In such a climate it is hardly surprising that Walter, given his diffidence with the opposite sex, should have experienced some feelings of sexual ambiguity. At first he became attracted to Lytton himself whom he teased after noting him 'in a punt near King's Bridge . . . pretending to write what would have turned out to be rather pretentious verse, when he was not calculating the capacities of the well-dressed genitals around him'. Whenever he was away he made a habit of sending Lytton, with partly ingratiatory intentions tantalising descriptions of male physical attributes, sometimes from real life encounters and some from more vicarious, aesthetic experience of works of art. On a visit to Milan, he described seeing 'a very brilliant "revue" or "Spettacolo Goliardico" given by a lot of students. We had Adam with his fig-leaf, the Virgin, and "Il Padre Eterno" making fine sport together: and as the whole company, even including the orchestra, was composed of unusually handsome young men, you may guess I had a very tolerable evening's entertainment.' And after seeing Raphael's frescoes in Rome, he wrote asking

Lytton, 'do you know the one called "The Driving Out of Heliodorus"?' adding provocatively, 'There is a divine young man climbing round a pillar, & his glorious back & bottom seem to *glow through* his cincture of greenish gauze . . . I could not help thinking it a terribly sad thing that the man (Raphael, I mean) had not more non-ecclesiastical patronage – for there he is a pure, unrestrained pagan'.

However, Walter soon aroused the shrill, sharp sarcasm of Lytton who nicknamed him 'The Corporal' because of his 'second rate officiousness' and thought him 'conceitedly obsequious' like 'a fellow with one leg who's not only quite convinced that he's got two but boasts of his walking exploits'.[5] Walter then, after falling in love with James Strachey – much to Lytton's disgust – turned his attention to Adrian Stephen who, in fact, seems to have preferred Henry – and Euphemia. After an evening with Adrian, Walter reported how they 'somehow got on to my brother, whom he apparently thinks beautiful as well as his fiancée; and he announced his intention of being a regular visitor to his garret in Chelsea'.

When he left Cambridge in 1907, Walter, as if exiling himself, became for two years an assistant master at Clifton College, Bristol, 'this queer patch of desert', as he called it, where, a generation before, Roger Fry had been a pupil. At first he was lonely and out of his element: 'the importunate minutiae and lack-lustre amenities of school-life allow me only an occasional hour of real existence for reading at ease: any good writing is out of the question', he complained to Clive Bell. Then there were the grotesque imbecilities of the Rev. Canon Blorings. Walter, like Henry, was no churchgoer and, with an agnostic background and atheistic inclinations, he soon found himself at odds with the school establishment. But, having 'shown a bold front to the Headmaster on the question of Chapel' they 'arrived at a comfortable arrangement' and Walter gradually became acclimatised to his temporary aberration more from the promise of a return to lecturing at Cambridge than to much adjustment on his part. He was to leave Clifton with relief though not without some affection: 'they are all very sweet to me in my last term', he wrote, 'and I have just written 25 reports which say in 25 graceful variations that they are very charming boys, and I came very near having a brass plate put up over my stall in Chapel.'

Meanwhile, as Walter in Bristol had pined to be in London or

Cambridge among, as he described them, 'a company of unharnessed wits and live imaginations', back in Bloomsbury, Virginia and Company had been verbally sticking pins in him. When in 1913, he was appointed to the Secretaryship of the Royal Academy, they thought him quite beyond redemption: 'his life now lies among respectable, semi-smart, rich people, whom he half despises, so that his accounts are always condescending', wrote Virginia in her diary.[6] Earlier, she had conceded that he had 'hopes of a more brilliant future than falls to most of us', although Walter had himself claimed not to seek fame: 'I am not great myself, nor think I am or maybe, nor hope to find greatness', he had written after leaving Cambridge, admitting, 'I shall have to resign myself to the fact that I am by nature a loafer, a button-holer, to whom the world is nothing but a great dingy music-hall, a vast street-corner, or – worse still – a perpetual Turkish-bath.' Leonard Woolf once called him 'a superior footman' and, in fulfilling his role at the RA, Walter could hardly have created a post more suited to his abilities. Though often accused of having an inflated opinion of himself, Walter told Lytton after his appointment, 'I don't quite know how I came to be here but I saw an advertisement in the paper, and as I felt rather despondent about the prospect of making any money in London, I sent in my name. I was unanimously elected out of 121 applicants.' He then went on to describe the new job: 'I have a handsome apartment and a Registrar & Clerks & Porters under me. The work is not heavy except at times if preparing the Spring & Winter exhibitions. I have £500 a year & a pension after 10 years. Everybody seems to treat me with the greatest respect. As to the great difficulty – how I am to take them all seriously as artists – I can say nothing yet, as I don't know how seriously they take themselves'. Certainly, his new office allowed him to develop fully his talents as a courtier: adviser, informant, confidant, Walter was the perfect power behind the throne. Rather than opting for a free-lance career using his initiative – as Henry chose to do – Walter fell easily into a subservient but influential role close to the right hand of the respective Presidents of the Royal Academy: that arch-reactionary Munnings was moved to call him an 'imperturbable and learned secretary',[7] and he was undoubtedly happiest nestling under a wing of the English establishment upholding tradition in a cocoon that he seemed able to keep warm for perpetuity. He enjoyed oiling the wheels of a large institution with his placatory manner subduing any tendencies to rebellion. Again, unlike Henry, he avoided any signs of contention and would usually subscribe to the prevailing opinion. T. S. Eliot was reported by Virginia to have been 'overcome with the charms of Walter Lamb'; and she told Vanessa, 'Whatever Walter says, has the same flat, smooth, grey, surface . . . his voice alone would dull the fieriest poesy in the world . . . The one passion of his life is for eighteenth century building.'[8]

As it happened, when he settled in London, he bought an eighteenth century house, on Kew Green, by coincidence, not far from Hogarth House, Leonard and Virginia's home at Richmond. Since Cambridge, he had been interested in collecting – particularly rare books – and was always fastidious as to his environment, once wondering whether Clive Bell might 'consider with Vanessa the best scheme of decoration' for his rooms. Virginia has left an acute, cruel account of her new neighbour at home in his bachelor pad in 1916:

> 'Watty, as spruce as a Bank Clerk, and as bald as an egg . . . took us back to tea in his exquisite residence, which has walls of ducks egg green, and delicately tinted engravings of 18th century buildings hang perfectly in order, and a green baize board with crowds of invitation cards. He goes to dances every night, and has become a sham man of the world. Art interests him less and less. And then he began upon the King and Queen, and the President [of the RA], and how wonderful the President thinks him, and his kidneys, and his rheumatism, and long, long stories about Princess Mary and her Lord in waiting, whom she made wear a gas mask and then gave orders to his man, in a corner of the R.A. – which Watty thought showed a fine wit – Poor creature! He knows he's but a slug, and all the time he tries to excuse himself.'[9]

For Virginia, in particular, Walter was always ripe for raillery and the only 'sympathetic' remark she seems to have made was towards the end of the First World War when she was much relieved to learn that both Walter's house and her own favourite target himself were spared in an enemy air-raid: 'Nine bombs on Kew; 7 people killed in one house, a hotel crushed', she reported to Vanessa, 'but not a hair of Wattie's head was touched'.[10] In failing to win Virginia, poor Walter seemed never to win *with* her either. Whatever Walter did – or did not do – and whenever he spoke – publicly or in private – she attacked and ridiculed him with some caustic comment: 'Owing to Wattie's influence', she informed her sister prior to the Summer Exhibition in 1918, 'the RA will be smaller than usual this year.'[11]

128

Whilst clearly, he was anathema to Virginia, at the same time it is doubtful whether her friends ever had much respect or regard for 'the much vilified Walter Lamb'. Certainly he was associated with the older, original Bloomsberries; but only briefly was he ever an intimate. In telling Clive Bell, as one of his 'intimate friends' that he had put his name down as a referee, Walter hoped it would 'serve to soften a little the stiffness of your present attitude towards me, and possibly to reopen our former pleasant relations.' But the friendship was never properly revived – if indeed there ever had been any great enthusiasm on the part of Bell – and when his interest in Walter was on the wane, he made no attempt to hide his disenchantment, which attitude drew a reprimand: 'you maintain a silence towards me that is very cold and discouraging', complained Walter after his return to Cambridge. Significantly, their separation, socially and culturally, became more obvious towards the end of 1910, when the notorious exhibition of *Manet and the Post Impressionists* opened at the Grafton Galleries and was making headlines in London. Earlier that year, the organiser, Roger Fry, had met the Bells, who soon were 'completely whole-hearted in their acceptance of Fry's views – if not all his theories'.[12] Walter asured Clive that he would make every effort to see the show but whether he did and what he thought of it is unrecorded. Inevitably though, the rift between them could only have widened after Bell had thrown in his lot with Fry on the side of 'modernism' and Walter had accepted the shelter of the Academy. By 1913, in English art politics, the way from Bloomsbury, with their francophile, avant-garde attitudes, to Burlington House, proud of its traditionalist values, could hardly have been stonier or stormier. As Walter was himself to write later, in defining – pompously but with absolute conviction – the purpose of his beloved institution:

'To keep the main body of art alive, through regular intercourse with the perceptions and feelings of ordinary people – who must be familiar with normal forms before they can appreciate the strange fruits of experiment – is one great duty of such an organisation as the Royal Academy.'[13]

After his appointment to the Secretaryship, Walter channelled most of his working energy into Academy business and, for leisure, into connoisseurship until, in October 1926, Henry announced 'the convulsing news that my brother Walter is about to marry a Russian

American'; and soon after, he reported, having 'twice met brother Walter's girl whom the rest of the family have been anxiously keeping out of my way'. Despite dismissing her as he did with most of his family, Henry, for a wedding present, painted her portrait; by the time it was completed, Rose Brooks from Chicago had become Mrs Walter Lamb. The couple settled to a cosy, cultivated, and relatively unchallenging existence; but in later life, Henry came to think more of Rose, perhaps growing fonder of her than of his own brother.

Walter continued to show a more than ordinary, fraternal concern for Henry and his career; but of nepotism, he was completely innocent: had Henry been less independent he could well have become an Academician long before his election to associate membership in 1940, especially having exhibited there since 1921, when he was already a well known artist. As always, Henry chose to reject, even at difficult times, nearly all the help his caring and influential brother would have been willing to give.

Ultimately, Walter remains a kindly, slightly sad, and – in spite of contentment in both marriage and a secure, prestigious career – a somewhat lonely figure. He seemed doomed forever to be an entrenched traditionalist and a nodding bystander of all that was culturally conservative. In the face of Bloomsbury's cruel intolerance and vicious gossip, he must either have feigned indifference or simply become inured to derision. After the First War, he was to see little of his former fellow students but, as Bloomsbury reputations grew, although he appeared to enjoy the comforting assurance of his placid existence, doubts regarding the validity of his chosen role would disturb him occasionally: 'I expect, if you think of me,' he wrote to Lytton Strachey, in 1928, 'you regard me as a very minor Secretary, quietly writing, passively watching the phantasque of passions and affairs', adding with genuine admiration and without any envy, 'I do see and hear some curious things, even where I am; but among the things that I observe with a special thrill of interest are your career and fame in literature.'

Henry's relations with Bloomsbury were hardly more equable than his brother's, although none of the charges of complacency, self-congratulation, nor impoverished imagination, that were brought against Walter, could justifiably be levelled at Henry. Also, unlike

130

his brother, Henry retaliated, at times becoming as much of an irritation to them as they were to him. For all the sincerity of their pacifist convictions they had a surprising taste for vituperation to which Henry would respond lustily: having little time for pacifism, he described the Bloomsbury war effort – or rather its absence – as 'scrim-shanking', an onomatopoeic expression of disapproval for their being conscientious objectors. And after one of his rare post-war reunions in Gordon Square he reported returning from a rather formidable dinner in Bloomsbury, congratulating himself on leaving without committing murder: 'I get suffocated by those people', he exclaimed, asking, 'why must they go on talking about their bloody little group?'

The term Bloomsbury to describe such a varied and complex group of exceptional individuals, though convenient and in common usage, is a quite inadequate and misleading over simplification. Yet even Henry resorted to it in referring to his former friends, despite his being well aware of how very different each was from the other and how his affections and antipathies were as varied as the characters themselves. What he called their 'squalid gossip' generated by 'some obscure cyclones in Gordon Square' became more than his patience could bear one evening: having casually discovered some of them 'drinking port & talking drivel', he soon realised his mistake and confided, 'I seldom feel at my ease in any *group* of people and was this time overtaken again by my old ferocity. I can't stand the restraint and I don't like port.'

Above all he hated the Bloomsbury attitudes to art and despised 'the false aesthetics of the Clive-Fry coalition' that exploded just before the First War and reverberated long after. Henry felt – quite subjectively and with bitterness – that the powerful and pervasive influence of Clive Bell and Roger Fry had become a monopoly which poisoned and perverted artistic taste in Britain to an extent that became a disservice to himself and to many of his contemporaries. In the October of 1912, when the Second Post Impressionist Exhibition opened in London, he reported reading 'the Times notice on the Grafton Show with a most greedy disgust', and complained, 'it is really getting time that Roger's fetid little bubble was burst.' And by the December, he was mentioning a dealer who had come to his studio 'but could be made to buy nothing. The Triumph of Roger is making him uncertain what to put his money on'. He retained some grudging respect for Roger as a writer, however: 'in an atmosphere of truce', he had given Henry a copy of his first long article on Cézanne which, in the summer of 1926 at Charleston in Sussex, Roger had first written in French for 'L'Amour de l'Art', and it was almost certainly this version that Henry described as 'the best thing I read on the subject, although he quite misunderstands the question of distortion.' But of Roger's lecturing, Henry was less kind, complaining how impossible it was 'to enjoy the slides to the accompaniment of that old rectorish drivel – patronising everybody – Cézanne (whom he can *never* understand) as well as the audience. Besides many of the pictures were cut about shamelessly as they are in his book & in the French article. What would a fugue sound like with 10 bars cut off at the beginning & end?'

Henry was no more appreciative of Roger as a painter. In 1911, when Roger was instructing him in the mysteries of tempera, he would have seen some of Fry's work in progress at Durbins, his house in Surrey; but Roger reported to Clive an unenthusiastic reaction from Henry: 'I've done more to the portrait; I rather like it', he wrote, adding, 'Lamb . . . doesn't much.'14 Which portrait is not known, but another that Roger worked on later that year was of E. M. Forster, which met more with Henry's approval when he saw it at Roger's one-man exhibition in January 1912 at the Alpine Club Gallery where, Henry reported, 'I was conducted & commented to by Miss Fry [Margery, Roger's sister]. Forster's portrait seemed to me the best picture', he decided, mentioning that afterwards, he went to tea with Lytton Strachey at his club where he 'met Forster & liked him.' But Henry came to have and maintain little or no respect for Roger's art. In the autumn of 1925, Roger spend some time with Vanessa Bell and Duncan Grant at Cassis painting the Mediterranean landscape. Henry would have seen five of the results in the following May at the first London Artists' Association Exhibition where Roger's work, unusually for him, was something of a success, both critically and commercially. The paintings could hardly have found favour with Henry, though, for the next year, while spending Christmas in the South of France in the same region, avoiding the traditional English festivities which to him were always abhorrent, he described Cassis as 'a nightmare although there is no denying its very great natural charms. But even these would not be any use to me for a long time owing to the numerous reminiscences of other people's pictures; the skeletons of several dreary Rogers & other Bloomsbury wraiths dancing in company much above them keep hiding the view.' Despite all this, Henry's own slight, undistinguished, but not unpleasing results from Cassis have a relaxed spontaneity that Roger, because of an innate insensitivity to oil paint – although he had a thorough technical knowledge of the medium – and perhaps, too because of the ponderous, theoretical constructions he put upon his painting, poor Roger, invariably lost. Yet he always wanted to be appreciated as an artist and continued to paint and to exhibit. Early in 1928, Henry, in London with Pansy, his young wife-to-be, described his comic retreat from a near encounter with an avalanche of Bloomsbury:

'we were going down Bond St. & saw Roger's Exhibition boosted and beflagged at a doorway to which we returned for political reasons after a natural impulse had carried us past. It was on an upper storey & as we drew near to the shrine a certain peculiar and suspicious hum seemed to catch my ear like one of those strange warning notes that sometimes issue from beehives. "Is this a private view day?" said I to the attendant by the door: "Yes, but that's no matter: do come in" (almost pushing me in by the elbow). I was down the stairs and in the street like a streak of lightning P. following with a fou rire and describing the grin on the doorkeepers face as he watched me fly.'

What in Roger, Henry felt to be increasing pomposity, provoked in him a thoroughgoing mischievousness that on April Fool's Day, 1927, was seasonally manifest in a daring, elaborate, but apparently successful ruse when he had tickets printed announcing a 'pianoforte recital at the Wigmore Hall to be given by Henry Lamb' at the end of the month. Roger liked Henry's painting no more than Henry liked his and always thought that Henry should have been a pianist. Complimentary tickets were sent to Roger who received them appropriately on the first of April, seeming, according to Henry, to have swallowed them whole. The only clue to their spuriousness was in the subtly clever insertion of the name of the concert agency as 'Tibbs & Billet'. Henry was delighted with the success of his little practical joke – worthy of one of his older acquaintances, that arch-joker and legendary character, Horace de Vere Cole – but in admitting later that he had been 'hard put to dodge' Roger, must also have felt some slight embarrassment at its effectiveness.

Clive Bell, the other half of 'the Clive-Fry coalition' and spokesman for the gospel of 'significant form' in the visual arts, soon became as unpopular with Henry as was his partner. Always averse to aesthetic programmes, Henry sniffed suspiciously at Bell's theories on art, searchingly held them up to the light, and rejected them absolutely. As early as 1911, he was refusing to take seriously Bell's – and Fry's – adulation of Cézanne and reported being shown by Boris 'the way of utilizing in the grand style the amusing tints one gets from the sort of Cézanne pochade that we can all make'. Though Henry was himself modestly represented in the British section of the Second Post Impressionist Exhibition in 1912, he came to use the term 'Post Impressionist' as a derogatory epithet. But Clive, despite his determined francophile taste in art, seemed to recognise Henry as one of the potentially more important contemporary British artists and tried to help him in his career – at least, until 1914 – often asking to borrow pictures for several exhibitions. Unfortunately, whilst the Post Impressionist Exhibition was on, he borrowed without asking, or, at least, misunderstood Henry's instructions and took the wrong picture from the collection of Lady Ottoline Morrell in both her own and Henry's absence. From Ireland, Henry wrote furiously to Clive in London, and to Ottoline, who in all innocence was in Paris. Henry apologised to Ottoline, but never forgave Clive: 'Bell's bad faith is bad enough', he told Ottoline, complaining that his 'original description of the pictures was . . . not so vague as Bell is now trying to make out'.

Henry had another brush with Clive when in 1913, as one of the first and most active admirers of Stanley Spencer, he bought the young student's Slade School Prize painting which Clive had declined to purchase for the Contemporary Art Society: 'Bell wrote a long balls-aching letter to me which I have kept for your inspection', Henry informed Lytton Strachey, and, 'I wrote him a short ball-crushing one, which must have worked from what he said'. Henry thought Clive something of a clumsy dilettante and asked, 'Why should that creature's shadow darken my days? . . . isn't it enough that I shall probably have to see him 2 or 3 times more in my life without hearing his insignificant pretentiousness discussed with unexplained relish and to its uninstructive end by the more enlightened of my friends?' Thus he was probably as much himself to blame for his work becoming neglected by Bell and Fry, for his sustained animosity could hardly have endeared him to them and must have stretched their objectivity and good nature unreasonably.

Even when Henry was in agreement with their praise of an artist he still reacted cynically: 'I hear Duncan Grant's very famous in London', wrote Henry from Doëlan in 1911, '& Clive Bell declares him the greatest artist since Cézanne.' Henry had known Duncan at least since 1907 when they were students together in Paris. Though historically and by definition a pillar of old Bloomsbury, Duncan, in Henry's estimation, stood slightly apart from his circle and, because he was unwilling to indulge in spiteful tittle-tattle or character assassination, Henry felt able to relax in his company, more than he ever could with most of Duncan's intimates. Thus he maintained a higher opinion of Duncan, if not always of his work: after seeing the London Group Exhibition of 1927, Henry thought 'they might be called School of Confectionary' but, in picking out Duncan's pictures as 'easily the best', he still complained that his designs were neither interesting nor original. Seeming to be totally lacking in neuroses, unaggressive, with a warm and loving disposition, Duncan took an optimistic pleasure in the basic goodness of life and, whenever Henry was alone with him, he found he could respond with ease to Duncan's kindly and generous good nature. Once, when Henry was convalescing, he mentioned Duncan having called and, while giving him encouragement in his work, made him 'feel better by his angelic sweetness'. For his part, Duncan recalled Henry as 'a very strong character – very forceful and a fine draughtsman'. In 1911, he made drawings of the gentle Duncan which the sitter seemed certain were done in Fitzroy Street: looking handsome, highly sensitive and subtly sensual, he so outlived his period that it is difficult to relate this clean-shaven young man to the bearded Duncan Grant in his very old age.

Before the First War, Henry saw several permutations of 'Bloomsberries', usually in twos and threes as he preferred not to be overwhelmed by 'rather too much of a crowd'. He must often have met the famous Maynard Keynes but Henry's sole reference to him was in a request to Lytton to 'fart for me under the nose of Maynard'.

Of the less well known figures in the group, Saxon Sydney Turner was for a while a close friend who retained Henry's affection and respect, on one visit, finding him 'so absorbing' that he admitted neglecting everyone else. Turner was one of the most intelligent and talented of the circle: an exceptionally wide range of interests and a formidable intellect; an erudite scholar who wrote '100's of lines of poetry', composed music, including a whole opera, and sonatas, some of which Henry played, thinking parts of them 'extraordinarily beautiful, but so desperately unequal'; and an armchair critic who, with Henry's encouragement and much to his delight, contemplated a treatise on art counter to the theory of 'significant form' because he was, reported Henry, 'sufficiently indigne' by the aesthetics of Fry and Bell. Sadly, however, Turner was to fulfil none of his brilliant promise: by settling for a safe career and spending a lifetime with the Civil Service he was to be something of a disappointment to all his circle, participating negatively in their interminable discussions and remaining a detached, inconspicuous observer of the Bloomsbury scene. Henry too, must have been saddened by his friend's capitulation and conversion to public administration and high finance, mentioning at the time, in 1913, his arriving 'in a top hat just promoted to the Treasury & resembling an iced wall-nut [sic]'. Before Henry joined the army the following year and loosened, if not actually severed, his connections with the Bloomsberries, he made a perceptive drawing of Turner looking exactly as he must have been, ruminating, sucking his pipe, on the sidelines, noting the action from the security of his chair. During the war, perhaps Turner underwent a traumatic personality change, for when Gerald Brenan met him in the twenties he thought him 'a curious, perverse creature and one of the greatest bores I have ever known', suggesting that he might have had 'an attack of schizophrenia . . . which had killed all that was human and vital in his mind and left only the machine.'[15] Henry had reported Turner having a wretched time with sciatica & neuralgia in 1912; and he gave an enthusiastic testimonial and a surprisingly accurate predictive evaluation when he called Turner 'so supreme that one only deplores in him the lack of power to record his supremacy more obviously'. But of his psychology, Henry makes no mention and after the war, they seemed to lose touch.

Turner had been one of the class learning Russian with Henry in 1912. Another classmate was Leonard Woolf and during that year they too became quite close: 'I dined with Woolf after Russian', wrote Henry, 'he was looking beautiful after a stay on Exmoor: I am getting to like him so much . . . He has quite a different combination of qualities from anyone I have met & that made him difficult to judge at first: he is like an unfinished sketch of a great passionate character. Most of the elements seem there only without their expected *apanage* & décor (spiritual, so to say). I must hurry up & do a picture of him'. Only a fortnight later, Henry made a portrait of Woolf, reporting on 24 March that he 'came to lunch today & sat for me & I did a head in oils very like but not so good as Lytton's I think.

W. is a dear & I get more attached to him at each meeting.' For his part, Woolf merely recorded in his diary for that day – a Sunday – 'Lunch with H. Lamb who painted'; and for the Monday, even more cryptically, he noted, 'Lunch with HL.'[16] The portrait was painted in Hampstead, at the Vale of Health Hotel, on the top floor of which Henry had rented a studio after his extended stay in Brittany in the summer of 1911 and, that autumn, a luckless search for accommodation in Paris. The studio, until the late twenties, was to be Henry's main workplace in London; and during that first winter of 1911–12, he was to entertain various combinations of Bloomsberries, including Turner and Woolf, Adrian Stephen, Duncan, and Lytton Strachey, with occasional dinner parties at Jack Straw's Castle, the hotel at the top of the hill overlooking the Vale of Health.

Woolf's portrait probably remained in the studio untouched after the sole, Sunday sitting, for it seems not to have been exhibited until Henry's memorial exhibition at the Leicester Galleries in 1961. Neither does Woolf appear to have been painted by Henry again, although sometimes he sat for Duncan Grant and Vanessa Bell. Technically, and in conception, Henry's version is not unlike several of the head and shoulders studies of Lytton Strachey made at about the same time in preparation for the more familiar, enormous full-length portrait. There is too, in the El Greco-esque elongation of Woolf's head and features, a further affinity with Lytton. But in his case, Henry was simply emphasising Lytton's naturally pronounced attentuation whereas the treatment of the Woolf portrait suggests a more mannerist distortion as though not quite convincingly growing out of the actual characteristics of the sitter. Indeed, as Henry himself wrote, the painting is very like Woolf but, despite his strong, near emaciated physiognomy set in an always spare frame, it is just possible that Henry's view of Woolf might have been affected by his vision of Lytton Strachey. Though apparently unfinished, the portrait has a satisfying completeness and perhaps it was fortuitous that Henry left well alone. At times, and particularly between 1911 and 1914, he was apt to overwork his paintings; but that of Woolf, being rendered simply and directly with broad, confident strokes of warm, mostly earth colour, and having the feel of a preliminary 'laying in', remains fresh, spontaneous, yet unified. The portrait also seems informed by the artist's admiration and affection for the sitter although, even in 1912, there existed a curiously childish, comic rivalry between them.

During the first half of that year, Henry would regularly go riding – on Wimbledon Common or Richmond Park – often with Woolf. Some fifty years later, in his autobiography, Woolf recalled Henry as 'a congenitally incompetent rider';[17] and at the time, Henry described Woolf as 'rather nettled' because he fell off more than he did. However, in August, Woolf married Virginia Stephen and Henry was to see less and less of his riding companion – and competitor. After one reunion after the First War, Henry confessed that, 'Although it was a pleasure to see the ageing Woolf after so many years, I shall never feel tempted to enter his shuddery den'. Perhaps partly attributable to the responsibilities of running a publishing business with the stringency essential to the then financial precariousness of the Hogarth Press, Woolf developed an obsessive concern for the dry, meticulous details of day-to-day expenditure and its attendant economies, to an extent that many found maddening and most put down to parsimony. Such calculation and frugality would have become increasingly inconsistent with Henry's unworldly randomness and his generous sense of values. More fundamentally, Woolf's marriage was soon to be alienating.

With Virginia, Henry rarely felt at ease. She had mocked his brother Walter, chided his friend Dodd, envied Euphemia, and generally reacted unpleasantly toward Henry who, whenever he discovered some liking for her, mistrusted his feelings. When seeing Woolf frequently, he would often see Virginia as well and, though he professed to enjoy talking to her, he complained of a thin and drifting conversation and felt there still to be 'a deep méfiance'. He would have met her first soon after his arrival in London when he attended the Friday Club meetings organised by her sister Vanessa. Virginia's only reference to his art is unhelpful and possibly ambiguous since, in a letter – undated but probably of March 1906 – she mentions that 'Lamb's portrait is finished and it is bad'.[18] She sat to Vanessa, Duncan and Dodd around this time of course; she may well have sat for Henry, too; but no portrait has appeared or seems to have been exhibited, so perhaps the result may really have been 'bad'. Yet Henry's seriousness as an artist may have given him some continuing credence with Virginia and possibly helped to circumscribe a little the excessive criticism to which Walter had been subjected, though not entirely: the suspicion she aroused in Henry was clearly mutual for she described him as having 'evil goat's eyes';[19] she told Duncan that

Henry reminded her of Wyndham Lewis and asked, 'Did you feel that he was master of horrid secrets, or merely quite ordinary? I do hope other people haven't some secret about life up their sleeves, which makes me appear to them an innocent lamb. Henry Lamb (talking of lambs) always gave me that feeling. Thank God, he's now exposed.'[20] And soon after her marriage she wrote from Sussex to Leonard in London saying, 'I broke off abuse of Henry Lamb to write this.'[21] One reason – or perhaps excuse – for some of her antipathy was because she really blamed Henry for seeming to manipulate and take advantage of Lytton Strachey, who conceived such a passion for him; as well too, although she made many cruel asides regarding Lady Ottoline Morrell, she also wrote empathetically and consolingly to her about Henry's capriciousness, mentioning 'all his whims' when he upset her.[22]

Virginia seems to have been relieved when Henry went off to war for she rarely failed to comment on his re-appearance – or even threatened re-appearance – and was at great pains to warn Bloomsbury of the impending danger. When his release from military service was imminent in 1919, she informed Vanessa, 'By the way, Henry Lamb is on our tracks, without success so far, and has sent a message . . . to say that he does not mean to renew his acquaintance with any of his old friends'[23] For his part, Henry had found that even before the war, Virginia could be unnecessarily offensive. To him, she came to embody the more vitriolic, less warm aspects of the circle. After what he called 'a deadly visit' in 1913, he described it as 'all so icy' and 'left hoping never to see any of them again!'

NOTES

1 Virginia Woolf – Lytton Strachey : Boxing Day 1912; *Letters* Vol.2, p.16.
2 Virginia Woolf – Vanessa Bell : 17 Mar 1921; *Letters* Vol.2, p.131.
3 Fitzgerald *The Knox Brothers* p.76.
4 Holroyd *Lytton Strachey* Vol. 1, p.208.
5 Holroyd p.131.
6 V. Woolf *Diary* Vol.1, p.14.
7 Munnings *The Finish* p.175.
8 Virginia Woolf *Diary* Vol.1, p.14.
9 Virginia Woolf – Vanessa Bell : 14 May 1916; *Letters* Vol.2, p.96.
10 Virginia Woolf – Vanessa Bell : 31 Jan 1918; *Letters* Vol.2, p.214.

11 Virginia Woolf – Vanessa Bell : 28 Apr 1918; *Letters* Vol.2, p.235.

12 Q. Bell *Bloomsbury* p.34.

13 W. Lamb *What the Royal Academy stands for* in *Art in England* ed. Lambert, p.47.

14 Roger Fry – Clive Bell : 26 Jan 1911; *Letters* Vol.1, p.339.

15 Brenan *Personal Record* p.59.

16 Leonard Woolf *Diary* : 24 & 25 Mar 1912.

17 L. Woolf *Beginning Again* p.55.

18 Virginia Woolf – Violet Dickinson : undated/end Mar 1906; *Letters* Vol.1, p.218.

19 Virginia Woolf – Lytton Strachey : 4 Jan 1909; *Letters* Vol.1, p.378.

20 Virginia Woolf – Duncan Grant : 26 Mar 1916; *Letters* Vol.2, p.85.

21 Virginia Woolf – Leonard Woolf : 8 Apr 1913; *Letters* Vol.2, p.21.

22 Virginia Woolf – Ottoline Morrell : end Jan 1911; *Letters* Vol.1, p.451.

23 Virginia Woolf – Vanessa Bell : 27 Feb 1919; *Letters* Vol.2, p.337.

NINE

OTTOLINE

―――――

'My immense picture of Ottoline is to begin: so my respiration may
be audible in Dorset', wrote Henry facetiously from Fitzroy Street
to Lytton Strachey staying at West Lulworth in the spring of 1910,
some months after first meeting the formidable, eccentric aristocrat,
Lady Ottoline Morrell. Patron extraordinary to the English avant-
garde of the early twentieth century, Ottoline was instantly
captivated by the engagingly handsome, intelligent and talented
Henry Lamb: 'I . . . saw standing . . . a figure that seemed to come
from a vision of Blake, a pale, slim man, dressed in an old-fashioned
mustard-coloured coat, a green and yellow silk scarf round his neck,
an almost transparent face and pale golden hair', she wrote
glowingly in her somewhat muted memoirs, recalling her first
glimpse of him late in the September of 1909.[1]

Towards the end of that summer, on returning to London from
Brittany and Paris, Henry – according to Ottoline, then living with
Helen Maitland – took the studio at No.8 Fitzroy Street, formerly
used by Augustus. There, for a moment, Dorelia – possibly with
some calculation – called, leaving Ottoline outside in a taxi. The
setting was not unfamiliar, for when Augustus had occupied the
studio she had been a frequent visitor, not only as a willing model,
but also in extending her patronage to encompass more than mere
connoisseurship. As Ottoline waited, ruminating on both the real
and imagined passions of the recent past with Augustus – who had

141

soon come to feel contained and threatened by her excessive, pestiferous demands – she was suddenly, and most pleasantly, returned to the present by the appearance of Henry at the window of the taxi. At Dorelia's suggestion, he had come downstairs to invite her in.

Dorelia herself, of course, was still emotionally involved with Henry but, nonetheless, felt she could no longer ignore Ottoline's assault on the home front, despite her spouse's uncharacteristic reluctance to respond any longer. Sensing danger, Dorelia, not without some encouragement from Augustus, felt it timely to divert Ottoline's attention. While Henry was in town, she thought, how better to deploy his considerable charms than to introduce him to the voracious Lady Ottoline? But the seemingly chance, casual, innocent meeting lit a rather longer, stronger flame than Dorelia could have hoped for or imagined. Immediately Ottoline invited Henry – with Dorelia and Helen – to tea at her house nearby in Bedford Square: thus the tinder was lit; but not at once was the fire fully burning for Ottoline's next invitation was graciously declined on account of Henry's imminent departure for a longish stay in Cornwall. 'May I look forward to the pleasure of visiting you when I return?' he asked.

Exactly why he went to Cornwall then, remains a mystery. But earlier in 1909, Henry had made some lively drawings of the poets A. E. Housman and John Masefield for the publisher and author Grant Richards, who had a cottage at Cadgwith, near the Lizard. Here 'c/o Mrs Grant Richards', as he informed Ottoline, Henry stayed for a little over a month. Years later, when Richards asked if he might use one of the drawings of Housman as a frontispiece to an edition of his poetry, Henry concurred, saying that Richards was his first patron. No drawings or paintings from this stay appear to have survived, nor, incidentally, any from Henry's occasional later visits to Cornwall – apart from the fine portrait of another poet, Quiller-Couch, 'Q', done in 1938 at Fowey, that included as a background a view through a window overlooking the harbour. Quiller-Couch had long been associated with the Cornish coast: it provided the setting of his first novel; and he was often a guest of Richards who, in his *Memories of a Misspent Youth*, mentioned the cottage at Cadgwith which, because of its many distinguished visitors – including Bernard Shaw, Laurence Binyon, E. V. Lucas, and Sickert – he thought 'should be provided with a tablet', and declared, 'its neighbourhood will always be the most beautiful for me with rocks to climb, crystal water in which to swim and boats from which to fish'.[2] Henry must have been reminded of Doëlan – he had not yet been to Donegal – and could have been inspired to draw the environs; or was he, as during the previous winter in Edinburgh with the Jamiesons, limner in residence to the Richards? And why was he 'c/o *Mrs* Richards'? Certainly he seems not to have been attracted particularly to Cornwall complaining after an 'atrocious' visit in the twenties how he despised it: thus, he may merely have taken a holiday in that autumn of 1909.

Back in London, Henry spent the winter living and working in Fitzroy Street, showing his work to prospective clients at Sickert's Saturday afternoon gatherings at No.19, nearly opposite. Sickert's intention to outwit the dealers by selling the work of contemporary artists direct to patrons must have had great appeal to Henry and he seems to have given unusually enthusiastic support to the venture – at least while it remained informal: but when the Fitzroy Street painters blossomed and began exhibiting as the Camden Town Group, his involvement became no more than nominal. In June 1911, when the first group exhibition opened at the Carfax Gallery, Henry was in Doëlan, sending his work by proxy after replying with some condescension to the invitation from the organiser, Spencer Gore, that he could show any of his 'old things'. For the Second Camden Town Exhibition in December, Henry was in London but seems to have derived more pleasure from the gossip concerning his old 'friends', Wyndham Lewis, Roger Fry and Clive Bell, than from the pictures themselves. 'It appears that Pissarro threatened to leave if Lewis's pictures weren't removed but didn't dare keep his word', Henry told Ottoline, 'but the best joke is Clifton's [owner of the Carfax and not one of Henry's favourites, either] having taken the wind out of Roger's & Clive's sails. An accomplished English Cubist sensibly liked & explained by Clifton was too much for them, they were stumped & behaved like ninnies.' In the third and final Camden Town show in December 1912 Henry showed two portrait heads but was in Ireland when it opened. Thereafter, he ceased to be associated with the group which, in any case, in 1913, expanded to become the larger, longer lasting London Group, a development that could only have been alienating to him.

Before then, however, when the gatherings were casual and unofficial, Henry had been happy enough 'to put in an appearance at

Sickert's & perhaps take some work' across the road where he was to sell several of his early, important paintings including *Purple and Gold* and *Death of a Peasant*. He also enjoyed some success with modest sales of drawings that, as ever, he was apt to dismiss: when Nan Hudson, friend of Ethel Sands, student of Sickert, painter and patron, bought a drawing for £3, Henry called it 'of course the sort of purchase which I don't consider should "count" or to be even fair'. But perhaps more importantly, Sickert's Saturdays introduced him to a number of helpful and later influential patrons such as Eddie Marsh, Hugh Lane, Michael Sadler and Ethel Sands, although Henry hardly had a good word to say for any of them. Ottoline, too, would come and buy, and Henry, as if pleased with the progress of Sickert's little ploy, reported to her, 'The Fitzroy Saturdays seem to be well attended & Gore said something about keeping the place open every day in March & April.' Unrealistic as he invariably was regarding the business end of his career, Henry was not entirely oblivious to the occasional need for gaining at least a toehold on the ladder of fame. Such rare moments of truth usually came when he was away from London, particularly when he was in France and, like a cool breeze of reason, would infiltrate and disturb the continental warmth in which he luxuriated. From Marseilles, after visiting Dorelia at Martigues early in the summer of 1910, he acknowledged to Ottoline that, 'in the most material way, I suppose I must establish myself a little more securely in London before I can enjoy this apparently jewelled existence. But the prospect of living under that smokey pall again a few days hence makes me feel like some privileged trans-Stygian shade whose lease is ended & who must return to his all but perennial doom.'

London had never been one of Henry's great loves despite his so enjoying what he called, 'cultural debauches'. Concerts, especially at the Queen's Hall, were always high on the list. He went regularly to Covent Garden, being 'quite transported by an amazingly fine performance of Elektra', and succumbing to 'Gluck's Elysian strains'; with Tristan he was bored the first time, but, as he advised Ottoline, reading the libretto added enormously to the enjoyment. He was too, something of a balletomane and became, as all his circle did, a devotee of the Russian dancers, particularly of Nijinski.

Henry liked London for its galleries, mainly the permanent collections. At the National, he coveted Hogarth, Reynolds, Hals and Ruysdael; of the Italians, among his enduring favourites were Titian, Tintoretto, Veronese, and Mantegna (despite shades of Euphemia); and in later life, he greatly admired Le Seuer. At the Tate, Blake was 'perhaps the most immense, admirable & perplexing figure to comtemplate,' and, he admitted, 'I have never got rid of a certain guilty sense of not having done justice to my natural enthusiasm for him'; Le Douanier Rousseau was 'always too quaint' for his taste but Seurat's *Baignade* he thought 'a soothing picture' and one of the little studies done for it 'exquisite'. He also got 'very grand feelings from Courbet's apples' – liking it better than any other Courbet – from 'the Renoirs, the biggish late Degas of the bending down dancer showing her shoulders, the little bright Sisley by the Seine, Monet's Falaise de Fécamp – & Van Gogh's chair. You know', he wrote, 'I believe that is the solidest most prismatic thing he ever did.' At the Courtauld, he was 'overwhelmed by 6 super Cezannes & the most lovely Manets' but before getting to the Renoirs he developed 'Impressionist Indigestion'. With the private, smaller galleries he was endemically ill at ease and always mistrustful of their motives, complaining, 'how these places compete with one another in their bumptious vulgarity'. Such prejudices may well have affected his judgement of the work in some cases, particularly of contemporary art, although he was never an enthusiast for post-Post-Impressionist experiments and was habitually averse to the modern practice of naming a 'movement' to describe a stylistic tendency. On seeing the Italian Futurists' exhibition at the Sackville Galleries in March, 1912 he exploded, calling it 'a grim amusement . . . *enfin ce sont des gens foncièrement bêtes*'. Normally he could only respond to individual artists, perhaps only to particular works of art, and refused to accept notions of collective creative endeavour – at least in painting. Whereas in the public collections he could relax, contemplate, inhale and re-live the experience of old familiars, the private exhibitions left him increasingly bewildered, irritated, despairing and sometimes, even when he knew the artist and his work well, he could be appalled at the results. A show of Sickert's recent paintings in 1928, Henry described as 'scrappy, attractive & disappointing as ever – really rather depraved in its opportunism: the signatures & inscriptions scrawled across them quite demented (at the kindest interpretation) "Rd.St. A.R.A.", etc.'

Before a concert or in between his gallery going Henry would often eat at Simpson's in the Strand, 'received with suspicious servility by the waiters & some stupefaction by the More Fortunate of England', to enjoy 'innumerable plates-ful of Saddle of Mutton'. Of the *embarras de richesses* in the metropolis he was neither unaware nor unappreciative and partook of as many of the social and cultural offerings as his taste suggested and his pocket would allow; but to live for long in the centre of London became dispiriting and unhealthy: 'There is clearly something in this town which poisons me', he told Ottoline, 'for I am now in much the same state of internal discomfort as before I last went to Peppard.'

Peppard Cottage, near Henley-on-Thames, was the small, country retreat of Ottoline and her husband Philip before they uprooted themselves from London and settled for many years more spaciously at Garsington, near Oxford. In the spring of 1910, Henry made several forays to Peppard *à deux* with Ottoline, intimate 'expeditions and picnics in the beech woods', as she described them later.[3] But the more ecstatic the excursions, the more he came to detest London, and asked, 'how can I escape?', eventually announcing to Ottoline in sheer desperation early that summer, 'I am giving up my studio here & shall have no fixed abode for some time to come: without the consolation and advantage of genuine vagrancy this is a somewhat desolating predicament.' Inevitably, naturally, Ottoline both took pity and took charge. Art for art's sake was a nineteenth century notion: she believed in art for the artist's sake and, though her motives were not entirely altruistic, as fairy godmother to the talent around her, she waved her wand and Henry was installed in a makeshift studio at Peppard Cottage, taking lodgings at the Dog Inn nearby. Here, for a little over a year, when not in Paris or Brittany, Henry stayed and worked, entertaining Kennedy, Boris, Turner, Duncan, Lytton and, of course, Ottoline, herself. 'You say my friends can be yours', he told her, asking mischievously, 'yes, but are you ready to make enemies of my enemies?'

At first Henry thought he was desperately in love, calling Ottoline, 'Dear Spouse' and declaring, 'I burn to embrace you & cover all your body with mine'. They spent a few days together in Paris and, the night after she left, he confessed to her, 'I lay down in your bed, plunged my face in the pillow & breathed myself to sleep in your scents. It was like dying – and the following night an attempt to repeat it resulted in something like an unsuccessful suicide! The smell

Leonard Woolf *1912   Oil on canvas   51.2×41*
Private collection

'When will he realize what he makes us
SUFFER?
*(Lytton, Self Portrait, Ottoline) from a letter
to Lytton Strachey: 20 August 1912
Strachey Papers, British Library*

Lytton Strachey and Clive
Bell criticising works of art
*c.1910/11
Pen and ink on paper
Stone Gallery, Newcastle-upon-
Tyne*

Ottoline *c.1910   Pencil and*
watercolour on paper   47 × 30.5
Private collection

Lytton Strachey, possibly taken by Lamb,
c.1912

Lytton Strachey *c.1912/13*   *Black chalk on paper*   *29.5×22.4*
Private collection

'Ka' (Katherine Cox) *1911/12*
Black chalk on paper   34.6 × 24.4
Private collection

Carrington *c.1926/27   Pencil on*
paper   35.9 × 25.6
Private collection

Stanley Spencer *1920* *Oil on canvas* *33.3×25*
Whereabouts unknown

Dear Hay Lane, Poole *1922*
Oil on canvas
Whereabouts unknown

Football Edition *1926   Oil on canvas*
139.1 × 177.6
Private collection

The Tea Party (The Round Table) *1926   Oil on canvas   184.6 × 143.6*
Lamb is seated in the foreground with the young, gesticulating Stanley Spencer opposite him.
Private collection

of your hair was fainter and the perspective of our separation much clearer.' From Paris, he wrote later, 'I kiss your face & your body all over but your face – where your beautiful spirit is most expressed – I return to & kiss all over again.' From Doëlan he sent his 'love again & a wonderful embrace as naked as you will permit'; and weeks after, still from Doëlan, the memory of Paris lingering, he bade her 'Goodnight' and promised to kiss her 'on the lips stretching out my hands in yours till our hearts touch & I smell your hair'.

Ottoline was some years older than Henry and their affair had oedipal overtones. She admitted it was perhaps a half-maternal instinct that drew her to him; and when the relationship was in decline, he inquired ruefully, 'what if I had pushed myself 10 years earlier into this old world? do you suppose I could have pushed myself into yours?' Unusual as it was for Henry ever to be submissive, with Ottoline he confessed an egoistic desire for domination and seemed happy enough – at least initially – to succumb to her nurturing. He was never one to elicit sympathy or be dependant but after a few years in the wilderness he began to enjoy some respite from vagrancy and bohemianism and, for a while, Ottoline provided a haven, both physically and emotionally. Although he had said to her that 'apparently vagabondage is my destiny' he nevertheless, temporarily, welcomed her support and described his feelings for her as, 'possessed with an immense adoring submitting love'. As if supplying an end-of-term report, he sent her his own assessment of her protegé's progress: 'Why my good creature,' he wrote,

> 'you have only to reflect that in something like a year's time you have managed to envelope me in every possible sense with your benevolence, you have clothed me from head to foot several times over in your livery; fed, doctored, nursed, housed, studioed & beflowered me; (nay, have you not, penned, papered, inked, chalked, painted me even?); you have advertised, secretaried, wire-pulled, bargained, heckled, haggled, persuaded, bewitched, for me – in short, you have put me on such a footing that I can look all material & most moral difficulties straight in the face; I can chirp, grow fat, live where I will & paint what I like'.

Henry had a great instinct for survival and his material needs were always simple; but Ottoline's succour provided a much-needed lift to his ailing resources and soon gave some edge to his confidence as an artist. The actual work surviving from the winter of 1910–11 at Peppard was undistinguished. There were many drawings and a few

147

paintings of friends who came to stay; some paintings begun at Doëlan were painfully completed and, Henry felt, without success; and he made several tentative trials with tempera. More, it was a period of gestation that was to bear fruit in the following summer chez les Favennecs where, despite the disadvantages ensuing from the abduction of Ede, he was enabled, largely as a result of the support - and encouragement from Ottoline, to establish the rudiments of a personal style. Her intervention could hardly have been more timely for, apart from the interruptions he brought upon himself by issuing open invitations to friends who would stay longer and with greater disruption than he unwisely anticipated, he could work undisturbed. Whilst he had longed to be out of the city and whilst appreciating the calm of the countryside around Henley, some strange, masochistic whim urged him to shatter his peace. Time and again in imagining that solitude was to his taste, once it was achieved, he would begin to crave for company. Sometimes his heaven-sent isolation would seem eerie and lacking in creative stimulus to an extent that found him reversing his good intentions and seeking companionship, only to regret it almost at once. Yet in spite of the ridiculous paradox resulting from his unconscious perversity, these months at Peppard mostly gave him a chance to recharge, relax, reflect, to focus and, above all, to experiment.

Perhaps the most interesting of Henry's productions from this phase were the drawings of Ottoline herself though few could rank with the very best of his work. She was not beautiful by any conventional standards; but she was memorably striking in both appearance and personality. Henry rather erred on the subjective, overly-sympathetic side, possibly betraying an untypical hint of sentimentality and tending to flatter her pronounced features. As later with Woolf and with Lytton Strachey, he elongated her head; but, possibly because of his emotional involvement, he was apt to minimise her formidable nose and credited her mouth with a sensuality that is hardly apparent from photographs. Since most of these drawings were done during their initial, passionate encounters, his view of her seems softened by the warmth of his feelings at the time and his lovingly lyrical line reveals none of the discord that was to punctuate their relations later, nor any of the resentment that he was to feel after briefly surrendering his independence. Her proportions scarcely conformed to the classical mould but generally he drew her as though she were a day-dreaming goddess. Perhaps that was how he saw Ottoline then. Certainly, Henry was kinder than some of his contemporaries: Augustus, for example, as if venting his disgruntlement at having succumbed to her, was cruelly perceptive, interpreting her as an eccentric, domineering, pantomime dame, resulting in a dazzlingly virtuoso painting and one of the great, unforgettable images in British portraiture; Simon Bussy exaggerated her already remarkable profile to a degree bordering on caricature and mocking her extrovert, overbearing tendency to sweep all before her. Apart from the several paintings, Ottoline was also featured in fiction, notably by D. H. Lawrence, as Hermione Roddice in *Women in Love*, and by Aldous Huxley, as Priscilla Wimbush in *Crome Yellow*, pen-portraits she thought so malicious as to be unforgiveable.

As a hostess and patron Ottoline was childishly competitive, vying for the attentions of as many of the famous and up-and-coming artists and writers as her enthusiasms and her setting could accommodate, something that at first greatly irritated Henry who demanded of her, 'Must I wait for the age & fame of a Henry James before I am to be allowed the general concession of private attention?' Henry, not without some self-interest, tried to wean her from what he deemed an excess of the artistic and social whirl and suggested, 'You will have to begin to limit your numerous activities in one direction or other', asking pointedly, 'what & whom will you forfeit? The old sympathies and interests as outworn, or the new ones whose roots are not yet struck?'

To begin with, Henry would have preferred some exclusive rights to Ottoline's affection and her patronage. And as a model, she became nearly as frustratingly unavailable as Dorelia and, like his drawings of her, the summariness of those of Ottoline may be attributed to the snatched nature of the sittings which were so often confounded by her overfull diary of cultural commitments and complicated amours, leaving Henry less and less time to do justice to her dramatic physiognomy. Thinking the move to Peppard would produce more favourable conditions he admitted, 'I am jealous enough, as you may imagine & angry with myself at the reflection that I have known you so long & produced no picture of you yet. Now I promise myself a real solution of this difficulty.' But despite the improved circumstances, he found no discernible progress in his drawings and still complained after a morning's scrappy unsatisfactory business how hard it was not to see more of her and draw her more often: 'you cannot quite realize what chagrin it is to work without results', he told his elusive sitter. Then, he began finding fault with Ottoline's posing and, though saying an accusing thought had never crossed his mind, expressed a wish that had she 'sat a little more steadily' it would have been 'a greater economy of strength in the end'; and enquired solicitously, and obliquely, 'Was it not possibly the long sitting yesterday which has tired you?'

Henry called these sessions 'sittings' but when he came to paint a full-length portrait of Ottoline – as he reported to Lytton – he breathed in deeply, steadied himself, and suitably and significantly, had her standing. The portrait was begun either towards the end of January or at the beginning of February 1911. It seems not to have been exhibited and its whereabouts remain unknown. Seemingly it was never properly finished for his glorious intentions were regularly thwarted. 'Your portrait must be a sumptuous thing', he told Ottoline, 'I will have nothing less: therefore don't grudge me the hours you have stood & will spend standing for a chiffon here & a pearl there for I can't imagine you painted in an indifferently coloured work.' But she remained elusive throughout: 'When are you coming to sit?' he asked, 'The green of the dress is sinking in so much it will have to be picked up again when all the other colours are in – which is a good thing. Don't dash my hopes of finishing that picture.' Then Kennedy came to stay at Peppard and Henry reported to Ottoline that of his recent work her portrait had taken his fancy most and 'he thinks it would be almost criminal of you not to contrive to sit again'. Still she was unmoved: 'I grudge very much the 3 days you plan to spend at Fry's', he complained, 'when I might be colouring your portrait as you come fresh from its décor. You know a "week-end" here hardly means more than a couple of sittings under the best of circumstances & how am I to paint face, hand, scarf, jacket & embroidery in that time?' Ottoline's spirit was willing enough: she was, after all, a most energetic, enterprising patron; but her physical stamina was limited and, in having to stand for her portrait, she tired easily. For what was to be the last 'sitting' – over a long weekend – Junia Anrep, Boris' first 'wife', was imported from Paris to talk and read to her while she posed. Ottoline was profoundly grateful for her company since it deflected some of Henry's ill-humour arising from the painting's slow progress: 'through my constant dyspepsia', he told Lytton, 'Ottoline's portrait came to an inglorious end'; and to the sitter herself he wrote from

Doëlan, towards the end of the summer, saying that he had decided to give up all idea of finishing it.

Judging by two of the full-length pencil and watercolour studies made probably in preparation for the painting, the pose seems perfect. Ottoline was a descendant of the Hapsburgs and Henry's conception emphasises the aristocratic in her: elegant, regal, imperious – despite her wearing, in one of the drawings, simulated peasant dress à la Dodo – the demands upon her patience and staying power must have been enormous, making her reluctance to continue more understandable. Both drawings, incidentally, also seem to have caught some infection – as Henry might have said – from Augustus, especially the Dodo-esque one which, at first glance, might be mistaken for a John. Ottoline, like nearly everyone in the circle, came under the spell of Augustus and for a while affected Dorelia's distinctive style of dress, although its simplicity was quite alien to her more usually rococo taste. Again, like many of the circle – Sickert, the Bloomsberries, Augustus himself – Ottoline had a childlike fascination for dressing up. The world was a stage to her and, though her remarkable face and figure were instantly recognisable in whatever extraordinary guise she chose, she ranged from prima donna flamboyance through *fin-de-siècle* filminess to the introspective mood of a long Russian winter – on her honeymoon in Paris in 1902 she could have passed for Anna Karenina. Her wardrobe was always exceptional but became increasingly idiosyncratic and archiac-looking as the years passed and, though just acceptable in 1910, among the shorter hair and skirts and altogether simpler styles of the twenties, looked more and more conspicuous and decidedly unfashionable. Her taste in art was clearly contemporary – at least until the First World War – and she was a founder member and leading light of the Contemporary Art Society through which she extended her patronage to most of the best known and promising British artists of her day including, of course, Henry. As for her taste in interiors, it too was distinctly extrovert and the pictures she purchased for her own collection had to compete with some outrageous colour schemes for she had a passion for daring colours, a trait soon noted by Henry who ventured to suggest to her that, 'you beat us all at colour!' However, he was not always enthusiastic about her colour sense. When in 1912, she sent him a present of a cushion, he politely thanked her, pleased with the comfort but doubtful about the appearance; 'I confess it has rather an exotic look in its dusty surroundings . . . but I am getting more used to it & like the colours very much at night.'

Later on, Ottoline's passion for bright colours found an outlet in an extravagant, near-theatrical use of make-up which, as age and ill-health took their toll of her complexion, she applied ever more liberally and daringly with striking contrasts. Her hair too, she began to dye in, for then, quite shocking colours and would crown it all with the most fantastic of hats, as if life were one long garden party. But when Henry drew her first, her appearance was infinitely less artificial and less obviously eccentric and, though he was apt to flatter a little and to circumscribe the peculiarities of her features, he caught her before the hectic round of social engagements and her overactive emotional life undermined her health to a degree that she began regularly attending clinics in Lausanne and Marienbad. After 1912, Ottoline seems rarely to have been fit for any length of time yet continued to entertain large parties of her more creative contemporaries and became celebrated as an ardently conscientious hostess. Untalented, uncreative in any tangible way she nonetheless had an alert and imaginative eye for a work of art. Thus, she alleviated the frustrations of not being an artist by applying herself to being a creative collector: but for her inspired patronage public collections in Britain – and many of the artists – could only have been poorer.

Ottoline was too, an avid reader and an inveterate, obsessive concert and theatre-goer, interests she shared with Henry. But her eye for the artists was even keener than for their productions, a tendency resulting in a string of intrigues bordering on farce in one of which Henry was, for a while, a leading member of the cast. The comedy in the situation and its extreme theatricality are exemplified by a simple, ludicrous enough occasion recalled by several visitors to the Morrells when Henry and Ottoline were discovered by her husband Philip embracing fervently. A zany send-up of the episode in a radio review by Alan Bennett of *Lady Ottoline's Album*, a book of photographs with commentary published in 1976, conveys the comic absurdity of the incident:

'aficionados of Bloomsbury . . . will need no reminding that Ottoline Morrell was the chatelaine of Oxford's Garsington Manor, famed rendezvous in its sylvan setting of artists, intellectuals and anybody who WAS anybody who happened to be passing. No Nobel Prize Winner was ever turned away.

The Album kicks off with some snaps of Ottoline herself and of the hubby, Philip. Well-to-do and six foot two, Ottoline was never a beauty in the conventional sense, but no one could deny she was possessed of a certain stentorian dignity.

This young man is the painter Henry Lamb. Now Ottoline was very smitten with Henry. Mind you I think he probably led her on – but one afternoon they were in the front room of Garsington. Well I'm saying the "front room" – I mean one of the front rooms, because there were rooms and rooms and rooms. It was a very detached house. Well, they were in the front room and Ottoline was giving Henry a French kiss. Suddenly the door opens – in walks hubby Phil. Ottoline never drops a hairpin. She just wipes her mouth and says "Henry has a temperature. I was just giving him an aspirin."'[4]

From the several versions of the escapades of Ottoline – indeed, from the two volumes of her memoirs – it might just be possible to overlook the fact that she had a husband and a daughter. Philip Morrell made a modest mark in public life but privately took a very back seat, at home being heavily overshadowed by his dominating, gregarious wife. Henry thought Philip 'charming & unbelievably naif' and felt that he had 'a way of making his weaknesses appear virtuous – by excessive frankness'. Henry developed a genuine fondness for him and made at least one drawing which is, as the sitter was, likeable but unremarkable. His affection was mixed with some sympathy and, as if she were taking her husband's good nature too much for granted and being grossly overbearing, he enquired of her, 'How is it he has no friends? Obviously he would love to have them, men, I mean, so I suppose people are either too suspicious or patronizing & if neither, *you* absorb them! What a sad sacrifice.' Sometimes Philip would join Henry and Leonard Woolf riding in Richmond Park or on Hampstead Heath at a time when Henry's enthusiasm for Ottoline was beginning to wane and romance was being supplanted by realism. It was then that his sympathy became tinged with empathy and Henry began to feel increasingly sorry for Philip. 'Poor fellow', wrote Henry, not without some identification, to Ottoline, 'I do like him so very much & feel acutely for him when I see him lonely or bottling up his uneasiness', adding rather pointedly, that he 'simply works on bravely against a certain doom of mistrust & ineffectual obscurity.' Henry saw most of Philip when Ottoline was abroad, often being treated for various ailments – including suspected tuberculosis – and recuperating at expensive sanatoria. In trying to compensate and fill the vacuum left by her absences, Henry would have lunch and 'a nice little talk' with Philip; or perhaps they would dine together, afterwards gossiping away 'without noticing the time'.

Also, when Ottoline was away, Henry, who got on well with children, would take an extra-paternal interest in the welfare of her daughter, Julian. He called her Junie and would send regular bulletins to her mother, reporting that he had managed to catch a few minutes with her before bedtime and 'she looked well & was in lovely appearance & spirits'. Another time, he would have tea with her and play games to keep her amused, especially when she was ill. Once he recorded her as recovering well but looking rather pinched and grey; later, during her convalescence, he mentioned seeing her for a moment resting and thought she looked plump and lovely and melting. Julian Morrell was about five years old when she saw most of Henry but she remembered his charm and that he 'used to romp with me, send me post-cards, and organised an electric light system for my dolls house'.[5]

When he returned from the war, Henry saw little of the Morrells and wrote to Ottoline imagining Julian by then to be an unapproachable flapper. She married in the early twenties and soon after, Henry was to paint her father-in-law, Sir Paul Vinogradoff, an impressive portrait, now at Oxford, in the Old Bodleian Library.

Long before meeting Ottoline, Henry had been prone to depression; but, in his late twenties, he contracted a series of alarming psychosomatic disorders that began to interfere with his work, and impinge on his social life. At first, Ottoline was inspiring company and encouraging to his art: she was so different to any woman he had known well – she was a unique woman anyway; but gradually familiarity bred in him a kind of contempt resulting, partly from his increasing disgruntlement at seeming to have surrendered too much of his independence to a somewhat gigolo-like situation, and partly from a wider, deeper disaffection with the world in general. All his friends suffered – Boris, Kennedy, especially Lytton – but Ottoline was to bear the brunt of his moodiness, what he called his 'sulky dark disposition', a fact she recorded rather heavily in her memoirs. 'I would ask your pardon for my atrocious sulkiness', he wrote in apology following a bout of irritability, 'alas it is my fatality', and explained, 'this slavery to moods makes me try to shun connexions, hoping no one else may be involved in them'.

For a while Henry thought Ottoline could provide a cure – could *be* a cure, in fact. 'I feel sure you could tame me & that with your help I could overcome myself', he told her earnestly, exhorting her to 'illumine, cheer & warm the cold crypts of my heart!' and declaring 'my whole existence appears to be in ugly disorder just now & I pine for something more settled & productive'. Ottoline agreed and she too thought that in arranging his move to Peppard, all his 'difficulties & black apprehensions must vanish'. He promised not to be obsessed by anything morbid and decided, 'I really think that my fuss & agitation is due to inexperience & impatience at the process of 'settling down'. I will also try to be more patient & self-possessed.'

Later in life, Henry became something of an insomniac, particularly just after the First War when he confided to Ottoline that he was still relearning the art of sleeping with the greatest difficulty. Even before the war, despite Ottoline's careful ministrations, he had been liable to terrible bouts of sleeplessness, lying awake 'groaning aloud for escape all night', crushed and worried by infernal pains in the head and guts that would incapacitate him for hours the next day. Henry's digestion was always troublesome and sometimes his 'refractory belly' would combine with his 'wretched head' to put him off painting for days on end. 'I always have to destroy work done in that state', he told Ottoline. Thus the vicious circle of headaches, sickness, depression and frustration worsened during the winter of 1911–12 as he touched the depths of cynicism, felt mastered by a black humour, and was horribly irritable and uncontrolled. Periodically, he was saddened by the approach of defeat and apologised again and again for his sulky, surly behaviour, for his being disagreeable, unsympathetic, and selfish while 'whole vistas of lovely, good ideas & desires were made inadmissable and had to be stifled', as he put it to Ottoline. 'Do, do, forgive me for this 1000 1st time', he pleaded with her, 'try to attribute it as much as possible to my naughty guts', and excused himself by suggesting that, 'it was partly the repeated thwartings which excited my devils'. As the attacks increased both in number and severity, so the excuses multiplied. Henry liked to think that his collapse was chiefly physical and, when he enjoyed good health, he only wished that his happy tranquillity would come more often. He should have found peace and some relief from aches and pains during the summer at Doëlan; but still he was plagued and explained to Ottoline,

'I have just finished another morning in bed tortured by a violent & inexplicable colic: it is really getting disastrous – the amount of time I waste through this sort of disablement. I begin to think of saving my resources for a visit to some well-attested digestion cure . . . I am feeling very dejected – all the work I do in the penumbra of these attacks, either before or after, has to be obliterated & so causes more real despair than the invisible effects of idleness.'

Just when he could have enjoyed some of the benefits ensuing from Ottoline's care and attention during the previous winter, so his peevish ill-humour got the better of him; and just when he was beginning to find some success with his work, so he proceeded to dismiss praise as forcibly as he did adverse criticism. At worst, he felt a victim of dark powers whose forces were plotting his downfall, his disintegration. Feeling victimised, he blamed Ottoline, as if, in some preposterous, irrational way, she were controlling the evil cycle of events which seemed his destiny. His intelligence and insight told him otherwise, of course, but his diabolical emotions so distorted his perception that, with the inevitable and extreme contradictions arising from imbalance, he told Ottoline, 'I feel in greater need of your help now than I ever was, so do try & rescue me from this besetting dejection.'

In that summer of 1911 – ironically, despite his disorders, one of his most richly productive periods – Henry became more withdrawn than usual. As a rule, he was too alert, too interested, and too busy for much introspection; but recognising something of his problem, he admitted to Ottoline, 'it is a question of being less wrapped up in myself or my work – which are becoming more & more identical' and, he decided, 'being perpetually crouched over the slow brew of one's resources' must be 'very bad for the nerves'. He then began analysing his friendships and cried, 'Ottoline, Ottoline, I told you none of my friends have any really imaginative affection for me, they all love me lazily & after their own halting fancy.' Normally he was sociable enough – in small, informal gatherings – but, staying with Boris in Paris, he had complained how 'much camaraderie does violence to my brooding soul'. He warned Ottoline how chary he was of guidance and the more he turned inward the more he rejected advice. In a sense, she became indirectly both the cause and the object of his bad temper. As a last resort, in the February of 1912 – a notoriously low, black month in the calendar of emotions – he attended, with some misgivings and a good deal of cynicism, a Dr

Bramwell in Wimpole Street, a pioneer of psychotherapy in London.

The notion of psychiatry as an alternative medicine was then growing and becoming fashionable, at least amongst the intelligentsia. Leonard Woolf has noted the interest in Freud even before Virginia's mental breakdown, soon after their marriage in 1912;[6] and James Strachey, later to be a student of Freud and his English translator, had also become interested in the subject at about that time. Indeed, it was Lytton Strachey who passed on the doctor's name to Woolf, warning him that, 'It costs 2 guineas even to see the man!'

After his first visit, Henry still felt apprehensive and sceptical: 'it is a ludicrous business', he reported to Ottoline, and though calling it 'a mumbo-jumbo game of quackery', wondered whether it was just what his guts were pining for: 'We never know how it has pleased God to make us. Certainly I left, after the 2 guineas quarter of an hour, in a very happy frame of mind, which lasted me all evening'. And at the end of his first week of treatment, despite his continuing reservations, he admitted to Ottoline that he had had 'great relief & freedom from the belly's tyranny: but it seems strange to connect those absurd little 10 minute interviews with the improvement. I don't mind them in the least', he wrote, thinking them 'quite painless'. But the following week, the impatient patient was again in the doldrums, complaining of the vicissitudes of life and feeling very sorry for himself. Then, as he regained his strength, he recovered his spirits, attributing none of it to the therapy: 'I feel pretty sure that my nerve centres are impervious to the advances of old Bramwell', he wrote obtusely and unfairly, 'I have no confidence in him: his stupid old groovy ways only irritate me', but conceded that 'the same treatment by a better man might be effective'. And a day or so later, when he was out and about again, he confidently declared his recovery to be totally independent of Bramwell's 'spells'. At his final interview, Henry 'almost fell asleep during his mumbles' and told Bramwell there seemed little point in continuing: 'he was very nice & recommended me not to come for a week, then to write & come back for a few more séances before he left for Easter, *if I felt inclined*', stating with certainty, 'But of course I shall not: I know he has absolutely no effect on me'.

Indeed, Henry never returned.

'The journey was the perfection of comfort from Corfe to Bournemouth', wrote Henry to Lytton Strachey in July 1911, after spending the few days in England breaking his stay at Doëlan:

> 'there I had to get out but had the unexpected consolation of seeing Bertie Russell performing the nimblest pirouettes & excursions on the platform to avoid me. When the other train came in he had to wait till I chose a seat & then tried to get in somewhere between me & the dining car. Finally it was by a terrific sprint (on his heels) that he managed not to be left behind. And then I doubt if the poor creature got any dinner: I did. Imagine lemon sole & partridges & red currant jelly . . .'

Henry would probably have first met Bertrand Russell when brother Walter was at Cambridge. There Walter helped Russell in founding the Association for Adult Suffrage but, unlike 'Bertie', was never a natural crusader and felt out of his element, at the time very much doubting his ability to become a successful political propagandist. Usually so bland and tolerant, Walter was fairly critical of Russell, whose tendency to lengthy sermonising he likened to the whine of a circular saw, a description borrowed from Lytton who was himself not overfond of Bertie. Though Walter thought Bertie very friendly and charming and 'not quite such an automobile of an intellect' as he had feared, he nevertheless suggested, rather patronisingly, that he had 'nerves and one or two feelings, one of which makes now and then a timid grasp of poetry'.

Russell was none too popular with Henry either. Never a great respecter of persons, Henry responded to people mostly for their intrinsic qualities of warmth and good humour and not at all for their eminence, wealth, or even intellect. He developed a rapport that grew from a mutual interaction of some unstated, deeper, common sense of values; but with Bertie, despite his being a little in awe of the power and range of his extraordinary mind, Henry was always suspicious and, in defence, reacted to his aloofness, as he did to Virginia's iciness, with an impish irreverence. 'I don't understand the necessity Bertie evidently feels to snub me every now & then and that is what makes me more nervous with him', he complained to Ottoline following one awkward encounter. The truth was that neither Henry nor Bertie could relate to each other without prejudice since, for at least a year, they were competing for the affections of Ottoline. Bertie wrote his first love letter to her in March 1911 at a time when Henry was still professing his love. Thus Henry, though never making moral judgements, was unable to reconcile the principled, public pronouncements of the philosopher Bertrand Russell with the wayward, private passions of the man he knew as Bertie, who seriously pursued Ottoline with the ardour and tenacity that he might have brought to an intellectual problem. Henry, on the other hand, despite the extravagantly passionate tone of his letters to Ottoline, could scarcely have been convinced of the likelihood of any permanent liaison.

Of course, none of this takes account of Ottoline's unobtrusive, patient, supportive husband Philip. When Walter first met him in 1910, he thought him 'merely handsome' but told Clive Bell he had to agree with Bertie Russell that Philip obviously did his best to demonstrate how to the outside world his marriage was not 'a hopeless mésalliance'. Russell, however, was exceptionally persuasive and besieged Ottoline for many months trying desperately to prise her from Philip. Henry never went to such lengths in spite of his avowals of love. Ottoline herself claimed she had been cautious in her friendship with him: 'His smile is angelic, but the mouth has long, curving, rather thin lips', she wrote, asking, 'what do they express?' and decided that, 'the slim visionary figure must not be looked at too much'. On the surface she thought Henry 'so enchanting; but as one knew him more intimately shadows of dark storms within would sweep across that fair face . . . this twisted and interesting creature . . . seemed to have surrounded himself with an entanglement of barbed wire to prevent anyone from knowing the real self, also to protect his own self-esteem.'[7] She had been taken with him for his beauty, his talent, and his life-style: 'I had not hitherto met anyone like him', she recalled, 'and I was intensely interested and attracted by him, for he had the rare combination of intellectual activity and the experience of artistic bohemian life.'[8]

Bertie too, was active intellectually; but he was neither beautiful nor bohemian. Henry never exactly relished the prospect of meeting his rival and was usually discomfited by his formidable presence despite seeming so truculent and cavalier towards him. He bemoaned the fact that Bertie was to spend another day at Peppard while he was there but was relieved that 'it looks as if it will be too hot to punch his nose'; and afterwards complained of having to endure the manuscript of 'Bertie's new popular handbook on philosophy', read aloud by Philip, which he found 'infinitely feeble and agaçant like a file working on a thin iron-sheet. B seems to have all pedagogues' insensibility to what the uninstructed person can or wants to know', he told Lytton. In 1913, Lytton sent Henry a copy of the 'New Statesman' containing an article by Russell that reawakened Henry's anti-feelings and which he likened to 'one of those preliminary speeches in a Plato argument – only suitably salted up with amusements in modern taste. Couldn't you write the Socrates reply dishing him & his narrow little scale of results'? he asked Lytton.

For his part, Russell appears to have ignored Henry as if he never existed – at least in retrospect – for nowhere in the three volumes of his masterly succinct autobiography of an exceptionally long, rich and varied life, is there the merest mention of him. Perhaps Bertie divined correctly at the time that Henry was not really serious competition and simply dismissed him as of no importance. As well too, despite the incredible string of his academic accomplishments and the superhuman extent of his preoccupations, Russell would seem to have given no more than passing acknowledgement to the visual arts and certainly Henry's activity as a painter is unlikely to have been of much interest to him.

Henry's attitude to Ottoline regarding Russell was amazingly tactful and reticent: 'I am glad Bertie's visits still give you pleasure', he wrote politely, explaining, 'the continued absence of comment from me means not hostility but merely a wish not to interfere – as I know that to express my feelings on the subject more clearly than I have done, would be very much like impertinence.' Again, at the height of her affair with Bertie, when they were the subject of tittle-tattle between family and friends, Henry simply told her how absurd it all was and asked, 'Won't they end by making the poor man desperately in love with you? And do you expect me to sympathise with your point of view . . . when I have always looked with apprehension on the coincidence of my "chute" & B's ascendance?!! Now speak to me no more on the subject! One exquisite moment's triumph has soothed all jealousy in the case.' Why should he be jealous? Envy was never a strong emotion in him. He envied what he felt to be Augustus' spurious success as an artist; but was not envious of his skill. Certainly he resented Augustus' possession of Dorelia, although he was not normally a jealous lover. Officially, he was married to Euphemia, whom he continued to see from time to time:

she and Bloomsbury had dropped each other but she was still very much a part of the less selective, less rarefied John circle being, by 1911, heavily involved with the young, dying Innes. Henry had soon tired of Helen; Dodo was always there in spirit but was rarely available in person; and Ottoline? The ascent of Bertie encouraged a more realistic appraisal and Henry began a lengthy disengagement.

Sometimes, the lonely spaces between painting, making music, concert-going, and the pleasures of enduring friendships, were occupied with lighter-hearted flirtations and occasional, less demanding conquests, what he described as 'the pursuit of *chimériques bonheurs*'. Temporarily, his spirits would be restored by 'a copious application of the most agreeable female society in all its phases' resulting in 'a delightful state of sleepy well-lubricated tranquillity'. He expressed gratitude for the 'partial solaces of lower class society' thinking 'its effect on the organs of inspiration . . . astonishingly powerful'. Of women in general, the more one loathes them, he declared, the more one is driven to regard them with undiluted lasciviousness. Yet he always regretted his lapses. One such suburban event occurred in Hampstead with an Olive Sharples who quickly became 'the least smiling part of the landscape . . . adorning the middle distance' for, when he saw her again, he was 'thoroughly *meurtu d'ennui*' and decided 'she must be promoted without delay to the rank of corpse. Is it possible that I could once embrace that creature?' he asked, thinking, 'I must indeed have been exceedingly ill last summer.'

Ottoline rather frowned on these frivolous divertissements. After one of her large Christmas parties given for her domestics and their connectives in the schoolhouse at Peppard, he reported to Lytton that he had 'danced with all the maids but was not allowed to kiss them'. He recounted everything to Lytton, including his capricious adventures with various *fillettes*; but to Ottoline he confessed only the more serious affairs. And as their relationship assumed its more obviously oedipal character, she became an increasingly important confidante: from initially calling her 'Dear spouse', he began referring to her as 'My angelic mother' and unburdened himself about his old loves – and some of the newer ones as well.

During the autumn of 1911, he became mildly attracted to Katherine Cox. Always known as 'Ka', she 'might have been described as ugly . . . but no one ever thought it of her'.[9] She sat for Henry several times in the latter half of 1911 and the earlier part of

1912, and one spirited drawing seems remarkably evocative of the sitter judging from contemporary photographs and from Christopher Hassall's description which could almost be of the drawing itself:

> 'She carried her strong shoulders bent slightly forward, habitually in the stoop of a woman nursing a child: her light brown hair was soft and long and gathered back, and her eyes, small and grey, were short-sighted, so that she had to wear pince-nez; her nose, rather turned up, was curiously flattened at the tip, which gave it peculiar character and her full and expressive mouth would hang open a little, showing her very white teeth, when she was slowly thinking; her complexion was very smooth and clear, and her low voice made one believe that she understood everything with a profound, almost maternal comprehension.'[10]

As with Dorelia and Helen and Ottoline, Henry again had fallen for a surrogate mother, a role well suited to Ka whose own mother had died when she was young, leaving her, with her elder sister, to share the household responsibilities for some years, even more when their father died suddenly in 1905, just before she went to Cambridge. There, while she was at Newnham, she was drawn into the Bloomsbury circle who called her 'the Bear' or simply 'Bruin', a nickname Henry also thought apt. Virginia assured Vanessa that Ka was 'a broad-bottomed, sensible, maternal woman'[11] and, when Virginia had her breakdown in 1912, Ka supervised her convalescence; and earlier, in March of that year, she tended Henry, applying fomentations and dressing his wrist, after he had fallen from a horse while riding with Woolf. Henry thought her the kindest of nurses; and a friend, Frances Cornford, gave her the most beautiful of testimonials,

> 'There was not one touch of strain about her anywhere. To be with her was like sitting in a green field of clover . . . She accepted everybody without criticism, as she did the weather, and then gave out, not knowing how much she was giving.'[12]

At first, Henry found Ka charming and sympathetic and told Ottoline how much he enjoyed talking with her: she was so encouraging, kind, and unsentimental. Once, she went with him to Manchester, proving to be just the right sort of companion for an always difficult visit. He thought he might be in love and suggested to Ottoline that since he felt 'not much advanced in virtue' he would have to take Ka 'a walk in the dark among all the other happy Sunday couples' on Hampstead Heath. But, though they remained friends and she married another painter, Will Arnold-Foster, the affair lasted only a matter of months, possibly weeks: soon Henry thought her 'too good & a tiny bit slow & plodding'; and complained to Ottoline of 'a lack of responsiveness in her . . . and a lack of intelligence that seems to dwarf every subject she talks over'. Very quickly he became bored, thinking her too principled: 'give me something more organic'! he cried, declaring, 'I must see very little of her if I am to be able to behave to her with mere *ordinary kindness*'. And the more Ka saw of the Bloomsberries, the less enamoured was Henry: observing her looking after Virginia in Woolf's rooms he noted, condescendingly, how 'the poor creature seemed so pathetic & daunted by all the people she now moves among' and thought 'their quicker currents keep her dazed & desperately trying to cling onto the drift'.

During some of the time he was involved with Ka, Henry was attending Dr Bramwell, of course, and his views were overshadowed by depression; he was, too, adjusting to a more realistic relationship with Ottoline; and Ka herself was going through an emotional crisis. At Cambridge she had met Rupert Brooke who also thought he had fallen in love with her. The strikingly handsome, godlike Rupert, whom age could not weary nor the years condemn, seemed attracted to women but was possibly more attractive to men: both Lytton and James Strachey were taken with his good-looks but had been heartbroken to find themselves rejected. Afterwards, Walter reported to Lytton that James had been in the most appalling state of despair and gloom and, for a few days, had done 'nothing but brood & brood . . . The mischief is that Rupert won't come to see him, and he daren't go there anymore without some encouragement'. Lytton too, was doomed to disappointment: 'I'm sorry the pink Rupert has deserted you', wrote Henry consolingly, but revealed little regard for the object of Lytton's passion: 'I can't recall him – unless he be a certain *beau jeunne homme* I saw in the distance at the Stephen's one night, who looked repulsively polished & cheerful'. Eventually, it was Eddie Marsh who became Rupert Brooke's closest friend and his greatest patron and who, incidentally, espied Henry at one of Ottoline's *soirées*, the next day asking Rupert, 'do you know him? he was in a rough brown suit, with tails, shaped at the hips, and had a red handkerchief round his neck, but looked far more elegant and fashionable than any of the men in faultless evening dress. I'm afraid he didn't take to me much, and I'm told he has a cold and selfish nature'.[13] Marsh was given no encouragement by Henry, who also seems to have disliked Rupert on sight, happily nicknaming him 'the Cauliflower' a while before Henry, unwittingly, became the corner of an emotional triangle with Ka and Rupert.

In 1911, Henry spent an unexpectedly amiable Christmas with the John family, their first since settling at Alderney Manor, near Poole. Further westward along the Dorset coast, Lytton Strachey was staying at Churchfield House, then a tiny inn, in the village of West Lulworth; also there, in the same village or strategically nearby, was a covey of Bloomsberries and associates – including Ka and Rupert. Henry was invited to join them for the weekend though no one knows how or by whom. Certainly he was met at Wool Station by Lytton with a carriage on December 30th. On New Year's Day 1912, Henry wrote to Ottoline, describing West Lulworth as 'divinely beautiful – almost too poetical & sweet; dreamy white, graceful cliffs with fantastic caves & arches, orange-red beach & green sea. The sky like Giotto's blue. The grass seems a more lovely tender green than I have seen before & the hedges fawn & blood red against it. The air is dizzily pure & strings me up like a harp, but who has the musician's cunning?' he asked, provocatively, suggesting he may have felt some tension in the atmosphere and sensed the dramatic potential of the setting and the circumstances, although the cast was hardly to his taste – 'practically the whole of that tea party without Stephens & McCarthies', is how he described the company. He had bed and breakfast at the inn with Lytton, but lunch, tea and dinner with the others, thinking they were 'rather too much of a crowd'.

Henry decided Ka was far the nicest there and lightheartedly flirted with her, greatly to the annoyance and upset of Rupert who, over that weekend, became insanely jealous, literally to the point of breakdown. Not only did he think Henry guilty of ruining his chances with Ka but suspected Lytton of being a party to the plot. For once, though, Henry appears to have been innocent of any conscious effort to inflame the situation, tempting as he might have found it, since he would have derived some slight, perverse pleasure from his accidental involvement. Rupert was beside himself and in desperation asked Ka to marry him; but she told him she was in love with Henry, whereupon he went hysterical, unburdening himself to James Strachey and returning with him to London to see a Harley Street specialist whose advice was simply rest and sunshine. Thus

164

Rupert spent the winter and spring of 1912 recuperating, first in Nice, then Munich.

Back in London, Henry was soon utterly disenchanted with Ka. She went abroad to visit Rupert who, according to Henry, gave her a trying time in Germany. On her return, Henry was resolved to do his best to be kind to her: 'she must suffer from a loneliness she will never admit. But what am I to do?' he asked. 'Practically nothing', he told Ottoline, 'my admirable intentions . . . were swamped, crushed, annihilated as if by a lump of lead!' Much as he still thought her 'very good and even admirably brave', and much as he wanted to reciprocate her solicitude, he now found himself unable to control his impatience at her plodding slow-wittedness. 'As for Ka', he wrote, 'I would continue the chart if there were enough paper to take it lower down'.

By the summer of 1912, it was all over.

Like many of the artists and writers who were to be indebted to Ottoline, Henry, once recovered from the first fine careless rapture, adopted a defensively flippant, cynical, mocking attitude towards her as if in retaliation for her seeming to have deprived him of some of his essence. Despite both her material generosity and her generosity of spirit, Ottoline's patronage was inclusive of a powerful element of possession, almost covetousness not only of the art, but also of the artist and, as soon as he sensed a surfeit of her attention and felt overwhelmed, he became less and less respectful. This marked change of attitude was just about coincident with the appearance of Bertie as a serious contender when Henry seemed deliberately to annoy Ottoline by exploiting his own charm and good looks and consequently play upon his rival's deficiencies.

Henry would take refuge and delight in coining nicknames, calling Ottoline 'Our Lady of B.S', and referring to her house in Bedford Square as the 'Throne Hall'. In Lytton Strachey, he found a ready audience and ally. When Ottoline's daughter, in later life, discovered to her horror and disappointment the import of what Lytton himself had written about her mother behind her back she, in an act of exorcism, disposed immediately of the portraits of him by Henry that she had inherited: 'I was so disgusted with the ingratitude that Strachey showed towards my parents in his letters to friends, (while at the same time writing fulsome letters to my mother) that I

165

did not want to have portraits of Strachey in this house',[14] she wrote. Lytton, for all his remarkably gentle forbearance, wrote of Ottoline – especially to Virginia Woolf – with unusual malice. Henry never went to such cruel lengths. He could write with as sharply a satirical pen as any of Bloomsbury; but he was not as hypocritical for, as a rule, Ottoline was left in no doubt as to his honest opinion, often to her intense annoyance and she responded to many of his letters by impetuously amending them with crossings out and contradictory comments. Initially, Ottoline had brought out the passionate in Henry; but as his ardour decreased, so she provoked the playful in him and he baited her to such an extent that she would storm at him. Several times he announced absolutely that he would not be visiting again: 'I have resigned my post of eclave non favori and shall in future be seen rarely in the Throne Hall', he told Lytton, 'You need not ask me for explanations: the amputation was done without anaesthetics and I have lost enough blood'.

In an already theatrical enough situation, Henry's withdrawal, like the positively final appearance of a performer retiring, proved rather more protracted than intended, and he continued seeing Ottoline and aggravating her for some time to come. The severance was only really effected when he joined the army a year or two later. On leave in France in 1915, during a lull, he wrote to her reflectively saying how he always thought of her 'in relation to great pleasure – or great suffering'. After the war, in the late Twenties, she underwent a serious operation to her jaw that left her permanently disfigured and necessitated her wearing a scarf to cover the awful scars. Henry, older, with the detachment of maturity and the sympathy of experience sent his good wishes, having only just heard in a roundabout way of the terrible time she had had: 'I would like you to know how sorry I am', he wrote, adding, 'How well I wish you could have been left in peace after so many trials.'

NOTES

1 Morrell *Early Memoirs* p.186; Darroch *Ottoline* p.75.
2 Richards *Memories of a Misspent Youth* pp.23–4 and p.55.
3 Morrell p.194.

4 Alan Bennett *The Book Programme* 1977 (transcript); Mahood *Secret Sketchbook of a Bloomsbury Lady* p.45.
5 Mrs Julian Vinogradoff – author : 7 Sep 1977.
6 L. Woolf *Beginning Again* pp.36–7 and p.160.
7 Morrell p.186 and p.194.
8 Morrell p.194.
9 Hassall *Rupert Brooke* p.271.
10 ib.
11 Virginia Woolf – Vanessa Bell : 27 Mar 1921; *Letters* Vol.2, p.461.
12 Hassall p.222.
13 ib.
14 Mrs Julian Vinogradoff – author : 7 Sep 1977.

TEN

LYTTON STRACHEY

With the fervour of a New Year resolution, Henry began work on his largest portrait of Lytton Strachey – and his best known picture – during the first week of January, 1912. 'Do come as early as you can', he pleaded, 'I want to make an elaborate drawing to scale, so that I need only to have to paint hands & face from you.' Lytton, he found a most stimulating companion and a magnificent model who had often posed for him, the first time perhaps as early as October 1908, just before his departure to paint the 'Scotch Lady' in Edinburgh. While Henry was there, Lytton wrote, offering to sit again, an opportunity Henry promised to take up as soon as he returned to London: 'I should much like to make a more adequate presentation of you than that sketch', he replied, dismissing his first attempt but adding encouragingly, 'Your posing is exemplary.'

Lytton's motives in proposing himself were undoubtedly more amorous than artistic. He had never attempted to disguise his sexual proclivities and, several years earlier while he was at Cambridge, his interest in Henry had been aroused by Walter who would make such provocative references to his beautiful younger brother that poor Lytton could hardly fail to be intrigued. Yet when they first met – probably in 1905 at the Stephens' in Gordon Square soon after Henry's arrival in London – Lytton felt able to admire Henry only from afar: 'I didn't speak to him', he told Leonard Woolf, 'but I wanted to, because he really looked amazing, though of course very very bad.'[1]

168

By the time Henry began to make drawings of him, Lytton had long since left Cambridge; but he would often return to stay with former colleagues and friends and, noting him in that milieu, Henry found him 'a different & happier person'. Henry himself, though, was never over fond of Cambridge nor ever felt quite at home there despite the entrée Walter provided to its intellectual and social life. Certainly he was appreciative of the buildings – 'much more beautiful than anything in Oxford', he decided – and came to particularly admire King's College Chapel. He made sketches of Wren's Library at Trinity, and loved the Blake drawings. However, these consolations were not enough and he thought he still 'wasted too much time in that odious place'. He was always too impatient with 'the old dons . . . grumbling & sighing' and felt it needed 'nothing short of a *coup de foudre* to shift those people out of the ruts ages have worn'. Lytton, he considered to be much the most intelligent individual there and was pleased that his friend's intellectual eminence was undisputed by his contemporaries. But Henry was as disparaging of some of the younger company as he had been of the old: 'I find myself getting into a comatose state sitting in those infernal college rooms, smoking, & listening to those endless drifting discussions which lead nowhere', he reported to Ottoline; 'Not knowing the people well, of course, I rarely take part in them. Perhaps that is why I am more struck by their futility. Everywhere there is the same paralysing fear of the sentimental, the scrupulous evasion of the commonplace. Ugh! how I loathe those timid, well-mannered, unambitious and unlovely existences.' He was never more than an observer of the Cambridge scene but, because of relations, friends, and, above all, portrait commissions, he was to have connections with the university for the rest of his life, even though he seems to have disliked being there nearly as much as he hated returning to Manchester. Some of his prejudices against both places may have had a common basis for, years later, in 1925, when he was doing a portrait in Cambridge, and stranded with a broken car, he was reminded how it filled him 'with strong and mixed feelings – chiefly unpleasant' though admitting, 'all its wretched suburban side is . . . much accentuated by the presence of a powerful bunch of relatives' who managed to upset him.

Lytton, on the contrary, had found Cambridge exhilarating. The intellectual climate had suited him admirably and, as well as the stimulus from tutorial contact, he had been profoundly affected by the contact with his exceptional peer group whose influence was formative and enduring. Cambridge developed and shaped his ideas and by the time he left he was just beginning to find himself and be aware of his inner strengths. Externally, so far as his appearance was concerned the university had made little impression on him: his features were still weak and unremarkable, his body limp and languorous, set on spidery limbs so long, so thin, as Virginia described them, that his thigh was no thicker than her brother Thoby's arm.[2] Lytton was always thin and looked frail; but when he and Henry first became friendly, he was characterised by an ungainliness out-of-step with the fluency of his thinking. As a young man he was conspicuous by an extreme bodily awkwardness far removed from the still eccentric, yet coordinated, stylised aesthete who inhabits the vast canvas of Henry's *pièce de résistance* and it was some while after leaving Cambridge, when Lytton began mixing with an arty, more bohemian crowd, that the familiar, mature image emerged. Exciting encounters with painters and their patrons – his cousin Duncan, Henry and Augustus, and Ottoline – encouraged him to be visually more aware, to experiment sartorially, to match and integrate mind and body, and to shape the appearance by which he has become indelibly identified.

When Henry first drew him, Lytton had a thick moustache, shorter hair, and pince-nez. In one of the early drawings, he looks aloof yet full of insight, slightly pompous but benevolent, tolerant and, of course, superiorly intelligent. In the eyes is a hint of that quizzical humour which Henry responded to and so appreciated in his unique and remarkable friend; but only in the slight elongation of the already elongated head is there any real indication of the extráordinary shape of things to come. He was then Henry's most patient, long suffering sitter but progress was slow. 'He has sat for me 2 or 3 times in the mornings but I don't get on very well yet', Henry told Ottoline, 'He sits admirably & doesn't mind. But we are inclined to talk too much . . . I have not had much stirring conversations since the early days when I had just left school . . . it is good to be stirred to one's mind's depth occasionally'.

Lytton made an extended stay at Peppard during 1910 and Henry was resolved that while painting he should be completely neglected. However, despite the willingness of his model, concentration in such an intellectually stimulating atmosphere was a continual problem. 'We sigh for you to take the burden of conversation from me', wrote

Henry to Ottoline, reporting, 'I have made a few indifferent drawings & begun a painted head which the weather has not allowed to dry enough to continue. Now that he is staying a little longer, it need not be abandoned I hope.' Henry would seem to have found the perfect model in ideal circumstances. Unfortunately though, he was too easily and too often distracted by both the demands of deep discussion and his sitter's unambiguous advances. Lytton so enjoyed the quiet seclusion of the countryside around Henley and, relaxing in Ottoline's armchairs, became so covetous of her cottage that Henry described him to her as 'in a perpetual state of beatified coma . . . unable to face the prospect of ever returning to other worlds'. On the other hand, Lytton felt thwarted by the attractive but unyielding artist drawing and painting a mere arm's length away and became terribly depressed at his total lack of sexual success. Previously, at the Fitzroy Street studio, Henry had tried firmly to establish his own inclinations, to Lytton's utter chagrin, as afterwards he wrote in his diary,

'Walked through Bond St. to H. He drew me . . . I tried to embrace him. Extreme severity. "Absolutely out of the question, impossible." I was bitterly disappointed. Managed at last to discuss. "Not enraged in the least – but chiefly wanted to draw me." I said, "You knew I was a dangerous character." He said, "I hoped to draw you first."'[3]

As a result of their respective frustrations the friendship suffered, yet withstood some severe tests and latterly at Peppard, Henry found that Lytton could only avoid sulks by their keeping as much apart as possible. Few drawings and no paintings from this spell at Peppard appear to have survived and it seems unlikely that Lytton sat again while he was shorter haired and merely moustached, and probably not until Henry returned to London in the autumn of 1911.

Earlier in 1911, in the spring, while staying in Dorset, Lytton contracted mumps and for some weeks had been confined to bed in the Castle Inn at Corfe. Being able neither to shave nor get his hair cut, he emerged from his incarceration looking more like the 'eminent Edwardian' he was to become. He told his mother he resembled 'a French decadent poet – or something equally distinguished'.[4]

Lytton kept his luxuriant red-brown beard and his long hair; but Henry would not have seen the transformation until the end of September, when Lytton spent his sulkily reclusive, disastrous few days at Doëlan. 'Lytton's visit was a failure', Henry wrote, 'he simply moped and whined and funked in his room except for the days of his arrival and his departure. I was frightfully bored and glad to shunt him on to Paris'. Henry had been so thrilled at the prospect of seeing Lytton again, after being separated for most of that summer: he had thought he could turn his memories of their conversation 'to still better account . . . in retrospect' and imagined, 'I . . . shall have time to sift out what of our frothy gabble may be worth assimilating'. Soon, though, he found himself very often pining for Lytton's luxurious intelligence and was delighted at having succeeded in persuading him to come to Brittany. 'He arrived well and with armsful of gossip', reported Henry, but admitted he would get less work done: 'he is rather helpless alone so I suppose he will be much on my hands – just a shade too much for my industrious conscience probably.' The next day, he realised his mistake. Again, anticipation had proved the better part and Ottoline heard the whole awful story of the realisation: Lytton 'lost his good humour after 24 hrs . . . and having caught a minute chill or touch of indigestion with practically no symptoms . . . got into a silly panic about his health. One has simply to humour and coax him as one would an idiot and it's too much trouble', decided Henry, 'I have done what I can, however, and not given a second to myself or work since he arrived . . . Now he declares he detests everything which obviously pleased him the first day: the twist is not amusing enough to excuse its extravagance & egoism.'

For his part, Lytton was relieved to be 'shunted on to Paris' and, twenty years later, walking again through the Luxembourg Gardens, was reminded of those fateful few days at Doëlan and wrote in his diary,

> 'after a night journey through Nantes . . . my remembrance of the gardens is vivid, and my sudden excitement in them. After the discomfort, illness, and emotional failure of the Brittany week, an extraordinary sense of vitality and excitement came upon me; a spring of self-confidence gushed up; I felt able to face the world – it was delightful and astonishing.'[5]

Under the circumstances, it is hardly surprising that Henry, then, failed to appreciate the pictorial potential of Lytton's new image. Also, there must have been something ridiculously incongruous about the effete Lytton against the basic, unsophisticated Breton

172

background, for he took delight in insularly and obstinately refusing to speak French although, before leaving London, he had just delivered to the publisher his first manuscript, ironically a study of French literature. Such a complete mismatch of sitter and setting combined with the emotional tension simmering between them must have blunted the artist's perception and it was not until Henry returned to London, following an unsuccessful search for a studio in Paris in October, that he was able to see his friend – actually and metaphorically – in a new light.

In the November of 1911, Henry rented a studio at the top of the Vale Hotel in the Vale of Health on Hampstead Heath. Here, in what he called his strange new lodging in the sky, although Lytton failed to achieve his earthier ambitions with Henry, Henry created the unforgettable image with which they both have become synonymous. In the more suitable setting of his Hampstead studio, no longer beholden to Ottoline, Henry was enabled to appreciate the stylish, new look of his most patient sitter and became inspired to capture Lytton afresh by embarking on his magnum opus.

First, he had to organise some heating in the new studio. It was winter and very cold on the top floor by the time he settled in, despite the glowing compensation of a view over the Heath. Though he acknowledged a need of warmth for work, Henry was always impatient with the mundane practicalities of life and complained bitterly that his 'lungs would have to feed on smoke' until the stove was fixed; and even when it was working properly he again complained that, in order to keep the place warm, he would 'have to burn fortunes of coke'.

However, by the first week of December Lytton came to sit every day. His features, when less hirsute, were not unfamiliar but, apart from the drawings done at Peppard, Henry appears to have made no others before moving to the Vale Hotel. Here, as a result of this week of intensive study and preparation, he became so fluent at drawing Lytton that he could well have made a substantial portrait of him from memory. As it happened, much of the painting was completed, uncharacteristically, away from the model, one considerable reason for its seeming unique and strangely difficult to relate to the body of Henry's work. Throughout, too, he was very conscious of the design element of the whole, perhaps more so than usual, and, although none of the studies of Lytton's head made during this intensive week seem to have survived, from the full length,

173

outline sketches it is evident how at the start compositional concerns were paramount. Once established, the idea remained fairly constant and there seem variations only in minor adjustments of detail. At the end of that crucial week, Henry announced to Ottoline with eureka-like enthusiasm, 'I think I have a good design for his portrait', adding ominously, 'it will be very big.'

Before the 1920s, Henry made few full-length portraits: the 'Scotch Lady' in 1908; a drawing of Helen in 1909; Ottoline a year or so later, although only the sketches remain; various studies of Ede but even the largest done at Doëlan in 1911 is really seven-eighths. So, undoubtedly, the Lytton was an ambitious project; but almost at once, it was delayed. Having decided firmly on the design and the scale, Henry tried in vain all over London for canvas large enough to take his grand, expanded vision, finally imploring Boris to send some from Paris. Boris replied promptly enough but the first parcel was lost in the Christmas post; by the time the second despatch arrived Henry just managed to stretch and prime the canvas before leaving for Dorset to spend Christmas with the Johns. Then there was the diversion of New Year at West Lulworth with Ka and Rupert and company. Lytton stayed on there for a few days while Henry, back at the Vale Hotel, put brush to canvas, blocking in the composition ready for the sitter's return.

In January and February 1912, between concerts with Ottoline, riding with Woolf, Russian with Turner, therapy with Bramwell, occasional consolation with Dorelia, finishing pictures begun at Doëlan, and working on several modest portrait commissions, as well as trying to make time for the Lytton, his 'Ritratto Grandioso' as he came to call it, Henry had a very busy start to the year. But by the beginning of March, he had almost given up the struggle and Lytton was resigned to visiting him 'at decently rare intervals'. Henry had thought he might despatch the whole thing quickly, certainly by the spring; but as usual, with any major work, Henry was over-optimistic. Even with encouragement from the sympathetic Duncan who, when he saw it in progress in the studio, admired it greatly, despite Henry making another life-size, oil sketch of Lytton's head which he thought looked very good in the distance but was 'too perishable', despite all this effort and resolution, Henry admitted to being still baffled by the large portrait.

Before the end of March, Henry sprained his wrist in the accident riding with Woolf and was forced to suspend operations while convalescing, tended by his 'kindest nurses' – Ka and Lytton. Ka he had tired of quickly but his relations with Lytton continued to be as variable as the differences in both their disposition and physique. The one, neat, agile, physically active and attractive, alert, involved, volatile and impatient; the other, ungainly, unathletic, given to moping, an acute observer and commentator capable of extreme bitchiness yet with an extraordinary tolerance and compassion. The injury and Henry's consequent inability to work produced in Lytton a remarkable solicitousness for which his patient was truly grateful. Lytton dressed his arm '3 times a day most tenderly & beautifully' and 'slept 2 nights in the spare bed on the new mattress just bought at Maples . . . He is only too ready to sacrifice his time for me & makes himself indispensable', Henry informed Ottoline; 'Also he is less touchy with me now & seems really trying not to provoke scenes. We often sit up past midnight in the throes of gossip & speculation'.

Heartened by this rediscovered serenity, Henry and Lytton, at Easter, set off for Dorset again, this time to Cerne Abbas. Henry was disparaging of the place but liked the setting. 'Certainly this stretch of country is a find', he wrote,

> 'there is a long range of elaborately varied downs broken up by deep valleys with primitive villages dotted about on the streams. The views are magnificent on all sides & very vast. Cerne is a dilapidated old place close up under the hills: there is a church & remains of an old abbey: half the houses are in ruin. A lovely fresh stream runs through one of the streets: people look uninteresting & melancholy: rather uncouth & distinctly hostile to us. There are no tourists & scarcely a picture postcard to be found. The inns are slovenly & unused to visitors . . . we are about 15 miles from the sea high up among the hills: it is Thomas Hardy's country only still more rustic & less populated than the time he wrote about. Cerne used to be a flourishing place with a glove factory. Now it is crumbling away & the stones rest as they fall since no one needs them to build new houses.'

They stayed at the New Inn in the main street. Henry told Ottoline that 'Lytton is behaving on the whole . . . *well*; though his treatment & intolerance of the poor fumbling Inn people revolts me occasionally.' Quite why they chose this now picturesque village is not revealed; but what was revealed when they awoke the next morning after their arrival was a great source of mutual pleasure and amusement. Graphically – in words and with a drawing – Henry described to Ottoline the delights of the view that lay – or rather stood – before them:

> 'On a steep hill above the village is drawn a vast obscene Giant dominating the place with his club & his OBELISK. No doubt this accounts for the absence of lady visitors, but the superstition of the village council is stronger than their avarice and they keep the gentleman in beautiful outlines & have lately even put up an expensive iron railing to prevent cattle grazing over him.
>
> Imagine Lytton's hysterical delight when on Saturday morning we saw the unblushing clearness of what we had only dimly & frivolously guessed at in the dusk of Friday!'

During the weekend, Henry took advantage of being near enough to the Johns to introduce Lytton to Augustus – surprisingly they seem not to have met before. 'I think John liked him', reported Henry with some relief, 'he was certainly respectfully impressed & invited him to call upon him in town', and thought, if ever Augustus 'could understand Lytton it would be an incalculable benefit to him, but mon Dieu! how chancy it must be.' Lytton had been gravitating towards a more flamboyant image ever since growing his hair and beard the year before, and it could well have been this meeting with Augustus that inspired him to add earrings as a final touch. Several of Henry's drawings of him dated 1912, show the earrings gleaming conspicuously although Henry himself had long since discarded such appendages and successfully cast off as many of the more Augustian influences even if his art was to remain infected. Augustus may also have influenced Lytton in his drinking habits for, until then, his alcoholic intake had been modest; but over that Easter, Henry reported that they were 'both in vigorous health & were able to booze valiantly with John without subsequent disaster'.

A few weeks later, in May 1912, they set off together for the Lake District. Here again, Henry reported that Lytton was 'well & gluttonous to a degree new to him' and mentioned how he had 'acquired the surprising faculty of absorbing immense quantities of beer with impunity'; but he also wondered how long he could put up with Lytton's snoring on the sofa afterwards, and warned Ottoline 'that our holiday is scarcely rolling on as blithely as the last'. The sweetness and light and good companionship they had enjoyed under the gaze of the Giant at Cerne hardly appeared in the 'very big & grand, but grim' greyness of Cumberland. The dull weather and the heavy-

176

going terrain affected them both but, for the more delicate Lytton, proved too much and after a day's arduous struggle over mountains and bogs, he began 'taking every precaution against exhaustion'. Within a few days they were back in London.

Just before their departure for the Lake District they had had another tiff and Henry, perhaps rashly but in an attempt to mollify Lytton, had told him, 'Mon vieux, I can't imagine any intimate friendship worth anything in which "efforts of magnaminity" are not occasionally necessary on either side – and to a degree expected. And if the friendship is not to be intimate, well "some people" can keep their bloody magnaminity.' Despite these worldly-wise, good intentions, Henry would still tease and provoke his friend, even beyond Lytton's unusual patience and endurance, especially whenever they were staying together: Doëlan, the previous year, had been a disaster; Cumberland was fraught; at Lulworth, Henry had been preoccupied with Ka; only Cerne was at all serene. In between these breaks, in London, their relationship was regularly punctuated by petty differences: 'his natural power of judging character is hampered by his unwillingness to be judged', Henry explained to Ottoline when she was beginning to wonder about the mysteries of Lytton, 'and he tries to explore without first opening his own gates to the stranger. I was for more than a year mistrustful about him', he wrote consolingly. But Henry's friendship with Lytton was not competitive – far from it, given their respective talents and attitudes to life – but often it took on the character of a tennis match in which the rallies of conversation became faster and faster as the finely tuned players responded more and more daringly to each other's brilliance until the fatal moment when one outrageous remark landed in too sensitive an area to be returnable and the wounded party – usually Lytton – would retire hurt. After one such bout, Henry admitted to him, 'I was . . . an ass to think you could stand an equal return of your daily banter.'

Their next away match was later in the summer of 1912 when Henry, against all the odds, invited Lytton to Donegal. Much as he pined for solitude, he missed his friends – especially Lytton who, despite receiving no more than a Platonic reciprocity, accepted the invitation simply because he was still intrigued and emotionally involved with Henry. Henry had this recurring attraction for isolated places. When he became stifled, particularly by London, he would yearn for a more primitive existence; but the primitiveness he sought was not really to Lytton's taste, a difference that became another source of conflict. Lytton liked peace and quiet and was happy with a measure of solitude: he had been happy enough at Peppard Cottage, but he was also infinitely more conscious of his creature comforts than Henry who often appeared quite oblivious of anything other than his most rudimentary needs. Henry too, was a natural athlete and altogether more physically energetic than Lytton, whose interest in sport and outdoor activities was mostly confined to an admiration of the muscular attributes of the participants. Although Lytton thoroughly enjoyed walking, Henry, at his most perverse, would set a cracking pace suited to his wiry frame but making impossible demands on his partner's frail, willowy physique. These paradoxes, incompatibilities and aggravations were hardly the best ingredients for a happy, trouble-free time together, and Donegal proved to be the worst debacle of all.

It was in the August of 1912, after a few days together in the hotel at Middletown, near the Donegal coast, that Lytton suddenly departed, returning to England to find sanctuary in the more sympathetic, maternal arms of Ottoline. 'I didn't want you to go away and I was aghast at the rapid failure of our holiday', Henry told him:

> 'I thought we might have managed a month together. There was only one thing that enraged me seriously – the perpetual raising of the question of our relationship. I believe that it is one of the plants that are apt to wither if one keeps digging it up to look at the roots.
>
> All the other disagreements were surmountable, however acute – with the aid of a proper faith in the roots. You were an ass to doubt me . . .
>
> But what shall I think of your trumping up an over-night's imaginary tiff (which must have been fancied when you were senseless with fatigue and dyspepsia) as an excuse for your retreat . . .?'

With the letter, Henry enclosed a witty, provocative, perhaps presumptuous but probably pertinent drawing of himself, angelic yet mischievous, floating in clouds and holding ropes from which in his right hand Lytton is suspended and in his left Ottoline. The two victims commiserate sharing a cartoon balloon saying of Henry, in unison, 'When will he realize what he makes us SUFFER?' The idea that Henry was holding the strings and could manipulate his friends at will would hardly have endeared him to either, certainly not Ottoline, who had a great need to control people, most of all artists.

Evelyn Waugh *1930   Oil on canvas   74.6 × 62.3*
Private collection

Opposite top: Tea Things *1932*
Oil on canvas   46 × 56
City Art Gallery, Birmingham

Bottom: River Ebble, Wiltshire *1937*
Oil on board   50.5 × 60.3
Fitzwilliam Museum, Cambridge

Lamb and Lady Pansy on honeymoon at
Souillac in the Dordogne, August 1928

The Artist's Family *1940–43   Oil on*
plywood   114.5 × 91.5
Tate Gallery, London

Rt. Hon. Neville Chamberlain *1939*   *Oil on canvas*   *129.5×94*
National Portrait Gallery

Fatigues, Canadian Forces *1942*   *Oil on board*   *51.3×41*
City Museum, Stoke-on-Trent

Self Portrait *c.1950*   *Oil on canvas*   *51.3 × 46*   *Private collection*

Opposite top: The Artist's Wife (Pansy reading) *1933*   *Oil on canvas*   *63 × 76*
Tate Gallery, London

Bottom: Afternoon Walk *1949*   *Oil on board*   *31 × 38.6*   *Private collection*

Self Portrait *1951*   *Pencil and red chalk on paper*   *38.7 × 27.9*
National Portrait Gallery, London

Three weeks later, Henry sent Lytton another cartoon, this time unquestionably for his eyes only. The two friends naked, hairy and ape-like as if romping in the jungle, have their backs, perhaps significantly, to each other. Lytton, preoccupied with his gargantuan penis, is distracted momentarily by Henry climbing a tree and farting into his crestfallen face the message: 'Best Friends are not always Best Companions.'

Flippant as these drawings – and others sent to Lytton – undoubtedly are, they reveal with graffiti-like directness the bawdier aspects of their curious relationship. Lytton was a lifelong admirer of Voltaire, but shared with Henry, when they were closest yet at their stormiest, a distinctly Rabelaisian view of the world and farts and phalluses would feature loudly and largely in their exchanges. They also had in common woefully unruly digestions and regularly compared notes on the relative merits of various diets. 'Health mild to changeable', he reported to Lytton, 'but I just keep going with the help of Paraffin, Cascara, Calomel, Ammoniated Quinine, Gall & Opium Ointment, Seidlitz powders, & an occasional touch of Fellows Syrup', and then complained of a devil of a North East Wind that 'reeves & harries my navel'. He then questioned the advisability of Lytton continuing with what he called 'strictly homely' fare and told him it 'must be based on God knows what jumble of your own empiric notions as to what is "fortifying" or "not undermining"'; then Henry warned him,

'As to my regime you had better think twice before adopting it . . . get up at 7 a.m. glass of hot water; exercises in pyjamas . . . dress in a set of very light clothes for running; run round the Heath for ½ or ¾ hour covering about 4 miles; cold water swabbed all over with bath towel gloves; drubbing exercises (naked) . . . then dress in ordinary clothes . . . I have reduced the strength of my tea about ¼: have given up smoking & sometimes go in for chewing my food. At night I sometimes do drubbing exercises again before getting into bed . . . I mean to keep it up for a long while because I believe that the particular diseases of my giblets can't be cured in a hurry.'

Henry must have been a pioneer jogger on Hampstead Heath and yet, although he tried 'some wonderful suppositories shaped like airships' which Anrep advised and practically reduced his 'desperate state of blood & agony', Henry's 'giblet's' continued to trouble him until, early in 1915, he was forced to have an operation for 'piles'. Afterwards, when he got up for the first time, he told Lytton, 'My

179

arse felt damnably sore & the general weakness quite astonishing: the moments of démerdement are still acutely painful, I feel aged & depressed.'

Sometimes Henry would apologise to Lytton for being captivated by the spirits of 'exuberance & youth' and regretted how he was 'tempted *tout de bon* into a fart & turd-competing Rabelaisian life; but in fact, much of his indulgence in earthy riposte was a defence against his friend's advances: by teasing Lytton and playing upon his homosexuality, Henry would both intrigue him and keep him at a distance. Following one of Lytton's more acute bouts of sickness, Henry suggested, 'I have no doubt it was nothing but your infernally slack life which induced the ills: you simply must take exercise regularly – and much of it . . . don't sin again: cork up your arse and begin to ride at once; it is much the best way of getting exercise'. To arouse Lytton's interest, Henry would send him postcards of Nijinsky – 'that lovely serpent'; a photo of bluecoat boys at Christ's Hospital, adding the caption, 'Their stockings are yellow'; and a photo of the young and beautiful H.R.H. Prince George, inscribed 'With love from me & George'. He would send enticing descriptions of attractive youths: of the blooming, thirteen-year-old Prosper Favennec, he wrote from Doëlan, 'Mon dieu, he has become 100 times more beautiful, coloured like a partially ripe plum, with a surface somehow both smooth & rough, clothed in light greenish blue, washed out linen things: very silent and flirtatious.' And after Henry had had to share his bedroom with Prosper, he sent photos of him telling Lytton, 'when he got into bed in the same room where I sleep, showing all possible invitation I felt no tremor lower than my corrupt intelligence . . . the photographs are all wrong about the character and miss the charm, but they do give some idea of the superb firmness and solidity of the limbs. Surely you must have found some passages to admire?' he asked, provocatively. While staying with the John family, he described to Lytton how very hot it had been and conjured up an image, reminiscent of a Henry Tuke picture, of 'lovely naked boys running about in the woods'. And in Hampstead, having put an advertisement for male models in 'The Evening News', Henry taunted Lytton with his fantasy regarding the outcome: 'when I wake up I shall expect to see all the eminences of the heath thronged with youths of all colours and sizes waiting in attitudes of agreeable anticipation for the dread moment of selection', he told him, asking. 'Don't you wish you were going to wake up in my spare bed armed with a rosy stand to help me choose?'

Another tease that Henry practised concerned Lytton's slender chances of ever forming a permanent union with the opposite sex. Virginia Stephen, somewhile before marrying Woolf, contemplated the possibility one day – and decided firmly against it the next. Ottoline, at her most maternal, had wondered about a continuing liaison with Lytton, but other pressures and preoccupations – particularly Bertie – forced her to make a realistic appraisal of the prospect. It was the unbeautiful, unpopular Ethel Sands – ever a butt with Henry and his circle – whom he exorted Lytton to take seriously. Sometimes, facetiously, Henry would address letters to his 'old mate', hoping his wife and children were well, as though Lytton were a happily married, family man. Once, when he had received no letters from either Lytton or Dorelia for an unusually long time, he accused them of running away together: 'The only . . . reason I can imagine for the lack of news from you', he told Lytton, 'is that you have at last persuaded Dodo to elope with you, cargo and all; and are too frightened to tell me. You know you would get a bloody nose. She also has not answered my last 50 letters and I consider things look suspicious. However', he conceded, 'if you will be a man, write quickly and confess all, I should be disposed to commute your punishment to a simple bush-shaving.'

One issue that united the two friends and upon which they both stood firm concerned the erection of Epstein's controversial statue commissioned for the Oscar Wilde tomb in Paris at the Cimitière Père Lachaise – the setting of Ida John's bizarre cremation witnessed by Henry in 1907. The sculptor Jacob Epstein, for whom around 1908 Euphemia had been a conscientious model, seemed destined to be a centre of controversy. The wind of modernism was already blowing hot from the continent during that summer of 1912 and the Wilde tomb simply blew it back again for, even before the carving left his London studio in Cheyne Walk where it was seen by several other artists and collectors – including Henry, who went twice, thinking it amazingly beautiful, although he was critical of what he called 'the other Gill-like figure' – Epstein ran into trouble with the French customs who wanted to impose an extortionate duty.

Henry was never really, in any formal sense, motivated politically; neither was he particularly admiring of Epstein or his work, despite calling a drawing he had seen at Dodd's house in Blackheath, 'very wonderful'. But in any dispute involving officials, dealers or patrons he generally sided with the artist and, as soon as he learnt of Epstein's dilemma, he began rallying support – from both France and England. And since the tussle also concerned freedom of individual thought and was soon to involve questions of obscenity, Lytton too was sympathetic and became a useful ally in the campaign. Lytton then, of course, was hardly known outside his immediate circle – his first best-seller was not published until 1918 – but he knew a lot of influential people who could lend weight to the argument. Indeed 'weight' was initially the problem, as Henry delicately outlined to Lytton: 'the weight of Epstein's stones is between 30 & 40 tons (*sans compter le scrotum*) & there were two estimates of the Douane's duties first £160 & afterwards £120 which is probably more correct (*ce qui ne me parait guère fabuleux – vu qu'il n-y-a point de verge*)'. Lytton drafted a letter of petition and, with Henry, invited signatories: Charles Holroyd, Ricketts & Shannon, Aitken and Bakst were among Henry's first suggestions, the last of whom he met at lunch in a Jewish household. He also thought Fry 'wouldn't dare to refuse his wormy signature – *sous titre de la plus pure philanthropie*' and, thinking 'Wells would be excellent', asked 'How about Yeats?' A week later, somewhat disheartened, having contacted Lavery and McColl, and Shaw having indicated his willingness to sign, Henry confessed to Lytton that he was quite stumped by the Epstein business and had no idea what to do next: 'I have been hunting up Bakst industiously & . . . he is coming with me to Epstein's having already agreed to add his modest name. But how to go further? If we only had the thing in French I should like to try leaving out these bloody British officials', and complained, 'John has never been heard of in France – nor Ross.'

This last named, Robert Ross, art critic of 'The Morning Post' and Wilde's friend and literary executor, had been instrumental in commissioning the tomb. He had also written good things about Henry's work, and before becoming a critic had been in partnership with Arthur Clifton, much maligned by Henry, Director of the fashionable Carfax Gallery in St James's. Ever alert to the faintest possibility of injustice to an artist, Henry piled agony on an already fraught situation by bringing to bear all his prejudices against any entrepreneur – especially one who was also an art critic – and privately accused them both of deviousness. 'Clifton & Ross have been behaving with rare blackguard-ry', he told Lytton, claiming they had tried 'to prevent the final payments of the commission after securing a bonus of £100 for themselves'. Epstein himself averred in retrospect that the disputes were settled in his favour but, despite the letter of protest which eventually was signed by Shaw, Wells, Lavery, Bakst, and Ross, amongst others, the Douane were adamant and the duty had to be paid.

The massive tomb carved from one block of stone arrived in Paris safely enough: but when Epstein began to work on it in situ and the design was revealed properly – or improperly, it seemed – he ran into further trouble with the French authorities. 'My dear Lamb', he wrote to Henry in desperation,

> 'The conservateur of Pere Lachaise & the Prefect of the Seine have decided that the tomb is immoral in its present state & must not be exposed to the public. I must so they say cut off the sexual parts or cover it with a bronze fig leaf. Can we do anything to avoid this odiousness? Do you know anyone in Paris who might bring influence to bear on these officials?
>
> The tomb is erected in place & for the present is kept covered with a tarpaulin, the sexual parts are covered over with plaster & all this sickening business must disgust you as it does me.'[6]

Twentieth century liberals might well have felt that the Victorian English had a monopoly on nineteenth century prudery, but the official Gallic response to the Wilde tomb was every bit as antiquatedly puritanical as had been the reaction in London to the unveiling, in 1908, of Epstein's first major commission – the carved stone figures for the facade of the British Medical Association building in the Strand. A few days after Epstein's entreaty, Dodd added his concern, asking Henry,

> 'Can your pal Strachey do anything with his French people to help Epstein in the Pere La Chaise affair, the authorities wont let him put up his Wilde or rather they have plastered it all over and wont let him uncover it till he has castrated it or bronze leafed it. He poor man is in Paris without funds and does not know a great many people and is with his back to the wall.'[7]

The protest against the French authorities gathered momentum and received support from both sides of the Channel but, as Dodd put it to Lytton, with the best of intentions though not without considerable prejudice, 'To fight French officialdom with Principles

183

and so on seems a perfect hopeless affair', and dismissed it as 'an ingrained habit of the French mind'.[8]

Whether Henry played any further, practical part in the campaign is doubtful. In 1912, from August until the end of the year, he was in Donegal; and it was not until the following March he reported that Epstein had been ordered to remove the statue from the cemetery within a fortnight or else it would be disposed of. According to Epstein, to avoid any more trouble,

'Ross had a large plaque modelled and cast in bronze, and fitted to the figure, as a fig-leaf is applied. A band of artists and poets subsequently made a raid upon the monument and removed this plaque; and one evening in the Café Royal a man appeared wearing this affair suspended from his neck, and approaching me explained its significance. The monument remained covered by the tarpaulin until the outbreak of the war, when it was removed without remark.'[9]

By giving in so easily Ross had let them down. His solution was not just a weak compromise but amounted to sheer capitulation. Although the war intervened, effectively ending the affair by default, the principles at issue had been important to both Henry and Lytton and, as a result, neither could have felt any better disposed towards Ross. Endemically, Henry saw every dealer as a potential crook and every critic as conspiratorial; and even well-intentioned patrons he would seem to despise: Ross, unfortunately, was something of each. One extremely black day in December 1911, Henry took great delight in dismissing all three categories, as he described with relish to Ottoline:

'I looked in on Neville [owner of the Stafford Gallery] who had been to see me yesterday & wants pictures from me in "response to numerous demands", "first refusal", "lots of people", etc. All to no good my little man! Then at the door Mrs. Stoop swooped down from a motor as I was leaving: wanted me to take her round galleries, to come here [Vale Hotel] & see my paintings etc . . . no good, either, my pretentious little lady! Then I went to Clifton to make him ask Sadler for a photograph of my picture & met Walter Bayes there who wanted a picture from me for some representative exhibition in Venice – no good my dear dull little man!'

Henry hardly had a good word to say for any of them. Charles Aitken, then of the Whitechapel, later Director of the Tate, he thought had 'antidiluvian charms' which, after observing him at a party, he felt to be 'rather at a discount in a crowd of other fossils'; and one of his excuses for failing to present a design for the Dublin scheme of murals was because he mistrusted Hugh Lane, having decided he was 'a slippery creature'.

In view of his attitude, it is hardly surprising that he should not have had a one-man show until he was thirty-nine. He had been first vaguely tempted in the summer of 1910 by an offer from the dreaded Carfax Gallery, but refused, telling Ottoline, cynically, 'Although the thought that my work could for an instant tickle Clifton's jaded toothless palate fails to inspirit me, I don't think the idea of a show at the Carfax a bad one. I have considered it before now: there is no hurry.' Again, in 1911, he was offered an exhibition, but decided firmly against it, saying, 'No I don't want to have a show if I can help it. I think it would be bad for me at this juncture when I am feeling my way for styles: so long as I can manage it let me slip through my creditors fingers, while I can buy brushes paints and canvas there's no need of a show.' Prone as he was to erroneous self-assessment, Henry was probably right: before the summer of 1911, he was in no way prepared; those months at Doëlan were a turning point. Yet being away from London for so long in that crucial year, meant that he was somewhat dependent – and rather more than he acknowl- edged – on friends to act informally as agents, especially since he trusted none of the dealers and always resented paying commission. Usually he saw that they had only his poorer work: an inferior drawing in Ottoline's possession, he suggested she should palm off on Ross for as much as she could get, and, promising to replace it with a better one, he explained to her, 'I . . . am much more anxious for you to have good things of mine than for him (Ross) who can take pleasure exactly in what you & Philip object to in that drawing.'

Robert Ross had always been encouraging to Henry in print and through his connection with the Carfax Gallery tried to market his work; but Ross received little or no thanks for his efforts and Henry reacted with surprising aggression. Although he conceded that it was very kind of Ross to be 'respectful' about his productions, he still obstinately declared, 'I'm afraid I can't return the attitude though I suppose he is very nice.' Even if they were complimentary, Henry consistently dismissed critics with contempt; dealers he would alienate with ease; and patrons, he often seemed unafraid to enrage. Arthur Clifton was no less unpopular with him than was Ross, both of whom he attacked for their pains: 'it is good of him to exert

185

himself so', Henry admitted, superiorly, after receiving Ross's review in 'The Morning Post' of the New English Art Club Summer Exhibition ot 1911, 'and I hope indeed he will find me buyers, though I swear it was equally disquieting to learn that the buyer of the first picture was Clifton & that the writer of my praises was Ross – or at least someone who smacks his lips over Steer and Tonks, admires the drawings of Lees and is *pâmé* by those of Orpen.'

As to a one-man exhibition, Henry managed to procrastinate until the outbreak of war in 1914 and then, being abroad and on active service, he was virtually *hors de combat* as a professional artist. Ross died in 1918 and, after the war, Clifton, understandably, seems not to have had any dealings with Henry's work – at least directly with the artist, who was not to commit himself fully to a major showing until 1922.

'I wish I could write to you', Henry told Lytton, somewhat unconvincingly, following months of a regular, lengthy epistolatory exchange, 'literary people make me so self conscious when I try to make a sentence.' For Lytton literature was in his blood and the written word his medium, his instinctive, natural mode of expression. Like most of his friends at university, he came rather late to an appreciation of visual imagery. After leaving Cambridge, he became surrounded by artists and it was first through his cousin Duncan Grant, then through Henry, thence acquaintance with Boris and Augustus and Roger Fry – whom he never liked and who reciprocated his dislike by calling Lytton 'that *mauvaise langue*'[10] – and ultimately, of course, through living with Dora Carrington, that Lytton's visual sensibility was developed. Yet his concern for the visual arts remained – a little like Bertrand Russell's – more in the nature of an academic acceptance and acknowledgement of their existence and importance as an example of man's uniqueness and a manifestation of his creative spirit, rather than being based on an informed, critical enthusiasm. In fact, of painting, Lytton seems to have been, for him, relatively uncritical. A possibly unfair, certainly unkind, frivolous example of his apparent lack of visual acuity came later, in 1929, when he fell victim, or so it seemed, to a hoax perpetuated by Tom Mitford who, at an exhibition by 'Bruno Hat', a bogus expatriate German painter, appeared in a wheelchair disguised as the artist, one of whose pictures was bought by Lytton.[11]

On the other hand, Henry, throughout most of his life, was an avid reader of all kinds of literature about which he would make a perceptive and intelligently written appraisal, usually either to Ottoline or to Lytton. At Doëlan he read Plutarch, Aristotle, and re-read Plato, whose logic he thought 'piffling sophistry' although he recognised the sublimity of the 'Phaedrus' and was captivated by the exposition of the 'Ideas'. He became entangled in the labyrinths of Spinoza and, when unable to sleep, turned to Goethe, finding 'orthodox excitement' in *Wilhelm Meister*, whose 'sententious reflections' he was 'not proof against in a melting mood'. A 'glance into Walt Whitman' was good for him and he decided he was 'a grand fellow!' Boris introduced him to the Russians – Tolstoy, Gogol, Gorky, above all, Dostoievsky – which he read first in French, recommending them to friends. Of French authors, he began some Maupassant tales and 'wasted some odd minutes on *Bel Ami*, calling it 'an absurd novel . . . quite bad & infinitely squalid'; he thought Flaubert, after reading his letters, 'a gloomy companion'; Racine, he knew he must come to terms with in the end and, in the Twenties, found Rimbaud 'attractive'; Proust tempted him, and he struggled: 'In some of the *temps perdu* of a week's mouldiness', he wrote, 'I took the fatal step of opening the first Proust volume. The first 20 pages produced the direst moral & physical heavings – actual *envies de vomir*: for 3 days I was on the brink of closing him for ever, but am now beginning to want to go on and I expect I shall go through with it – which means many months of constancy so slowly do I read, & the survival of various interruptions.'

Of English writers, Webster he read hastily when younger, but reading the plays again in 1912, though still preferring *The White Devil*, *The Duchess of Malfi* reminded him 'vividly' of Ottoline, 'the tones of your voice & your rich dresses', he told her, 'particularly the last scene where she is murdered'! He was 'ravished' by a volume of Donne, and became 'absorbed' in the life of Coleridge; he read and re-read Blake with all his 'old enthusiasm'; but Gibbon he looked forward to in his mellower old age when, 'who knows but a willing spouse may then be reading him to me to soothe my idle decrepitude?' *Wuthering Heights* he read 'with the greatest astonishment & pleasure . . . in spite of that preposterous style!' When, in 1911, he thought Ottoline to be suffering from an epidemic of Hardy he asked her, 'is he really worth it? I thought most of *Jude* not above a Railway magazine level'. Arnold Bennett's 'little style' he at first found pat and vulgar, and after finishing *Clayhanger*, which exceeded his expectations but not his hopes, decided, despite some wonderful scenes, that it was 'execrable' and wanted no more of 'all that overloaded picturesqueness of expression and excess of cheerfulness'.

Besides taking a critical interest in literature generally, Henry took an encouraging and analytical interest in Lytton's writing. During the more intense years of their friendship, Lytton would send Henry draft manuscripts upon several of which, while saying he was often 'disabled from writing', he made detailed comments. Before Lytton achieved fame and was in demand as a biographer, he would write lengthy poems, one of which Henry returned with a critical commentary 'in symbolic copulating envelopes' finding himself 'smiling indulgently'. And when he began writing prose, Henry told Ottoline, 'Lytton's writing . . . has some special quality – c'est fin, très fin – the analysis very searching and then it all goes down so easily on account of that peculiarly captivating way he has of making it sound "strictly confidential". But I think he has long voyages to make to discover an individual *style*. One feels that it is inexperienced and wobbly and unequal and not subordinate enough'.

Early in 1915, while Lytton was working on the biographical essays that were to become *Eminent Victorians* and Henry was away in France, Lytton sent him a draft of 'Cardinal Manning' for which Henry thanked him a thousandfold, sending his congratulations and saying that he read it nearly all night, finishing it in the small hours of the morning. But later that year, when Lytton sent his study of his hero Voltaire, Henry, though reading it 'with a great deal of pleasure', was more critical and asked perceptively, years before Lytton's then original, witty, tongue-in-cheek style of biography became familiar to a wider public, 'Are you always going to make such ludicrous mannequins of your characters? You only hint at what is not paltry in Voltaire and the similarity of this treatment to your Manning and other quasi-satirical pieces makes me wonder if you will ever care to expose & develop what you do respect in people. Is it always going to be foibles? You never seem to miss whipping it up to an exciting pitch, but', he pointed out subjectively, almost as if he knew Lytton too well, 'I cant help noticing a nasty taste in the mouth at the end.'

Henry had always enjoyed sharing Lytton's bawdy humour and was thoroughly in tune with his irreverence, but he sensed in his friend's writing a trend towards an over-use of satire and an undue attention to the 'warts' of his subjects, criticisms that were often to be made of Lytton's technique but which also contributed to his remarkable success. Significantly perhaps, Henry's sharper comments came after they had been separated for a time by the war which effectively ended their old intimacy.

Although he was always telling Lytton that he felt overawed by literary types, Henry never seemed lost for words, either written or spoken. He was a lively and prolific correspondent but maintained a lifelong aversion to writing, complaining of the limitations of his conventional pen. His verbal ability, he would denigrate: 'the right answers do occur to me at odd moments of the day & piecemeal', he admitted, 'but it's another matter when one comes to range them together.' He was impatient with words, despite volumes of letters suggesting the opposite. 'I feel it such a godly art to speak & write properly', he declared, 'something demanding one's whole concentrated force.'

Literature was never a discernible influence on Henry's painting: rarely was he moved to illustration and hardly ever did he use literary themes as inspiration for his pictures. In his formative years, his work, though neither a conspicuous nor definable part of any movement, nevertheless showed a clear avoidance of narrative and constituted a reaction against the tenor of nineteenth century academic English art. He was never a literary painter, remaining essentially and consistently visual. He hated narrative painting, having little time for the Pre-Raphaelites; but he could still find virtues in the Madox Brown frescoes in Manchester Town Hall, familiar since childhood, and, on a return visit, thought they all had charm, whilst two or three he decided were 'very beautiful . . . a great accomplishment – unique in England . . . real frescoes done on the plaster while wet.' Most of all he despised the later Victorians, even criticising the staging of Gluck's *Orfeo* at Covent Garden because it reminded him so much of Leighton, Alma Tadema and B. W. Leader.

To assume any obvious, inevitable connection between a visual artist's fondness for literature and a direct reflection of it in his art would be simplistic. At times, Henry would have intense spells of reading but found that the more he painted the less he read books: 'the more I work the slower I work', he wrote and, as though disclaiming any literary connections, added, 'I get less and less satisfied with "faking" rapid work and more patience in the search for abstract essentials.'

Meanwhile, back in Hampstead, at the Vale Hotel studio, Lytton's portrait was still unfinished, gathering dust in the summer and autumn of 1912; and not until early in the new year, some weeks after his first extended stay in Donegal, did Henry turn to it again, making an almighty effort to complete what he called 'the Ritratto Grandioso'. Ordering a new stretcher for the giant canvas – a stronger one, presumably, since neither the size nor the design were altered – and satisfactorily completing a 'colour rehearsal sketch', in February 1913, he announced to his long suffering sitter that now he was 'only dying to leap ahead with the Magnum Bonum'.

Again, in imagining that the portrait could be completed in a few days, Henry was wildly optimistic: 'I think from Wednesday until the end of the week should be enough', he told Lytton, asking him to bring his old suit when he came to sit at the beginning of March. But by the end of March he was far less certain and told Lytton, 'the last stages of your picture must necessarily be slow and I get unduly spleenful and impatient over them'; and he admitted how very scared he had been feeling once or twice about 'the conclusion of the grandissimo. Somehow or other it is very nearly finished, though, and at times fills me with incredulous pride – that I could ever get it so far complete . . . You would scarcely believe how amazingly unified the later operations have made it look: and I don't think the choice of style was wrong!'

Lytton went to Naples during the first week of April – his presence was no longer essential although Henry complained that he was rather left in the lurch; and Henry's own departure for Donegal was imminent. Nevertheless, he pressed on, having to contend with the seasonal arrival on Hampstead Heath of the fair that traditionally set up beside the Vale of Health Hotel, just below his studio window. The cacophony seemed even louder than the previous year and Henry became convinced that the proprietor had taken the opportunity of a change of patron at the hotel 'to restore the drum & cymbals to his orchestra' since when, he claimed, 'I have had no intelligible communication from my cranium'. He also had to cope with what he called, 'the small grey villainies of Mrs Enderby, his new landlady, whose dishes, mounted up and threatened him 'with a perfect *frayeur mystique*'. Finally, Kennedy arrived for a few crucial days. However, he still promised himself an early completion, telling Lytton, 'With 3 good days of light, health & quiet, I'm certain I could finish your picture to the immortal glory of us both'. Then suddenly, at the beginning of April, he announced, 'The Grandissimo became finished at an unexpected juncture last week', explaining to Lytton, 'I had the highest possible complement of obstacles to overcome – dark & cold weather, belly in revolt, steamband, & the wasting effect of K[ennedy]. But I watched, prayed, starved & took Sanatogen and did somehow manage to wind the thing up to a sort of conclusion. I had almost decided to leave the face over until you returned: the studies were so unsatisfactory in expression. I thought I could fly back from Donegal to meet you & draw your Italicised looks: but that would have been quite out of the original gamme. Ultimately I . . . allowed myself one last try at the head on the very morning of the départ. The result was so far better than the previous versions that I took the exeat. I have hardly dared to look at it since: I know it is far below our combined deserts *mais que faire*? I ought to have painted the face just after you left but was afraid of getting it splashed during the other labours and was too cocksure of my memory and didn't reckon enough on the dissipating effect of Kennedy's idleness . . . At any rate there is a sort of completeness and a certain amusement though it looks rather clumsy & inexperienced and as I say not nearly representative of *you.*'

Whilst Henry made his way via Dorelia in Dorset to Kennedy's house in Donegal, Kennedy stayed on at the Vale Hotel studio, taking a rest after giving up painting and before starting his new profession – architecture. His first commission was supposed to be designing a house for Lytton, a project that never materialised. Kennedy's ideas came slowly and uncertainly and, after a further fortnight in Henry's studio overlooked by 'the Grandissimo' on the easel, he wrote to Lytton with a conscience but without results: 'Your silent presence in the room haunts me every time I look at it with a patient reproach and I am very grieved not to be able to send you a better account of my stewardship.'[12] In Donegal, at Cashelnagor, Henry anxiously awaited his sitter's verdict on the repainting of the portrait and suggested that Lytton, on his return from Italy, would be able to interview it and Kennedy together, though warned of what he called a 'bedimnedness' and 'a misfortune . . . in the way it has dried – rather dead & sunken: but I hear say of a temporary varnish which might buck it up for exhibition. The proper thing would be to keep it for a year before varnishing & showing it.'

After the warmth and light of a Neapolitan spring, Lytton,

191

apparently, found it difficult to adjust to the damp and smog of London and even the clearer air of Hampstead failed to illumine the portrait to his satisfaction. Almost literally, his judgement was clouded to a degree that found Henry defending himself: 'I'm not astonished that you saw a Carrière mist over my poor Grandissimo coming fresh from Mantegna', he replied, 'Some of that is a mere chemical accident & will disappear with varnish a year hence (and for that reason I'm not in a hurry to show) but there is also some that crept in quite unintentionally – from a cowardice that makes me simply crumple up to remember', and, he added ominously, 'I'd like to repaint the head someday'.

Almost exactly a year later, following an extended stay in Donegal, Henry came back to the Vale studio, 'quickly turned round the Sinfonia Gillestica' – Lytton's first name was Giles – from where it had rested, face to the wall, and, with what he called 'a heroic determination', began another series of revisions to the giant work. 'The whole thing must be completely repainted in quite another vein', he decided, 'in fact it will be a new picture' and explained at length to Lytton, 'As an elephantine sketch or bagatelle it was not done with enough fluency or verve to be worth keeping but what is there will make an excellent underground for what I mean to do – i.e. build it all up in terms of the deepest possible solidity and realism. Nothing vapoury or arty in the treatment: but frank colours & solid forms studied *au fond* & which will be bound to move (as Gluck asserted of Alcestis) "because it was founded on Nature". I believe that the proper attenuated & subtle expression of the piece will prevail the stronger for it.' Not only was Henry still dissatisfied with the head but also felt the background needed attention, telling Lytton, 'I want to remove the pot and brushes and might put – a chair with your hat which could keep that useful round form and there might be some books somewhere as you once suggested.' He never pursued the idea of books – they could have been too obvious a biographical reference – but he put Lytton's hat on the chair with, leaning against it, an umbrella, all relevant and complementary to the figure. As well he began making further studies of trees and bushes on the heath but was 'uncomfortably hurried by the pace at which the leaves were appearing and bothered by the absence of fog darkness and winter effects. If I cant see my way through the thing', he reckoned, 'I shall prefer to wait till winter'.

This was the spring of 1914. Lytton must have groaned, inwardly if not audibly. Since December 1911 he had been sitting for the 'magnum bonum', either for preparatory drawings and paintings and alternatives to the design or for work on the face and figure done directly onto the canvas: 'For all this, of course, Henry warned his model, 'a multitude of studies will be necessary and . . . I would like to make new drawings for face & hands – when you next come, and a few other things.' But it was not until the middle of summer that he managed to bag Lytton again: 'I got some canvas today', he wrote on a confirmatory postcard, 'and I hope you will come in the morning. I shall not expect you after 10.30 am.', and added, 'It would be a good thing if you could bring those brown slippers'. And only a few days later, he asked Lytton to 'bring the reading specs next time'. Until then, Lytton had been wearing *pince-nez*; but the change to spectacles was a radical change of detail, making him strikingly reminiscent of El Greco's 'Cardinal', a picture mentioned by Henry then, when he was doing a self-portrait after acquiring his own new glasses, and a not entirely coincidental connection in view of his continuing admiration for the artist.

During the final stages of the 'Grandissimo' – the absolutely final stages – Turner, and Lytton's other brother Oliver, came to read and talk to the model to ease the burden of conversation for the artist as Ottoline sometimes had done at Peppard. That summer, of course, nationally there was a general frenzy from the threat of war in Europe. More locally, apart from his having a desperate time not able to sleep, owing to the heat and the fairground proprietor's dogs and his landlady's cats, Henry had to contend with his sitter suddenly deserting him in a fit of pique. 'I'm afraid your a bloodier ass and a feebler one than I imagined', Henry told Lytton the day after, in no uncertain terms and with fulsome eloquence: 'Your affairs were brought up for consideration on two occasions yesterday: and on the first were discussed with an adequate amount of respect to their conclusion and on the second when I began to joke about them you pretend to keep up for some minutes and then slough away into a pulpish huff, nursing your bloody little scratched vanity till you were brought to the valorous point of making a written protest. Well sir, all I have got to say is that I agree and that it is "absolutely hopeless" for you to *épaucher* if you can't do it more vigorously than that. And . . . don't let yourself imagine that . . . if you can joke and rally with success and I can't, it is because you do it so much more artistically. Remember that as much indulgence can be used in receiving a joke as delivering it . . . Moreover if you're the sort of cove that can behave genially for 2 or 3 entire days with a fellow and then go off mortally offended by the unfortunate conversation of a few seconds, then I advise you to keep away for 2 or 3 entire years and I will paint your picture with an imagination sharpened by this experience; otherwise the pillory will be ready for you as usual at 10.30 tomorrow morning.'

That Lytton buried his wounded pride and obeyed the instruction seems unlikely, but Henry continued working on the portrait and it was to be another month before Lytton proposed himself, agreeing to sit again. '*Pour ne parler pas de la peinture*', replied Henry, 'The picture goes forward very slowly and I have never had a fair opportunity to do another head on it . . . I did not feel up to the *vultus ipse*, but other parts have crept on making it look alarmingly complete. It will be good to see you again and I'm sure I will do the head better for it'. He worked on it through most of August as if sensing that it must be brought to a conclusion before events overtook him. Towards the end of the month, not unexpectedly, he 'got a very military summons to go and enlist at Putney', at the same time informing Lytton that the portrait was practically finished but he just wanted to alter the colour of the floor, outline the bare boards on it, and mark the pattern on the cloth, presumably the tartan rug draped over the basket chair. Two days later, on the twenty-eighth of August 1914, it was done, just in time, for by the first week of September, Henry had volunteered for medical duties at Guy's Hospital.

Some images, intrinsically banal and individually unworthy of serious attention, become, through the multiplicities of repro-duction, as familiar and subliminal as a commercial jingle. The *Portrait of Lytton Strachey*, though reproduced many, many times, has never been subjected to mass exposure nor trivialised by the proliferations of popular culture. Yet it is a well-known picture and, being far from banal and full of import, holds the attention to such an extent that 'once seen' it would seem to be 'never forgotten', for usually the name of the sitter is remembered, sometimes that of the artist, but nearly always, like an eidetic image, the gestalt is recalled and, with a little coaxing, the details conjured up and pieced together, often vividly. Remarkably, its fame and familiarity have come almost entirely from encounters with the picture itself, from the unforgettable experience of being enveloped in its vastness, from memories of the mirth engendered by the wit implicit in the near caricature of that extraordinary figure. Wit in fine art is rare; even rarer is for the humour to be enduring: more than seventy years on, 'Lytton' continues to amuse, to raise a smile, a chuckle, if not an occasional belly-laugh. Whether it is liked or disliked, reactions to it have always been positive, one of the strongest being from Stephen Spender's father: 'The only pleasure I ever saw him get out of a modern painting was once when we went to the Tate Gallery and saw Henry Lamb's large portrait of Lytton Strachey', recalled Spender,

> 'My father stared at this in silence for a long time. Then hatred for the painter suddenly clicked in his mind with hatred of the most irreverent and iconoclastic of modern essayists, as he said in a loud voice: "Well, Lytton Strachey deserves it! He deserves it!" And he strode away, meditating on the poetic justice which had ordained Henry Lamb to place Lytton Strachey in the inferno of those rooms which my father labelled "the lunatic asylum" in the Tate.'13

The portrait is the largest Henry painted and he spent longer on it than any other picture – at least, the time spent was spread over a longer period, since after the first war, he again made some small adjustments – partly explaining its uniqueness, both to him and to portraiture in general. The composition is highly original, or was, thinking of some recent portrait painting in Britain – Sutherland, Hockney, Organ, for example – which perhaps makes the unusual balance between figure and ground, and the telling, cunning use of space seem a little more commonplace. However, it still works and remains enigmatic; and for Henry, the whole conception was one of his most imaginative and the design a daring departure to which he never returned. The canvas measures eight feet in height by nearly six, barely a quarter of which is occupied by the sinewy, sprawling figure. The artist was frequently overawed by the sheer labour of covering and controlling the enormous area but it is the dis-proportionate use of the background – in academic theory – that contributes to the incredible likeness to Lytton and, more remark-ably, mysteriously evokes his milieu. Seeming to border on caricature, the relationship between the subtly emphasised attenu-

195

ation of the figure set against the exaggerated expanse of window is in itself a visual joke; but the whole, having been treated with such deadpan seriousness despite what William Gaunt called 'a certain artificiality of style',[14] still convinces. David Garnett likened the figure to 'an etiolated plant soon to die for lack of fresh air, light and the watering-can',[15] and any doubt that Lytton could have looked other than exactly like this is overruled by the many who knew him and have attested to the striking resemblance, so much so that often descriptions of the sitter seem informed and sharpened by memories of the portrait and the perceptions of the artist. When, in 1923, Lytton attended a writer's conference at Pontigny, André Maurois recalled how the French contingent of *penseurs* were immediately startled by his resemblance to the Henry Lamb portrait, which up till then most of them had regarded as simply a caricature.[16]

The portrait is also an interesting fusion of art and life. The shaping of Lytton's appearance was in itself something akin to the creation of a work of art though its realisation took a little less time than that of the painting. He was neither extrovert nor dashing but in growing his hair and beard, and sporting an earring, a broad-brimmed hat and a cloak, he had veered temporarily towards the flamboyance of Augustus: the influence is evident in the portrait, but it is assimilated, re-interpreted and Lytton appears essentially himself, much as he was to be for the rest of his life. He was thirty-one when the great work was begun but the artist can be forgiven for making him look older. When Lytton left Trinity, it 'marked, so he felt, the end of his youth, and the premature onset of a dull and dusty middle age'.[17] Ottoline too, described him, even as a young man, as 'looking indeed far older than he is . . . a combination of frivolity, love of indecency, mixed up with rigid intellectual integrity'.[18]

Lytton was extremely complex – there was no sure way of responding to and coping with the contradictions in his make-up: Henry tried, but always lost patience; at first, Ottoline was a sympathetic, surrogate mother but decided later that,

> 'The steeds that draw the chariot of his life seem to be curiously ill-matched, one so dignified and serious, and so high-stepping, and of the English breed, so well versed in the manners and traditions of the last four centuries; the other so feminine, nervous, hysterical, shying at imaginary obstacles, delighting in being patted and flattered and fed with sugar.'[19]

His most intimidating aspect was being prone to long, apparently inexplicable silences – a habit not unknown with Virginia – at least those who knew Lytton less well would find them intimidating, and even Ottoline admitted to feeling shy with him,

> 'for he said so little and he seemed to live far away in an atmosphere of rarefied thought. His voice so small and faint, but with definite accentuations and stresses of tone, giving a sense of certainty and distinction, appeared to come from very far away, for his delicate body was raised on legs so immensely long that they seemed endless, and his fingers equally long, like antennae.'[20]

Even when interviewed for Cambridge, he was recalled twenty years later as, 'very silent, but uncannily quick and comprehending.'[21] And Diana Mosley, who would not have met him until the late Twenties, remembered Lytton as 'not quite easy as a guest and I think he rather wished he had stayed at home . . . He had a way of retreating behind spectacles and beard which was rather alarming; in this mood he could not be reached.'[22] Osbert Sitwell thought he had an 'air of someone pleasantly awaking from a trance . . . Certainly he was both one of the most typical and one of the rarest persons in this assembly [of Bloomsbury]. His individual combination of kindness, selfishness, cleverness, shyness and sociability made him peculiarly unlike anyone else . . . I remember comparing him to a benevolent but rather irritable pelican.'[23] Sitwell admired Lytton's work but his appearance and personality he found even more admirable and intriguing: 'his emergence into any scene, whether street or drawing-room, lifted it to a new plane, investing it with a kind of caricatural Victorian interest', he wrote, and went on to sketch a verbal cameo that could almost be the portrait itself:

> 'the lanky, bearded figure, with his high, incisive gift of few words; for in company he spoke little and to the point – though sometimes to a point that only he saw . . . Usually . . . he was kind, and somewhat silent. I have seen him sit with a kind of eager silentless and sense of waiting . . . But, to show him as he looked in his life, and as he is most certainly to be seen, too, in the portrait of him by Henry Lamb . . . I choose . . . to make him pose for an instant . . . a figure more striking than any . . . alive, able to move, to turn and look: the lean, elongated form of Lytton Strachey, hieratic, a pagod as plainly belonging as did the effigies to a creation of its own. Well muffled, as usual, against the wind . . . His head was crowned with a wide-brimmed brown hat. He had by nature a narrow, long-shaped face, and his narrow, rather long beard,

which extended it in similar fashion and showed itself to be chestnut-coloured in the sun, exaggerated this characteristic . . . Lytton's long brown tweed coat seemed . . . typical of a literary man, and since he held his arms in an inert way, the effect was . . . of a cloak. Humour and wit were very strongly marked in the quizzical expression of his face, and also, I think a kind of genuine diffidence as well as a certain despair and, always, a new surprise at man's follies . . . Though of a type so rare, and therefore unnational, as well as deliberately un-English in style, he yet could have belonged to no other country, and was pre-eminently Anglo-Saxon . . . His long nose, the colour of his face and beard, his rather arched angular eyebrows, and his brown eyes, the sense of a cultured, scholarly man that permeated his entire outward aspect, all these characteristics and qualities, though highly individual, essentially English. It is important to look the part one plays, and he gave consummately the impression of a man of letters, perhaps rather of one in the immediate past: a Victorian figure of eminence, possibly. Yet, examining him carefully, it became clear too that he would have been at ease in the England of an earlier age, when his beard might have been tinted a carnation hue. It was an Elizabethan as well as a Victorian head that peered aloft.'[24]

In reminiscing some twenty-five years after the encounter, Sitwell's observations were clearly informed by hindsight, by knowledge of Lytton's literary success, and most of all, with memories of the portrait, details of which have subtly infiltrated his prose.

In others, Lytton often aroused strong feelings of dislike, notably and ironically, in Edith Sitwell who, unlike her brother, saw in him all the faults of Bloomsbury, 'the home of an echoing silence', as she called the group:

'Some of the more silent intellectuals, crouching under the umbrella-like deceptive weight of their foreheads, lived their toadstool lives sheltered by these . . . One intellectual lighthouse . . . was immensely tall, and if he had not been so inert one would have supposed him to have been involved in a death-struggle with a lamp-post. They seemed to be inextricably entwined. From the top of this edifice from time to time a few dim sparks emerged, but they did not cast much light on anything.'

And in a more personal vein, she continued,

'Lytton Strachey was a major Bloomsbury idol . . . I knew him but slightly, and don't like his work . . .

Visually, he made the impression on me of having strayed from the companionship of the kindly demons in the Russian ballet "Children's Tales", who existed only in profile, and had long beards of gardener's bass – (actually I think he saw the beings of whom he wrote, with the exception of Queen Victoria, in profile only, never full face). He seemed to have been cut out of very thin cardboard. He wasted no words in conversation.'[25]

Frank Swinnerton called him 'a bookish dilettante' and 'a male bluestocking';[26] and to Dmitri Mirsky, he was the 'author of "artistic" biographies' whose 'method' is simply the irony of an aesthete looking down with amusement from his highbrow eminence on the marionettes of history . . . full of respect for poets and dreamers, but scornfully condescending to all practical activity, especially political.'[27] Vita Sackville-West hated him, thinking the drooping Lytton must have done a great deal of harm to the Bloomsbury cause.[28] Her husband, Harold Nicholson, was no less forthright, as Michael Holroyd has recorded with some amusement:

> 'Lytton, he told me, had resembled a bearded and bitchy old woman, rude rather than witty in society, injecting with his unnaturally treble voice jets of stinging poison into otherwise convivial gatherings.'[29]

Most of the less kind remarks seem to have been made at a slight distance by those who knew him, but not well, the one exception being the ubiquitous Bertie: Russell retained an aversion to Lytton in particular and to homosexuality in general and, in assessing his one time friend, he dismisses both:

> 'Lytton was always eccentric and became gradually more so . . . He dressed very oddly . . . He talked always in a squeaky voice which sometimes contrasted ludicrously with the matter of what he was saying . . . he liked to appear lordly in his attitude towards human affairs.'[30]

But his real friends saw through and penetrated what William Rothenstein called 'some defensive armour to cover up his extreme sensitiveness'.[31] David Garnett counted Lytton amongst his 'Great Friends', saying he 'was very gay, enjoyed what he saw, and was a delightful companion, eager to explore'. He had first been struck by 'his gentleness and his hospitality . . . I could see that he was very much alive and very responsive' although Garnett stayed 'warily conscious of his capacity for boredom'.[32] Desmond McCarthy thought Lytton's 'friendships were more like loves' and that,

> 'His influence, especially upon his younger contemporaries, was to fix their attentions on emotions and relations between human beings. He was a master of what may be called psychological gossip, the kind which treats friends as diagrams of the human species and ranges over the past

and fiction as well as history, in search of whatever illustrates this or that side of human nature.'[33]

Virginia Woolf called 'The Strache . . . the essence of culture . . . exotic, extreme in every way';[34] And Stephen Spender considered him to be 'certainly the most astonishing of the Bloomsbury group' who,

'like the last kick of an enlightened aristocratic tradition . . . made moderate but distinct claims on society . . . Strachey . . . combined strikingly their gaiety with their intermittent chilliness . . . Often he would gossip brilliantly and maliciously. At times there was something insidious about his giggling manner; at times he would sit in his chair without saying a word.'[35]

Frances Partridge, who perhaps came to know him as well as anyone, described him as,

'by no means ugly, as some have implied. Tall, willowy, and with very long and beautiful hands, he displayed a peculiar elegance in the way he used to walk, or rather stalk, across the lawn under a white sunshade lined with green, and fold his legs away into a deck chair. His velvety brown eyes were full of expression.'[36]

Recollections of Lytton are generally of him seated. The chair in the portrait was originally Ottoline's and she remembered seeing him 'sitting in a long basket-chair by the . . . the gas-fire leaning forward . . . holding out his long, thin hands to warm.'[37]

Several artists besides Henry, and all of them friends, made portraits of Lytton. An early example by his brother-in-law, Simon Bussy, shows him in *pince-nez*, with moustache, wearing an overcoat, writing at a folding table under which tucked awkwardly are his long legs, hinting at his characteristic entanglements with furniture and suggesting something of the humour of Henry's version. For Vanessa Bell, Duncan Grant and Roger Fry, Lytton was a vehicle for post-impressionist improvisation, in each case the likeness being subordinate to expressionist technique and the colour embodying the 'significance of the form'. To Dora Carrington, he was a frequent but informal and incidental sitter, usually reading against a background of books, and though his eyes are rarely in detail, her many beautiful, sensitive drawings and paintings reveal her affection and adoration and emphasise his wisdom and benignity. Carrington's vision of Lytton is made manifest collectively, each study building on the next, unlike the comprehensiveness of Henry's portrait which alone seems to say all. Perhaps its closest rival in this respect is a late, last bust by the brilliant, neglected sculptor and poet, Stephen Tomlin, himself a sitter of Henry's in the early thirties. In his unpublished study of Tomlin, Oliver Garnett has called the *Head of Lytton Strachey*, 'his most remarkable achievement. For not only is it an extremely good likeness, but it also captures more of his character than any other portrait or photograph I have ever seen.'[38] Tomlin also did a very fine, almost complementary head of Virginia Woolf conveying what Garnett calls her 'desperate energy' which, together with the 'self-effacing nobility' of Lytton, comprise two of the most potent images of Bloomsbury.

There is no denying genius in the work of Tomlin, particularly the head of Lytton, and any comparison between two- and three-dimensional imagery is unequal; but the sculptor was observing the mature, successful Strachey whereas Henry's sitter was virtually unknown. Despite the agonising prolongation, his painting was realised in all its essentials by 1914, some years before Lytton had become a celebrity. Apart from symbolising the height of an unusual, affectionate, yet abrasive friendship, Henry's portrait looks back to Lytton's early uncertainties, shows him exactly as he was in the immediate pre-war period and, incredibly, anticipates the career to come. Embodied in that image, in the contrivances of the design that now seem unalterably perfect, in the curious relationship between the high camp of the languishing figure set against the near impossible expanse of window through which, wilting as if in sympathy with the sitter, is seen such a calculated, stylised Hampstead Heath, in effect close to the painted flats of a stage set, embodied in all that artifice and theatricality is more than a mere likeness and the interpretation of a moment, a day, even a decade. For the whole embodies a whole life and, self-conscious as the affectation of style might seem, Henry put more than he knew – in any conventional sense – into the making of 'Lytton': like an exhaustive biography, the picture contains the whole world of Lytton Strachey, perhaps explaining further its satisfying completeness, its definitiveness. It remains the unique summation of a person, a period, and a cultural milieu.

It is surprising too, how closely it corresponds to William Plomer's memoir of him towards the end of his life:

'Strachey was then still in his forties, but his beard and spectacles made him look older . . . [seeming] to create a certain distance between himself and others. About Strachey's eyelids, as he looked out through the windows of his spectacles over the quickset hedge of his beard, there was a suggestion of world-weariness: he had in fact just two more years to live. To me he did not seem like a man in early middle-age, and although his beard made him look older than he was, I did not think of him in terms of a sum of years but as an intelligence alert and busy behind the appendage of hair and the glass outworks. A glint came into his eyes, the brain was on the move as swiftly as a bat, with something of the radar-like sensitivity of a bat, and when he spoke it was sometimes in the voice of a bat.'[39]

All of which is implicit, if not explicit, in this extraordinary portrait. Moreover, it is a 'speaking' likeness in a literal sense, for it is possible to imagine the legendary falsetto emanating from 'the quickset hedge of his beard'. Some mention Lytton's wider range of voice; but his habitual tone was high-pitched, like the 'breathless squeak of an asthmatic rabbit.'

Technically, many of the preparatory drawings are superior to the finished picture which, as a result of so much laborious reworking, has somewhat darkened and sunk, something of which Henry himself was fearful: 'the look of the superstructure begins to make me feel uneasy', he told Lytton when he thought he had nearly finished, and confessed, 'I fancy I was betrayed by those freakish dryings'. The preparatory studies of Lytton, rather than an end in themselves, seem more than usually a means towards painting which gives them a directness, a feeling of urgency, as though the result were pretty clearly in view however far away it seemed at times. The drawings and paintings are also quite stylised at an early stage – by then, of course, Lytton himself was stylised – and even in those of the head alone, there is an awareness of the relation of the parts to the whole, an aspect that became vital to the finished picture with its precarious balance of figure and ground. Henry continued to repaint passages – certainly some of the foliage and sky – when he returned to the Vale Hotel studio in 1919 and until the public showing at his first one-man exhibition in 1922. Seemingly, his sole concession to his sitter's rise to fame was to add two tiny figures walking arm-in-arm across the path in the background, decidedly turning away from their biographer. Representing Queen Victoria and looking very like her companion John Brown, the two are pencilled in and painted over some slight simplification of the fence and bushes, a witty reference to Lytton's success with his irreverent study of the late

Queen, published in 1921, and unobtrusively becoming a part of the larger joke of the whole portrait.

In the final analysis, given some beautifully inspired, witty details – the folds of the blanket draped over the basket chair echoing Lytton's legs in reverse and echoed further by the drooping branches seen through the window, the studied precision in the placing of the hat on the chair against which leans the tightly rolled umbrella, a symbol of industrious respectability, contrasting with the notoriety the sitter attracted, the addition of the two passers-by – all this incident works, is fascinating, very amusing; but ultimately, it is the sum of these parts that succeeds so superbly. Despite the daunting deliberations during its progress, and whatever weaknesses emerge from close scrutiny of the handling, the conception is masterly and is carried through to a triumphant conclusion. If not a great painting, it is surely a great portrait.

The *Portrait of Lytton Strachey* is a landmark in English painting. Yet no parallel comes to mind and it seems without either precedence or subsequence. Within the oeuvre of Henry Lamb, it remains virtually isolated though, so far as its whimsy is concerned and to some extent its treatment, there is a connection with *The Kennedy Family*. Otherwise, it stands apart, which fact Henry came to resent. Like the fictional ventriloquist whose dummy takes over and dominates him, there is something surreal, unnerving, irritating, even demoralising, about a creation that subsumes its creator. For an artist to be identified too soon and too completely with a particular work may prove disastrous to his development. Perhaps this occurs more often in literature where an author may have enormous difficulty in following up a successful first novel, indeed may never succeed in doing so, and his career dwindles because of an inability to emulate that initial enterprise.

Not that Henry was particularly young when he painted 'Lytton'; he was nearly forty when it was exhibited. But from then on he lived with the frustrating paradox of a picture more famous than he was. Later, much later, he would dismiss it as a youthful indulgence, an extravagance, for during the Second World War, when asked about paintings representative of his career, he was reluctant to suggest 'The Strachey' and referred to it as 'a vast juvenile piece of inexperience' that 'looks well enough in a photograph, but is terribly éffacée in reality'. In reality, it never was 'éffacée'.

NOTES

1 Holroyd *Lytton Strachey* Vol.2, p.7.
2 V. Woolf *Moments of Being* p.166.
3 *Lytton Strachey By Himself* (19 Mar 1910) pp.122–3.
4 Holroyd, Vol.2, p.16.
5 *Strachey By Himself* p.182.
6 Jacob Epstein – Henry Lamb : 15 Sep 1912.
7 Francis Dodd – Henry Lamb : 20 Sep 1912.
8 Francis Dodd – Lytton Strachey : Sep (?) 1912.
9 Epstein *An Autobiography* p.54.
10 Fry *Letters* Vol.1, p.47.
11 Sykes *Evelyn Waugh* p.395n; Guiness *Potpourri from the Thirties* pp.16–17.
12 George Kennedy – Lytton Strachey : 21 Apr 1913.
13 Spender *World Within World* p.76.
14 Gaunt *Concise History of English Painting* pp.207–10.
15 D. Garnett *Great Friends* p.150.
16 Holroyd, Vol.2, p.471; Maurois *Memoirs* pp.123–5.
17 Holroyd, Vol.1, p.239.
18 Holroyd, Vol.2, p.19.
19 ib.
20 Holroyd, Vol.2, p.4.
21 Holroyd, Vol.1, p.427.
22 Mosley *A Life of Contrasts* pp.79–80.
23 O. Sitwell *Laughter in the Next Room* pp.16–23; Rosenbaum *The Bloomsbury Group* pp. 254–5.
24 O. Sitwell *Noble Essences* pp.12–13.
25 E. Sitwell *Taken Care Of* pp.81–7; Rosenbaum pp.256–9.
26 Rosenbaum p.387.
27 Mirsky *The Intelligentsia of Great Britain* pp.111–20; Rosenbaum p.387.
28 Sackville-West *Harold Nicholson's Diaries and Letters 1930–39* pp.350–1; Rosenbaum p.249.
29 Holroyd *Lytton Strachey* preface to revised edition 1979, p.19.
30 B. Russell *Portraits from Memory* 'The Listener' 17 Jul 1952; Rosenbaum p. 249.
31 Holroyd Vol.1, p.319.
32 Garnett *Flowers of the Forest* p.17.
33 Rosenbaum p.32
34 V. Woolf *Moments of Being* p.166.
35 Rosenbaum pp.261–2.
36 Partridge *Memories* pp.76–7.
37 Holroyd, Vol.2, p.3.
38 O. Garnett *The Sculpture of Stephen Tomlin* p.31.
39 Plomer *At Home* pp.43–6; Rosenbaum p.297.

V

Palestine and Poole

1914–1928

ELEVEN

STANLEY SPENCER

———

'I walked to Cookham and brought back Spencer with me', reported Henry to Lytton in the spring of 1914: 'I understood his origin & genre much better this time and he was much less nervous and trying; so that I really got to like him tremendously'. His first encounter with the young Stanley Spencer early in November, the previous year, had not been an unqualified success. Afterwards Henry had admitted feeling '*écrasé* by the double weight of Spencer and the hell of a chill. Indeed it was one of the most terrible days of my life', he wrote, 'and has left me considerably aged.'

Henry was eight years older than Stanley, though because of the worldly experience of the one and the negligible experience of the other, the gap then seemed wider. Darsie Japp, a Slade student contemporary of the younger and friend of the older, had brought them together by drawing Henry's attention to Spencer's Slade School prizewinning picture *The Apple Gatherers* when it was first shown publicly during the summer of 1913. So impressed was Henry that his comments were passed on to the artist: 'Dear Mr Lamb', wrote Stanley in his ponderous copperplate, 'Your friend Mr Japp told me that you like my picture at the Contemporary. It gives me pleasure to enclose herewith a photo of it. I think it looks better in this photo than it does in the original. I hope to see you some day – I don't go to London now so I hardly ever see anybody or any works of art. Japp comes to Cookham sometimes, and tells me about everything – you know he knows everything.'

Meanwhile, in July, Henry went to Manchester to begin his father's portrait; in August, he was in Donegal for the second time that year, thence to Gola until the end of October, by which time, by proxy, he had clinched the purchase of *The Apple Gatherers* with a cheque sent direct to the artist: 'Thank you very much for the £30', wrote Stanley in acknowledgement enclosing a formal receipt, 'Of course if you at any time should feel you could give me more I should be very glad to receive more but I do not want you to feel obliged to give more, because you are not. For the sum you have so kindly sent the picture is yours.' Henry had no intention of keeping the picture. He had been irritated and disappointed at failing to persuade the Contemporary Art Society to take an interest and buy it from their summer exhibition; he was even more annoyed at Clive Bell, one of the purchasers for the C.A.S.: 'It is *absolutely essential* that Clive should buy it', he had told Lytton, 'The price is £100, though as you see the *oeuvre* is *impayable*. The fellow is far poorer than Lewis I shld. say & immeasurably more worth encouraging so unless you can manage to bring off that purchase, I command you to become instantly unbearable to Clive again or . . . whish whish whish . . . *cent-mille coups. Mais pense donc* – Spencer *on n'a que vingt ans!*'

Bell's refusal was like fuel to Henry's ire so, to embarrass one of his *bêtes noires*, to bypass any middle men, and, most of all, to help the struggling young artist, Henry decided to bait prospective clients himself and to pursue a dark plot of his own which, as he put it to Lytton, 'should dang Clives loathsome carriage down to Hell'. The grapevine of the artworld must have been working well for, not long after Henry announced his little plan, Stanley reported, 'Mr Edward Marsh wrote to me a day or so ago asking me if, in the event of my Apple picture not being sold, I should be willing to let him have it for £50. I told him it was sold, and asked him to communicate with you'. Only three days later, Stanley, with his mixture of whining innocence and calculation, of humility and self-interest, again wrote to Henry saying, 'I feel crossed about that picture, because all the time I am wanting money I am wanting you to keep the picture. You understand that I can wait, you see for another year or so I shall not be having to spend a lot, I seldom do, and if I live as I have been doing until now I shall be able to go through a year without danger, and I tell you, that I do not worry about money but I think about it.'

Soon after Henry's return to London, Stanley, on Monday the Third of November, delivered his picture to the Vale Hotel studio.

He had warned Henry many people had tried to convert him to Hampstead Heath with all its pine trees and wonderful views, but that he always got 'horribly deppressed [sic]' whenever he went there. Yet it was a district he was to become associated with intimately, after the First War; and despite having studied at the Slade for four years he was still surprisingly apprehensive about finding his way: 'You will give me full directions as to how to get to your place etc', he had asked Henry, explaining, 'as I am not used to London and get very puzzled, sometimes . . . Japp tells me to "fight against it" but I cannot somehow . . . I wish the National Gallery was in Cookham'. He also asked to be taken everywhere in the big city, particularly to the National, and Henry gave him a guided tour, even fitting in a visit to Japp whose grand home in Tite Street in Chelsea rather overawed him but whose new baby he had wanted to see. It was perhaps as well for his host that Stanley had refused an invitation to stay the night, preferring to return to his beloved Cookham that evening, for by the end of the day, Henry was far 'too *épuisé* to describe' his first meeting with this restless genius, this genuine original, this incredible talking head, whose pictures were so wonderfully inventive but whose conversation quickly turned into a monologue. '*Tu sais que ce n'est pas un homme*', decided Henry, whilst continuing to be ecstatic about *The Apple Gatherers*, and telling Lytton: 'everyday I think it better'.

Stanley soon caught on to Henry's little ploy, becoming keener by the hour to profit, literally, from its success. Only two days after delivering the picture to Henry and spending the day with him, he called on Eddie Marsh, saying there was no political significance in his visit. But Marsh, who had risen to the bait, showed Stanley his collection of pictures, including a pen and ink drawing of Henry's which he looked at three times and liked best of all he saw. Then in the same breath, typically, he negated such tactfully diplomatic praise by adding ingenuously, 'except a drawing by Roberts that he did when he was 12 years old' and asked Henry, 'have you seen it? It is a head & it is good, one of the best he has ever done.' He also said he liked Marsh very much – something that would hardly have pleased Henry – and hinted that Marsh 'was always spending and . . . never knew at what time he might have to spend a lot . . . he is holding his offer open for a certain time, I do not think there is anything to fear from his saying this. But,' Stanley suggested, 'if you cannot raise more money than Marsh offered and cannot manage to keep it yourself, let Marsh have it.' A week or so later, the grapevine had reached Yorkshire: 'Spencer's picture is at present at Leeds being inspected by Sadler who will probably buy it', Henry informed Lytton, explaining, 'I am auctioning it & have so far only got one bid – £50 from E. Marsh . . . John wrote rather snottily when I suggested he might buy it for his millionaire' – Augustus' American patron, John Quinn. But then, thought Henry, after arousing so much interest, if he and Japp became joint owners and offered it to the National Gallery, that would let them all down and really annoy everyone!

In the meantime, Stanley, with increasing confidence, wrote to Henry, bringing him up to date,

> 'Dear Lamb (can I drop Mr.), Marsh says . . . that Pro 'Sadler has offerred [sic] £50, he also says that if there is such a difference made between his offer & Mr Sadler's such as £50 & 50 guineas, that he (Marsh) would also offer 50 guineas, that is what I understood him to say. If you must part with it I want Marsh to have it because he was first to make the offer & he kept it open for a good time'.

By the first week of December 1913, the deal was done: Marsh was the owner of the magnificent 'Apple Picture', though he had had to raise his offer; Henry had derived enormous pleasure and amusement – as he always did – from the success of his little scheme, especially since the abominable Bell had been out-manoeuvred, and above all, the artist was richer than he had ever been in his twenty-two years. In acknowledging the first instalment, Stanley had told Henry, 'I have just been to the post office with the cheque and I find I am too wealthy. I cannot put it in the Post-office Savings Bank'; and on receipt of the balance of £25, he announced, 'I opened my Banking account today. I shall be able to write out cheques like Japp does, only I must get a nice desk like his.' With the letter he again enclosed a proper receipt signed over a penny stamp: 'I always write formal receipts', he explained, 'because Tonks [the Slade Professor] says it is right to be businesslike'. Also, he enclosed his first drawing for *The Apple Gatherers*, a present to Henry in appreciation of his trouble.

Henry was ever admiring of Spencer, the artist; but of Stanley, the man, he was very unsure and remained ambivalent. Initially, Stanley's striking naivety was a great source of fascination and amusement. Early in 1914, when Clive Bell's *Art* was published, Lytton, possibly suspecting that Henry was unlikely to buy it, sent

Irish Troops in the Judaean Hills Surprised by a Turkish Bombardment *1919* *Oil on canvas* *184.6 × 220.5* *Imperial War Museum, London*

Advanced Dressing Station on the Struma 1916   1920   *Oil on canvas*   *186.6 × 212.3*   *Manchester City Art Galleries*

him a copy. In thanking him, Henry, probably still haunted by that exhausting day in November when the 'Apple Picture' was delivered, simulated Stanley's lumbering copperplate and his child-like mode of expression: 'Mr Bell's book looks just as rotten as I expected', he wrote, promising to 'write him a letter to thank him for his Information.' Thus *Art* was succinctly sent-up and summarily dismissed forever, but Henry's acquaintance with Stanley was renewed soon after when, in March, Henry walked from Marlow, where he had been staying a few days, to Cookham, on the Thames.

Stanley had explained at length about their being a large family and the difficulties of having people to stay, although his parents were always pleased to see any of his friends. He had apologised for having no room of his own but, nonetheless, wanted Henry to see him in his natural habitat, as if sensing that he had not been at his best at their first meeting in Hampstead. In Cookham, however, the 'domestic scene was too remarkable to describe . . . I loved it', wrote Henry. Stanley was the eighth surviving child of a somewhat impoverished late Victorian household living at Fernlea, in the High Street. His father was an organist making a modest living as a music teacher; he would read aloud to the family, chiefly from the Bible, and had fixed ideas on education, as a result of which all the Spencer children were educated at home. Biblical texts and the village of Cookham were to be the profoundest and most enduring influences on young Stanley. Henry found the whole experience enthralling, and was inspired to take Stanley back to London where they wandered round together again. Having seen Stanley in the family setting, Henry was able to look at his new friend in a different light and with a greater understanding, discovering in him a streak of pure Calvinism and, most rewardingly, a desperate passion for music to which Henry responded with tremendous enthusiasm. 'I like playing to that sort of cove', he happily admitted: Bach Preludes and Fugues, a Mozart Minuet and, what Stanley called, 'the Diabelly Variations', were in Henry's repertoire and regularly requested by his young admirer. 'Will you get anytime to play', he asked Henry before coming to see him, and when they met up in 1919, after the war, Stanley declared how wonderful it was to hear Henry play again, 'the effect on me is something of the same sort of thing as the sun & planet. The planet gets its impetus from the sun and I get mine from your playing. It does me a world of good' and he suggested, 'Can't you write a great treatise . . . on piano playing?'

211

Henry must have been a little flattered by the attention. It was a new experience for him: with Dodd and Augustus, his role had been that of a student, at least at first; Boris, Kennedy and Lytton were his peers; but Stanley was his first disciple. 'I rather liked the way we mooched about London didn't you', wrote Stanley to Henry, after returning to Cookham and reflecting on his pleasure from their day together going round the galleries. Until then, he thought, Japp, knew everything, but now, his omniscience was overshadowed by Henry who, to this provincial innocent, was such a supremely confident, variously talented, articulate, widely-read, well-connected man-of-the-world. Henry, for his part, rather enjoyed his guru-like position and at first, Stanley absorbed all he could from the friendship, including some of Henry's own antipathies. Roger Fry, for example, was an inevitable target. His growing influence as an arbiter of taste was a continuing cause of concern to Henry who would have had no inhibitions in letting off steam about him to his attentive companion. Fry registered the Omega Workshops as a company in May 1913. By November, Stanley was telling Henry that William Roberts was working for Fry and asked, clearly playing upon his mentor's prejudices, 'Did you ever hear of his "Omega" workshop. It fell through; soul [sic] survivor Duncan Grant', an item of news some years ahead of the actual demise, though Stanley may have assumed that the dramatic departure of Wyndham Lewis and other Vorticists from the workshops in July had signalled the end of Fry's project.

Aside from his aversion to Fry and Bell and their aesthetics, Henry showed a sensitive appreciation of Stanley's natural talent and inclinations, and was influential in diverting his attention from Post-Impressionism by steering him towards the older masters, especially the earlier Italian and Flemish painters with whom he seemed to have most in common. *The Apple Gatherers*, in both treatment and mood, is probably the most Gauguin-esque of all Stanley's paintings and it is tempting to see some connection between this and Henry's own brief but intense Gauguin period; but the 'Apple Picture' was done before he ever met Henry who, in any case, by 1913, had become disenchanted with Gauguin especially and abandoned most Post-Impressionist notions. Stanley knew what and how he wanted to paint and pursued his visions relentlessly; but Henry's encouragement in the direction of the early Renaissance would have been a welcome confirmation of his intuition. Whenever Henry sent him books and reproductions that would match his ambitions, he would worry for more. 'If you have any Lorenzetti's you can give me, give them to me by return of post if possible', pleaded Stanley, 'I am getting a very good collection of postcards. I do not put them into a book because I like to look at them separately. I take them out according to how I feel & I put it somewhere in the room so that I can look at it if I feel inclined; it sort of keeps me company & makes me work.' Stanley, after leaving the Slade and isolated in Cookham, became dependent on such stimulus, 'It relieves the monotony of seeing the same people everyday to receive things like that now & again', he confessed. He also became inspired by a book on Assisi that Kennedy had lent Henry who passed it on to Stanley: 'If you cannot get another book like it ask Mr. Kennedy to let me have this one because I want to keep it very badly', he implored Henry; and towards the end of the summer of 1914, after war had just been declared and conscription looked likely, he was resolved that, 'If I go to war I go on condition I can have Giotto the Basilica of Assisi and Fra Angelico in one pocket and Masaccio, Marsalino and Giorgione in the other.' As it happened, when he was called up, he took with him – in addition to Chaucer, Shakespeare, Blake, Keats, Milton, Borrow, Dickens, Marlowe, and the Bible – books on Giotto, Fra Angelico, Carpaccio, Giorgione, Michelangelo, Gozzoli, Raphael, Claude, Velazquez, Early Flemish painters, and (given to him by Henry), the coveted Basilica of Assisi.

Stanley was always excessively, obsessively demanding. 'Do not forget the Lorenzetti's', he would plead. 'Any incorrect spelling please correct', he would ask. Again and again, he would implore Henry to play for him: 'I shall want to come to London to see you and hear you play before you go back to Ireland', he requested. And during the war, when he felt deprived of music, he asked Henry, 'Don't you just ache for Gluck, Mozart, Bach, and Beethoven', and complained, 'You remember you did not get the chance of letting me hear much of Gluck up at Hampstead'. A close parallel to their relationship – at least in fiction – might be to that of the tragic couple of central characters in Steinbeck's *Mice and Men*: though the plot and circumstances are vastly different, the simple Lennie in his persistent pleading with his mate and mentor George to repeat their plans for a settled, sublime, but sadly never to be realised future, is not unlike Stanley, particularly in the early days of their friendship. 'Go on now George', asks Lennie for the umpteenth time, 'tell me, tell me about the rabbits – like you done before.' Similarly, asks Stanley, 'play me the Diabelly Variations and a lot of other things you *have* played to me'.

Such nagging dependence, whilst initially flattering to Henry and to some extent inevitable given the differences in their age and experience, carried with it a one-sidedness that could only be abortive. Although Henry derived much pleasure from Stanley's naive, intensely personal view of the world and continued to admire and wonder at his work, he also found his company increasingly wearing and so exhausting that eventually he came to hold a higher regard for the productions than for the man, thus reverting more to his original opinion. They remained friends for many years and, despite differences, there were none of the great ruptures that punctuated Henry's friendship with Lytton. But Stanley's perennial preoccupation with his own problems that, with his success, seemed to multiply, was a real obstacle to any profound growth in their relationship – perhaps in any of Stanley's relationships. His was such an extreme case of egocentricity and his concerns, apart from those of his family, were so exclusively his own that he seems to have been totally unaware of any needs that Henry might have had. Henry continued to be remarkably enabling, but his generosity of spirit was never properly returned and of all his relationships with men, it was the only one that failed to be significantly or tangibly reciprocal.

For a long time Stanley, even in his thirties, continued in some way to depend on Henry: despite his scrupulousness, he would ask for money, for accommodation, for help with patrons, for advice on painting. During the first war he had told Henry, 'I love the idea of your getting a commission . . . & taking me for your servant but do you think it could possibly be done.' On the surface he seemed content to be subservient; but his subservience was manipulative and masked an astonishing determination and near arrogance: qualities that contributed greatly to the power and extent of his output as a painter but rather detracted from his personal relations. Again, superficially he might have appeared lacking in confidence, but beneath his monotonous ramblings was a surprising certainty bordering on complacency, a trait soon noted by Henry. Following one admonishment, Stanley replied compliantly but without any feelings of contrition, 'I quite agreed with what you said about me . . . I am in danger of becoming smug.'

'I very nearly disgraced myself in the O.P. surgery', reported Henry to Lytton, explaining in some detail, 'when my friend pulled for about 5 minutes at the gory end of a youths mangled finger, vainly attempting to tear the nail off. I had to pretend to look for another friend in the next room, and though I soon came back and bandaged the thing up, I felt wrong for an hour afterwards.'

At the end of August 1914, Henry had experienced what he called, 'a certain return of military feelings occasioned by the bad news' and found himself almost unable to resist enlisting. But after confirming his more cautious principles and deciding that he was too much of a crock to do anything but the ambulance service, he withdrew his name from the recruiting office in Putney. The next morning, as if to vindicate his decision, his ever troublesome piles reasserted themselves. He then tried to make his medical attainments acceptable, spending nearly a whole day visiting various offices, writing to the Red Cross in vain, and approaching the St. John's ambulance who strongly advised against going abroad in view of 'the state of his guts'. Eventually, in the first week of September, he landed 'an ordinary dresser's job' in the out-patients' department at Guy's Hospital.

'The horror & repulsiveness of it all seem far greater than they used to be', he told Lytton, 'and in addition I have all the boredom of becoming socially a medical student again without the curiosity. But there are of course plenty of interesting characters (not among the students) and dramatic moments'; but, he admitted, 'I have been doubting sometimes if I shall ever be able to learn the trick of attending to what I am meant to, or of sacrificing more general interests to particular ones, well enough to become efficient again'. There were consolations, however: he enjoyed getting to know some of the city and the environs of the hospital; he was too, surrounded by pretty nurses providing numerous opportunities not all of which he neglected. One of the trainees, the devastatingly beautiful Nurse Manners, later to be Lady Diana Cooper, remembered how 'it was lovely to cross the court and the so-called gardens and hope to see Henry Lamb . . . then a gold-thatched student.'[1]

During his first week at Guy's Henry travelled daily from the Vale of Health but found the fares – fivepence each way – a steady drain on his resources. By the end of the second week, he was living in the hospital but his piles were becoming persistent and very painful. 'I am hoping that a good opportunity will presently turn up for treating them with the K-nife', he told Lytton; 'I saw the operation yesterday and thought it looked satisfactory. I am getting used to blood. It is much harder to bear when the people are not anaesthetised', something also felt by Nurse Manners who, 'Dreading operations . . . had never expected some dressings to be worse, but', she wrote, 'they . . . are much more terrible – the patient's own consciousness and shame and pain, the smell and the realism and all the horrors the theatre overcomes by its unearthliness.'[2] By October, Henry decided that the work itself was the least objectionable part – especially since his gore-sickness had subsided. But as he became familiar with the hospital routine he was appalled at the general slackness, calling it 'inconceivable', and finding 'it hard to believe that the place couldn't be run as well by ⅔rds of the men if they would buck up.' He was then promoted to 'full-dresser' which involved more arduous, responsible and interesting work. On the second day of his new appointment he had to do an operation for hernia and soon found himself desperately reading medicine and surgery to try and keep pace with it all.

Christmas 1914, he spent on duty at Guy's, finding the hospital festivities 'quite agreeable, only fatiguing'. Then, for the first fortnight of the new year, he became a patient in Evelyn Ward and underwent the operation for his piles. 'Nothing terrifies me', he had told Ottoline, 'but I have slight misgivings about the anaesthetic – unreasonable enough since the whole thing should be finished in quarter of an hour. After that I expect to have to lie up here about a fortnight and will soon be quite comfortable. The nurses . . . compete in spoiling me, and I am to have the best surgeon and anaesthetist in the place.' His convalescence was more painful than he had expected and during one sleepless night he finished reading, with tremendous excitement, Lytton's draft of 'Cardinal Newman'. Kennedy was a conscientious visitor, coming everyday until Henry was discharged towards the end of the month when he spent a weekend in Dorset with Dorelia before going off to work in France at l'Hôpital Anglais du Casino in Fécamp.

Starting there at the beginning of February 1915, Henry described it as, 'a more or less official private establishment financed by female aristocrats and wealthy doctors' with '100 beds &, at present only one medical man – the brother of Rowlands who repaired my bum. So I will have plenty to do', he informed Lytton, 'Screw £2 a week and expenses, a building on terra firma to live in, and best of all, they are allowing me to bring Kennedy as an orderly and will pay his expenses.' He thought Kennedy, though attending a First Aid course, would probably be useless as an orderly, but had to admit, however, that his company would be a great asset. The hospital was pleasantly situated, below the cliffs overlooking the bay at Fécamp, 'a compact little town . . . among hills with a superb cathedral', wrote Henry, 'at the coast are fine white cliffs & occasional pebbly beaches. On the top the country is monotonous enough but the valleys are divine. I should quite well like to stay here at other times'. The job was less to his liking: he was not overworked and, he told Lytton, was 'well fed, housed (bitched if I wanted them) and paid'; but, what he called his 'sufferings', consisted of, 'primo the métier, secundo the absence of my own métiers and leisure, tertio the boredom of the people I have to live with, quarto the ignorance of my chief, and quinto the disturbance and uncertainty caused by the quarrels of the beau monde . . . we do not find any of this lot sympathique. There is not a spoonful of brains to be found in the whole collection, beau-monde, doctor, matron, or nurses. Only Lady Guernsey has a sort of accomplished energy: she is our directrice and I dislike her. She is as barbarous as the rest and I can see no hope of wars ceasing while such people abound'. His medical chief, he described as 'a worm of the blindest and most subterranean kind' although he felt Kennedy's existence to be even more difficult than his own since his job was less defined: 'everybody charges him with odd duties', he told Lytton, and you can guess how easily he allows himself to be put upon.'

Sometime during the summer of 1915, Kennedy left to enlist in Lord Derby's recruiting scheme, but Henry stayed on at Fécamp until the beginning of November when at last he got leave to return to Guy's and, as he modestly put it, 'read for the lowest qualification' to get a temporary commission in the Royal Army Medical Corps. Meanwhile, at l'Hôpital Anglais du Casino, by the end, with the nondescript company he had become horribly bored, but resigned: 'I love my patients', he told Ottoline, 'but for real consolation and joy I starve.' In August, after six months without a break, he spent four days in and around Rouen, which he pronounced 'superb . . . the architecture gives me such delight particularly in some of the village churches' that he had discovered on walks. Yet he was more than ready to get back to England again, even though it meant months of cramming for the examinations, and he left Fécamp without much regret.

London, of course, despite his past complaints, now meant many of the things of which he had been starved – concerts, opera and ballet, galleries, lunches at Simpson's, suppers at the Well's Hotel in Hampstead, or further up on the Heath, occasional dinner parties at Jack Straw's Castle. Though he was living at the Vale Hotel studio, there was no time for painting: 'I have just got through the 2nd and hardest part of my final examination', he announced to Ottoline, in the middle of the summer of 1916, 'a month hence I should finish all, with luck, and be at last in the Army.' On the twenty-third of August, he was commissioned as a Lieutenant in the Special Reserve of the R.A.M.C. and posted, with the Northumbrian Field Ambulance, to Salonika.

'I hear . . . from men in this ambulance that your ambulance is in this country', wrote Stanley, with the British Salonika Forces, to Henry, in the summer of 1917, 'so I conclude you must be somewhere near me' and, he added, 'I got your photograph and have it with me . . . Please write and let me know if this reaches you, with much love from Cookham.' They had kept in touch since the war began and Henry knew that Stanley 'had gone to clean lavatories', but he must have been very surprised to learn that Private Spencer was also in Salonika, only a few miles away. 'If there is any chance of my seeing or getting with you do what you can to arrange it', pleaded Stanley, pointing out, 'I think it would be too exasperating to think of you and I being perhaps so near and yet not getting a glimpse of one another'. Henry had been promoted Captain in the February of 1917, but Stanley stayed a Private throughout, conjuring up an Arthurian image of his grand friend and suggesting, 'if you have a noble charger, you might be able to get to see me'. In fact, they were to meet only once during the war, in the summer of 1917. Henry arrived, as Stanley had hoped, on horseback.

'Are you doing any painting or drawing?' asked Stanley. Sadly, for Henry, the war was to be mostly a period of gestation. His work as a surgeon was both demanding and dangerous, leaving little time or energy for drawing and none at all for painting. Next to nothing done on the spot survives from Salonika though the experience there was to be the basis of his quietly monumental *Troops on the Struma* recreated afterwards in 1920, mainly from memory. Towards the end of 1917, when he was transferred to the 30th Field Ambulance (attached to the 5th Royal Inniskilling Fusiliers) and posted to Palestine until May of the following year, he produced a number of small drawings in pencil, pen, or watercolour – and sometimes combining the three – that in themselves may not be of much more than documentary interest; but in the charm of their whimsy, they point to one of the minor directions he was to take as an artist many times again. In both their strengths and weaknesses, they are typical of any number of Henry's later groups of figures – usually on a small scale, occasionally very large – set on Hampstead Heath, in Poole, or in Wiltshire and, during the Second World War, at Service bases and camps all over the South of England. Their strengths are in the 'classical', almost Poussin-like, displacement of the figures and in the often witty observation of character; the weaknesses lie in the summary carelessness of detail, the lazily evasive drawing, and in a lack of imaginative power in the conception.

Perhaps the best, certainly the most finished, drawings done during this artistically inactive, but not infertile, period are the meticulous studies of Palestinian plants. These could be seen simply as botanical exercises; but they might also be interpreted more deeply, and unconsciously, as an antidote to the horrors of war. In Palestine, compared with Salonika and despite the tension and frustration of service life, Henry had a little more time to reflect, and doubtless the involvement in the mechanics of recording as faithfully as possible the plant form in front of him would have been therapeutic, providing a welcome respite from the misery and pain that surrounded him. Like objects of contemplation, the tiny plants would have become a focus for his more sensitive awarenesses that had been endangered by the cruder, harsher realities of battle, the terrible aftermath of which was his concern. For Henry, the drawings are exceptionally, painstakingly analytical, detached, nearly clinical, yet with a Gothic intensity reminiscent of Dürer; beautifully crafted, they stand apart from his mostly sketchier work done on active service – and also from his work in general. After the war, when he tackled flowers, he used broad brushes and oil paint, seeming less interested either in recording information or in visual analysis and more concerned with capturing as swiftly as possible the freshness of his subject matter, lest it should fade. Here, in these snatched moments from hospital duties, his choice of subject may not have been accidental, for such close concentration on nature in its innocence and serenity was a positive counterpoint to so much aggression, futility and despair, perhaps encouraging a more optimistic frame of mind and giving him a glimmer of hope for the future.

During his seven months in Palestine there had been the occasional lull until, in the May of 1918, Henry was posted, via Egypt, to France, still with the 30th Field Ambulance and still attached to the Inniskilling Fusiliers but, this time, thrown into the thick of battle. In September, he was awarded the Military Cross,

> 'For conspicuous gallantry and devotion to duty when an outpost company were suffering numerous casualties from enemy bombardment. He proceeded to the locality at once and under heavy shelling got all the wounded moved to shelter remaining with the company until the bombardment ceased. During a trying time he showed splendid devotion to duty.'[3]

Afterwards, in October, he was badly gassed and returned to London, recuperating at a military hospital in Grosvenor Square until the start of the new year when he suddenly announced that he was about to be demobilized as unfit for further service.

To have been incapacitated in the penultimate month of the war was doubly tragic and Henry was permanently weakened by the awful experience. Now, at the beginning of 1919, with diminished energy and reduced circumstances, he had the difficult, delicate task of picking up the threads of his career as an artist. He was thirty-six. Unlike many who returned to civilian life and took the opportunity to change direction he seems to have had no doubts about wanting to be a painter again. He had, after all, changed direction quite dramatically once before, only reverting to medicine in the emergency. However, he had little chance to brood, for his immediate future was almost wholly circumscribed by a major commission that was to take him until nearly the end of the year to complete.

It had taken most of the previous year to extricate him from medical duties in order to set him up as an official war artist. The wheels of officialdom ground so slowly that by the time he was appointed, the armistice was signed and Henry was in hospital. In

220

fact, but for the procrastinations and obstructions to his release, he might never have spent his last few months of active service in France for, early in February 1918, Robert Ross had written to Campbell Dodgson, Keeper of Prints and Drawings at the British Museum and wartime adviser to the Ministry of Information's Pictorial Propaganda Scheme at Wellington House, asking,

'What do you think of Henry Lamb, who is now at Salonika? He was suggested to me by Dodd. I admire his work very much, as I am sure you do; but, of course, the question is, would he do what was required? He would certainly work in pencil and water-colour. Dodd is going to send some of his drawings which Lamb has done in the East.

As you know, he has been working as a surgeon, but apparently tired of that.'[4]

The dauntless Dodd – and his benevolent brother-in-law Bone – had been drawing at the front in France since the beginning of 1917. By October, Dodd reported to Wellington House that, after completing at least a hundred portraits, he was in need of a holiday; and Muirhead Bone, no less energetic, was said to be a great success in England and selling his work like hot cakes. The enabling brothers-in-law in their kindly, encouraging way, did their best to rally support for Henry's early release. And Bone's brother James, the London editor of 'The Manchester Guardian' for whom Henry had done the drawings published in 1905/6 wrote forcefully and glowingly to the Controller at the Ministry, Lord Tweedsmuir (John Buchan), suggesting, that Henry was,

'really a big swell, I mean that he is easily amongst the first dozen artists we possess, and I would put him personally in the first flight of these. He is a very quick worker, and everything he does has distinction. He is really a much bigger man than McBey . . . his brother is Secretary of the Royal Academy (although that should not be used against him). He was a member of the New English Art Club, and one of his pictures was accepted for the Tate Gallery (that, too, should not be used against him). He has not exhibited much, and that is the only reason why he is not already well known . . . I know that what I am writing about Lamb's art expresses the views of nearly every responsible writer on art.'[5]

Such a magnificent testimonial and the support of Charles Aitken, by then Director of the National Gallery, Henry Tonks, Professor at the Slade, and Lord Tweedsmuir himself, could not persuade the War Office to release Captain Lamb. At the same time, Lord

Beaverbrook, Chairman of the Canadian War Memorials Committee, had applied to the War Office for Henry's services, but without success. Eventually, at the end of 1918, after nearly twelve months of negotiation, Henry was commissioned 'to paint a picture of historic importance'.[6]

Rather than spend the first few weeks of 1919 in a convalescent home recovering from 'flu and the after effects of gas, Henry preferred to paint, believing it would restore him to health more quickly. When he was proposed as a war artist, there was some suggestion that he be sent to Mesopotamia; but now, with the war behind him and the Palestine drawings to hand, combined with the vivid memories of his recent months in the Middle East, he began designing the first of his two large war pictures. 'Ross saw the sketches & approved', it was noted by the War Museum on the sixth of January, 1919, though considering Henry's already low opinion of Ross, especially following the Epstein affair, he is hardly likely to have found the news inspiriting. The scheme was Ross's conception and Henry's contribution was to be one of a group of large paintings by a number of artists including Stanley, Walter Bayes, the brothers Nash, and Sargent, a diverse selection to be hung in a memorial hall. The scheme was more or less carried out and the pictures were all hung – and still hang – together, but in the Imperial War Museum. When the plan was described to Henry, he reported to Wellington House that he was still unclear as to the requirements and took the liberty of telling Ross he did not think the memorial scheme could 'possibly succeed as at present planned. A hall to be decorated by so many different artists is bound to fail', he wrote, pouring cold water on the idea. However, reluctantly, if it had to proceed, he instructed Ross to 'set a scale of light and dark for everyone as that is the sort of unity that will matter far more than harmony of media.' Strictly speaking, Henry was right. The commissioned pictures have little or no conceptual or stylistic unity, but each in itself is a remarkable and powerful painting, the result of a splendid and unique chance for the artists, no less for Henry, who, putting aside his prejudices against the 'architect' of the scheme, accepted and rose to the challenge. After all, Ross's ideas and opinions were simply hurdles to be overcome, a mere means to an end. Henry was raring to paint again and this was his moment to climb back in the saddle: *Irish Troops in the Judaean Hills surprised by a Turkish Bombardment* was underway.

Intended originally to be more than ten feet in length the finished picture is actually a little over seven feet by six in height. Painted entirely in the Vale Hotel studio, it was destined – prior to its permanent resting place – for an exhibition of war paintings to be held at the Royal Academy in the winter of 1919–20. The summer before, Henry must have been otherwise occupied, preoccupied, or more likely, unfit, for he seems not to have made a start on the canvas until the autumn of 1919, barely three months to the deadline, although the idea and design were largely shaped by the end of 1918. He may just have made a false start earlier, but he was probably still suffering from being gassed. At the outset he had anticipated requiring models for life studies and needing at least three months to complete the picture; he promised to work as hard and rapidly as possible in order 'to benefit by the freshness of impressions.' At the end of August, the War Museum, already getting a little anxious, offered to lend some steel helmets for him to draw, tactfully trying to speed things up; but he declined saying he had a tin hat of his own and required nothing more in the way of material – 'only health'. Soon he found himself painting against the clock and told the Museum, 'I am working regularly and hard at my picture and hope it will be finished about the end of Oct. but cannot promise for any date'. In September, he was warned that active preparations were being made for the exhibition and that they were hoping to complete the photographs for an illustrated catalogue as near the end of October as possible. By the middle of November, he was writing to the Museum,

'My picture is nearly finished but requires at least a week more work, perhaps more. Unfortunately I cannot go on with it owing to lack of coal. My studio is heated by an anthracite stove for which I can find no fuel and believe it to be now unobtainable from any merchant. Can you, I wonder, use your influence to help me in any way? Perhaps you know of someone who could spare a cwt. for the time being, and that amount would just pull me through: that is to say if you cannot induce any government department to come to my rescue.'

The Museum were unable to help directly but fortunately the weather turned milder making the studio more bearable. Again, Henry pleaded, 'Not quite ready can you give me another week?' Finally, the frame having been ordered in October, the picture was delivered to the Academy at the beginning of December, too late to be photographed but just in time for the exhibition opening.

Irish Troops in the Judaean Hills is romantic, almost expressionist, in its design, with strong diagonals hurtling across the scene. But in its setting, it is strangely classical – in an historic rather than stylistic sense – since the action takes place in what is virtually a natural amphitheatre and the figures move like startled marionettes playing a Greek chorus. The drama is enacted well below the audience as if seen from on high in the gods. But, dramatic as 'Irish Troops' may appear, unlike *Lamentation* of nearly a decade earlier, it avoids theatricality. And despite the complexity of its rhythms, it has a deceptively chilling simplicity, perfectly appropriate to the theme and contributing greatly to its effectiveness as an evocation of war. Eleven men sprawl, stagger, or writhe angularly from right to left over the lower half of the composition, at least four of whom are either dead or dying. The smallness of the number comes as a surprise for there is a feeling of many more participants and the few are cunningly representative of a multiplicity of reactions to the disaster that is overtaking them. The absence of skyline heightens the tension and the whole is lit with the blinding, searing flash of an exploding shell. The entire picture is highly original in conception but, of the detail, it is the treatment and use of the billowing, swirling, suffocating smoke that is so virtuoso: it is both threateningly solid and mysteriously transparent: it works as form and as atmosphere, concurrently cutting the design and holding it together. The dynamic strength of the composition apart, it is pleasingly unified by the consistency of treatment: each part relates perfectly to the next and to the whole; and the whole achieves a satisfying completeness with which Henry, for once, should have been content. Delaying the start allowed him no time for changes of mind yet, formalised, stylised as it is, no passages are overworked. Indeed, the entire picture is done with such fluency and sureness of touch that it belies the fact it was his first major painting since the portrait of Lytton, five years before.

In his letters, Henry often mentions Giotto, but rarely Uccello: *The Rout of San Romano* comes most readily to mind in connection with 'Irish Troops', partly because of the similarity of subject, but also because they share a similarity of treatment and mood. In both the horror of battle is portrayed, not with expressive passion, but with a coolly objective, near clinical detachment. Indeed, in Henry's picture, the cool handling of the terror stricken figures, the sharpness of the unfriendly boulders, the delicate precision of the plants growing against impossible odds, all work as dramatic irony; a striking contrast to the bloody reality of the actual event. Man's vulnerability is vividly conveyed in the balletic poses of the soldiers signifying pain, fear, and despair. Stylised as they are, they are not contrived, and their angularity echoes and integrates perfectly with the volcanic, crater-like landscape. The viewpoint and the scale of the figures in relation to the setting are also slightly reminiscent of Breugel, another of Henry's favourites who, some years before the war, he had declared a wonder. Undoubtedly though, the closest connection of all is with his own younger contemporary and friend Stanley Spencer.

Stanley had as much difficulty and took just as long to get out of the army as Henry and, similarly, it was through being incapacitated that he was eventually released. He too had been proposed as a war artist in 1918, while still serving in Salonika. This was in May, but it was not until October, when he had contracted malaria, that there seemed any serious likelihood of his demobilisation. 'It will be a cruel disappointment to me if I can't do any painting', he wrote from hospital to Henry, not knowing at the time that he had been gassed and was also in hospital. Stanley was commissioned to paint his war picture in December, spending Christmas, 1918 at home in Cookham, and early in the new year, catching up with Henry's news. 'I was wondering where you were until I had your letter yesterday', wrote Stanley on the fourth of January, suggesting that he might come to London to see him. However, they seem not to have met again until March when Henry went to Cookham for a day and played the piano, much to the satisfaction of Stanley. A week or so later, Henry invited him to Hampstead. Stanley still asked, 'Let me know what station I get out at when I come . . . and the direction from thence to your place. I forget it.'

That they corresponded so little during 1919 suggests they may have seen quite a lot of each other. In the autumn, Henry was hard pressed to complete 'Irish Troops' whereas Stanley, having made a quicker recovery, had begun his large war picture, *Travoys with Wounded Soldiers in Macedonia*, early in January, completing it by June, shortly before he had a further attack of malaria. Stanley was never reticent of his intentions and Henry surely heard all about and must have been shown every prospective detail of 'Travoys' well before it reached the canvas. Henry's advice is also likely to have often been sought though, taking account of their respective behaviour

225

patterns, it is equally unlikely for Stanley to have volunteered advice on 'Irish Troops' – he was usually too preoccupied with himself and his own work to help others. Precisely who influenced whom is a tricky question and perhaps not one to be answered precisely. The certain similarities are in the treatment of the two paintings and to some extent in their scale, possibly indicating a measure of collaboration since, despite the uniformly high quality of the individual works included in Ross's original scheme, the visual disunity that Henry feared is evident in all but 'Travoys' and 'Irish Troops'. Though each is strongly personal and they are not exactly a complementary pair, they still hang together happily, enjoying a close interdependence. Some significance may attach to the fact that although Henry's was conceived at about the same time as Stanley's, 'Travoys' was finished months ahead of 'Irish Troops'.

Where they differ most is in the colour: 'Travoys' is set apparently at night with a rich, golden glow coming from the improvised operating theatre in the middle distance and illuminating the wounded in the foreground; 'Irish Troops' also has strong contrasts of light and dark but is altogether colder, with a preponderance of chalk white and grey, pale blues, and some of the now familiar, characteristic khaki that Henry continued to use until long after the war, indeed thereafter. The paintings differ too, in their degree of abstraction and ambiguity. As much because of the explosive nature of the subject, 'Irish Troops' is inevitably the more dynamic in design; but, apart from the mysterious menace of the enveloping smoke, one shaft of which extends across the foreground like the stretched skull in Holbein's *Ambassadors*, the shapes are almost immediately and wholly explicit. As an artist, Henry was not given to being ambiguous and, although in later work he was sometimes to leave areas unrealised, his shapes are invariably open to only one interpretation. On the other hand, with 'Travoys' the shrouded wounded, perhaps the ambulance men, and even the mules, are not all at once intelligible and, at first, are an intriguing jigsaw of shapes and colours: only after looking again, do we begin to read and interpret them for what they are and as integral to the incident. 'Travoys' has been described as 'one of the exceedingly few Spencers that show a conscious interest in pattern and design as the principal formal elements of a picture.'[7] Stanley's consciousness of these elements might just have been heightened through discussion with Henry; but in the absence of documentation, the connections and influences, other than the obvious stylistic affinity, remain conjectural.

The exhibition of war pictures that opened at the Royal Academy in the first week of December 1919 attracted large crowds. It was a remarkably varied, comprehensive, artistic response to the experience of war and 'Irish Troops' was an instant success, clearly confirming Henry's claim to being a serious, and potentially important, contemporary painter. It introduced him dramatically and significantly to the postwar public. 'The Studio' Magazine, in retrospect, called Henry's picture, 'the most striking' with 'real intensity of expression. The painting of the detail is admirable and keeps its place in the decorative whole. His use of the clouds of smoke is very effective.'[8] Even Clive Bell in his review in the 'Burlington Magazine' was moved to favourable comment. Ever since it was exhibited, 'Irish Troops' has remained one of the most telling, potent images of its period. In a recent study of *The Arts in Britain in World War I*, the incident depicted is described as 'seen . . . almost with divine compassion . . . as smoke drifts mystically across the scene.'[9] 'The Times' thought it 'so treated as to suggest a momentary arrest of time in which apparently irrelevant details are stamped upon the mind.' And Mary Chamot, in a survey of *Modern Painting in England*, published in 1937, referred to it as having 'great beauty of line and pattern' suggesting 'a moment of severe mental strain or terror'.[10]

Irish Troops in the Judaean Hills surprised by a Turkish Bombardment has been shown and reproduced often. Yet, despite its continuing critical acclaim, it is far less well known than some of the others in the scheme, the Nashes, the Nevinson, and indeed the Spencer, for example. However, for Henry, the success at the time very soon led to another major commission – amazingly from Manchester – the second of his war compositions that was to occupy him for much of 1920.

The summer of 1920, Henry spent at Stourpaine, a tiny Dorset village near Blandford. He had soon tired of London again. His health was indifferent; he slept badly, worse than ever, and was unsettled; feeling rootless, he was encouraged to explore the countryside, to look for somewhere more remote, more peaceful. In London, since the war, the stage had revolved: rarely was he nostalgic and he had been loathe to pick up many of the threads of his former existence. In joining up, he had effectively closed a number of doors and some that were still ajar he was reluctant to open. Temperamentally, culturally, and because of their unwavering pacifism, he felt even further from Bloomsbury. In any case, they had spread to Sussex – apart from Lytton who, now well known and well off and though living in the country in an extraordinary ménage, had taken up with Carrington. Ottoline, from whom he had disengaged himself just before the war, was now preoccupied with a new, younger generation, many of them writers such as Siegfried Sassoon, T. S. Eliot, and Aldous Huxley. Dorelia, in nursing him through some of his convalescence, had demonstrated her affection, but, were he honest, what hope was there there? Kennedy was almost literally rebuilding his career as an architect. Boris, ostensibly living on Henry's doorstep in Hampstead, was buzzing to and from Paris. About the only consolation to living and working at the Vale Hotel studio in those immediately postwar years was provided by a new circle who gathered informally nearby, at No.47 Downshire Hill, the home of the Carline family.

'Do you know *Richard* Carline?' Stanley had asked Henry just prior to the opening of the War Artists' Exhibition, saying, 'I saw his work before the war & thought him a most promising young artist.' Richard, and his brother Sydney, had been students at the Slade, had been in the war, had pictures in the Academy exhibition and attended the preview at Burlington House, with Stanley. It seems probable that this was Henry's introduction to the Carlines, whose gatherings at No.47 were a focus for the artistic and intellectual life of Hampstead in the Twenties. Richard and Sydney lived there, with their sister Hilda, another Slade student, and their mother, Ann who, inspired by the artists around her, took up painting in 1927, at the age of 64. Their father, George Carline, who had died suddenly in 1920, was also a painter. Others who came to the house were James Wood, philosopher and co-author with C. K. Ogden and I. A. Richards of *The Foundations of Aesthetics*; the painter Ethelbert White; the sculptor Leon Underwood; Randolph Schwabe, later to succeed Tonks as Professor at the Slade; Kate Foster, a Slade student contemporary of the young Carlines; Henry Rushbury, draughtsman, etcher, and friend of Dodd and Bone; Mary Adshead, painter, later to marry Bone's son Stephen; Robert Bevan, painter veteran of Camden Town, and his artist wife, S. de Karlowska; and many others living in the area. The group was never formal and the discussion never consistently definable – had it been, Henry would not have stayed; but, as Richard Carline said, they 'were largely swayed by antagonism to academic officialdom and by some scepticism regarding movements like "Futurism" or Clive Bell's "Significant Form"', sentiments with which Henry would have been wholly in sympathy.[11] In fact, their talk ranged widely and Kate Foster noted in her diary for the summer of 1923, Henry discussing 'Nietzsche over supper in the garden' with Francis Macnamara, the Irish poet and sometime husband of Ede McNeill, and David John, son of Augustus, both of whom Henry had introduced to the 'cercle', as Henry liked to call them affectionately.

The nucleus of the group was recorded in a large painting done between 1924 and '25 by Richard Carline. It includes mother, brother, and sister, James Wood, Kate Foster, Stanley, and Henry, to whom the artist sent outline sketches of the proposed composition, more for information and interest than for advice and comment. 'Your new group fills me with lively & sanguine apprehensions – apart from the infallible lure of a chance of featuring in a contemporary masterpiece', replied Henry, suggesting several alternatives to the design of which Richard declared he 'took no notice at all'!

Aside from the stimulus of lively conversation at these gatherings and the relief of coming down from the isolation of his studio at the top of the Vale Hotel, the Carline home became, for a few critical years, another home from home. Having rejected most of his own family – Richard Carline was unaware, all the time he knew Henry, that he had more than one brother and one sister – to adopt a family was for Henry a recurrent need. This postwar period was a difficult time for artists, no less for Henry, yet, with the struggle, he did some of his best work and re-established an individual, recognisable style, attracting favourable critical attention, although he remained as usual, uncertain of the direction he was taking. In this generally unfavourable climate, the contact with the Carline family was an enormous help, providing much needed moral support. Mrs Carline, in particular, was fond of Henry, instinctively mothering him at a time when he began to experience terrible pangs of loneliness.

Henry was a little older than most of the visitors to Downshire Hill and Richard felt, in retrospect, that he rather took advantage of his position by sometimes being unnecessarily perverse and manipulative in the company. He was still noticeably handsome but his youthful good looks had the imprint of experience, his features lined with war weariness and drained by the effects of continuing ill-health. Still there was great personal charm but he could be unpredictably awkward and was described as 'decidedly waspish' by Kate Foster who eventually became the unwitting object of a sharp disagreement between Henry and Richard. Both men undoubtedly found her attractive and Richard became increasingly exasperated and affronted as Henry paid excessive attention to his mother whilst conspicuously ignoring Kate. Richard made his feelings known outspokenly to Henry and relations were never quite the same again. The trivial details of the tiff are unimportant: Henry's irritability and perverseness of mood were largely attributable then to his regular lack of sleep and his general debility. More significant was how, whenever earnestness and profundity were unrelieved by wit, Henry always became impatient, often flippant, and it seems likely that his so-called rudeness on this occasion was totally misconstrued. The outcome of the incident may have been symptomatic of a major deficiency in the 'cercle' as a whole, the tenor of which was characterised by a near Teutonic intensity and a notable absence of humour – unlike the Bloomsberries, for example, whose high seriousness was complemented by their unfailing ability to laugh at themselves and rarely to take offence.

Stanley, before his emotional involvement with Hilda Carline, was well-matched to the character of the group. He liked talking and, although he seemed Chaplinesque in stature, was almost totally without a sense of humour, a deficiency upon which Henry loved to play. In the spring of 1927, having already perpetrated the April Fool's trick on Roger Fry who turned up at a bogus piano recital at the Wigmore Hall to be given by Mr Henry Lamb, Henry then turned his attention to Stanley who, during the February and March had had a first, highly successful one-man show at the Goupil Gallery. Then, Stanley was living and working at Henry's studio at the Vale Hotel and, to annoy his young friend, Henry arranged for a Rolls-Royce to be driven round by a salesman who was convinced that he had a genuine customer. The victim was absolutely livid and, soon suspecting that Henry was a party to the ruse, wrote him pages and pages of complaint: 'I have often made it clear to you, or at least tried to', he began his long-winded admonishment, 'that I hate ragging or jesting of any kind. What irritates me is your presumption in thinking you knew me to the extent of making me the subject of a jest. There is one thing I know, & that is that whoever did write to these people . . . it was certainly not a Christian Scientist that did it. You are quite incapable of knowing or calculating what effect your "jest" might have on me apart from having no right to do it.

If you do not send me the name of the person who wrote or told RRs to write to me, I shall be put to the terrible trouble of finding out & I certainly shall find out.

It does not matter in the least to me your saying I am making heavy weather or being absurd in this matter. You are *utterly incapable* of knowing what I am feeling at all. I dare say that I was explained to RRs as being a very wealthy & a likely client which would have been a LIE told with intent to deceive. Without being in the least degree morally prudish, this kind of thing makes me more wild than any malicious or slanderous lie, because this last has been done in hot blood & the other kind has been done as a result of having at some time been a university under graduate or Public School boy. I know that all such as these last are expected to take jests "in good part" "be sportsmanlike" & all the rest of it.

If there is a time when I wont 'join in' in a jest it is when some such attitude as the above mentioned is expected of me. Would you believe it possible for a person *with* a sense of humour & a generous outlook to dislike anything done in jest & for a "rag"? You've got a lot to do before you can answer this question. First you have to know what a sense of humour means & then to know what a jest means & entails & that last would take you a long time.

You need not feel anxious on my behalf as to the possibility of my being or appearing absurd in this matter. To appear an ass in the eyes of yourself or any of the people you mention as being some of my best friends would not worry me in the least. If the person was any that I have mentioned I'd make them spit blood, though I feel you are (the) person to attack.

If you & your friends idea was to give & cause me annoyance & irritation, you have both succeeded admirably, but that is the irritating part of it: that you neither of you did it for this purpose but expected me to "enter into the joke"! Making me a party to a jest (a thing I loathe) which entails lying, deceit & the desire to make a fool of somebody!

Oh & I dare say I would be thought to be lacking in heaven knows what for looking at this in this way . . . I don't want any apology that is no use to me: I want to ensure against this kind of thing happening again & that is why I am put to the inconvenience of trying to show you what my feelings are about these "rags".

> . . . Keep saying to yourself & everybody else if you must that I . . .
> have no sense of humour, that I cant see a joke, or that I am mean petty
> or anything you like, any of that great heap of "clever" "cutting"
> sarcasms, witticisms, Oh Christ knows what anything only in return for
> this . . . leave me alone.'

Stanley would never forget an ill turn and Henry's jest he used to
recall till the end of his life. When Henry was painting his portrait a
year later, he even took the opportunity at one sitting to blaze away
at Henry.

What Stanley utterly failed to appreciate from between the
blinkers of his extreme self-centredness was that Henry, almost in
the same breath as devising his practical joke, had written to his
friend Lawrence Haward, Curator of the Manchester City Art
Gallery, saying, 'I was so much struck by Stanley Spencer's
exhibition which opened last week at Goupil's that I cannot help
suggesting a visit to it on the part of you and your Powers in case one
is not already arranged. The vast Resurrection picture which I had
seen at various stages during the past 4 years at his studio, and
generally without enthusiasm, produced an overwhelming impression
seen as it can be now in a larger room and at a proper distance'.
Stanley was also apt to overlook the extent to which Henry had
helped him more directly for, apart from the saga of the 'Apple
Picture' and Henry's continuing to find and encourage patrons on
Stanley's behalf, he also, during the war, purchased by instalments
The Centurion's Servant which Stanley had shown at the N.E.A.C.
Winter Exhibition in 1915 and which is now in the Tate.

Henry was helpful as well to Stanley's younger brother Gilbert,
whose 'Crucifixion Picture', now also in the Tate, he bought from
the Slade summer show of 1914 for £20. 'Lamb, with Muirhead Bone,
and Francis Dodd', recalled Gilbert Spencer,

> 'was one of those selfless artists who though not rich themselves were
> prepared to offer the pictures of young artists for sale inside their own
> studios. I did not have to wait long before I received a characteristic
> note from him telling me that Lady Ottoline Morrell had bought it for
> the Contemporary Art Society for £100, which he hoped I did not
> mind!'[12]

Gilbert was as outgoing, generous and witty as brother Stanley was
not. Lytton, after meeting Gilbert, was moved to tell Henry that he
was like a breath of fresh air and even in old age he retained the
earthy ebullience of a music hall comedian referring, with the most

suggestive winks and nods, to Henry's amatory prowess. Gilbert also had continuing affection for Henry and praise for him as an artist: 'Every penny he owned he earned', he wrote, admiringly,

'and yet there never was a more ruthlessly independent painter. He was very selective when portrait painting. It was not the faces that primarily interested him, and in conversation one discovered that he had all sorts of odd reasons for agreeing to paint his subjects.'[13]

In his memoirs, Gilbert claimed to have been influenced by Henry's use of light figures against a dark background, citing particularly the second of Henry's large war pictures. There is no reason to doubt the veracity of the assertion, but only the vaguest influence is discernible in Gilbert's work; rather it would seem a genuine attempt to record a tangible acknowledgement of his indebtedness to Henry. Moreover, Gilbert was a witness to much of the planning and painting of that second war picture, most of which was done during the summer of 1920 while Henry was at Stourpaine and Gilbert and Stanley were in the nearby village of Durweston. 'Would it disturb you if Gil & I came to stay in your district for a few weeks', Stanley had asked Henry, 'If you could find us any old room we could both come and do some landscape.'

Earlier that year, Henry had exhibited in Manchester a small study called *Succouring wounded in a wood on the Doiran Front*, a memory of Salonika, which, combined with the success of his 'Irish Troops', prompted the City Art Gallery committee to commission him to paint a picture based on the study 'for the definite sum of £300'. In June, after a reconnaissance trip to Dorset, Henry informed Manchester that he had been fortunate in securing good lodgings in the country, where he hoped to start on the picture as soon as his sketches were returned: 'I shall then be free of the annoyances which interrupted the progress of the War Picture I painted in this studio for the Government last year . . . I appreciate greatly the liberty with regard to size etc . . . Under such conditions I think I can promise you the picture well under the 12 months.'

The 'studio' at Stourpaine, near the church, was no more than a large wooden barn, but in its size and peacefulness was ideal although, at the time, Henry may not have been fully aware of how near-perfect it was. In his previous quests for quiet and solitude he had gone far further afield, often to find the company of the 'natives' an intrusion. Here, the gentle villagers were sympathetic, helpful even, interested but not inquisitive, several of the men posing as soldiers for the more detailed studies of the finished picture. Hitherto, in Brittany and Ireland, his attempts to import friends for company had usually proved disastrous and disruptive. In Stourpaine, he was safe from interruption since, for once wisely, he had found lodgings for Stanley and Gilbert a mile or so away in the next village where, during the day, they were busy painting landscape. But he had their company in the evenings when they would wander over to see Henry and discuss the picture's progress. Henry stayed barely a quarter of a mile from his makeshift studio, at Havelins Farm, with Mrs Draper. Her son, who still lives in the farmhouse, remembered being invited, with other children of the village, into the barn to see the painting. Occasionally, Henry would join the Spencers, painting out-of-doors. One result of these diversions – actually of Havelins Farm and done on a return trip the following year – he gave as a present to Mrs Draper. Modest in size, small in scale, the picture hangs in the farmhouse kitchen: at first glance it could be mistaken for a Stanley Spencer; second glance suggests a Gilbert Spencer; only close inspection reveals the signature, 'H. Lamb 1921'. Though a slight example, the picture, full of charm, confirms how close was the affinity between the three painter-friends in the early twenties. 'Young' Mr Draper recalled Augustus, Dorelia, and T. E. Lawrence visiting Stourpaine to see the war picture. Later, Lawrence was to commission Henry to draw Gen. Dawnay for the first privately printed edition in 1926 of *The Seven Pillars of Wisdom*.

Troops on the Struma was completed, more or less, during that summer before its removal to Hampstead in the autumn. In the following February, 1921, Henry reported to Manchester, 'There are some fairly serious alterations to the picture which I must try to finish before it starts on its journeys. I doubt if their necessity would be noticed by others, but having lived now for many weeks with it, my conscience will not spare me the job. Otherwise I think it is my best picture so far and I am feeling bucked at receiving the same verdict from two opinions I most value in the world.' One of those valued opinions might well have been that of Gilbert, who, at the Academy opening the year before, had been a great admirer of 'Irish Troops'; the other could have been Kennedy's, although, in his published, more considered opinion, in the monograph of 1924, he tended to prefer the earlier painting, saying of *Troops on the Struma*,

'This picture is essentially more of a generalisation than the Palestine one, and it is impossible not to feel that the Pre-Raphaelite treatment which reinforced in the latter the impression of intensity, suits this work less well, and appears to have a slightly confining effect. To judge from a preliminary sketch ... its beautiful colour would seem to have demanded rather more adjustment in translation to a more epic scale. One feels that a quality is lacking which might have carried this noble conception a stage further.'[14]

Rather appositely, Kennedy went on to describe the 'Struma Picture' as 'almost Shakespearean', quoting from the First Scene of Act Two in *Henry IV Part I*, in which the carriers are tightening the girths of their pack-horses in the small hours of the morning, all the while exchanging small talk and complaining as they wait. Waiting, and its ensuing boredom, are very much the theme of the painting and anyone with experience of the frequent longueurs of life in the services would recognise how effectively it is depicted. Not that the achievement makes it a great painting. If it were simply a portrayal of ennui it might succeed merely as illustration, a trap that here has been skilfully avoided. In calling it 'essentially more of a generalisation', Kennedy was absolutely right, though it is arguable whether the 'Struma Picture' is *more* generalised than 'Irish Troops'. What is certain, in continuing the analogy with Shakespeare, is how superbly Henry has risen above 'the trivialities of the homely dialogue'; parochial as the models for the soldiers must have been – and most would have been ex-servicemen returned to Stourpaine – they are movingly representative of a much wider section of humanity. These anonymous villagers, impassive, patient, despite airing shared grievances, are monumentalised, not pompously or superficially, but profoundly, symbolising the vulnerability and suffering that is the common lot of the conscripted man in wartime.

The mood of *Troops on the Struma* could hardly be more different to *Irish Troops in the Judaean Hills*. In portraying the polarities of war – violent action and boring passivity – the two pictures are exactly complementary. On the one hand, the dynamics of shock and fear, on the other, the tension and anxiety of waiting; extremes that are reflected in their respective designs. In direct contrast to the high viewpoint and strong diagonals rushing across the Palestine picture, the Salonika one is made up of the verticals of the soldiers and trees that occupy the upper, greater part of the canvas and grow out of the horizontals lying across the lower, lesser part. The change of

235

direction is made just about on the golden section, the two parts linked by foliage. The whole is seen from below eye level, as if from the front row of the stalls, but in fact from the trench in the foreground. The design has a classical stability and a quiet strength that belie the sinister atmosphere of unease and tension, a tension increased by the steely light and the balance of colour, a preponderance of bluish purple contrasted with the warmer, khaki foreground, evoking perfectly the chilling alienation of the moment before dawn. Kennedy called the treatment 'Pre-Raphaelite' which seems wide of the mark since the only faint similarity to a group of painters Henry heartily disliked is possibly in the degree of precision in the execution, though even this is a superficial connection and, in none of his major paintings was Henry subsumed by anecdote or narrative nor was he ever a microscopic naturalist. In the 'Struma Picture', every detail is stylised consistently and integrated with the whole. Though it lacks something of the spontaneity and directness of the earlier war picture, only in the slight, unobtrusive overpainting of the right hand group of plants is there any visible evidence of changes of mind; and the 'fairly serious alterations' that Henry mentioned are nowhere noticeable. 'The seated figures on the left . . . are combatants . . . suffering from Malaria', Henry told Manchester, suggesting that the full title – 'correct in military language' – should be *Advance Dressing Station on the Struma 1916.*

The painting was first shown at the Royal Academy Summer Exhibition in 1921. 'I have in front of me a gradually increasing pile of curled up press notices referring to your picture', wrote Lawrence Haward, Director of the Manchester City Art Gallery, to Henry after the opening, 'Most people seem agreed that it is what in old days used to be called the picture of the year, and even those who don't like it thoroughly respect it'.[15] Henry Tonks, not given to praise lightly, had already complimented Manchester on their imaginative patronage: 'I am so pleased you have given Lamb the commission', he wrote, 'In doing so you are doing good to him and to the Town in making your own artists take a pride in their native place. Your policy is bound to lead to good results.'[16] And Dodd, in June, 'just back after 4 weeks holiday', wrote,

'I have at last seen the Lamb picture. You are to be congratulated very much indeed and I think the courage your chairman showed in commissioning so young an artist has proved so successful, that I hope it may lead (of course with discretion) to the purchase in the same way of other works, for there is no doubt at all that it is a cheap picture as well as an excellent one'.[17]

The summers at Stourpaine had convinced Henry that he must move to the country. Since demobilisation, his health had worsened: 'I have been recommended to chuck work for 3 months and go walking in Spain in order to cure my sleeplessness which gets no better', he wrote, after completing the picture for Manchester and thinking the prospect a 'horrible proposition'. Gilbert Spencer recalled, at the time taking 'ten-mile walks with him in an attempt to ease the effect of his glassy-eyed insomnia . . . which knocked him off painting for days at times.'[18] After months of looking for somewhere in the Dorset area, in February 1922, he finally lighted upon Poole.

Poole was not an arbitrary choice: the old town and harbour were quaint and charming, but unpretentious, intimate, small in scale and accessible, and, with the townsfolk, seemed appealing and promising subject matter. And though, intending to shake forever most of the London dust from his feet, it was a not inconvenient distance from the Vale Hotel studio, which he continued to rent. Above all, Poole was only two or three miles from Alderney, and from Dorelia.

'My first two months of Poole have been terribly unproductive as far as quantity goes', wrote Henry to Richard Carline on Easter Sunday, 1922, 'but I daresay I can allow myself some discount for the move of headquarters, the new cares of property etc.' For the first time in his life, almost to his surprise and rather reluctantly, in purchasing No.10 Hill Street, Henry had become 'a man of property'. A modest early Victorian terraced house, now demolished, No.10 was 'in a slum street, which was once genteel . . . very near the quay', having 'a sort of narrow town-garden with a cottage at the far end' which he converted to a studio.

Once settled, he began a series of rooftop views from the window of his new workplace, similar to several he was to paint during his five years at Hill Street. After these initial essays in the genre, he decided that townscape suited him better than landscape, which he painfully discovered, 'making a snail's progress', was not his game. In Brittany, he had felt the same, although sometimes in Donegal he had been encouraged by the occasional *paysage*. But, despite his enthusiasm for and sensitive awareness of landscape, and despite an appreciation of landscape painting, it was never his *métier*. By the

Thirties, he came to be convinced of the value of spontaneity in painting – sometimes to his detriment – and although he loved to get out of the studio, into the countryside with easel and oils, enjoying the direct contact with nature, the results fall short of his excitement and expectations, and show him not to be a convincing *plein-airist*. For him, landscape painting became a refreshing, but minor, antidote and it is significant that, though landscape motifs frequently played an important part in his pictures, none of his major works is exclusively in that genre.

In Poole, it was the townscape, literally on his doorstep, that immediately captured his imagination. The rooftop series, and other townviews, were a successful departure. Unconsciously, they may have been sparked off by Stanley's *Mending Cowls, Cookham* of 1915, a small pencil sketch for which he had sent Henry during the war. The picture, a view of oasthouses from the nursery window of Fernlea, is now in the Tate and may also have been in Henry's possession for a while. In conception, in scale, and to some extent in treatment; there are similarities; but whereas Stanley has abstracted and stylised the shapes into a simplified, dramatic pattern, Henry is most interested in the varieties of angle and texture and, where figures occur, in the human incident, although it is never obtrusive. To describe these delightful pictures as *intimiste* might be misleading since it is a term usually associated with interiors by Bonnard, Vuillard, and the Camden Town painters. However, there is an intimacy about them, so close are the houses opposite, as if they could be touched by leaning out of the window. Paradoxically too, it is as though the outside were brought indoors, suggesting that *intimiste* might not be too inappropriate a description.

Being a small port, Poole was especially vulnerable economically in the post-war period and had a high rate of unemployment, culminating in the General Strike of 1926. At the time, Henry, so used to seeing dole queues and men standing idle in the streets, declared that he saw no difference. Living on the street, as it were, he was prone to disturbance and tamed one persistent irritant by painting his portrait. *The Doler* of 1923, sits tense, tight-lipped, broad-shouldered, uncomfortable in an alien context, as though doing penance for his wrongdoing – as, in a sense, he was. Unfortunately, the sitter's dis-ease, the peculiar circumstances, and Henry's lack of sympathy and patience, made for an unappealing, uninteresting portrait and an indifferent painting.

Boats, Henry had rarely drawn, despite having had ready access to them at Doëlan and Gola, but in Poole, with Hill Street leading towards the quayside, he was inspired to make studies of sailing ships, although he took the ideas little further. Nevertheless, *Football Edition* of 1926, set near the quay, is one of the major compositions from this period. Nearly five-and-a-half feet by six, it has the warm glow of an autumn evening and with a touch of pathos is beautifully unified. The groups of figures are integrated and take on a deep significance, representing a moment of simple excitement in the humdrum lives of habitually bored, probably unemployed, underprivileged men and youths. Poignant as the message might be, any social comment is contained, implicit, and the result remains a satisfying painting, powerfully evocative of an epoch and a place.

The house in Hill Street, unlike the Vale Hotel studio, was big enough to accommodate visitors without encroachment on Henry's workspace. His longest-staying, most dependent guest at Poole, was Stanley who, for the latter half of 1921, had been living at Steep, near Petersfield in Hampshire, with Muirhead Bone. Even the kindly, enabling, long-suffering Bone, who had invited Stanley to paint a series of panels for a war memorial in the village hall, had had enough of him by the end of the year. 'I have just had an interview with Bone', wrote Stanley to Henry, just before Christmas, 'in which he had the ordeal of announcing to me that he was afraid I should have to . . . "take lodgings"'. Stanley moved to The Square in Petersfield until the summer of 1922, when he mentioned to Henry wanting to leave: 'do you think I could go to your rooms in Hampstead or come to you in Poole where I could get a room?' he asked.

Over the next few years, Henry was to be a haven, a rescuer, a 'father confessor', as Richard Carline called him, to Stanley, whose frequent emotional upheavals were becoming – despite the constancy of his love for Cookham – a counterpoint to his activity as a painter. Sometime in the summer of 1922 he stayed with Henry at Hill Street, moving to Hampstead to the Carline home in the December when his relationship with Hilda Carline seemed blooming. Early in the new year, he again wrote to Henry, 'Would it be possible for me to live at Vale Hotel Studio, as it has now become imperitive[sic] that I leave 47 Downshire Hill.' Having said that he had definitely finished the affair with Hilda and packed up everything, making ready to leave, almost immediately after he announced that there was no great hurry: 'I hate doing drastic things and everything seems to be cooling off nicely'. Eventually, he stayed in the Vale studio for most of the winter of 1923–24 whilst, at Downshire Hill, the Carlines endured the ups and downs of Stanley's lovelife. 'Cookham & Hilda are the limit', wrote Henry, with heartfelt sympathy, to Richard, 'and I am sorry for all you Downshires daily feeling the brunt of these limitations & having to put up with them. As far as I am concerned I have found the "upset of balance" to which you refer has greatly spoilt my interest in Cookham as a person.'

Stanley married Hilda in 1925, and they continued to live together at the Vale Hotel studio. But, they were not happy for long and soon, Stanley was unburdening himself again to Henry – in Hampstead, and in Poole. In the spring of 1928, Henry reported from Hill Street that Cookham had spent nearly a week there, 'Rather an addling time', he wrote; 'When he had gone for two or three days I had the whirling feel in my ears & brain like the result of a too long motordrive. He simply can't stop babbling and seething. When it was too dark to paint . . . I did a head of him which turned out better than could be expected seeing that he never stopped his chatter . . . However he can be very charming & it is impossible not to pity him in that desperate ménage to the failure of which he freely confesses'. A few days later, having recovered more fully from Stanley's visit, he called it 'a very pleasant echo of old times'.

The most historic moment and Henry's greatest achievement in helping Stanley as an artist came during a prolonged stay at Poole in the summer of 1923. 'Stanley sits at a table all day evolving acres of Salonika and Bristol war compositions', Henry told Richard, and it was these drawings that were seen by the Behrends, two visitors to No.10 who were to give Stanley his largest and most prestigious commission. Henry had known 'the faithful, generous, undemonstrative Behrends' since 1911. 'They are very nice', he had told Ottoline, 'She is dark and pleasantly featured, lively, naive and sincere, but not striking in any way. The man is thick and curly haired also dark but reserved and rather intelligent and very nice. Both very young.' Mary and Louis Behrend spent most of their lives in helping young and impecunious artists of genuine talent and originality and Henry had been one of the first to benefit from their patronage and he was probably one of the last when, in 1947, they commissioned him to paint the portrait of Benjamin Britten, a composer they had already helped.

Back in 1912, at the beginning of that busy and often black year, Henry began a portrait of Mary. 'I am to do a ¾ if possible but to please myself in everything', he wrote Ottoline, mentioning that Louis Behrend 'did not think £25 too much for head & shoulders and I think I'm to get £50 for the ¾ length if I do it, instead.' The light was so bad at the second sitting that the painter and his model retreated to Simpson's in the Strand to try, what Henry called, 'the mutton, cigar & chess cure'. By the middle of February, he began a new canvas and, for encouragement, Mary brought him a pot of flowers and some new jewels to paint on her bosom. But a week later, he was onto another canvas, the third edition, 'it is much fresher & livelier than the old-one and the colours are interesting though subdued and simple', he told Ottoline, saying how, 'To-day Mr B startled me by sending his cheque for it. £50! it is altogether too fabulous and kind and I am returning £20 on the best conscientious grounds: they are such angelic people and not at all rich, I like them very much and won't allow them to have such manly feelings of generosity. Last night they took me to a big Symphony Concert after dining with them.' After the final sitting in March, however, Henry felt he had failed with Mary's portrait: during a touching struggle of mutual generosity he was paid £40 and did a quick oil-sketch of her husband as a present. 'They are thoroughly nice people and I am glad to know them', he wrote, 'I feel as if I could call there once a month for the rest of my life. I am sorry in a way that she doesn't come any more: her quiet intelligent ways often used to beguile me out of reprobate humours.'

Mary had rather fallen for Henry; he was flattered too. They both were disappointed that the sittings were at an end and only a few days later, she turned up at the Vale Hotel studio 'looking dewy and winning'. Often they musicked away very agreeably, he on the piano, she the violin, in Mozart Sonatas, though he thought Mary played too stiffly. The Behrends would take him to concerts, opera and ballet and, when they lived in London, at No.90 Adelaide Road, Swiss Cottage, he would go for lunch or dinner. Once, he took Lytton to tea: 'it seemed to delight her ambitious young heart to have a real intellectual author in her drawing-room', said Henry, 'She was outwardly bright & happy, but I could see the tortures of self-consciousness blighting the pleasure and racking her within.'

The portrait of Mary Behrend, though admired by Duncan, is a curious, fumbling affair, painted as though Henry was unable to define her social role – perhaps because then, Mary couldn't either, before she was known as a patron and collector. Certainly, it is one of the most Greco-esque of all Henry's portraits, not only because the sitter wears a mantilla, but also in the dramatic use of light and shade, in the pose itself, and in the treatment, although Henry was never happy with it. After he had delivered it, framed, he confessed that he was glad to be rid of it and hoped to replace it someday. What her husband thought is not recorded but Henry did mention, after painting him one Sunday morning, that, 'He got a shock on seeing his wife's portrait which he survived and then steadily liked it better gazing at it during his sitting.' Henry never liked the one of Louis Behrend either and it was to be another fourteen years before he was to try again.

In 1918, the Behrends moved to Burghclere in Hampshire, where their collection of contemporary British painting grew considerably. By the Thirties, they had acquired at least twenty of Henry's pictures, including the vast 'Strachey', and they were already admirers of Stanley's work before seeing it at Poole. Shortly after Stanley was demobbed, Henry had taken him, with brother 'Gil', to tea with the Behrends and Stanley had pronounced them 'extra-ordinary sensible people'. But it was their visit to Hill Street in the summer of 1923 that effectively sowed the seeds of their most inspired patronage. The story of the Burghclere Memorial Chapel is well documented and well known but Henry has not always been given proper credit for his role in the initial stages of the scheme. For once, Stanley appears to have been genuinely grateful, for on hearing the news that he was to be commissioned to decorate the interior of a chapel to be built in memory of Mary's brother who had died during the war from an illness contracted in Macedonia, he wrote to Henry, 'Of course I expected to hear something nice when you said the Behrends were getting keen as the result of your efforts but I did not expect quite such glorious news as I received this morning.'

The chapel project was to occupy Stanley for much of the following decade during which time, doubtless to Henry's relief, he was to move to Burghclere to live and work. But during the planning Henry was burdened with every detail, every minute change: 'If you fealt[sic] you could come and healp[sic] with the plans while I was

242

Hon. Mrs. Bryan Guinness (Lady Diana Mosley) *1932   Oil on canvas   133.3 × 101.3*
Alexander Mosley

The Level Crossing: Souvenir of Poole 1922   1953   Oil on canvas   92.3 × 123.7   Private collection

there', he suggested to Henry, 'I would like you to as I am thinking of some judicial alterations'. Originally, Kennedy was to have been the architect: 'his idea is . . . that you should be director of the scheme', Stanley told Henry, 'as you would in that way be holding a more aloof position than either Kennedy or I, and would therefore be better able to deal with and controle[sic] the more knotty parts of the scheme'. In the event, Kennedy withdrew and Henry, after being such an inspiring and effective mediator between patron and painter, seems to have played no further, active part in the project.

Whilst Stanley had been evolving the many war compositions, Henry was working away at his Poole pictures, one of which he had just finished at about the time the Behrends called. 'After announcing his complete dislike of it in one devastating little sentence', wrote Henry to Richard, 'Cookham then goes on to praise it for hours at a time with seeming enthusiasm.' Henry found most praise and most blame resistible, but Stanley had an unfortunate, unnerving, and ultimately cruel way of pouring cold water on eulogy. Like a child, he could not help but be honest in his criticism and never took account of the other person's feelings, a refreshingly healthy attitude in many respects but sometimes disabling to Henry. 'I went to Oxford and saw your portrait of the Don', wrote Stanley, probably of Henry's portrait of the Provost of Worcester College of 1923, 'I like the Don portrait best of all your portraits which I have not seen . . . At first when I saw your Don portrait from the far end of the room I thought how bad, but you will be relieved to hear that this first impression did not remain above a moment.'

Although Stanley acknowledged his gratitude to Henry by letter, he seems not to have been demonstrably appreciative of the unique opportunity provided by the Burghclere commission and it was left to the Behrends themselves – always kindly, thoughtful, sensitive, unobtrusive, and scrupulously fair – who, thinking they must in turn do something for Henry, commissioned him, in 1926, to do their portraits, this time, a family group, for they now had two children, Juley and George. Henry made several studies of each of the family separately and at least two preparatory studies for the group which seemed to go from bad to worse. Privately, and irreverently, he had nicknamed the Behrends, 'the Barebums', and he began calling the family group his 'Bums Symphony', complaining, 'I have been rather gloomily plodding away at my eternal Bums . . . Oh! such ups and downs. So many days are washed out from mouldiness derived from the guts, throat, insomnia – not to speak of the embittered heart!'

Henry was concurrently in the throes of having his hopes raised and alternately depressed by Dorelia, though none of the fluctuations are evident in the finished portrait, which is surprisingly serene, untroubled in its treatment, cosy and affectionate. 'The picture shows the frame (centre) of Spencer's well known *Marrow Bed* over the piano where Lamb would play sonatas with my mother whose violin performance was not of his standard, as I recall my mother saying almost tearfully on several occasions. Hence the prominent fiddle case', wrote George Behrend in 1977.[19] He, sitting on his father's lap, looking the image of his mother, would have been about four at the time, and his sister, a year or so older. The single portraits and much of the group were done during the summer, at The Grey House, the Behrends' home at Burghclere, until Henry, rapidly losing patience, declared, 'I don't feel capable of staying an hour longer here as soon as I am able to flit . . . If Bum can find me a warm room large enough somewhere near Newbury I am willing to try again in the autumn . . . Otherwise he must be content with the studies for his money and I must prepare for a winter of bankruptcy.'

The Behrends were never difficult, demanding, arrogant, or interfering patrons and Henry's remarks seem unfounded and unfair. Again his irritability had got the better of him and, 'After a few more days desperate encounter with the Bums' group' he 'finally abandoned it'. Perhaps partly because of this, the result is more satisfying than he ever realised, with a pleasing completeness and charming freshness, despite the impatience, despair and bad feelings surrounding its later stages. Less immaculate than *The Anrep Family* of six years earlier, *The Behrend Family* is indicative of the looser style of brushwork that Henry was to adopt from the Thirties onwards. It is too, less ambitious in scale, less complex in design, less stylised, and certainly less witty than *The Kennedy Family* of 1921. Yet, is there not the faintest hint of humour in the handling of the perplexed seriousness of Mary Behrend? Does she not gaze wistfully at the artist as she must have in 1912? Or has the picture simply and unconsciously been infiltrated by Henry's mockery of the sitter's continuing susceptibility to his charms? In the 'Behrends' as well, there is a happier relationship between the group and the background than in, for example, *The Japp Family*, painted only a few months later at Rooksnest Farm, Darsie Japp's home and riding stables, near Lambourn in Berkshire. Being much larger with the group further away, the space around the Japps seems vacuous, merely a backdrop to an already uninteresting composition. The Behrends, on the other hand, sit close to the picture frame, not an inch is wasted, and the 'business' in the minimal background is telling, contained, and never obtrusive or boring. Modest in size – 22″ x 27″ – and painted thinly with a quick, sure touch, the luminous colour is almost like watercolour and reminiscent of Gainsborough, one of 'the old stations' where Henry always halted in trips round the National Gallery. A lovely balance between portrayal of character, composition, colour, handling and scale, *The Behrend Family* remains among the best of Henry's portrait groups.

His portraits of Stanley, though of historic importance, are less successful than suggested by the personality. A magnificent subject, he was apparently an appalling sitter and neither Henry's continuing admiration for the artist nor his reservations concerning the man are reflected in the examples of 1921 and '28. Competent likenesses that they are, they make no comment nor reveal any great insight into the complexities of character, unlike those of Lytton or Kennedy, for example. 'I expect you will make a "Velasquez dwarf" portrait of me', wrote Stanley to Henry before he started, admitting, 'that would at least distinguish it from Stracheys.' This was in the later Twenties, sometime after Henry's interest in him as a person had passed. The earlier portrait is the more probing and more complete; the latter was severely hampered by the sitter, still seething at the artist for having been the victim in the Rolls-Royce affair.

But throughout, Henry was unfailingly generous in his assessment of Stanley's painting. Even when he thought Stanley had produced a bad design, he still praised what he called his 'powers of realization & an erudition of style equally amazing'. And in 1924, when the 'Spencer' volume appeared in the series of 'Contemporary British Artists', having thoroughly denigrated the *Henry Lamb*, he went on to say of 'Cookham's book',

'I was the reverse of disappointed I think the result is overwhelming & the public ought to be overwhelmed. The "noble constancy" of the little gentlemans work. . . together with the astounding novelty of such a personality stepping in at this time of day to restore narrative art to its primitive purity lost in history since Fra Angelica & in every child after the age of 12 or 13 – Not *rescued* nothing so conscious, but just frankly stated & reestablished.'

NOTES

1 Cooper *The Rainbow Comes and Goes* p.129.
2 Cooper p.123.
3 Army Records
4 Robert Ross – Campbell Dodgson : 3 Feb 1918.
5 James Bone – John Buchan : 7 Mar 1918.
6 Ministry of Information – Henry Lamb : 12 Nov 1918.
7 E. Rothenstein *Stanley Spencer* pl.4, notes.
8 Galerien *The Renaissance of the Tate Gallery* 'The Studio' Jul 1921.
9 Ferguson *The Arts in Britain in World War I* p.112.
10 Chamot *Modern Painting in England* p.76.
11 Richard Carline: notes to his painting of the Downshire Terrace group.
12 G. Spencer *Memoirs of a Painter* pp.33–4.
13 G. Spencer *Stanley Spencer* p.170.
14 G. Kennedy *Henry Lamb* p.28.
15 Lawrence Haward – Henry Lamb : 12 May 1921.
16 Henry Tonks – Lawrence Haward : 24 June 1920.
17 Francis Dodd – Lawrence Haward : 4 Jun 1921.
18 Spencer *Memoirs* p.68.
19 George Behrend – Christie's : 19 Dec 1977.

TWELVE

CARRINGTON

———

'I find I can not get on with any work unless I plant & cultivate myself carefully in one place', Henry once wrote. After four years in Poole, he had done a lot of good painting and some of his best, most personal pictures came from the house in Hill Street. In 1922, he had had a modestly successful one-man show, his first, at the Alpine Club Gallery in South Audley Street; he exhibited at the Academy; portrait commissions were coming his way, particularly from the Oxbridge colleges; and Kennedy's slight but significant monograph was published in 1924, putting him among the leading contemporary artists in Britain: Henry Lamb was becoming known.

Poole, initially, had offered him, as an artist, wonderful material and he had been carried away with the pictorial scope of his new surroundings. He had kept in touch with London through an occasional portrait combined with a cultural debauch, but he was beginning to feel his age and to be more conscious of his singleness. Nominally he was married to Euphemia but he had no children, no family of his own. The house was not large, but the longer he lived there, the emptier it seemed and the more aware he became of a sense of isolation. Despite his success as a painter, as a man he felt in limbo.

At first too, being neither of a practical nor technical disposition and forever impatient with bureaucracy, he had been preoccupied, perplexed, overwhelmed with, as he put it, 'the new cares of property'. He was not inhospitable, making friends with

Christopher Le Fleming, 'a nice Bretonesque youth – nearly blind but beautiful and very musical. He comes and musicates with me for hours and in this way I have been spared many solitary pangs'. He entertained various groups of old friends – and enemies: Helen came, with her 'Ma' and Roger, Boris, Kennedy, the Behrends, the Bonavias from Manchester days, Stanley, of course, Gilbert, Richard, Dodo, as often as she could escape 'the August clutches', T. E. Lawrence – 'Henry Lamb is in Poole', he wrote, 'and will play wonderfully to me if I go over';[1] and, a new friend, Carrington.

Dora Carrington had been a student at the Slade, a contemporary of Gilbert Spencer and Mark Gertler, having had a long and troubled affair with the latter. In the autumn of 1915, inexplicably, she had fallen in love with Lytton, setting up house with him and their respective loves two years later in a remarkable ménage. Considering the mutuality of their friends and acquaintances, it is extraordinary how she and Henry seem never to have met before 1925, for during and immediately after the war, she encountered, often in quite intimate circumstances, many of his circle. In December 1916, after a hectic party, she reported to Lytton, probably with some exaggeration, that Euphemia had 'played the most prominent part in all proceedings' and, in 'a debauche of white arms and bosoms', had discovered Boris, the Armenian (her nickname for Augustus), 'and even more degraded specimens'. The following summer, after another party, she suddenly found Boris becoming aware of her charms and starting 'some very heavy and moist amours'. Augustus too, though it was hot and he could hardly stand, made further attempts at satisfying his lustful inclinations, and on the way home at three in the morning, the indefatigable Boris did 'as much heavy work as a hand from the opposite side of a taxi will permit'. That same summer, she mentioned speaking to Richard Carline, but was disappointed: 'he was not so beautiful as I had imagined', she told Lytton, 'Not my type of good looks I am afraid. Still we had a long conversation. He seemed pleasantly simple and easy to get on with.' Carrington had also met Dorelia, likening her to 'some Sibyl . . . smiling mysteriously . . . so amazingly beautiful.' And once, in November 1919 at Covent Garden, her attention was drawn to 'Henry in the Heights', when he was convalescing and awaiting demobilisation. But, despite the many connections and coincidences, they still did not meet until the beginning of 1925, when she wrote to Gerald Brenan,

'I was interested at meeting Henry Lamb. Mostly because of Lytton's past relations with him . . . He looks like an Army doctor who has seen "life" on the Tibet frontier or who has suffered from low fevers in Sierra Leone and also has a past murder, or crime, which makes him furtive and uneasy. He has a most unhappy face. But he is amusing and very charming sometimes . . . He is a most perverse man in his opinions.'[2]

Carrington – after she went to the Slade, she dropped the Dora forever – came upon Henry when he was depressed, not as badly as in 1912, but just at the point where, with continuing ill-health, he felt time to be running out: 'I am feeling so dejected by results in general & other things', he told her, 'I would like to down tools and disappear for some voyage'. Where, though? Before the war, he had seemed so much younger and fitter, and escaped easily to Doëlan, Paris, or Gola. Already, he had 'taken the exeat' to Poole. What next? Painting was going well; but the abortiveness of his social life with its emotional vagaries began to impinge on his work and, 'although abandoned by all outer resources', he confided to Carrington, 'I have managed to prevail against the dread pangs of loneliness'.

Between 1925 and '27, she played, mostly by proxy, a near-sisterly role in his often solitary existence. They wrote to each other regularly and she became his chief confidante. He encouraged her in her painting, admiring a portrait she was doing of E. M. Forster: 'I mean it shows a combination of all your best Haydnesque qualities with the true beginnings of the kind of amelioration that is needed to make them all eventually turn into Mozartian masterpieces.' When she sent him the present of a picture, he claimed not to have 'had such delight . . . for ages!' and told her, 'So far I cannot decide where it will be hung: at present it just features on a chair back for me to gaze on while munching my solitary meals. Probably it will go to my bedroom to appease the much more painful solitudes of that apartment.'

She came for a weekend: 'do come and dine here on Friday evening', he had suggested, 'Saturday morning could easily be filled with "pottering" – in fact there are 2 potteries here.' But when she accepted, he was apprehensive, saying there was very little to do in Poole in bad weather. Again he wrote, warning her that if it were wet, she would be bored. As he expected, she was bored – at first – telling her friend Julia Strachey that she had been for a dismal walk along the sea shore with him but rather revived after 'a lovely supper of broad beans and claret'.[3] He drew her, sensitively and, though viewed with the hindsight of her tragic end – after Lytton's death in 1932, she took her own life – poignantly.

Plants were a passion Henry shared with her, exchanging notes on their treatment and progress. Once, he took her a present of a most superb Mexican Lily, a great red lily on the top of a thick purple stalk of which she made a large painting.[4] He too painted several flower pieces, dahlias, hollyhocks and gladioli were some of his favourites, diversions done robustly and spontaneously. The last time he concentrated on plant form had been in Palestine, significantly during a lull in the fighting when he had had time to reflect on the pointlessness of life, to brood, and generally turn in upon himself.

Music became a refuge and playing and listening assumed even greater importance for him, whilst at Poole. Being near Bournemouth, he found some consolation in concerts by the Symphony Orchestra. Later, in 1936, he was to paint a portrait – singularly unpopular with the sitter – of Sir Dan Godfrey, the Bournemouth conductor for many years: when exhibited at the Royal Academy, it had the distinction of being satirised in 'Punch', with the caption 'Muscular development of the neck induced by the continual acknowledgement of applause', pointing up the portrait's caricature qualities which so annoyed Sir Dan.[5] Henry, in the Twenties, also made studies in oil and watercolour of the orchestra and ensemble, charming divertimenti, though underdeveloped and never fully combining his skill and experience as a painter with his knowledge and enthusiasm for music. At Hill Street, he listened a lot to records, a subject depicted in *The Gramophone*, a small panel of 1923, and again, a theme he seems not to have taken further. Above all, he had a beautiful piano that he played endlessly whenever he was unable to settle to painting and which, sometimes, after thoroughly loosening his fingers, he found 'maddening to leave . . . like a new bride in the middle of a honeymoon.'

Marriage and families, he referred to frequently during this spell of acute loneliness. 'Weddings seem fashionable', he complained to Carrington with some bitterness when his admirable housekeeper deserted him to get married: 'my perfect Gracie has left me' only returning to cut the grass and water the small plants and 'occasionally repress the various blights by means of a squirter', he reported, conceding that her husband was 'allowed to cut the "verges".' The excellent Gracie's replacement, he found hopeless, cruelly calling her 'a large pink cow'.

Nothing was right. The demands and successes of painting, the pleasures of music and plants, the comforting assurance of a home of his own, the diversion of old friends visiting, the stimulus of new friends, none was enough and Henry remained lonely and unfulfilled. The house was bigger than he needed and its emptiness accentuated his void. He observed his 'old mate' Lytton tended by his new confidante Carrington, and confessed feelings of jealousy, telling her, 'I . . . dote with admiration and envy on the way in which you cosset him'. A large picture of 1926, the largest of the Poole period, fully six feet in height by more than five and a half, eloquently expresses and seems to summarise his sense of isolation at the time.

At first called 'The Round Table' and known subsequently as *The Tea Party*, the setting is the living room of No. 10 and the focal area, an enormous dining table around which sit five, strangely assorted characters as if invited by chance. In the foreground, his back to the spectator, sits the artist, his balding pate painted conspicuously, a self-mocking acknowledgement of the advancing years. To his left and right, sitting bolt upright in their Sunday best, are two neighbours. Further round the table, to the left, leaning on his elbow, listening attentively, is Leverton Harris, writer and critic. And holding the floor, his back to the window, talking and gesticulating characteristically, is Stanley. Visually, constitutionally and socially, the people are so unrelated, so arbitrary, and quite how the idea arose to paint such a curiously ill-matched group is a mystery. What could they all have had in common other than knowing Henry and trying to follow the drift of Stanley's interminable monologue? Like five characters in search of an author, they sit together, yet so far apart and so separately, for the distance between each and their relationship with the table and the room is exaggerated by some perspectival distortion making the interior much more spacious than it could have been – judging from the area left by the demolishers of No. 10. Almost literally, the picture is a kind of conversation piece but concerns the inability to communicate. Though never exhibited at the Academy, it might have made an ideal, newsworthy, problem picture and it continues to intrigue and to be enigmatic. The reasons why are hardly aesthetic. The design is slightly unusual, the colour mostly warm and pleasant; technically and stylistically it is unexceptional, having some affinity with the brothers Spencer. Ultimately, it is unique, both to Henry and perhaps to British painting. More than he could ever have imagined, it is an autobiographical picture. The very disparateness of the group hints at his personal fragmentation and the extent of the spaces separating them suggests his alienation, uncertainty, and difficulty with relationships. Unconsciously, he has expressed his sadness and fear at life slipping away. In the last analysis, *The Tea Party* is about loneliness.

But Henry couldn't brood for long. Working on the large, ambitious 'Tea Party' during the summer of 1926 had been, indirectly, therapeutic and, as a result, he had worked through some of his depression. But it was not readily saleable and financially, he was no better off. He still had a living to make and sitters were waiting for portraits. One was his old friend Darsie Japp, who commissioned a family group to be painted at their home in Wiltshire, which Henry always called 'Japp-an'. Good-natured, tolerant Japp, who before the war had introduced him to Stanley, was about the only person Henry actively discouraged from painting, although he had been a Slade student and had some work in the War Museum: 'he should not paint', Henry had told Lytton decisively, 'In time there is hope he will grasp this truth also, and retire to the country and breed horses: which will be altogether advantageous'. Japp continued to paint, albeit modestly, but, as well, with some success, bred racehorses for a living. Furthermore, he kindly put Henry in the way of a stockbroker friend who was keen to have the fair features of his famous daughter immortalised. Eileen Bennett was an attractive young Wimbledon star whose portrait he began in the autumn and fortunately completed before her poor father lost everything in the stockmarket crash of the following year, 1927.

'The Tennis Girl', as Henry always referred to her, was painted in the Bennetts' sitting room with a north light, high up, overlooking the Brompton Oratory. Henry called the setting, a perfect bourgeois interior which, he declared facetiously, he loved. He had been left without a base in London when, earlier in 1926, he relinquished tenure of the Vale Hotel studio. While painting 'The Tennis Girl', he stayed on the edge of Hampstead, at 3 Arkwright Road, with his sister Dorothy, then Mrs Brook, and her pompous husband: 'London is too much for me', he told Carrington, 'I shall die of respectability going from this house to Brompton Rd. daily.' Luckily he made an auspicious start and pronounced the tennis girl a charmer, with the help of nothing but her lovely looks and good heart. But after reporting the stockbrokers continued to treat 'with solid magnificence', things began to go wrong. Then, with so many dark and foggy days spoiling the light, and his delightful model abandoning him for a holiday abroad, he postponed the finishing touches until the following March.

The painting was first shown at the R.A. Summer Exhibition in 1928, entitled 'Portrait of Miss Eileen Bennett', since when it has disappeared. Henry's private name for it seems the more appropriate, especially as it is so subtly evocative of the period. 'I feel worried about the question of painting pretty people', Henry had said to Carrington when he began and asked her, 'Have you never felt as if something gets in the way as soon as fascination occurs and causes you to paint differently? At any rate for years I have fled from the Eternal Famine in art & am in dread of it creeping in subtly to what I do.' Despite his now old-fashioned prejudices and fears, and despite 'so many days . . . wasted through darkness & disease', judging from the reproduction in 'Royal Academy Illustrated', Henry would appear to have successfully captured the freshness, innocence and charm of the young and pretty Eileen Bennett. It looks too, as if he responded momentarily to the spirit of an age – at least to a perhaps frivolous aspect of the Twenties. Admittedly, the fashionably shorter hairstyle and skirt-length condition one's perception, but even in an indifferent photograph, the handling looks to have a deftness and grace and a simplicity worthy of Wodehouse, and so typical is it of its time and milieu, that the model might be about to deliver a devastatingly inconsequential line in a Coward play. Perhaps too, the portrayal anticipates something of the sun-tanned sensual energy of Betjeman's 'Miss J. Hunter Dunn', bearing in mind that, successful a Wimbledon star as she was, Eileen Bennett remained an elegant amateur. Henry was never in tune with the so-called Jazz age and would have rejected any notions of an affinity with Art Deco, but in *The Tennis Girl*, it is just possible to see him lifting himself into the period, moving with the times, and producing a politely syncopated, *Thé Dansant* painting. Maybe, after all, he had been overwhelmed by the prettiness of his subject and the perfectly bourgeois setting.

On being forced to abandon *The Tennis Girl* towards the end of 1926, Henry clinched another portrait commission that was to occupy him until the New Year. He had tentatively, perhaps presumptuously, thought he could paint it at Dorothy's, but as she, and doubtless her husband, suspected that his stay might then be a long one, he was, he told Carrington, given 'useless and very offensive reasons to clear out' of No 3 Arkwright Road. In some ways he was not sorry to have been evicted, Dorothy's had been convenient, but the atmosphere had been unsympathetic. In the November, he rented a studio in West Kensington, at No 20 Gordon Place. The contrast could hardly have been greater and he took a while to adjust to the peculiar charms of his squalid surroundings: 'a bed as damp as the bottom of a ditch', he reported to Carrington, 'on the stairs a suffocating smell of mice, sinks, Germans, and stale cooking; and in the studio every few seconds there is an earthquake caused by the underground trains which I hadn't noticed on first inspection.' Soon though, as ever, he began to adjust and to find his new abode surprisingly acceptable: 'I am settling down after all to this place', he wrote, admitting he was,

> 'quite astonished to find out how comfortable it is & quite the most convenient spot in the world – for almost every activity. The staircase smells are greatly diminished since I won a battle with the window as the top which used to be shut as often as I opened it. Now it remains open & actually I have the top storey of the house to myself – except on Thursday at 7am when the huns – mother & son – come up & have baths. There is also an intervening *étage* with no one on it. The resident mollusc makes my bed cleans my shoes & tidies away the breakfast things without seeming to need payment, so really the rent cant be considered high.'

Since the gas heater seemed not to cope at all well with such a vast area of cold and damp, and fearful that his sitter might freeze, he bought an oil stove – 'to place at her back'. The portrait, of Pernel Strachey, Lytton's sister, was for Newnham College, Cambridge, where, at the time, she was a Don and was to become, Vice-Principal. 'I'm sure this Pernel picture will be my last donnish commission and I'll be hung for a sheep not a Lamb', joked Henry, when he began on the sixteenth of December. He made some drawings at the first sitting giving him ideas for the design but complained, 'It is hateful having to hurry' and told Carrington, he would be 'sweating at Pernel till the end of the month' and was resolved not to 'budge for Xmas', for his sitter had to leave London on New Year's Eve, giving him barely a fortnight. The 'angelic' Pernel, came to the studio every morning. 'I find her quite fascinating', decided Henry, but felt the whole enterprise to be 'absurdly hurried – having to make up one's mind about a composition – in a strange room and unexplored lighting – so as to order the canvas immediately. However all has gone very well so far and the only difficulty is to keep the dear lady amused. She is rather inclined to go to sleep unless I talk and when I do that, somnolence is liable to overtake the painting'.

The result is far from somnolent. *Miss Pernel Strachey* is a delightful, lively, even gently witty, portrait, a happy fusion of Henry's previous, precise style with the looser, more vigorous, approach of his mature years. Again, the urgency of the whole commission was to be a fortunate restriction, allowing no time for revisions to ruin a promising start. The painting also shows a sensitive appreciation of the sitter and perhaps some incidental charm comes from the family resemblance – how like Lytton she looks: the *pince-nez*, the quizzical, intelligent gaze, the attenuated features; what a sense of *déjà-vu* for Henry. Though the large 'Lytton' is the more remarkable, original image, 'Pernel' is technically the superior painting.

Working in London again brought Henry back more often to the centre of things. Poole was desperately provincial and although he had the comfort of a house there, it still wasn't a home. Now, he met many of his old friends and was welcome in Hampstead, in Chelsea, even Bloomsbury, very occasionally, despite his reluctance. After finding the studio in West Kensington, and just before starting Pernel's portrait, he spent an evening at the Kennedy's where, he told Carrington excitedly, he met 'a charming beau-monde blonde . . . who with her brightness and stoutness combined with some languishing glances, succeeded in half-ravishing me'. It was an encounter that was to markedly change the course of his life and banish loneliness forever.

NOTES

1 T. E. Lawrence *Letters* p.416.
2 Carrington *Letters* pp.49–50.
3 Carrington p.339.
4 Carrington p.315.
5 Miller *The Bournemouth Orchestra* pp.104–5; 'Punch' 12 May 1937.

VI

Coombe Bissett

1928 – 1960

THIRTEEN

PANSY

The 'charming beau-monde blonde' Henry met in the November of 1926, had not long been working as 'a sort of apprentice' to George Kennedy in his architectural office above the Chenil Galleries in Chelsea. Lady Pansy Pakenham was twenty-two, the eldest daughter of the Earl of Longford, an Irish family from County West Meath. Depite the imaginative potential of the work and the promise of a career in interior design, she was at heart a writer and bookworm, a thinker and dreamer, unsuited even to Kennedy's ideas of office routine and business efficiency. As well as being clever and creative, she was very beautiful and, before the year was out, had succeeded in fully 'ravishing' the susceptible Henry, who soon was calling her 'an archangel'.

Until the summer of 1927, Pansy stayed with the Kennedy family – by then there were five children – in Ebury Street, no distance from the office in the King's Road. Because of the interest he began to show in Pansy and the attention he gave her, Henry thought Kennedy 'behaved terribly auntishly' towards him. Certainly by the spring, the family and friends were becoming aware of a closer, more serious relationship between them to the extent that, on April Fool's Day, Henry received a telegram – supposedly from Lord Longford, Pansy's father – which he admitted, succeeded in giving him 'a slight tremor for 2 minutes at breakfast'. It was unusual for Henry to be the victim of a practical joke: he suspected that 'busybody Kennedy' who may have had feelings of *in loco parentis*, but the author of the telegram remained undetected.

Henry, however, continued to see and to correspond with Pansy. She went to Italy at Easter and home to Ireland, to Pakenham Hall, in August, before returning to London and moving to a furnished maisonette at 54 Sloane Square which, 'after an inquisitive tour of inspection by her Ma' – as Henry tactfully described it to Carrington – she shared with a friend, Evelyn Gardner, during the winter of 1927–28. Meanwhile, Henry rented a studio and more permanent *pied-à-terre* at 28 Maida Hill West, in 'Little Venice', near Paddington, convenient for the train from Poole. With 'just enough quaint & derelict charm', he said he was very delighted with it, though thought the sunlight might be troublesome in summer. 'There is a canal in front and a prospect of mangy gardens at the back', he told Carrington; 'I am on the first floor – a large double (divisible) room, a cupboard, half each of a sink; bathroom and W.C. Underneath lives an elderly wealthy bachelor, overhead an empty flat, & level with me an elderly bank clerk & his wife.'

Whenever in London, Henry was a frequent visitor to Sloane Square. Another regular caller was Evelyn Gardner's friend, the young writer Evelyn Waugh. In the December, they became engaged – to be known as 'she-Evelyn' and 'he-Evelyn': Pansy thought the news 'charming and a great relief except that they have no money so cannot get married for some months'.

During that winter, too, Henry began introducing Pansy to his friends, to Lytton and Carrington, telling the latter it seemed 'rather natural' Pansy 'should not want to go alone into your group among your rustic glades' and that she 'would have gone down the intellectual groves shaking with terror – to begin with at least.' Inevitably perhaps, Pansy was in awe of Lytton but got on well with Carrington, who offered to paint her portrait, though nothing appears to have come of the idea. Instead, Henry began to draw and paint her, but too often was frustrated by the bad light of a London winter and Pansy's unavailability.

In January of the new year, 1928, she went with Henry to Provence, to a little port near Toulon, 'a bewitching place with radiant weather', making it, as he said, 'easy to sympathise with those who hibernate in these regions'. Back in 'Little Venice' again at the end of the month, in his studio he tried 'to make the most of London charms . . . the hygenic arrangements, the chat of the char &

the mouldy view of the canal in fog'. By then, Pansy and he were engaged – unofficially – forcing him to put his mind to making sense of the labyrinth of the law and, by starting divorce proceedings, to contend with what he called, 'the bunglings of solicitors'.

He and Euphemia had not lived together for more than twenty years yet neither had been paricularly motivated to seek a divorce. Henry had sometimes been cynical of his wife's liaisons, one of whom he called 'a typical Euphemia's man – rich & revolting'. She, in turn, had seemed tolerant of – or was merely indifferent to – his own digressions. Thus, it still is surprising, even allowing for the greater complexities and relative harshness of the law at the time, that the formalities of separation and divorce should have been so delicate and taken so long. Too often he had to endure 'terrible doses of Euphemia' in which she chose either to change the subject or ignore it altogether and it took months of sometimes devious negotiation and occasionally acrimonious wrangling to effect an official, permanent severance.

In London, at a concert, they bumped into Ottoline, 'ambushed in the Aeolian Hall', was how Henry put it, being hard put to dodge her inquisitiveness, and even more so when he went to tea the next week. Ottoline was more than convinced of some truth in the gossip she had heard that summer. But, under orders from his solicitors, he denied everything, protesting innocence, not very convincingly, to everyone.

For the summer, Pansy and her flat-mate she-Evelyn, both girls to all intents and purposes affianced, stayed at Wimborne in Dorset, within striking distance of Poole, waiting for confirmation of their respective futures. He-Evelyn went to Poole, too: 'I am at present staying with Henry Lamb', he wrote to Harold Acton, 'who is painting my portrait & delivering illuminating discourses on Cézanne'.[1] The result (still untraced), from reproduction, looks cursory and uncertain in its handling: apparently an unexciting portrait and indifferent painting, it was first exhibited in 1929, to a lukewarm reception. Waugh was away in Egypt at the time, but a friend reported to him, 'Lamb is having his show and there is a portrait of you, not one of his best things, hanging on the walls of the Leicester Galleries. You look highly suspicious of everything in it'.[2]

At Wimborne, Pansy struggled with her first novel, *The Old Expedient*, rewriting large parts of it, which she found much more difficult than writing the first draft. When it was finished, still anxiously awaiting news of the divorce proceedings, she wrote to Carrington with humour but somewhat disconsolately, 'At the moment I am absolutely idle though I try to sketch a little as it seems a suitable occupation for a young lady of refinement in the country. Not so suitable I am afraid for the wife of an artist but by that distant date I shall be no longer young or refined.'

Meanwhile, despite the delicate balance of his affairs, Henry made an offer for a house at Coombe Bissett, a village three miles to the southwest of Salisbury, that was to be their home until his death in 1960.

'You may be surprised to see what a distance I have travelled since my last letter: or perhaps you saw in the papers that I married Pansy Pakenham last week', wrote Henry to Ottoline in August 1928, on his honeymoon at Souillac in the Dordogne; 'Yes, the rumours with which you charged me that day at Gower St. were true; but', he explained, 'in the all-uncertainty of the issue of my procès, I was unable to discuss it with anyone. Immense damage would have been done had I broken the strictest rule of secrecy which was practicable. Well, now all those troubles are at an end.'

The house at Combe Bissett – called 'Brookside' but rarely by Henry – was of early nineteenth century origins. Set slightly back from a charming bend in the village street with a garden at the rear reaching down to the River Ebble, a tributary of the Avon, it was – and still is – a picture-book dwelling in an idyllic setting. Despite its beauty, in the course of the move from Poole, Henry, trying to cope with and being 'very much muddled up furnishing, dealing with electricians, agents, carpenters, gas men and company's and always shopping', had wished for a moment that the whole of No 10 Hill Street 'could have been transported bodily to the country'. However, once settled, he began to enjoy the advantages of his new state. 'I have a lovely companion – an archangel indeed – the greatest blessing possible for the "afternoon" of my life', he wrote proudly of his young bride.

Henry was forty-six. He 'threw himself into family life with the same sort of energy and enthusiasm that he brought to everything else he did', wrote Anthony Powell, to become in 1934 by marriage to Pansy's youngest sister Violet, an immensely likeable brother in-law.[3] Soon, Henry was welcomed into a large circle of new relations

262

for, as well as gaining a beautiful wife, he had also acquired three lovely sisters-in-law and two brothers-in-law, one of whom, Frank Pakenham, he immediately thought 'charming'. The house quickly became a home. 'There was no show, it was very simple with bare boards in the dining room and books and pictures everywhere', most of the latter by other artists, recalled Gwen, one of the villagers who, as a very young girl, had helped with the cleaning, learned to cook 'under Lady Pansy's watchful eye', and became nursemaid to the children.[4] The family for which Henry had seemed to crave – albeit unconsciously – came during the next decade: Henrietta in 1931, Felicia 1933, and Valentine 1939. He behaved 'as if no one else had ever produced children – at least none like his own – confounding all who had shaken their heads about his reactions to domesticity', wrote Anthony Powell.[5] Gwen would often accompany Pansy to shop in Salisbury – meat from Snook's the butcher, fish and game from Macfisheries; there was always wine in the cellar – usually French. The Lambs entertained a lot: 'never mind the dust and dirt', Henry would say, 'it's the food that matters': in fact, 'dinner before dust' became a sort of motto.

In marrying a much younger woman, Henry became part of a much younger circle. He had introduced Pansy to those of his generation: the Johns – the ever elegant Dorelia who always wore long skirts, – the Spencers, Boris, and certain of the Bloomsberries, though she was no longer in awe of them and developed her own, serious reservations about the group. But Pansy herself, having just emerged from 'coming out' and renounced the trappings of a debutante, was a near-contemporary and one of a circle of talented, soon-to-be-famous people of the Thirties, many of whom came to Coombe Bissett. Among these young visitors were Bryan and Diana Guinness, Lord David Cecil, Cecil Beaton, a neighbour at Broadchalke, and another at Odstock, Hugo Pitman, L. P. Hartley, Kenneth Clark, and John Betjeman who, on one visit, wrote a verse:

'Oh, the calm of Coombe Bissett is tranquil and deep
Where Ebble flows soft in her downland asleep
And beauty to me came a pushing a pram
In the shape of the sweet Pansy, Felicia Lamb.'[6]

Many of these friends were also sitters to Henry who, through the Thirties, continued to establish himself as a reliable, moderately successful portrait painter, increasingly academic, yet still distinctive and, though a regular exhibitor at the R.A., still not an Academician. In the course of a few years, he was commissioned to draw or paint all in the several generations of the very large family of Pakenhams – 'La bonne affaire', he told Lytton, when he began the task. Purely for pleasure and for what he thought relaxation, he painted Pansy and the children endlessly; and for a change, he would turn his attention to the village and villagers, to the garden, the river and the surrounding countryside, and, very occasionally, to still-life. Gwen was never allowed to touch the studio at Coombe Bissett, a ramshackle shed in the garden joined to the house by a covered way and cluttered with canvases and folders of drawings piled high. He painted many academics during the decade – and continued to do so – a role with which he became easily and naturally identified through his many links with university life. From time to time he would venture to an Oxbridge college to draw or paint the odd don *in situ*.

Henry kept on his studio in 'Little Venice'. One of his sitters there in 1930 was Evelyn Waugh who, that summer, had been shattered by the sudden collapse of his marriage to she-Evelyn. Afterwards, Waugh had stayed at Coombe Bissett while Pansy and Henry were in Ireland with the Guinnesses, managing to complete the manuscript of *Vile Bodies* but sleeping very badly. The first portrait, two years before at Poole, had not been a success, but now, in getting to know his subject better, the combination of ecstatic artist and depressed author produced the right chemistry for a penetrating study with which the younger Waugh has become synonymous.

The sittings for *The Portrait of Evelyn Waugh* alternated with those of another writer, David Garnett, who remembered watching the progress of the other with great interest, though at the time neither of them was to meet. Garnett, quite accurately, felt his to be the less successful and certainly, it is less sympathetic and less intense than that of Waugh, who sits full square, facing the artist, staring at him intently, an unusual choice of pose for Henry, who seemed rarely to paint such uncompromising frontality. The deceptively simple design works aesthetically but also helps illumine the sitter's personality. The mouth sucks, slightly petulantly, at a pipe but the focus is clearly on the hypnotic stare in the eyes set in a face that bespeaks determination. There is more than a hint of conscious superiority in the expression of imperturbability suggesting how much a force to reckon with was the young writer: that he would obviously survive and succeed, whatever personal disaster befell him and however change overtook him, is the quite explicit message of the portrait.

The 'Waugh', on the one hand, is an admirable example of that stylistic change in his painting that Henry made in the late Twenties and with which, apart from minor digressions and experiments, he was, as a portraitist, identified ever after. On the other hand, for reasons having little to do with painting, the image has acquired a wider, popular significance because of the legendary, hectic lifestyle of the society portrayed by the sitter, the supposed gaiety in the decade before the horror of 1939, and since the portrait's inclusion in the *Thirties* exhibition of 1979, it now seems strangely symbolic of the period and associative of the people. In his *Potpourri from the Thirties*, Bryan Guinness has drawn a proper distinction between observers and observed:

> ' "The Bystander" implied that we belonged to a set called the "Bright Young People". I remember at the time considering that this set was entirely alien to us and to our friends, and even suggested that the appellation was libellous. The "Bright Young People" were those we read about in the newspapers and who were rightly satirised by Evelyn Waugh. We saw an immense difference between our group of talented friends and the sensation mongering crowd to whom the name was applied. It is possible that the distinction was less evident to others than to us.'[7]

In spite of this essential awareness, in looking at the *Portrait of Evelyn Waugh*, it is still difficult to distinguish objectively between subject, style, and associations.

Another of Henry's portraits of this period, and possibly more directly expressive of the decade, is that of Diana Guinness, née Mitford, now Lady Mosley, one of the world's most beautiful women. Painted in 1932 at Biddesden this near full-length portrait of the sitter with her legs curled-up in a chair, through association and to some extent stylistically, is so evocative of its time that again it is difficult to separate content from treatment: the colour is bright, the technique almost pointillist, not as a theory of optics, but in the way the paint is applied. During the early Thirties, Henry, as if trying to break fresh ground and reflect the spirit of the age, adopted somewhat erratically the manner of pointillism. There seems no other, obvious, tangible reason for its sudden appearance, though a few connections come to mind – not ones that Henry would have sought consciously or appreciated at all. Similarly Augustus, in a portrait of Lady Adeane of 1929, had anticipated something of the next decade; Duncan Grant and Vanessa Bell, long after the failure of the Omega Workshops, were producing textile, fan and screen designs in a mode that often infiltrated their pictures, a mode that would have been abhorrent to Henry but which has distinct echoes of passages in the *Portrait of Diana Guinness*, notably the flowers to her right and the mantlepiece behind, to her left. A most striking similarity is evident in Boris Anrep's portrayal of Diana as 'Polyhymnia' in the mosaic floor of the National Gallery. Any link between the technique of mosaic and pointillism is merely superficial but, in this instance, the position of the sitter's head and the interpretation are surprisingly alike; and is it purely coincidence that Anrep's 'Awakening of the Muses' was completed in 1933?

As an expression of its time, Henry's painting is nearly perfect; but as a portrait, if falls some way short of the excellence of likeness with which he was usually associated. 'I feel worried about the question of painting pretty people', he had said when painting *The Tennis Girl*. Diana was not just pretty, she was a ravishing beauty and doubtless Henry found himself even less at ease confronted by such natural perfection. The sitter herself declared that, although he had wanted to paint her, he made her 'immensely fat, which', she insisted, I have never been'.[8] The portrait's success was also limited by the way events began to overshadow the sittings. At a fancy dress party at Biddesden that summer, one of the guests had been Oswald Mosley, to whom Henry took an instant dislike but Diana found 'thrilling . . . like having a crush on a film star.'[9] That year, Mosley had formed the British Union of Fascists and though not commanding wide support, was very much in the news. During the autumn, he became a regular guest of the Guinnesses and, while the portrait was being painted, the artist not only had to do justice to his model's exceptional good looks, but also had to cope with – to him – an alien presence.

Two years before, while Evelyn Waugh stayed at Coombe Bissett, Henry and Pansy had visited the Guinness family's Irish home at Knockmaroon, near Dublin. There, Henry made studies for what Bryan Guinness has called 'a prophetic family group' in which Diana is holding Jonathan, their firstborn, looking away to her left and Bryan looks towards the artist. Carrington thought the portrait of Bryan 'very pretty' but felt that of Diana 'gave one no impression of that Moon Goddess effect.'[10] Many years later, Bryan Guinness, now Lord Moyne, was to describe Henry's painting of the family group in a sad, reflective poem called *The Composition*:

'This picture that was here,
Was carefully composed:
Husband and wife looking their different ways –
He, lying on the ground with open book,
Unquiet in his happiness,
And anxious as he broods
Over the pattern they have made,
The pattern forming which they find themselves,
A pattern forged in fire of first hot love –
While she sits up in wonderment,
And listens, watching like a startled doe,
To see what next will come
Out of the thickets of the years,
The tangled woods of time.

The group sits picknicked on a bank
Above the ancestral Liffey,
Where dreaming Celt has brought
Falxen Northumbrian.
Over the river stands a neighbour's house
Of Georgian simplicity,
Grace and balanced symmetry,
Order and stability.

But, shaped in purple shadow, overhead,
Incongruous, an Irish wolfhound looms,
Dark with foreboding, shaggy as a cloud,
He hangs his head in sad affection,
And guards the pattern of the Composition.'[11]

Diana's wolfhound Pilgrim, was mentioned by John Fothergill in his reminiscences as an innkeeper at Thame, near Oxford, calling the dog one of the tallest, 3ft.6in., and very lovable.[12]

But, as with the portrait two years later, Diana's beauty was to elude Henry in 'The Composition'. Her younger sister Jessica described her 'as a "Vogue" cover-artist's conception of the goddess of the chase, with her tall, rather athletic figure, her blonde hair, and perfection of feature'.[13] However, the portrait of 1932, though apparently a less accurate interpretation than usual and whilst failing to fully capture the person, remains pleasingly, but uncharacteristically, decorative rather than truly analytic and is, incidentally, a remarkable period piece. The artist's 'stuffy' feelings while painting it were not altogether unwarranted, for within a year, Diana had left Bryan and, in 1936, in Berlin, secretly married 'that bounder' Sir Oswald Mosley.

Henry was not always to baulk at painting beautiful women; he had, after all, married one and, during the Thirties, his most available, long-suffering sitter was indeed Pansy. She adored reading, but appears rarely to have been allowed to indulge in her passion while posing. She was a continuous study, augmented first by a daughter, then another, and later, at the end of the decade, a son. Of the innumerable drawings and paintings of her – alone, with Henry, walking, seated, reading to herself, to Henrietta, bathing Felicia, teaching Henrietta to walk – probably the best known and the one that most characterises Pansy Lamb is called simply *The Artist's Wife*, dated 1933, and now in the Tate.

More developed than the majority of Pansy, yet not at all overworked, it is a touching summary of her personality as well as a sensitively handled painting, striking a nice balance between insight, informality and precision. The design – for Henry, relatively unusual – is in a landscape shape, with an easy flow from the head, through the shoulders to the hands and back again: nothing is obtrusive. A homely, straightforward portrait but nonetheless, very good of its kind and successful because of its affectionate observation and absolute sincerity: modest, unpretentious, lovingly painted, it is as if the wandering artist really has come home to stay. After a few years at Coombe Bissett, Henry confessed, 'I become more & more hermetical and would like to hear the good news that I need never again leave this house.'

NOTES

1 Waugh *Letters* p.27.
2 Waugh pp.31 – 2.
3 A. Powell *Messengers of Day* p.70.
4 Mrs. Gwen Castle (née Kerley) – author : 6 Apr 1979 (interview).
5 Powell p.70.
6 Sir John Betjeman – author : 14 Jun 1979.

7 Guinness *Potpourri* p.18.
8 Lady Mosley – author : 27 May 1979; 2 Dec 1978 (interview).
9 Pryce-Jones *Unity Mitford* p.48.
10 Carrington *Letters* p.453.
11 Guinness *Potpourri* pp.46–7.
12 Fothergill *An Innkeeper's Diary* p.229.
13 Skidelsky *Oswald Mosley* p.340.

FOURTEEN

HENRY LAMB

———

'I must face the fact that my contact . . . is just that of a journalist and the experiences can hardly come from within as they did in my pictures of the other war', wrote Henry to the Ministry of Information in the summer of 1940, after he had been working as an official war artist for some months. He was then fifty-seven and well known, having been elected an Associate of the Royal Academy. His role was quite different to that in the earlier conflict when, from 1916 till 1918, any drawing had been heartfelt but 'unofficial', notes made in moments of respite from active service to be used later in support of his vivid memories of the horrors of war. Then, the amalgam of his experience had been composed and worked up in the aftermath; now, in the Second War, he remained in Britain throughout and in making portraits of servicemen from life and studies of the action on the spot, all his work was 'official'. Yet, as he so rightly sensed, despite his genuine concern for the men involved and his identifying with the activity in front of him, he still felt detached from his observations. In a sense, in 1940, he was something of a voyeur.

The year before, Henry had had an ironic prelude to his work as a war artist. Towards the end of 1938, he was commissioned by the Friends of Birmingham to paint a portrait of the Prime Minister, the peacemaker, Neville Chamberlain, to commemorate his 'success' after Munich. The painting was begun at Downing Street in

February 1939. Sitter and artist got on well together and, although Henry 'was absolutely uninterested in world affairs', he 'liked Neville very much personally', said Pansy, and, 'rather to his surprise, found him lively and interested in the arts'.[1] Meanwhile, the turn of events during the course of that critical year heavily overshadowed the ill-fated painting and Henry was very astonished one morning when Chamberlain, replying to his remark that there was not much to enjoy in the picture yet, said in 'a voice of ashes', 'The time for enjoyment has gone by'. The Germans had marched into Prague the day before.

Thereafter, the portrait's history is a shade uncertain. At the end of the summer Parliamentary session Henry took back to Coombe Bissett a small preparatory study and the beginnings of a life size version; but before he could resume work on it, war had been declared. In any case, by September, it would have become a rather painful subject and the initiative by the Birmingham Friends, headed by William Cadbury, something of an embarrassment. According to Chamberlain's daughter, at the outbreak of war, the unfinished painting was in the possession of her mother, not the artist, and went with Mrs Chamberlain's effects into store in a Furniture Depository in the city that was destroyed by fire.[2] The whole tortuous tale has a double, perhaps triple, irony for, in 1940, the sitter died and in December, Henry mentioned to the Ministry of Information, 'trying to do something for Birmingham of Chamberlain posthumously'. It was this posthumous version, the copy, as Pansy called it, that went to Birmingham and would have been destroyed, presumably in the bombing of the city, explaining why the version in the National Portrait Gallery, acquired from the artist's widow for £200 in 1962, looks a little unfinished.[3]

However, it has a satisfying completeness and was of historic significance to both artist and sitter. For Chamberlain, it marked the sad summation of a peace mission that ended in tatters and resignation, although Pansy remembered going to a cocktail party at Downing Street earlier in the summer of 1939 when he seemed 'perfectly cheerful and unaware of the impending doom'; and for Henry, it was the culmination of a decade of sometimes brilliant portrayals that had begun, more or less, with the second version of Evelyn Waugh. He had painted and continued to paint, many prominent academics and others well known in the arts and sciences; and during the Second War, he was to draw and paint numerous, newsworthy servicemen – and one or two women; but Chamberlain, in spite of his fall from grace and popularity, was easily Henry's most famous subject.

It was unique for him in another respect too, since he made so few portraits of professional politicians, not a race he warmed to habitually. Here, he responded to the challenge and his interest in and feeling for the person comes over. Even allowing for the more than usually formal nature of the commisson, Henry has penetrated the position of power, the aura of high office, and not only painted the Prime Minister but also revealed the vulnerable, soon-to-be disillusioned man. The little preparatory study would seem an adequate likeness until comparison with the larger version shows how subtly and effectively Henry has modified and stressed certain of the proportions and relations. In the larger, his body is turned a fraction further towards the artist; the head is smaller, relatively, and the thin spare frame just suggested though engulfed by the slightly exaggerated, capacious overcoat, emphasising Chamberlain's physical frailty and, albeit unconsciously, symbolic of his political precariousness. In the larger one too, he shows more of the inside of his top hat, like a conjuror with 'nothing up his sleeve'; and his neck, rising out of the sharply defined, characteristic, passé wing collar, is scraggier still. By 1939, Chamberlain looked out of his time, probably out of his depth, an entrenched Edwardian straying too far into the twentieth century. In Henry's painting, as in so many contemporary photographs, he appears distinctly unhappy; he may too, even then, have been unwell, for within the year he had resigned and died shortly after.

Though lacking conventional 'finish', the handling of the Chamberlain portrait is impeccably balanced, strikingly confident but never careless, forceful without being facile. Often when it all came too easily, Henry, like many artists, would be suspicious, get worried and, on his own admission, force a struggle, eventually overworking and undoing some of the advantages gained; but with Chamberlain, there was no time to do so, fortunately, and the result, which came from five sittings of one hour each, looks like one of those occasional, swimmingly ideal paintings that from the start was complete. In a portrait, Henry was ever at pains to 'find the thing that matters', as he put it, to seize the essence of a person. Here, he succeeded in achieving a perfect gestalt of a fading, sad and probably sick man slipping from power.

272

The only other portrait that Henry made of an especially well known politician – unless that of Sir Ian Gilmour and family of the 1950s is included – was of Lady Megan Lloyd George, originally commissioned by the Carnaervon Liberal Association. This too, had a curious history: exhibited in the Royal Academy of 1953, its progress had been so slow that by the time it was completed, the sitter had joined the Labour Party!

Portraiture was Henry's main work as an official war artist and, between 1940 and '42, he made more than a hundred drawings and paintings of servicemen as well as numerous genre studies of service life. 'He was the most reliable of all those who worked for us on the War Artists Advisory Committee', wrote the Chairman, Kenneth Clark, instrumental in commissioning Henry.[4] At first, he was a little unclear as to his role and was concerned, 'for the purpose of historical records to try and choose subjects distinguished by something more than the accident of service uniforms'. He thought it might be difficult in the early stages of the war to find such outstanding characters and proposed a set of drawings of the War Cabinet, in view of his recent experience of Chamberlain and his having met Churchill and Lord Halifax; but nothing came of the idea and it was not until April 1940 that officially he set pencil to paper for the Ministry of Information.

The Director of Medical Services for Southern Command, Major General Casement, was his first subject, an excellent sitter who, living scarcely a mile away from Coombe Bissett, would drop in to be drawn on his way to work. The following week, Henry drew Major General Hill, convalescing in a nearby nursing home and conveniently accessible, 'at least for preliminaries'. However, after two attempts at each, Henry was still dissatisfied and promised the Ministry that he was hoping to improve on them 'in a further offensive'. In May, he went to Plymouth, to HQ South Western Command, where he had more luck with his drawings but was infinitely less enamoured with his sitter, Major General Green, whose wife he thought 'the most offensive party'. So peeved was Henry, 'since they couldn't produce', what he called, 'the least solvency of manners', he specially requested the Ministry to make Gen. Green pay for any photographs of his drawings. 'In fact it was the mortification from this milieu', as he put it, that provoked him into applying to be sent to Harwich where, towards the end of the month, he spent a few rewarding days in a more sympathetic atmosphere drawing minesweeper men, whom he pronounced 'sublime'.

In June, he spent a week in Scotland as External Assessor to the Colleges of Art in Glasgow, Edinburgh, Aberdeen and Dundee – 'very interesting as well as exhausting', he wrote, 'The temper of the people is a wonderful tonic just now'. Glasgow he found the most inspiring place and envied Stanley there, making studies for his mammoth project, *Shipbuilders on the Clyde*, though he had no time to hunt him out. In July and August, he was again at Harwich, among the minesweeper and trawlermen; and spent September and October, back home at Coombe Bissett, drawing more servicemen.

At the end of October, he was invited to apply for a full-time appointment as a portrait painter with the War Office, to succeed the late R. G. Eves. 'As I can see no possibility of alternative work I suppose I shall accept', he grudgingly admitted, 'with gratitude but no inspiration as yet because what one sees of the army round here doesn't provide any.' He signed an immense form asking the colour of his hair, father's name and address at birth and decease, the same details of mother and his wife, and 'some other curious facts' but, he complained, 'Nothing about my previous military service or qualifications'. He need not have bothered for, twelve weeks after accepting and despite a visit to the War Office, he still had not received a pass giving him entry to military camps and practise, as he put it, his 'suspicious avocation', and neither had they decided whether he should have a petrol allowance for his duties.

Back in London, Walter's house at Barnes was bombed in the blitz but he and his wife were safe – and most of the furniture; and soon after, Henry reported Boris in Hampstead being shifted by the enemy from his studio which was in ruins; but in the country at Coombe Bissett, there was 'an occasional thud – and sometimes a noisy and even illuminated night' though 'still nothing nearer than a mile and no gunning' and Henry claimed to be 'getting terribly softened'.

It was not until May, 1941, having felt very uneasy about the unproductiveness of the first three months of his new appointment, that he began work again, this time with portraits of airmen stationed conveniently near, at Old Sarum in Wiltshire. Then, in July, he was in Hereford, drawing Indian soldiers; and later that month, in Sussex, with the 40th Tank Battalion at Ashdown Forest. In October, in London, he met the Canadian High Commissioner,

Vincent Massey, to discuss portraits of Canadians serving in Britain. These he began in November, in Surrey, with the 12th Tank Battalion, continuing them in December and in January of the new year. In February 1942, he followed the Canadians to Sussex, near Worthing, and in March, made his first trip to a Canadian Battery on the Thames estuary at Hadleigh in Essex 'which', he thought, 'in spite of Dantesque darkness appeared to have possibilities'. At the end of March, at Coombe Bissett again, he was able to forget 'all the winter miseries' and, with the arrival of crocus, catkins and red shank in the garden, enjoy the 'sudden glories of spring'. In April, he had to return to Essex and the Canadians: 'I am in a most wonderful place', he wrote to the Ministry,

> 'On some hills that break away south to the Thames estuary. There can be nothing more lovely in England. Hadleigh Castle – wasn't that the subject of that late large & over-dramatic Constable that came to the National a year or two before this war? – is on the next green hill to the East & the ground on which this camp stands has been saved from the developers by the Salvation Army, to which force I shall hence subscribe heartily. The Canadians here are better company than my tank friends but less Homeric. They have given me an excellent room *with adequate stove* in the sergeants' mess where I have 3 portraits already going strong. I have also ideas for 3 pictures of the doings . . .'

These 'ideas' were in fact, small genre studies of servicemen at work – and sometimes play – which, between portraits, he had been making in Essex, Surrey, and Sussex. Aside from portraiture, Henry had been worried as to how he could record interestingly and convincingly the various activities of service personnel. 'The possibilities are vast but very diffuse: the difficulties heart-breaking', he wrote; and, after 'nosing around incessantly without however succeeding in nailing myself down to one particular idea', he decided it would be best if he offered a series of small incidents rather than one single canvas intended for a comprehensive record. Although he could work rapidly, he was not in tune with capturing the fleeting moment and found, against his will, that, for this purpose, he had to resort to a camera. That the results, mostly in oil on board, though thoroughly personal, should also be reminiscent of similar subjects by Edward Ardizzone is really no accident, for Henry suggested to the Ministry his studies might be 'something of the sort that Ardizzone has given you though mine would be less humorous and I'm afraid much less stylish.'

275

The Ardizzone connection is a curious and, at first, surprising one: a blend of respect for the artist and his productions and a genuine pleasure in the person. The youngish illustrator and the older painter would have known each other's work for some time before meeting in the summer of 1940. Ardizzone was drawing servicemen stationed near Salisbury and called on Henry at Coombe Bissett: 'The Italiano . . . I liked', reported Henry afterwards; and when, at the end of July, Ardizzone left the area 'feeling he didn't thrive there', Henry said how pleased he was 'to have got to know such a charming fellow'. More recently, Ardizzone recalled Henry as 'a *real* artist. . . someone who really could draw', obviously sharing a modest, mutual admiration;[5] and Henry, despite some reservations, continued to praise Ardizzone's work. In the spring of 1941, after seeing one of the changing exhibitions of war pictures at the National Gallery, he found nearly all of them 'too germanic' for his taste, and registered nothing in front of Barnett Freedman's, failed to be excited by John Piper's views of ruins, quite liked Paul Nash's little watercolours of airplanes and John Nash's submarine, noted an Eric Kennington, admired Lord Methuen's moonbeams, but decided, 'As for the show itself I think Ardizzone again appealed to me most.' The reservations, he aired a little later, as if he had been thinking it over and was trying to define exactly what he found appealing – and unappealing:

> 'No the trouble with Ardizzone is not the very obvious derivation which doesn't matter a hang if the things "live" as they do – besides we're all derivative only in a more intricate and multifarious way – no, with him it is the constancy of mood which tends to monotony in the long run. Also the derivation is a bit insecure as far as the VERITIES go (given the style). Very probably he will come across them in time more or less instinctively.'

In assessing the Ardizzone influence, it would be a pleasure to record it as beneficial, an exciting injection of adrenaline rejuvenating an ageing artist. Tempting as it is to try to see these genre studies as a late flowering, sadly – unlike Sickert, for example, whose late works were reviled and dismissed until recent reappraisal[6] – they remain obstinately opaque, unyielding, unattractive essays in a charmless mood, revealing little concern for the serviceman's lot and no feeling for the period. In the past, Henry could evoke a milieu or encapsulate a decade, sometimes brilliantly. After the First War, he had distanced himself successfully yet

276

paradoxically conveying his involvement; but these wartime little Lambs of the 1940s communicate nothing of what he must have felt, admittedly, on his own admission, by proxy, and fail utterly to be inspiriting. Prosaic and uninventive, to see virtue in them would be so rewarding, like discovering profound poetry beneath the unpromising, unsympathetic surface of a plain exterior. But, apart from weaknesses in conception, they also lack structure and design and are, uncharacteristically, weak in drawing. Some are more evocative of the earlier war; most merely acknowledge the peculiarities and privations of service life in the Second War.

At the time, Kenneth Clark, perhaps out of loyalty to a friend, was overly kind, describing how Henry as a war artist had 'been consistently successful in oils, and in addition to his portraits' had 'painted some good small pictures of army life, full of character and pictorial intelligence.'[7] Much later, however, and on reflection, he revised his opinion radically, thinking very few of these 'genre incidents satisfactory' and saying that Henry 'was not an illustrator and his paintings showed no evidence of imagination.'[8] Disappointingly too, there is a conspicuous lack of humour in this phase, although Henry had anticipated that his 'would be less humorous' than Ardizzone's. But whereas Ardizzone, in spite of the repetitiveness already noted by Henry, could deftly depict with gentle wit and grace the most trivial of incidents, Henry was diminished by the prospect and failed to respond to the challenge he so unwisely brought upon himself.

It could be irrelevant, unfair even, to dwell destructively on what amounts to a minor, negative aspect of Henry's work. Should not an unhappy digression, such as this seems, best be ignored and left safely buried? Indeed, few of these little wartime pictures are ever on view, most remaining in the cellars of the Imperial War Museum or stored in museums and galleries elsewhere in Britain and Canada where many were dispersed after the war. But their importance is enlarged by taking on a sad significance, for at times during the war, he very clearly and poignantly expressed his doubts concerning his abilities and his work, especially when he saw it exhibited publicly. Referring to artists in general, he suggested that they '*have to* get rid of far more paintings than they ought' confirming 'the superstition that usually supervenes about them not being judges of their own work.' Henry was habitually an appalling judge of his own work: sometimes from impatience or simply despir, sometimes from a sheer self-effacing Englishness, he would adopt an unwarranted, ridiculous, false modesty, and summarily dismiss many of his worthier efforts.

At least, this was true largely until he was approaching sixty when, though at no great age, he seemed able occasionally to take a more Olympian view of himself and observe his work with a more rational insight. In 1941, after seeing another exhibition of war pictures at the National Gallery that included some of his, he reported being, for the first time ever, 'disappointed in Stanley S.' though, not having enough time to look round properly, he couldn't say why, but added that he had been 'much more disappointed in HL, not the drawing – the paintings.' Kenneth Clark called him 'a sharp critic of modern English painters' and certainly his comments on his contemporaries were always lively and original. But now, many of his judgements, though of interest and often inconsistent, would seem out of step with the consensus of posterity. Later in 1941, again at the National Gallery, he spent a long time marvelling at Stanley, but failed to appreciate either Graham Sutherland or Henry Moore – although in the early Thirties, he had purchased a Moore carving[9] – liked the landscapes of Edward Bawden, thought Vivian Pitchforth was churning them out too fast, and, despite feeling that some of his drawings looked all right, confessed how, 'The paleness of my own things gave me a nasty shock.' And the following year, he complained of his paintings all looking 'the colour of cardboard: they nearly always sicken me in mixed shows', he wrote.

Of his paintings that sickened him, several were portraits. The list of his wartime sitters was impressive, historically – Generals, Commanders, an Air Marshal, the Prince of Luxembourg; but Henry was never impressed with rank and, almost perversely, was happier painting the other ranks and less well-known officers. He enjoyed the minesweeper and trawlermen; a Soldier of the Free French Forces; the Canadians – especially a Redskin of the Canadian Royal Artillery; a Serbian Officer of the French Foreign Legion – a charming guest whose portrait was marred by his vanity; and civilians, decorated for gallantry – the portrait of one he had thought so poorly of that he consigned it to a group of canvases to be re-coated for future use until it was rescued by the War Museum in 1948.[10] Some of these were painted at a new studio – Flat 6, on the top floor of No 49 Roland Gardens in South Kensington – which he rented in July 1943, at first staying nearby at Bailey's Hotel in Gloucester Road until, towards the end of the war, after some windows shattered by bombs were repaired, he took over another room adjacent and was able to sleep there. This was his studio and *pied-à-terre* in London until, in 1960, he was no longer able to paint.

By 1944, Henry was still busy as a war artist but he painted no more 'official' genre pictures and portrait commissions were spaced, enabling him to pick up the threads of his professional career. At the end of 1945, when asked by the War Artists' Advisory Committee to paint Air Marshal Cochrane and the physicist, Lord Cherwell, he replied, temporising but accepting, more or less: 'I am really for the moment too bloated to need the commissions', he told the Secretary, 'and yet it seems heartless to spurn a moribund committee for whom I sweated hard in my purer days . . . As for Cherwell I am willing. I sat next to him at Christchurch once and met him elsewhere without developing a burning desire to immortalize him so if another painter would like to do him I should not grieve.' He painted the Air Marshal in between other commitments but his obvious lack of enthusiasm for the latter must have sent the committee elsewhere. Though officially he was 'bowler hatted', as he put it, in 1944, his last commission was not completed until two years later, by which time he was in the thick of painting academics again.

After the war, he became almost exclusively identified with portraiture, at least publicly, since, in the fifteen years until his death, of the 82 pictures he showed at the Royal Academy, 73 were portraits. Back in Coombe Bissett, he finished an ambitious family group of Pansy standing with baby Valentine, Felicia looking up at them, Henrietta standing to one side and Henry himself playing the clavichord on the other side with his back to the group. It was a picture he had been working on since 1940 and, admirable as the likenesses are, perhaps because of the protracted nature of the execution and the fact that the 'baby' was walking by the time it was completed, the figures remain surprisingly separate and the composition fails to cohere. But, for all its faults, *The Artist's Family* is like a celebration of his being home again.

Henry was fairly selective as to sitters and in this postwar period he attracted an interesting number. In 1945, Manchester commissioned him to paint his old friend Lawrence Haward, on his retirement from the City Art Gallery; in 1947, for the Behrends, he painted the composer, Benjamin Britten; and at about the same time, made drawings of Robert Lynd, the essayist, and Peggy Ashcroft, the actress; in 1951, he started the portrait of Lady Megan Lloyd George and completed one of Sir Maurice Bowra, Warden of Wadham College, Oxford; and in 1956, he painted Lord Moyne, whom he had last painted as Bryan Guinness in 1930. Despite evidence of some impairment in the handling in the later ones, largely attributable to his failing physical condition, he suffered no falling off in his observation and insight into character. An example of particular interest is that of Miss Skillikorn, Principal of Homerton College, Cambridge, done in 1953, for she was so well known to several generations of students, many of whom recall the painting hanging in the College dining hall and testify to 'a speaking likeness'. It is also interesting since the making of the portrait was witnessed by the then Head of Art at Homerton, Miss Melzi, who accompanied the sitter to London for each session at the studio in Roland Gardens. 'He was a somewhat small, but vitally dynamic person – seeming to dart about here & there in his studio, with an immense air of purpose', she wrote,

'He seemed (as far as I can remember) to mix the paints on his palette on the *floor*, crouching down easily to do this, and then back up to the painting – he moved to and fro a lot as he painted.

During the sittings he had so placed a *mirror*, so that Miss Skillikorn could see roughly what was happening, thus keeping her expression alert and lively.

He made a lot of conversation with her as he painted, discussing any current matters of interest, but especially relating to music. If he had been to a concert the night before, he would discuss the music and performance in great detail, even referring to the interpretations of specific themes or bars. All this time he was rather darting to and fro to the painting, working on it with an intensity of concentration, even whilst keeping the conversation (rather a *one* sided conversation from him) going spontaneously and smoothly.

Whilst we were considering various artists to do the portrait, he came to see us at Homerton. He and Miss Skillikorn took to each other and his final painting of her is based on a very characteristic position of hers, which must have struck him early on. He also liked the chair she happened to be sitting in – certainly a favourite one of hers – so the chair was brought to his studio too!

Henry Lamb seemed such a v. likeable, witty, kind and sincere person.'[11]

For the Festival of Britain Exhibition, 'Sixty Paintings for '51', he painted *Night Life*, a large composition of youths and bicycles, reminiscent of the Poole period and similar to many he did thereafter at Coombe Bissett. During this late phase, he reworked several old themes, exhibiting at the Academy in 1954, *The Level Crossing: Souvenir of Poole 1922* and *Mourners: Souvenir of Brittany 1910*; and in 1955, *Souvenir of Donegal*, a revision, almost a replica, of *Fisherfolk*, the 'Group Among Rocks' in Gola of 1913. This last lacks the finesse and poetry of the original; and the later Poole picture has an unspatial opacity that fails to bring it alive. It is not uncommon for artists to rework themes, especially in old age. Unfortunately Henry neither improvised nor improved upon the originals and the later versions are merely sad, tired reminders of a vital past.

After 1945, when it became easier to travel again, he returned to landscape. Ever since moving to Coombe Bissett, he had painted in and around the village, and further afield in Wiltshire; but now he went on painting holidays to Ireland and France and though the results were rarely dynamic or distinguished, they usually had charm. But perhaps some of his most original and best works from the last fifteen years were the many genre studies of village and town life. They too have charm; yet they also have some of that lightheartedness and deftness that so eluded him during the war. *Afternoon Walk* of 1949, for example, and *Woman with Perambulator and Four Men* and *Hat Fever* of 1950, are much closer to the feeling of Ardizzone than any done whilst he was fresh in the memory. Maybe, for Henry, the peacetime atmosphere was simply more conducive to this kind of painting and certainly it represents a worthy body of work for which he was little known.

As a war artist he had not made much money and afterwards, was always busy with enough commissions, selling his work at the Academy and at his regular one man shows at the Leicester Galleries. But he had a growing family and lived solely on the income from his painting, sometimes being hard pressed and hard up. He was well enough known in a wide enough circle, established, though not quite of the establishment, an outsider uncompromisingly independent to the end, despite becoming a trustee of the National Portrait Gallery in 1942, of the Tate in 1944, and being elected a full Academician in 1949. At this time, Henry became something of an elder statesman, a sort of unofficial alderman of the arts, though very much behind the scenes. At the Tate, 'He was outstanding', wrote Humphrey Brooke, then Senior Deputy Keeper, 'I greatly respected his integrity and judgement.'[12] It was also a time when Alfred Munnings was active as one of the most reactionary Presidents ever of the Royal Academy. Henry, to his surprise, found himself a leader of the younger element within the R.A. Not that he was at all overtly political: he abhorred what he called the 'matey luncheons' at 'the public market place', declaring his interest in the R.A. elections as 'below zero' and becoming 'suffocated . . . with boredom & disgust'. But in 1951, he was helpful to the appointment of Humphrey Brooke as Secretary in succession to his brother Walter.[13]

Henry never went out of his way to attract commissions. Unlike more commercially minded portrait painters, he was not a socialite, and had little or no business sense. He cursed the carelessness of Augustus, loathed the flashiness of De Laszlo, hated the 'photographic' likenesses of James Gunn and, superficially, envied the success of Gerald Brockhurst: 'How rich I shd. be if I could paint like' that, he joked, after seeing one of Brockhurst's glossy renderings of a society beauty. He was always scrupulous about money, sometimes ridiculously so, and had an endemic aversion to profit, even when he was in need: money was solely a means of survival, so uninteresting that he was almost careless with it; and he never asked more for a picture than his own lowly estimate, sometimes even forgetting whether a cheque had been received or not. While in intellectual discourse he could be assertive, stubborn and downright difficult, in any business affairs, he was diffident, self effacing and quite unworldly: 'I am bad at the thrusting part', he admitted. As a rule, he would have to feel some rapport with a sitter before accepting a portrait commission even though visually the prospect might not be too inspiriting; but were he absolutely honest – and normally he was mercilessly so – he would have to admit, inevitably, undertaking some for which he had no great enthusiasm. Hence his advice, like a paraphrase of Polonius, given in old age to a young painter struggling with a difficult sitter:

'have confidence that your natural geniality will triumph over the hard expression. Try twitting her! Try to enlist the services of an "amuser": avoid theology: develop the degree of schizophrenia that enables one just to *seem* to attend to what she is saying while really preoccupied with the determined task of the moment. Really there is nothing so useful as an independent interlocutor(tress?) & keep them well sherried! And you must pay no attention to the people hustling you about date of completion – you should grandly cite the precedent of the great Titian on this point.'[14]

Henry was efficient in the way that he could usually produce work more or less on time – or at least, he came to be able to do so, for in his first few years as an artist, he found it difficult to deliver things to order. But he was utterly disorganised at home and in his studio confessing that, 'my untidy, irrelevant habits seem to communicate themselves to my surroundings', and before he married again, and his cleaner left, he declared, unashamedly, 'the dust & untidiness must remain . . . but of course it only mildly grieves me!'. But where a commission was concerned, he became thoroughly dependable, however doubtful he was of some of the results. Some painters leave a trail of work unfinished, but he seems to have completed most of what he undertook and normally arrived at deadlines, with reluctance, yet with a feeling of professionalism. Above all, he was a professional both in the way that he handled paint and because his sole source of income was from the sale of his work, for he made no attempt to supplement it by teaching. He painted nearly every day and, after his early days in Chelsea and Paris, and other than as an external examiner in Scotland, he appears never to have again darkened the door of an art school. Nor was he tempted to make money from other sources such as illustration or writing criticism. As to writing, prolific and lively as he was in letters, he seems to have enjoyed neither the prospect nor the process and forever retained feelings of inadequacy regarding literary expression. Unlike several of his English contemporaries – Fry, Sickert, Lewis, for example – he suffered no tension between the demands of the visual and the verbal.

Tension might have come from his passionate and continuing love affair with music but there is no evidence of any conflict. As soon as he had abandoned notions of becoming a professional musician he seems never to have performed publicly: playing the piano was something he did in private, though no less seriously, as relaxation and an antidote to painting. Several sitters mention his habit of humming – often Mozart – while he worked, and much of his conversation was about music.

He is conspicuous amongst his peers in being consistently and almost exclusively an easel painter. Of his artist friends alone, nearly all at some time or other deviated from 'pure' painting and worked in another medium or context. Even that persistent easel painter Augustus was potentially and by intent, if not actually, a muralist, although his visions of vast, ambitious, decorative schemes were often begun but rarely completed. Augustus was also a considerable etcher; so too, were Dodd and Muirhead Bone, but Henry, despite hearsay of a print of his changing hands, could never have practised etching to any extent, nor any other means of printmaking. Neither did he pursue any of the crafts, or turn to carving or modelling, as Augustus did briefly in his last years.

Craftsmanship was not a particular concern. He was not a bad craftsman but the technicalities of painting were no more than a means to becoming fluently expressive. Unlike Sickert, for example, who into his very old age was continually experimenting and showing interest in the craft of his art. When Henry first began painting, naturally he worried over problems of technique; later he indulged, somewhat indiscriminately, in a kind of pointillist mannerism that was never unified or integrated convincingly with his work. Other than this though, and an essential awareness and understanding of materials, he betrays no particular preoccupation with technical effect or surface texture. He took care in choosing canvas, usually preferring a fine grain. As to priming, colours, oils and varnishes, he was cautious; with the last, so cautious that he could be offputting to patrons: 'a whole year should elapse', he would rightly warn them, but then go into such intimidating detail of all that could happen and despite his offering to do the job himself, many of his pictures, especially the later ones, to their detriment, remain unvarnished. With regard to framing, he was fairly fastidious, sometimes giving elaborate advice to patrons – this he enjoyed; but preparing for an exhibition was always hell. Prior to a one-man show, he would become touchy, impatient and defensive, regretting he had ever committed himself: it was either upon him too soon, or he couldn't get enough of the frame moulding he wanted, or he would find some other excuse, someone else to blame, but he could never enjoy it. Of course, all this was linked with, was part of, his unwavering aversion to profit, his indifference to money; above all, his dislike of dealers.

Neither had he any more respect for critics who, he felt sure, must be in league with the dealers. 'I never bother with press-cuttings nor feel I can esteem the judgement of any of the accredited pundits in the daily or weekly journals', he wrote in 1956.[15] Not that it is uncommon for artists to despise professional critics; but with Henry, harbouring these grudges, somehow indirectly and obliquely, justified his continual reluctance to become involved in exhibitions, institutions, and the whole business side of art. Unconsciously, it was a vindication.

Yet in fact, after his second marriage, he exhibited regularly. He had to, it was his living and it attracted commissions but he was never good at putting his art across and, in eschewing critics and dealers, underestimated the value of public relations, especially towards the end of his life with the increasing growth and importance of the media. His admirable independence was a strength but – it also contributed to his neglect. In some ways, he was his own enemy – like Wyndham Lewis, though for very different reasons. He was so absolutely his own master, rarely taking advice and if ever he did it seems it was, as when the kindly but unreliable Kennedy gave his opinion, misguided. On seeing some of his later paintings, particularly of the last decade, it is clear what he really needed was a sympathetic, perceptive, enlightened and, most of all, honest critic; an editor, an agent of sorts, who could direct him, promote him even, to make the most of his ability and experience.

Given his personality and disposition, the idea is impossible, although, during the later years, he must have sometimes wondered where his art was going and how he could break out of the mould that had begun to set after 1945. After the First War, his health had been permanently weakened and he never fully recovered from the effects of being gassed. At the end of the Second, he was still only sixty-two, but from then on became steadily, and eventually acutely, arthritic, until, in the last year of his life, he became almost unable to paint. The tragedy was that, in his sixties, he was already in decline, in health and creatively, although he continued to show an agility of mind and to be physically active. His brother-in-law, Anthony Powell, remembered him at this time in the garden at Coombe Bissett taking hold of stilts, running a few steps with them and perambulating round, 'wearing a soft felt hat with a broadish brim, the crown crushed down to the level of the ribbon. He looked exactly like a stilt-performer – probably Breton – doing a turn at a French fair.'[16]

In later life, with thinning hair and weaker sight, he took to wearing a hat and glasses. For painting, he had a sun hat with a green lining that features in a number of self portraits, portraits which make an interesting, and in some ways sad, contrast to the earlier ones. The eyes are still bright, alert, intelligent; the mouth, tense; the face sharp, spare, angular; but mingling with the grace and charm of the handsome proportions is a bitterness. Carrington noted him as a man with a past; Anthony Powell called him fractious; countless friends recall him with the greatest affection, admiration and respect, but many of them also refer to the bitterness beneath his considerable charm. When he married Pansy he put his past behind him, deliberately, resentfully, as if he were ashamed of what he called his bohemian *beaux jours*. In rejecting his previous, sometimes wayward existence, he naturally wanted to start afresh – as a man, and to some extent, as an artist. In both, he was successful: the settled life and the family for which he had yearned were his and he continued to support them from the sale of his paintings. Yet, to suppress the past was a strain, and the strain, allied with poor health, shows in these later self portraits. 'He much disliked any quizzing about his earlier work', wrote Humphrey Brooke, 'he said that such pictures reminded him of a period he would like to forget'.[17]

Remarkably, in view of his being well known for much of his life, his rich experience in medicine and art, and his latterday involvement in some of the major art institutions, he remained unrecorded – either by microphone or cine camera. In Henry's mature years sound radio was well established and in his last decade television emerged as an omnipotent medium. But he seems not to have broadcast at all, as did Fry, Bell, Woolf and Lewis, for example, nor was he committed to film as was Stanley, who fairly wallowed in the late attention he received from the media. However, Henry was never one to reminisce and radio, in particular, thrives on reminiscence. Also, his reticence about the past would have been no encouragement to journalists. His voice was evidently quite mellifluous – 'inimitably soft & musical', a friend called it[18] – and his movements agile and aesthetic – 'one of the most sensitive and graceful men I have ever known', said another friend and portrait subject.[19]

He was not properly at ease in the postwar world: after 1945, technological changes were of little interest to him; he was neither of a practical disposition nor mechanically minded and machinery was mostly a mystery. A car, for instance, was simply a means of getting around as quickly and conveniently as possible and when it broke down, leaving him stranded, he called the vehicle beastly.

Henry's dis-ease with the period is also reflected in some of the later self portraits and assessing the whole person and his art is almost like looking at two different men and two different painters. 'As an artist Lamb comes less easily than most into any classification', wrote his obituarist;[20] and yet, even now he is still difficult to 'place', both in relation to his contemporaries and in the development of British painting. No artist succumbs conveniently to an easy label; in any case, categorisation can be a superficial exercise. But some are associated with groups closely or for long enough to be identified with a particular movement. With Henry, this may be less true than with most. When he first came to London, he attended Friday Club meetings but could rarely have exhibited with the group. Bloomsbury would seem an obvious connection but any link is solely biographical, not at all stylistic. Furthermore, apart from lightheartedly making designs for Ottoline to work in tapestry, he was never a decorative artist as were Duncan Grant and Vanessa Bell and for Henry ever to have worked at the Omega is inconceivable. He showed often at Sickert's Saturday afternoons while the gatherings were informal but almost as soon as it became the Camden Town Group, he backed out.

In several of his paintings completed before 1914, there are strong hints of symbolist influence, not surprisingly, in view of his working through Augustus, Gauguin, Vrubel, Puvis de Chavannes, and Picasso. And it is noteworthy that one historian has placed Augustus amongst the 'English Symbolists', mentioning particularly his *Way Down to the Sea* and linking it with Puvis.[21] Not that Henry fits too comfortably under the symbolist umbrella; but the influence via Augustus, and to some extent the mood, stayed with him for some time and, to look again at *Fisherfolk* of 1913, it is still reminiscent of Puvis, even more of Maurice Denis.

After the First War, the strongest connection is with Stanley Spencer, though the interaction may have been more mutual than it seems at first. Thereafter, Henry begins to look like a rebel turning into a reactionary, but he was never quite either. In the Twenties, he was in the forefront of British painting, though not part of the avant-garde; by the Fifties, he was a Royal Academician, but he never painted Royalty. In showing such a marked change of style in mid-career, he is not alone among his contemporaries. David Bomberg was always dynamic, but ranged from Vorticist, geometrical, near optical abstraction to vigorous, near gestural expressionism. Christopher Nevinson too, made his mark as a Vorticist but soon after, produced some potently 'realist' images, dwindling eventually into a kind of Cubist naturalism. But with Henry, what began as a lighter, freer, more spontaneous approach to painting, too often became slack and careless and lacking in vitality. This last can be explained by his failing health but it doesn't explain the predictableness and lack of invention, for Renoir and Matisse, even from wheelchairs, continued to be inventive, and nearer home, Sickert, though usually working from secondary sources, maintained a liveliness in old age. Whatever happened to Henry Lamb?

He was always a natural draughtsman: to the end, his drawings were sensitive, sharply observed, and vital. His portraits were usually good likenesses, some exceptionally so. His use of colour remained essentially personal and instantly identifiable. But too many of his later paintings are weak in conception, in design, and in handling. So far removed do they seem from the best of Doëlan, Gola, Hampstead, Poole, or Coombe Bissett in the Thirties that, at times, they could almost be by another hand.

Yet Henry had painted in this looser, less realised manner before, almost from the very beginning; throughout his life he made preliminary studies in oil bearing a strong resemblance to the 'finished' works of his later period: studies for Lytton, sketches from Gola, from France, in the streets of Poole, early flower pieces, studies for the Kennedy family, and for many other portraits of the Twenties, stylistically, are surprisingly similar to many paintings of the Forties and Fifties. It was an innate style, but an inelegant one. Unlike Degas, for instance, who in the merest scribble or in the tiniest *pochade* never failed to be stylish; or Sickert, who always seized the essentials in every sketch as an *aide-memoire* to working away from the subject, each mark being meaningful, a deliberate, careful notation; or Picasso, who could improvise endlessly in a multiplicity of media and modes – unlike them, Henry was often impatient in preparation, as if he were over anxious to move onto the larger canvas. In the early years, he would draw assiduously from the model and, at least until the Thirties, would make many preparatory studies, working exhaustively on the finished picture, sometimes actually overworking the surface. But between these extremes of beginning and ending a painting there seems with him a wide, unsatisfactory, rather clumsy gap in the creative process. Few of his preparatory studies are satisfying in themselves and any strengths they gain are from their relationship with the finished picture. In itself, this may not be important: not every mark an artist makes needs to be a work of art or aesthetically pleasing, but with Henry it is of some moment because, as he grew older, he made fewer and fewer preliminary studies and would begin the final version at an ever earlier stage until, in the last decade, he sometimes made none at all.

To compare like with like over some fifty years of a working life is difficult, especially since much more of his later work was commissioned, a simple difference that may have a bearing on the style. And after 1945, too, he seems to have been more hard pressed, more rushed, and there is a greater urgency in his work, despite his intention not to be hurried. By comparison, the early years seem more leisurely, the work more reflective. For the exceptional Lytton portrait he made innumerable studies in pencil, pen, watercolour and oil between 1912 and 1914, and some even later when he turned to it again; for each of the Anrep and Kennedy family groups of 1920 and '21, there exist at least four compositional studies in both oil and watercolour, besides several of individual figures. But later, in 1951, for the excellent likeness of Maurice Bowra at Wadham, and for the protracted portrait of Lady Megan Lloyd George of about 1952–53, he appears to have made no more than two accurate but slight pencil drawings before starting on the canvas, and for the family groups of Professor Hewer of 1951 and of Sir Ian Gilmour of 1955, the sitters recall no bouts of intensive drawing and only limited preparation is evident. Thus it seems, the distinctions between conception, inception and completion narrowed successively throughout his career. In part, it accounts for some of the weakness and slackness of the later period.

Although it is chiefly for some of the earlier paintings that Henry has been remembered, it is also true that the whole of his oeuvre has been overshadowed and to some extent negated by the prolific, but nonetheless, diluted output of his declining years. Yet an artist must surely be judged on the best of his work: failures need not negate successes. Towards the end, sadly with failing health, perhaps he failed too often. Without the energy to break fresh ground, without the stimulus and excitement of adventure, perhaps too often he was reduced to working through known routines. But in his attempt to remain a professional painter, he remains heroic. And undoubtedly, nothing can erase the stunning, unique, memorable images that he produced at his best, pictures which hang happily alongside, and bear comparison with, the best of any of his contemporaries.

One of his very last sitters, the young and beautiful Vanessa Lawson, was painted at Roland Gardens in 1959; but he was hardly fit then to do her justice. Even though he was desperately unwell and 'often frantic with the pain in his hands', she found him utterly charming and 'quite fell for him'. He made no preliminary drawings, as she recalled.[22] Despite his condition, as ever he had no care for his wellbeing and she would take picnics to the studio. It was after one of these sessions, on the return journey to Coombe Bissett, that he met a neighbour, Lady Radnor, who remembered arriving at Salisbury station and trying to help him from the railway carriage to the platform. So disabled was he that she had to call for help and whilst they waited, he wept, knowing his painting days were soon to be over.[23] He was given cortisone, became quite irrational, even uncharacteristically abusive, and was taken to the hospital in Salisbury, then moved to a nearby nursing home where he died on October, 8th 1960. He was 77.

In the more lucid moments of his last months, one of the books he read with great interest and macabre significance was the recently published *Memento Mori*, Muriel Spark's moving but gently amusing novel of life and death in a ward of arthritic patients.

> 'The coffin began to slide slowly down the slope towards a gap in the wall while the organ played something soft and religious. Godfrey, who was not a believer, was profoundly touched by this ensemble, and decided once and for all to be cremated when his time came.'[24]

It was a case of harrowing identification: 'Being over seventy is like being engaged in a war', says one of the patients, 'All our friends are going or gone and we survive amongst the dead and the dying as on a battlefield.'

Henry Lamb outlived a number of his old intimates: by 1960, Lytton, Ottoline, Dodd, Kennedy, and Stanley had died; but Augustus and Dorelia, looking sad and bewildered, attended the funeral in the church at Coombe Bissett although, in the last years, he had seen little of them. And of the younger generation, at the graveside among other friends and family like a portrait retrospective, were many of his sitters including Lord David Cecil, L. P. Hartley, and Anthony Powell. On Henry's tombstone, below his name and dates, is inscribed,

'PAINTER, DOCTOR, MUSICIAN.'

NOTES

1 Lady Pansy Lamb – National Portrait Gallery : 24 Oct 1969.
2 Birmingham City Art Gallery – National Portrait Gallery : 28 Jan 1963.
3 Lady Pansy Lamb – National Portrait Gallery : 5 Jul 1962; 30 Oct 1962.
4 Lord Clark – author : 22 Oct 1977.
5 Edward Ardizzone – author : 21 Jun 1979 (interview).
6 Richard Morphet (catalogue introduction) *Late Sickert* 1982.
7 K. Clark *War Artists at the National Gallery* 'The Studio' Jan 1942.
8 Lord Clark – author : 22 Oct 1977.
9 Henry Lamb bought the Henry Moore carving from the Dorothy Warren Gallery c.1930. It was later on loan to the Manchester City Art Gallery for some years. Henry sold it to Manchester for the price he paid originally.
10 Henry Lamb – Imperial War Museum : 26 Nov 1948.
11 Miss Kay Melzi – author : 23 Nov 1977.
12 Humphrey Brooke – author : 18 Mar 1980.
13 ib.
14 Henry Lamb – Guy Roddon : 22 May 1959.
15 Henry Lamb – Guy Roddon : 7 Apr 1959.
16 Powell *Messengers of Day* p. 71.
17 Humphrey Brooke – author : 18 Mar 1980.
18 ib.
19 Lady Caroline Gilmour – author : 20 May 1983 (interview).
20 *Henry Lamb* obituary, 'The Times' 10 Oct 1960.
21 Hamilton *Painting and Sculpture in Europe* p. 146.
22 Vanessa, Lady Ayer – author : Jul 1982 (interview).
23 Isobel, Countess of Radnor – author : Jul 1982 (interview).

SELECT
BIBLIOGRAPHY

Books

ABSE, Joan *The Art Galleries of Britain and Ireland* Sidgwick & Jackson, London 1975
ACTON, Harold *Nancy Mitford: A Memoir* Hamish Hamilton, London 1975
ANSCOMBE, Isabella *Omega and After: Bloomsbury and the Decorative Arts* Thames & Hudson, London 1981
ARNOLD, Bruce *Mirror to an Age: Sir William Orpen* Jonathan Cape, London 1981
ASHCROFT, T. *English Art and English Society* Peter Davies, London 1936
AYERST, David *Guardian, Biography of a Newspaper* Collins, London 1971
BARON, Wendy *Sickert* Phaidon, London 1973
BARON, Wendy *Ethel Sands and her Circle* Peter Owen, London 1977
BARON, Wendy *The Camden Town Group* Scolar, London 1979
BEAUMONT, Cyril W. *The Diaghilev Ballet in London* Adam & Charles Black, London (3rd edn) 1951
BEHREND, George *Stanley Spencer at Burghclere* MacDonald, London 1965
BELL, Quentin *Virginia Woolf: A Biography* Hogarth Press, London 1972
BELL, Quentin *Bloomsbury* Futura (fp.1968) 1974
BERTRAM, Anthony *A Century of English Painting 1851–1951* Studio, London 1951
BLANCHE, Jacques-Emile *Portraits of a Lifetime 1870–1914* Dent, London 1937
BRENAN, Gerald *A Life of One's Own: Childhood and Youth* Cambridge University Press (fp.1962) 1979
BRENAN, Gerald *Personal Record 1920–1972* Cape, London 1974
BUCKLE, Richard *Jacob Epstein: Sculptor* Faber, London 1963
BURY, Adrian *Oil Painting of Today* Studio, London 1938
CARLINE, Richard *Stanley Spencer at War* Faber, London 1978
CARRINGTON, Dora *Letters and Extracts from her Diaries* Cape, London 1970
CARRINGTON, Noel *Carrington: Paintings, Drawings and Decorations* Oxford Polytechnic Press 1978
CECIL, David *Augustus John: Fifty-Two Drawings* Rainbird, London 1957
CHAMOT, Mary *Modern Painting in England* Country Life, London 1937
CHARLTON, H. B. *Portrait of a University 1851–1951* Manchester University Press 1951
CHITTY, Susan *Gwen John 1876–1939* Hodder & Stoughton, London 1981
CHRISTIE, O. F. *A History of Clifton College 1860–1934* J. W. Arrowsmith, Bristol 1935
COLLIS, Louise *A Private View of Stanley Spencer* Heinemann, London 1972
COLLIS, Maurice *Stanley Spencer* Harvill, London 1962
COOPER, Lady Diana *The Rainbow Comes and Goes* Hart-Davis, London 1958

COOTE, Colin (intro) *Army: War Pictures by British Artists* Oxford University Press 1942

CRABTREE, Derek & THIRLWELL, A. P. (eds) *Keynes and the Bloomsbury Group* Macmillan, London 1980

DARROCH, Sandra Jobson *Ottoline* Chatto & Windus, London 1976

DEGHY, Guy & WATERHOUSE, Keith *Café Royal: Ninety Years of Bohemia* Hutchinson, London 1955

DEVAS, Nicolette *Two Flamboyant Fathers* Collins, London 1966

DOBBS, Brian *Art in London* MacDonald, London 1975

DUNLOP, Ian *The Shock of the New* Weidenfeld & Nicolson, London 1972

DUVEEN, Joseph *Thirty Years of British Art* Studio, London 1930

EASTON, Malcolm & HOLROYD, Michael *The Art of Augustus John* Seeker & Warburg, London 1974

EASTON, Malcolm & JOHN, Romilly *Augustus John* National Portrait Gallery HMSO, London 1975

EDEL, Leon *Bloomsbury: A House of Lions* Hogarth, London 1979

EPSTEIN, Jacob *An Autobiography* Vista, London (fp.1955) 1963

FARR, Dennis *English Art 1870–1940* Oxford University Press 1978

FERGUSON, John *The Arts in Britain in World War I* Stainer & Bell, London 1980

FRY, Roger *Letters*: 1 & 2 Chatto & Windus, London 1972

FURST, Herbert *Portrait Painting: Its Nature and Function* John Lane Bodley Head, London 1927

GADD, David *The Loving Friends: a Portrait of Bloomsbury* Hogarth Press, London 1974

GARNETT, David *The Flowers of the Forest* Chatto & Windus, London 1955

GARNETT, David *Great Friends* Macmillan, London 1979

GARNETT, Oliver *The Sculpture of Stephen Tomlin* Unpublished BA dissertation, Cambridge/Tate Gallery Archives 1979

GAUNT, William *A Concise History of English Painting* Thames & Hudson, London 1964

GIBSON, Robin & ROBERTS, Keith *British Portrait Painters* Phaidon, London 1971

GRANT, Duncan *Paris Memoir* Unpublished, Charleston Papers, Cambridge nd.

GRAY, Camilla *The Russian Experiment in Art 1863–1922* Thames & Hudson, London 1971

GUINNESS, Bryan *Potpourri from the Thirties* Cygnet Press, Burford, Oxfordshire 1982

GWYNNE-JONES, Allan *Portrait Painters* Phoenix House, London 1950

HAMNETT, Nina *Laughing Torso: Reminiscences* Constable, London 1932

HAMNETT, Nina *Is She a Lady? A Problem in Autobiography* Wingate, London 1955

HARRISON, Charles *English Art and Modernism 1900–1939* Allen Lane, London 1981

HASSALL, Christopher *Edward Marsh, Patron of the Arts* Longmans, London 1959

HASSALL, Christopher *Ambrosia and Small Beer: Hassall-Marsh Letters* Longmans, London 1964

HASTINGS, Michael *The Handsomest Young Man in England: Biography of Rupert Brooke* London 1967

HOBHOUSE, Janet *Everybody Who Was Anybody: A Biography of Gertrude Stein* Weidenfeld & Nicolson, London 1975

HOLROYD, Michael *Lytton Strachey: 1 – The Unknown Years 2 – The Years of Achievement* Heinemann, London 1967, 1968

HOLROYD, Michael *Lytton Strachey and the Bloomsbury Group* Penguin, Harmondsworth 1971

HOLROYD, Michael *Augustus John* Penguin, Harmondsworth (fp.1974) 1976

HUBBARD, Hesketh *A Hundred Years of British Painting 1851–1951* Longmans Green, London 1951

HUTCHISON, Sydney C. *The History of the Royal Academy 1768–1968* Chapman & Hall, London 1968

JAWORSKA, Wladyslawa *Gauguin and the Pont-Aven School* Thames & Hudson, London 1972

JOHN, Augustus *Chiaroscuro* Cape, London 1952

JOHN, Augustus *Finishing Touches* Cape, London 1964

JOHN, Romilly *The Seventh Child: A Retrospect* Cape, London (fp.1932) 1975

KENNEDY, G. L. *Henry Lamb* Ernest Benn, London 1924

KENNEDY, Margaret *The Constant Nymph* London 1924

KENNEDY, Richard *A Boy at the Hogarth Press* Whittingham Press, Andoversford, Glos. 1972

KENNEDY, Richard *A Parcel of Time* Whittingham Press, Andoversford, Glos. 1974

LAMB, Walter R. M. *The Royal Academy: A Short History of its Foundation and Development* G. Bell, London 1951

LAMBERT, R. S. (ed) *Art in England* Pelican, London 1938

LAMBOURNE, Lionel & HAMILTON, Jean *British Watercolours in the Victoria & Albert Museum* Sotheby Parke Bernet, London 1980

LAWRENCE, T. E. *Letters* Cape, London 1938

LEACH, Bernard *Beyond East and West: Memoirs, Portraits and Essays* Faber, London 1978

LEHMANN, John *Virginia Woolf and Her World* Thames & Hudson, London 1975

LEHMANN, John *Rupert Brooke: His Life and Legend* Weidenfeld, London 1980

LEWIS, Wyndham *Blasting and Bombardiering: Autobiography 1914–26* Eyre & Spottiswoode, London 1937

LEWIS, Wyndham *Wyndham Lewis the Artist: from Blast to Burlington House* Laidlaw & Laidlaw, London 1939

LEWIS, Wyndham *Rude Assignment: A Narrative of My Career up-to-date* Hutchinson, London 1950

LEWIS, Wyndham *Letters* Methuen, London 1963

LEWIS, Wyndham *A Soldier of Humor and Selected Writings* Signet, New York 1966

LILLY, Marjorie *Sickert: the Painter and his Circle* Paul Elek, London 1971

LUDOVICI, Antonio *An Artist's Life in London and Paris 1880–1925* T. Fisher Unwin, London 1926

MAHOOD, Kenneth *The Secret Sketchbook of a Bloomsbury Lady* Bodley Head, London 1982

MARRIOTT, Charles *A Key to Modern Painting* Blackie, London & Glasgow 1938

MARSH, Edward *A Number of People: a Book of Reminiscences* Heinemann, London 1939

MARGETSON, Stella *The Long Party*, Gordon Cremonesi, London 1976

MAUROIS, André *Memoirs 1885–1967* Bodley Head, London 1970

MAYES, W. P. *The Origins of an Art Collection* Unpublished, Imperial War Museum 1961

MEULI, Jonathan *Henry Lamb: a survey of his life and work* Unpublished BA Dissertation, Cambridge/ Tate Gallery Archives 1980

MITCHELL, Donald *Benjamin Britten: Pictures from a Life 1913–76* Faber, London 1979

MORHANGE, Angelina *Boris Anrep: The National Gallery Mosaics* National Gallery, London 1979

MORPHET, Richard *British Painting 1910–45* Tate Gallery, London 1967

MORRELL, Ottoline *The Early Memoirs of Lady Ottoline Morrell* Faber, London 1963

MORRELL, Ottoline *Ottoline at Garsington: Memoirs of Lady Ottoline Morrell 1915–18* Faber, London 1974

MORRELL, Ottoline *Lady Ottoline's Album: Snapshots and Portraits* Michael Joseph, London 1976

MOSLEY, Diana *A Life of Contrasts: An Autobiography* Hamish Hamilton, London 1977

MUNNINGS, A. J. *The Finish* Museum Press, London 1952

NEVINSON, C. R. W. *Paint and Prejudice* Methuen, London 1937

NEWTON, Eric *War Through Artist's Eyes* John Murray, London 1945

NEWTON, Eric *In My View* Longmans Green, London 1950

ORMOND, Richard (ed) *The National Portrait Gallery in Colour* NPG/Studio Vista, London 1979

ORPEN, William (ed) with RUTTER, Frank *The Outline of Art* George Newnes, London (fp.1923) 1950

OWEN, Roderic & DE VERE COLE, Tristan *Beautiful and Beloved: the Life of Mavis de Vere Cole* Hutchinson, London

PAKENHAM, Pansy *The Old Expedient* Chapman & Hall, London 1928

PARTRIDGE, Frances *A Pacifist's War* Hogarth Press, London 1978

PARTRIDGE, Frances *Memories* Gollancz, London 1981

PIPER, David (ed) *The Genius of British Painting* Weidenfeld & Nicolson, London 1975

PLOMER, William *At Home* Cape, London 1958

POWELL, Anthony *To Keep the Ball Rolling* 2: *Messengers of Day 3: Faces in My Time* Heinemann, London 1978, 1980

POWELL, Violet *Five Out of Six* Heinemann, London 1960

PRIESTLEY, J. B. *The Edwardians* Sphere, London (fp.1970) 1972

PRIESTLEY, J. B. *The English* Penguin, Harmondsworth 1975

PRYCE-JONES, David (ed) *Evelyn Waugh and his World* Weidenfeld & Nicolson, London 1973

PRYCE-JONES, David *Unity Mitford: a Quest* Weidenfeld & Nicolson, London 1976

REWALD, John *Post Impressionism from Van Gogh to Gauguin* Museum of Modern Art, New York (2nd edn) 1962

RICHARDS, Grant *Memories of a Misspent Youth 1872–1896* Heinemann, London 1932

ROBINSON, Duncan *Stanley Spencer: Visions from a Berkshire Village* Phaidon, Oxford 1979

ROSENBAUM, S. P. *The Bloomsbury Group* Croom Helm 1975

ROSS, Margery (ed) *Robert Ross, Friend of Friends* Cape, London 1952

ROSS, Alan *Colours of War* Cape, London 1983

ROTHENSTEIN, Elizabeth *Stanley Spencer* Beaverbrook Newspapers, London 1962

ROTHENSTEIN, John *British Artists and the War* Peter Davies, London 1931

ROTHENSTEIN, John *Modern English Painters – 1: Sickert to Smith 2: Lewis to Moore* Eyre and Spottiswoode, London 1952, 1956

ROTHENSTEIN, John *British Art Since 1900* Phaidon, London 1962

ROTHENSTEIN, John *Autobiography 1: Summer's Lease 1901–1938 2: Brave Day, Hideous Night 1939–1965 3: Time's Thievish Progress* Cassell, London 1965, 1966, 1970
ROTHENSTEIN, John (ed) *Stanley Spencer: the Man – Correspondence and Reminiscences* Paul Elek, London 1979
The Royal Academy Illustrated London 1921–1961
RUSSELL, John *British Portrait Painters* Collins, London 1946
RUTTER, Frank *Some Contemporary Artists* Leonard Parsons, London 1922
RUTTER, Frank *Evolution in Modern Art: A Study of Modern Painting 1870–1925* Harrap, London 1926
RUTTER, Frank *Since I was Twenty-Five* Constable, London 1927
RUTTER, Frank *Art in My Time* Rich & Cowan, London 1933
RUTTER, Frank *Modern Masterpieces: An Outline of Modern Art* George Newnes, London 1940
SHONE, Richard *Bloomsbury Portraits* Phaidon, Oxford 1976
SHONE, Richard *The Century of Change: British Painting Since 1900* Phaidon, Oxford 1977
SICKERT, W. R. *A Free House! or the Artist as Craftsman* Macmillan, London 1947
SITWELL, Osbert *Laughter in the Next Room* Macmillan, London 1949
SITWELL, Osbert *Noble Essences or Courteous Revelations* Macmillan, London 1950
SKIDELSKY, Robert *Oswald Mosley* Macmillan, London 1975
SPALDING, Frances *Roger Fry: Art and Life* Paul Elek/Granada, London 1980
SPALDING, Frances *Vanessa Bell* Weidenfeld & Nicolson, London 1983
SPARKE, Muriel *Memento Mori* Macmillan, London 1959
SPENCER, Gilbert *Memoirs of a Painter* Chatto & Windus, London 1974
SPENCER, Gilbert *Stanley Spencer* Gollancz, London 1961
SPENDER, Stephen *World Within World* Faber, London (fp.1951) 1977
STRACHEY, Lytton *Eminent Victorians* Chatto & Windus, London (fp.1918) 1979
STRACHEY, Lytton *Lytton Strachey by Himself: a Self Portrait* Heinemann, London 1971
SUNDERLAND, John *Painting in England 1525–1975* Phaidon, London 1976
SYKES, Christopher *Evelyn Waugh* Collins, London 1975
WATNEY, Simon *English Post Impressionism* Studio Vista, London 1980
WARNER, Oliver *English Literature: a Portrait Gallery* Chatto & Windus, London 1964
WATERS, Grant *A Dictionary of British Artists 1900–1950* Eastbourne Art Society 1975
WAUGH, Evelyn *Diaries* Weidenfeld & Nicolson, London 1976
WAUGH, Evelyn *Letters* Weidenfeld & Nicolson, London 1980
WILENSKI, R. H. *English Painting* Faber, London 1943
WILENSKI, R. H. *An Outline of English Painting* Faber, London 1969
WOOLF, Leonard *Beginning Again: An Autobiography of the Years 1911–1918* Hogarth Press, London 1964
WOOLF, Virginia *A Writer's Diary* Hogarth Press, London 1953
WOOLF, Virginia *Moments of Being* University of Sussex 1976
WOOLF, Virginia *Diary 1: 1915–1919 2: 1920–1924 3: 1925–1930 4: 1931–1935* Hogarth Press, London 1977, 1978, 1980, 1982
WOOLF, Virginia & STRACHEY, Lytton *Letters* Hogarth Press, London 1956
WOOLF, Virginia *Letters 1: The Flight of the Mind 1888–1912 2: A Question of Things Happening 1912–1922 3: A Change of Perspective 1923–1928* Hogarth Press, London 1975, 1976, 1977

Articles

BELL, Clive *The Imperial War Pictures at Burlington House* 'The Athenaeum' Jan 1920
BELL, Graham *Art in the 'Island Fortess': a review of Contemporary British Painting* 'The Studio' Oct 1940
BENNETT, Alan *Lady Ottoline's Photograph Album* 'The Book Programme', BBC Radio 4 broadcast transcript 1977
BONE, James *Contemporary British Painting: Henry Lamb* 'The Studio' Mar 1929
BROWN, Frederick *Recollection: The Early Years of the New English Art Club* 'Artwork' Winter 1930
BURY, Adrian *Who's Who in British Portrait Painting* 'The Studio' Aug 1938
CHAMOT, Mary *Recent Paintings by Henry Lamb* 'Illustrated London News' 1931
CLARK, Kenneth *War Artists at the National Gallery* 'The Studio' Jan 1942
DONNELLY, Frances *The Bloomsberries: snobbish, sniping and self-absorbed* 'The Listener' (also *A Boom in Bloomsbury*, BBC Radio 4 broadcast) Aug 1982
FRY, Roger *Modern Mosaic and Mr Boris Anrep* 'The Burlington Magazine' Jun 1923
GAUNT, William *English Painting of Today* 'The Studio' Jul 1937

Henry Lamb

GINNER, Charles *The Camden Town Group* 'The Studio' Nov 1945

GOODISON, J. W. *Cambridge Portraits IV, Later Nineteenth and Twentieth Centuries* 'The Connoisseur' 1959

GORDON, Cora *Henry Lamb: the Leicester Galleries* 'The Studio' Feb 1946

HIND, A. M. *Recent Portrait Drawings at Trinity College, Cambridge* 'Artwork' Winter 1929

HORTON, Percy *War as Inspiration to the Artist* 'The Studio' Dec 1939

LAMB, Henry *The Mesoblastic Layer* 'The Manchester Medical Students' Gazette' 1905

McGREEVY, Thomas *The Decline of Portraiture* 'The Studio' Feb 1938

McGREEVY, Thomas *Henry Lamb: the Leicester Galleries* 'The Studio' May 1940

Portrait of the Artist No. 68: Henry Lamb 'Art News & Review' Sep 1951

POWELL, W. Egerton *News, Nature and Art: Some Recent Exhibitions* 'Artwork' Autumn 1927

RAWSON, I. M. *Patrons of Talent: The Behrends of Burghclere* 'Country Life' Oct 1978

ROBERTS, Keith *Augustus John: National Portrait Gallery* 'Burlington Magazine' May 1975

RUSSELL, Bertrand *Portraits from Memory* 'The Listener' Jul 1952

RUTHERSTON, Albert *From Orpen and Gore to the Camden Town Group* 'Burlington Magazine' Aug 1943

RUTTER, Frank *Henry Lamb: some examples of his recent paintings* 'The Studio' Nov 1931

SHONE, Richard *Henry Lamb: Retrospective* 'Arts Review' Apr 1973

SHONE, Richard *Camden Town* 'Arts Review' Oct 1976

SHONE, Richard *The Friday Club* 'Burlington Magazine' 1975

TATLOCK, R. R. *British Art at Millbank* 'Burlington Magazine' Dec 1921

VAIZEY, Marina *Ottoline: Edward Harvane Gallery* 'Arts Review' Nov 1971

VERTUE, H. St. H. *Henry Lamb at Guy's* 'Guy's Hospital Reports', London 1961

WEBBER, Michael *English Painting 1900–1940: New Grafton Gallery* 'Arts Review' Nov 1972

WHITTET, G. S. *Ottoline: Edward Harvane Gallery* 'Art and Artists' Nov 1971

WHITTET, G. S. *Henry Lamb: Memorial Exhibition* 'The Studio' Feb 1972

Catalogues (in chronological order)

The New English Art Club RBA	Winter 1905
Some Examples of Independent Art of Today Agnew's	Feb–Mar 1906
Allied Artists' Association: The London Salon	Jul 1908
The New English Art Club RBA	Summer 1909
The New English Art Club RBA	Winter 1909
The New English Art Club RBA	Winter 1910
The Camden Town Group Carfax	Jun 1911
The New English Art Club RBA	Summer 1911
The New English Art Club RBA	Winter 1911
The Camden Town Group Carfax	Dec 1911
The New English Art Club RBA	Summer 1912
Second Post Impressionist Exhibition Grafton	Oct 1912
The Camden Town Group Carfax	Dec 1912
Boris Von Anrep Chenil	Oct 1913
The Camden Town Group and Others Brighton Public Art Gal	Dec 1913–Jan 1914
New English Art Club RBA	Spring 1914
Twentieth Century Art: a review of Modern Movements	May–Jun 1914
War Artists RA	Dec 1919
Contemporary Art Society Künsthaus, Zurich	Aug 1918
Gallery Salon Goupil	Nov–Dec 1921
Spring Exhibition Goupil	1922
Henry Lamb: paintings and drawings Alpine Club	May–Jun 1922
Modern British Art Goupil	Summer 1924
Present-Day British Art: Inaugural Exhibition New Chenil	Jun–Jul 1925
Gallery Salon Goupil	Nov–Dec 1925
Seven Pillars of Wisdom Leicester Galleries	Feb 1927
Henry Lamb Leicester Galleries	Mar 1927

Henry Lamb Leicester Galleries	1929
Henry Lamb Leicester Galleries	1931
Henry Lamb Leicester Galleries	1933
Henry Lamb Leicester Galleries	1935
Henry Lamb Leicester Galleries	1938
British Empire Exhibition Glasgow	1938
British Painting Since Whistler National Gallery	1940
Paintings, Drawings and Sculpture from the Collection of the Late Sir Michael Sadler Leicester Galleries	Jan–Feb 1944
War Pictures National Gallery	1944
Henry Lamb Leicester Galleries	1945
National War Pictures RA	Oct–Nov 1945
Portraits Arts Council	1945–1946
British Painting: Modern British Pictures from the Tate Gallery Arts Council	1947
From Sickert to 1948: the achievement of the CAS Arts Council	1948
The Chantrey Collection RA	Winter 1949
Henry Lamb Leicester Galleries	1949
The Private Collector: the CAS at the Tate Tate	Mar–Apr 1950
British Painting 1925–1950 Arts Council	1951
Sixty Paintings for '51 Arts Council	1951
Early Years of the New English Art Club 1886–1918 Birmingham Museum & Art Gallery	1952
Edward Marsh Collection Leicester Galleries	May 1953
British Paintings 1900–1930: A Picture Book Manchester City Art Galleries	1954
Cambridge Portraits: 1 The University Collection Cambridge	1955
Pictures from Garsington Leicester Galleries	Mar 1956
Henry Lamb Leicester Galleries	1956
British Portraits RA	Winter 1956–1957
Henry Lamb MC RA: Official Artist in Both World Wars Imperial War Museum	Feb–May 1958
British Painting 1720–1960 British Council, USSR	1960
Diploma and Other Works by Academicians RA	Mar–Apr 1960
Henry Lamb: Memorial Exhibition Imperial War Museum	Feb–May 1961
Henry Lamb: Memorial Exhibition Leicester Galleries	Dec 1961
The Behrend Collection Leicester Galleries	May 1962
A Painter's Collection: Edward Le Bas RA	1963
Modern British Paintings, Drawings and Sculpture: 1 Artists A – L Tate	1964
Paintings, Drawings and Sculpture of the Second World War Imperial War Museum	1964
Decade 1910–1920 Arts Council	1965
Vision and Design: the life, work and influence of Roger Fry University of Nottingham/ Arts Council	1966
Decade 1890–1900 Arts Council	1966–1967
Art In Britain 1890–1940 University of Hull	1967
Bicentenary Exhibition 1768–1969 RA	Dec 1968–Mar 1969
Bournemouth Symphony Orchestra: 75th Anniversary Exhibition Russell-Cotes Art Gallery, Bournemouth	Jun 1968–May 1969
Decade 1920–1930 Arts Council	1970
The World of Lytton Strachey Gallery Edward Harvane	1970
National Portrait Gallery: Concise Catalogue 1856–1969 HMSO	1970
British Art 1890–1928 Columbus, Ohio	1971
Ottoline Gallery Edward Harvane	Nov 1971
Fitzwilliam Museum, Cambridge: handbook Cambridge University Press	1971
Cambridge Portraits Fitzwilliam Museum	1972
Painting, Sculpture and Drawing in Great Britain 1940–49 Whitechapel	1972
The Café Royalists Michael Parkin Fine Art	Sep–Oct 1972
Twentieth Century British Art Agnew's	Nov–Dec 1972
Boris Anrep Gallery Edward Harvane	Jan–Feb 1973
Bloomsbury: a Summing Up Gallery Edward Harvane	Feb–Mar 1973

Henry Lamb

Hampstead One c.1915–c.1925 Gallery Edward Harvane	Mar–Apr 1973
Henry Lamb: Retrospective New Grafton	Mar–Apr 1973
Hampstead Two c.1928–c.1938 Gallery Edward Harvane	Apr–May 1974
Henry Lamb and His Friends Gallery Edward Harvane	May–Jun 1974
British Drawings 1900–1930 University of Sussex	Jun–Jul 1974
Henry Lamb 1883–1960 Salisbury Festival	Jul 1974
English Painting 1900–1940 New Grafton	Oct–Nov 1974
Face to Face: Portraits and Self Portraits 1880–1940 Fine Art Society	Dec 1974
We are Making a New World: Artists in the 1914–18 War Scottish Arts Council	1974–1975
One Man's Taste: The Duke of Devonshire Theatre Gallery Chatsworth	1975
British Painting 1900–1960 Sheffield City Art Galleries	1975–1976
Camden Town Recalled: Centenary Exhibition 1876–1976 Fine Art Society	Oct–Nov 1976
Stanley Spencer Gallery Cookham	1976
The Bloomsbury Group National Book League	1976
Sickert to Hockney: 20th Century British Drawings University of Sussex	1976
British Art 1910–16: A Terrific Thing Norwich Castle Museum	1976–1977
The Camden Town Group Southampton City Art Gallery	1976
Bloomsbury Painters and their Circle Beaverbrook Art Gallery, New Brunswick	1976–1977
The British School: Catalogue of Paintings Vol. 3 Fitzwilliam Museum, Cambridge	1977
Masters of Modern British Painting 1890–1945 Belgrave Gallery	Sep 1977
Art in One Year: 1935 Tate	Dec 1977–Feb 1978
25 from '51 Sheffield City Art Galleries	May–Jul 1978
Concise Catalogue of British Paintings Vol. 2 Manchester City Art Gallery	1978
The Camden Scene Camden Arts Centre	Feb–Mar 1979
The Tate Gallery Room by Room Tate	1979
Paintings of London by Members of the Camden Town Group Anthony d'Offay	Oct–Nov 1979
Arts Council Collection: purchases 1942–1978	1979
Post-Impressionism RA	Winter 1979–1980
Royal Society Catalogue of Portraits Royal Society	1980
Stanley Spencer RA	Sep–Dec 1980
National Portrait Gallery Catalogue Stainer & Bell	1981
Southampton City Art Gallery	1981
Modern British Paintings Thomas Gibson Fine Art	Oct–Nov 1981
Henry Lamb New Grafton	Nov–Dec 1981
British Drawings and Watercolours 1890–1940 Anthony d'Offay	Jan–Mar 1982
Edwardian England Spink	Oct 1982
The Tate Gallery: an illustrated companion Tate	1983
Richard Carline 1896–1980 Camden Arts Centre	Jun–Jul 1983
Henry Lamb 1883–1960 Manchester City Art Gallery	1984

Index

Italicised numbers indicate illustrations.

Index

Index

Index